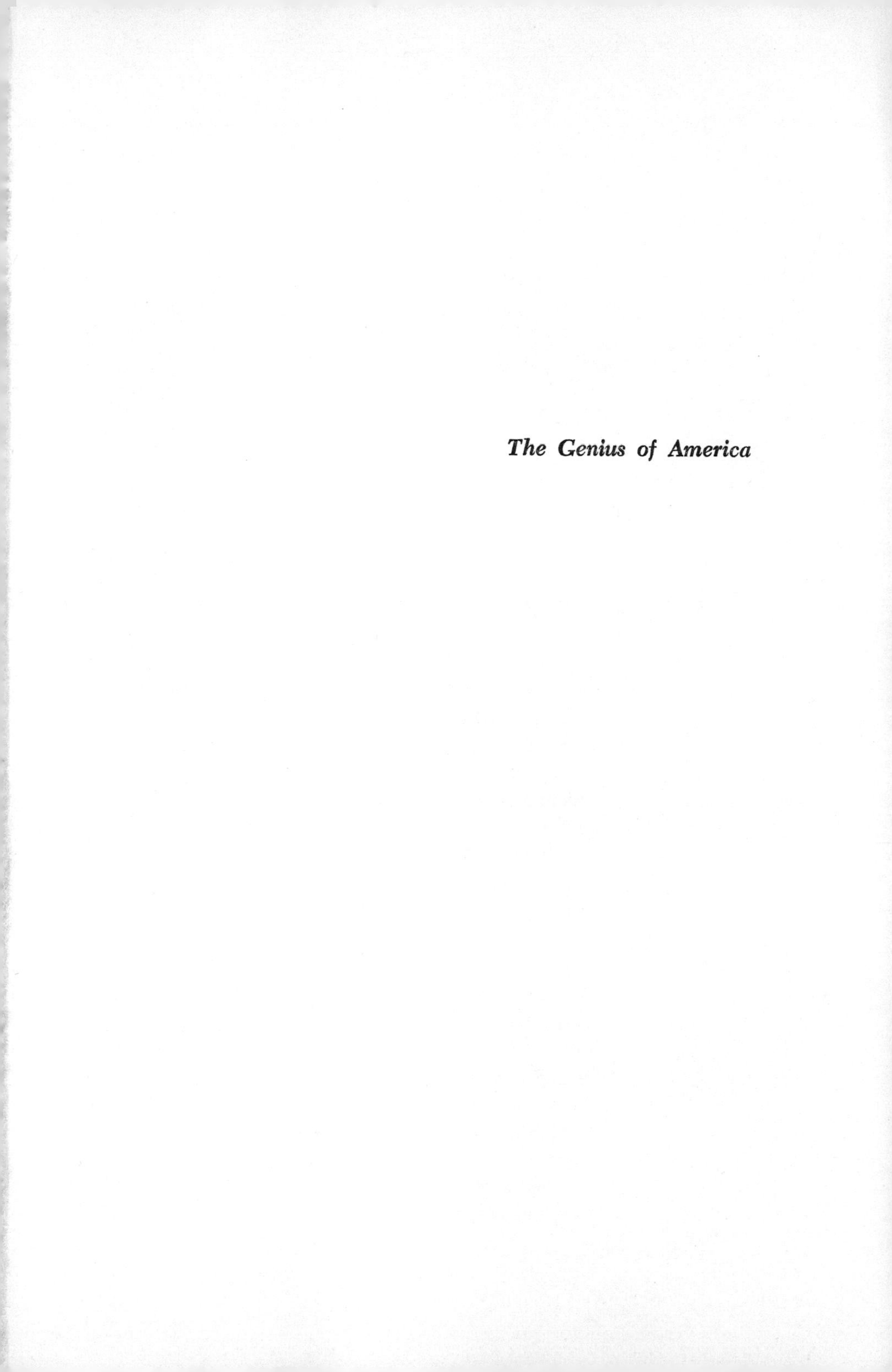

*The Genius of America*

*Books by Saul K. Padover*

THE GENIUS OF AMERICA
THE REVOLUTIONARY EMPEROR: JOSEPH II
SECRET DIPLOMACY
THE LIFE AND DEATH OF LOUIS XVI
WILSON'S IDEALS
EXPERIMENT IN GERMANY
LA VIE POLITIQUE DES ETATS-UNIS
FRENCH INSTITUTIONS
THE LIVING U.S. CONSTITUTION
THE COMPLETE MADISON
THE WASHINGTON PAPERS
THE MIND OF ALEXANDER HAMILTON
CONFESSIONS AND SELF-PORTRAITS
THE WORLD OF THE FOUNDING FATHERS

*On Jefferson:*

DEMOCRACY BY JEFFERSON
JEFFERSON (A BIOGRAPHY)
THE COMPLETE JEFFERSON
THOMAS JEFFERSON AND THE NATIONAL CAPITAL
A JEFFERSON PROFILE

# THE GENIUS OF AMERICA

*Men Whose Ideas Shaped Our Civilization*

SAUL K. PADOVER
*Professor, Graduate Faculty,
New School for Social Research*

*McGraw-Hill Book Company, Inc.*
NEW YORK TORONTO LONDON

Library of Congress Catalog Card Number: 60-14225

First Edition

48071

Madison as a Political Thinker, vol. 20, no. 1 (Spring 1953). George Washington—Portrait of a True Conservative, vol. 22, no. 2 (Summer 1955). The "Singular" Mr. Hamilton, vol. 24, no. 2 (Summer 1957). The Political Ideas of John Marshall, vol. 26, no. 1 (Spring, 1959). Reprinted by permission of *Social Research.*

Excerpt from *The Mind of Alexander Hamilton*. Copyright © 1958 by Saul K. Padover. Reprinted by permission of Harper & Brothers, New York. This essay was published as the Introduction to Saul K. Padover's *The Mind of Alexander Hamilton* (Harper, 1958).

Article on Emerson. Vol. LXXIV, no. 3, September 1959, edited by the Faculty of Political Science, Columbia University, for the Academy of Political Science. Reprinted by special permission from the *Political Science Quarterly*.

*To Peggy*

# Contents

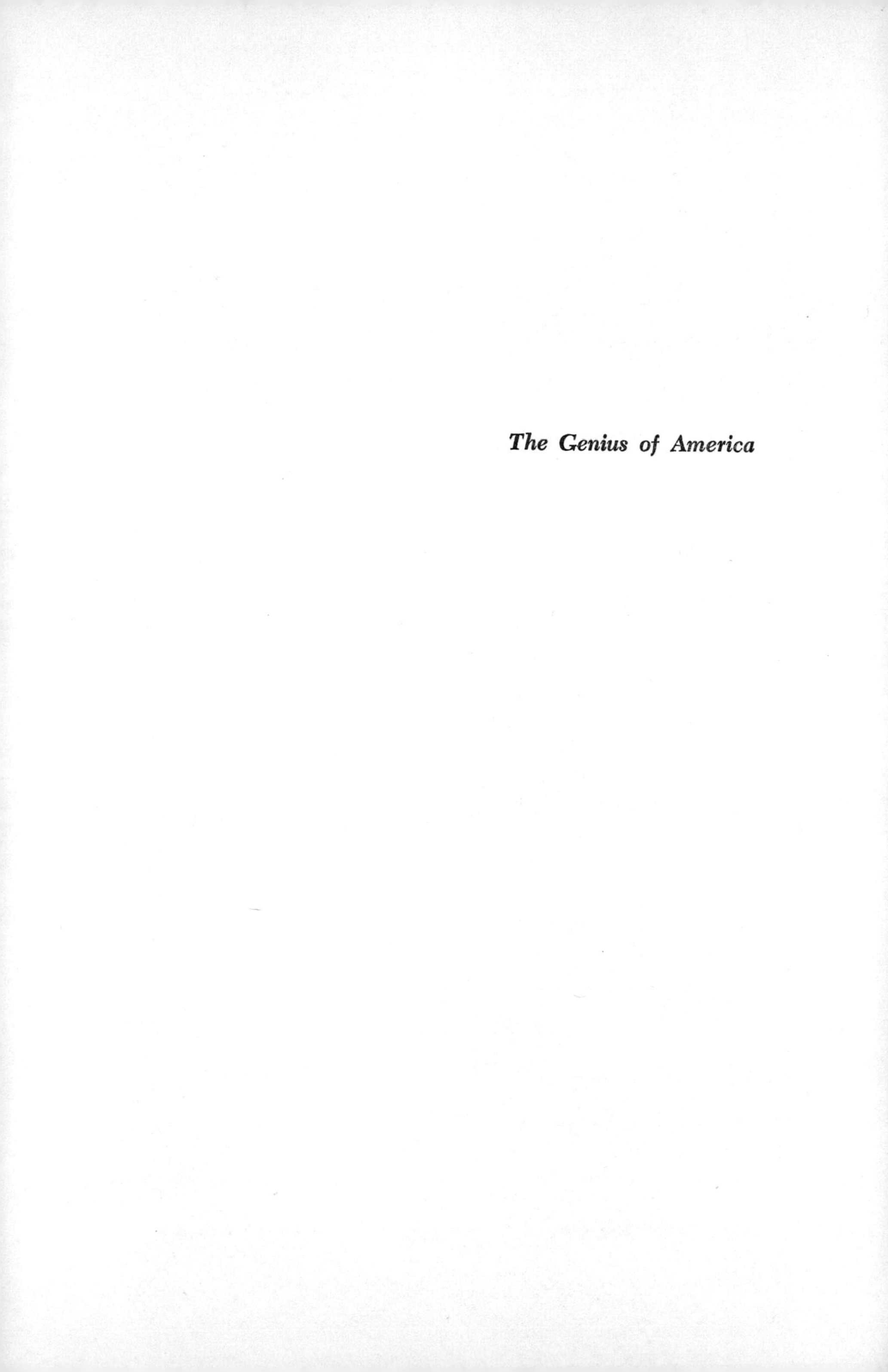

*The Genius of America*

# 1

## *THE NATURE OF AMERICAN POLITICAL THOUGHT*

*Our political thought always lags behind our practice. Our performance is wiser than our policy; and we are more virtuous than we claim to be.*
—*Reinhold Niebuhr,* "Liberty and Equality" in *Pious and Secular America* (1958)

This is a book about a group of men who molded America's political mind and institutions. It is not a history of political thought. Nor is it a story of political philosophers. It is, rather, a study of men who have had a special impact on the formation and development of what is historically a unique polity: the United States of America.

The strength and durability of American civilization in the political sphere has derived from an uncommon historic phenomenon of unity between idea and action. In the realm of political thought, the major formulators of what may be called the "American idea," which may be defined as individualism operating through self-government, were the practitioners of that idea. To put it in different terms, American political thought, insofar as a coherent body of doctrine may be said to exist, has been mainly the product of America's leaders. The country's distinct political character was shaped in the first place by men who became its Presidents, legislators, and judges, and secondarily—on a different level —by its philosophers and professional writers. A William James or a John Dewey, whose interests in any case were not primarily political, came after such statesmen as Thomas Jefferson and John Marshall had laid the foundations in both action and formulation.

The role of writers, as distinct from that of political leaders, has been mainly inspirational and critical. Philosophers and poets, notably

Emerson, Thoreau, and Whitman, provided insights and challenges that enriched the American mind, but they transcended the immediately political. Some of them, in fact, found "politics" distasteful and political participation unattractive. But their function was indispensable, especially in an earthy, vigorous democracy that has always been impatient with restraints. Literary men such as Emerson raised the quiet voice of reason amid the noisy bustle; poets like Whitman, embracing the prevailing democratic torrent, attempted to show in it a deeper meaning.

The role of the leaders in the shaping of the political mind has been direct and pervasive. These were the men who created the political institutions, supplied their rationale, and, in general, kept them viable within the constitutional framework and its underlying republican-democratic philosophy. The leaders were not as a rule original philosophers, although there are strands of originality in Jefferson and Madison and, certainly, in Calhoun. With few exceptions, a notable one being John Adams, they were not particularly interested in political theory or speculation.

Primarily, the leaders have been molders and adjusters, on a bold scale when the occasion required it. Thus neither John Marshall nor, a century later, Franklin D. Roosevelt was in any sense an original mind, but the scope of their operations, in transcending established political assumptions in their respective spheres, amounted to acts of creative endeavor. In that sense, a number of the leaders made what may be called original contributions to the nation's political thinking. In the main, however, the vital function of the leaders has been to harmonize prevailing ideas and aspirations and to shape them successfully to reality. What Jefferson said of the Declaration of Independence may be regarded as applicable to the role played by America's leaders in general: "Neither aiming at originality of principle or sentiment, nor yet copied from any particular and previous writing, it was intended to be an expression of the American mind. . . . All its authority rests . . . on the harmonizing sentiments of the day, whether expressed in conversation, in letters, printed essays, or in the elementary books of public rights. . . ."

The political leaders have not only shaped and articulated prevailing currents of opinion and sentiment; they have also served as living symbols which in turn influenced the stream of thought and behavior. The granite character of George Washington, the brooding humanity of Abraham Lincoln, the cheerful boldness of Franklin D. Roosevelt—such figures have been the permanent embodiments of American political civilization. They have been its makers and its image. As both shapers and symbols, therefore, the political leaders present an especially rewarding field of study.

It has been said that America's most original contribution to political theory has been to have no theory. In a special sense, this is true. American political thought is an aggregation of concepts, phrases, slogans, creeds, shibboleths, and traditions that has never been—and in the nature of things probably cannot be—distilled into symmetrical theoretical architecture, unless one wishes to follow the example of Procrustes. For one thing, pervasive democratic practices, affecting every aspect of human life, defy manageable theory. For another, the American national character, whatever its nature at any given time, has not been hospitable to intellectual speculation, especially in regard to ultimates. America has produced no Aristotle or Locke or Montesquieu or Marx.

Perhaps they did not have to, if Edmund Burke's observation is true: "One sure sign of an ill conducted State is the propensity of the people to resort to theories." In this regard, fate has been kind to Americans. Almost from the first they have been reasonably well governed. Certainly they have never been truly oppressed by conquerors or autocrats. Consquently they have felt no urgent necessity for elaborate theoretical explanations of the root meaning of their troubles. Having had no Cesare Borgia, they have had no need to produce a Machiavelli.

This does not mean that political theory has not played an important role in American thought and institutions. Actually, theory came into play in at least two of the three major crises in the life of the American nation, the American Revolution and the Constitutional Convention. In the third great crisis, that of the Civil War, theory was muted, except possibly Calhoun's. But that interesting "cast-iron" Carolinian found himself, so to speak, in a one-sided argument. The Civil War was not fought on his theoretical terms. Instead, whatever political thought underlay that conflict revolved around the idea of freedom derived fundamentally from America's experience and premises as a nation, as Lincoln reminded his hearers in the Gettysburg Address.

But in the two earlier crises, those that led to the creation of the American nation, well-established political theory was at the base of much of the thinking and action. There was political philosophy and rationale behind both the American Revolution and the Federal Convention of 1787. The thought was not indigenous. The basic ideas that guided the Americans of that period were those of Europeans, primarily Englishmen and Frenchmen—notably Thomas Hobbes. John Locke,

Thomas Paine (who was both Englishman and American), and the Baron de Montesquieu. Locke, in particular, provided eighteenth-century Americans with a theoretical arsenal in defense of their revolutionary action against Great Britain. The arguments of Locke's *Treatises on Government* were sonorously echoed in Jefferson's Declaration of Independence.

The triumph of political theory is most clearly seen in the Constitutional Convention. There, leading ideas of important thinkers were incorporated into the charter that has remained the cornerstone of American political institutions.

The founders of the American republic in the eighteenth century were most deeply influenced by about half a dozen juridical and political writers. In the field of law, the most seriously studied authors were the English jurists Sir Edward Coke, Lord Kames, and Sir William Blackstone. In the realm of political philosophy, the most influential books were Hobbes' *Leviathan* (1651); Locke's *Letters on Toleration* (1689), *Treatises on Government* and *Essay Concerning Human Understanding* (1690); and Montesquieu's *L'Esprit des Lois* (1748). The latter in particular was a best-seller in the Western world; within a year and a half of its publication twenty-two editions, in most European languages, had appeared.

The chief appeal of these European authors for the Americans of the Revolutionary and Constitutional period was their rationalism. They had in common a rational approach to politics. They rejected the mystically based state and the notion that government was divinely ordained. Their major premise was that men were of this world and were influenced by human attributes, including their passions and interests. Hobbes constructed his political analysis on a psychology that assumed the existence of human hate, greed, and violence leading, in a natural state, to "war of every man against every man." Only a mighty government with absolute powers, a *Leviathan,* could keep human passions under control. Without a powerful government, Hobbes wrote, human life was "solitary, poor, nasty, brutish, and short."

Hobbes was absorbed by the American founding fathers, many of whom accepted his realistic analysis with regard to human nature and the need for strong authority to bridle passions and selfish drives. Alexander Hamilton was Hobbesian in his frankly stated opinions that the human animal was too corrupt to be entrusted with uncontrolled self-government. Even James Madison, a moderate conservative with Jeffersonian leanings, accepted much of Hobbes in his political thinking.

He too felt that human nature should not be trusted altogether where political power was concerned. Indeed, strands of Hobbes are woven throughout the federal Constitution, with its system of "checks and balances" which sprang from a lack of confidence in the human character. This Hobbesian skepticism concerning human nature was expressed with illuminating candor in *The Federalist* (No. 51): "It may be a reflection on human nature that such devices [checks and balances in the federal Constitution] should be necessary to control the abuses of government. But what is government itself but the greatest of all reflections on human nature? If men were angels, no government would be necessary. If angels were to govern men, neither external nor internal controls on government would be necessary." The federal Constitution was constructed on the far-reaching assumption that men are not angels.

But the practical-minded Americans of the eighteenth century accepted only one half of Hobbes' theory—his psychology. The other half, that which advocated an absolutist (preferably monarchist) government, they rejected in favor of Locke's philosophy of natural rights. Locke's fundamental position, shared by the founding fathers, was that men came into the world with "inherent" rights, which they voluntarily relinquished when they formed a "social contract" for the maintenance of order and the preservation of property. Insofar as the American Constitution was concerned, the crucial idea in Locke was the one relating to the governing power, the legislature, which he regarded as servant rather than master. The legislature had no independent powers, only duties and obligations assigned to it by the social contract. This meant that government, being the creature of men, remained subject to their will. Otherwise, its actions were unlawful.

Thus, by a peculiar dialectic of history, the American leaders of the eighteenth century wedded Hobbes and Locke to create the original political mechanism known as the federal Constitution. They took Hobbes' premises about human nature but not his solution. They accepted Locke's assumption of natural rights but not his reliance on a unitary government. They agreed with Hobbes that human beings were, actually or potentially, nasty; and with Locke that men were born with inalienable rights. But they drew different conclusions from these assumptions.

In effect, the founders of the United States said that since human nature was untrustworthy, then *no* person or group could or should be entrusted with absolute power. If man were corrupt by nature, then it was too dangerous to endow him with the means of wreaking his unbridled will on his fellow creatures. Jefferson put it with his customary felicity in his first inaugural address: "Sometimes it is said that man cannot be trusted with the government of himself. Can he, then, be trusted with the government of others? Or have we found angels in the forms of kings to govern him?" Americans, therefore, concluded that the logic of the situation required limitations on governmental powers. Since men were not angels, they must not be provided with any opportunity to tyrannize over others. The tigrish appetites in men were not to be nourished or tempted with unrestrained power. To Americans in the eighteenth century, a *Leviathan* government was unthinkable.

How was government to be checked? Here Montesquieu, the scholarly French provincial judge, supplied the theoretical basis and the practical answer. The ideas of his *Spirit of the Laws,* which were finally embedded in the federal Constitution, were derived from a systematic study of comparative government through history. In the annals of mankind he discerned three types of government: the monarchical, the despotic, and the republican. He admired the first (if it was moderate), disliked the second, and was somewhat dubious about the third. The prevalence of despotism in the history of humanity he explained on the ground that it was an easy form of government, whereas moderate monarchy or republicanism was difficult. Governments that protected liberty were rare because they were hard to establish and required special efforts to maintain.

Montesquieu's main concern was with political liberty, which he considered the highest good. The way to establish and perpetuate a government which would protect freedom was to balance its operations in such a way that no single body or act could permanently outweigh the rest. That, Montesquieu thought, required rare political skill. He wrote, "To form a moderate government, it is necessary to combine powers, regulate them, temper them, activate them; to give, so to speak, a ballast to the one so as to enable the other to resist. This is a masterpiece of legislation which rarely happens by chance and is seldom left to prudence."

To attain such a masterpiece, Montesquieu proposed a system of laws that would restrain those who exercised political power and at the same time protect the liberties of the citizen. This made a separation of governmental powers absolutely necessary. It was vital that the legislative, executive, and judicial functions be entrusted to three separate branches of government, independent of one another. Where powers and functions were concentrated in the same hands, Montesquieu pointed out, liberty for the citizens was impossible. James Madison echoed this when he wrote in *The Federalist* (No. 47) that such an accumulation of powers "may justly be pronounced the very definition of tyranny." On the other hand, a careful and judicious distribution of political powers worked against the possibility of any one person or group developing into a tyrannical master. Each of the three branches was not only to operate separately in its own sphere, but was to have enough power to serve as a counterpoise—or ballast—to the other two.

Thus was Montesquieu's principle of "checks and balances" built into the federal Constitution. It has survived great strains and has remained the keystone of the American system of government.

The federal Constitution has significance on many levels. It knit the states together and formed a nation. It furnished a fundamental legal and political system. It set a pervasive example. But its main importance, so far as the American political character is concerned, lay in the fact that it created a special atmosphere.

The written federal Constitution moved into a sphere that in other civilizations is occupied by sacred literature and enshrined dogma. Apart from being a practical and successful scheme of government, it has also served as a documentary model. Following the Constitution, American thinking has tended to revolve around documents—utterances, speeches, inaugurals, declarations, and declamations—and has sometimes endowed them with magically evocative powers. They have crystallized opinion, supplied orientation for action or inaction, and have given a distinct shape to the American political environment.

Next to the federal Constitution and its state replicas, the most notable, quotable, and reliable quasiofficial documents are the Declaration of Independence (which, of course, preceded the Constitution), Washington's Farewell Address, Monroe's declaration in regard to the Americas, Lincoln's inaugurals and Gettysburg Address, Wilson's Fourteen Points, and Franklin D. Roosevelt's "Four Freedoms." There were others, but these serve to illustrate the point that public statements, in the wake and under the overarching roof of the federal Constitution, acquired a unique political authority.

The American political character, as it has developed under the canopy of the federal Constitution, may be described in three words: laic, libertarian, limited. In one way or another, the men who shaped American political thought and policy have subscribed to the ideas of secularism, liberty, and a varying degree of limitation on government. The institutions have, of course, reflected those characteristics. Without exception, America's responsible political and intellectual leaders have supported the idea of the separation of church and state. All of them have believed in individual freedom. Few of them have questioned the need for limitation on governmental power, at least in principle. These qualities of laicism, personal liberty, and governmental limitation also define the American conception and ideal of democracy in general.

Insofar as religious freedom is the first of all freedoms, separation of church and state under the Constitution has been one of the monumental achievements of the American people. It has had two primary objectives: to eliminate dogmatic obstacles to intellectual experimentation and the free flow of ideas, and to secure religious liberty for all sects. The separation of church and state has struck at the root of all despotism—mental enchainment—and has provided permanent institutional safeguards for liberty of mind and spirit. It has made possible the creation of secularized political and social institutions—foremost among them the educational system—free from clerical meddling and ecclesiastical domination. It has encouraged the growth and development of that multiplicity of religious organizations and practices (there are more than two hundred Protestant denominations in the United States today) which James Madison regarded as "the best and only security for religious liberty in any society." Freedom, he argued in the Virginia Ratification Convention in 1788, would find safety in the numbers of different churches: "For where there is such a variety of sects, there cannot be a majority of any one sect to oppress and persecute the rest." In a letter to Edward Livingston in 1822, Madison restated his lifelong belief in church–state separation, saying that "Religion flourishes in greater purity, without than with the aid of Government." The successful separation of church from state has been a major factor in the energizing of American civilization.

The establishment of a secular polity under the Constitution was neither accident nor sudden inspiration. It was the end product of a long and difficult process, during which the American character was being formed. The struggle for freedom of conscience began with the establishment of America. Its roots reach back to the 1630s when a bold young clergyman, Roger Williams, challenged the Puritan theocracy in Massachusetts and was forced to flee the colony. Williams, who may rightfully be considered the first American democrat, set a precedent for religious (and consequently political) liberty in his own Rhode Island, where he set up a "democratical" government. He took the daring position, which he propagated in books, sermons, and debates, that it was the "command of God" that all "consciences and worships" be granted full freedom, and that it was not the business of government (the "civil states") to meddle in spiritual matters. As he wrote in his classic tract, *The Bloody Tenent of Persecution for Cause of Conscience* (1644): "God requireth not a uniformity of religion to be enacted and enforced in any civil state; which enforced uniformity (sooner or later) is the great occasion of civil war, ravishing of conscience, persecution of Christ Jesus in his servants, and of the hypocrisy and destruction of millions of souls."

It took about a century and a half for the spirit of Roger Williams and other more or less like-minded men such as William Penn and Jonathan Mayhew to gain a large measure of acceptance in America. The conflict for religious liberty was unceasing, and it underlay the widespread opposition to civil tyranny in both England and America, as John Adams pointed out in *A Dissertation on the Canon and Feudal Law,* in which he wrote that it was this "great struggle that peopled America." The road to religious liberty was marked by marytrdom, especially in seventeenth-century New England, where Quakers were publicly maimed and hanged and so-called witches were executed.

The tone of martyrdom can be detected in the letter which William Robinson and Marmaduke Stevenson, two English Quakers, wrote from the "Common Gaol in the Bloody Town of Boston" before their execution in October 1659:

"O ye Rulers, and Chief-Priests . . . , consider what you are doing: Are you so blind that you cannot see you are persecuting the Saints of the Most High? . . . Do you thus requite the Lord for his Loving-kindness, to whip, to imprison, and cut off the Ears of his Servants . . . , Oh! thou New-England . . . : Is thy Religion come to no more than whipping, imprisoning, burning in the Hand, and cutting off Ears, and banishing upon Death . . . Oh ye Hypocrites! How can you sing, and keep such a Noise concerning Religion, when your Hands are full of Blood, and your Hearts full of Iniquity . . . Wo! Wo! to thee, thou Bloody Town of Boston . . ."

Even where there was no direct persecution for cause of conscience, discriminatory practices prevailed throughout the colonies, with the exception of New York and Virginia, until the era of the American Revolution. In many colonies Catholics and Jews were disfranchised or excluded from public office. In Massachusetts and Maryland the governorship was open only to Christians, and in Pennsylvania and South Carolina a belief in God and in a system of future rewards and punishments was a requirement for voting. In New Hampshire, New Jersey, and South Carolina, both the governorship and membership in the legislature were closed to non-Protestants, and in North Carolina and Georgia the same was true of the suffrage in general. In Delaware, voters were required to believe in the Trinity and in the sacredness of the Scriptures.

The liberating currents of the American Revolution swept away most of these religious tests and cleared the path for the establishment of the constitutional principle of church–state separation. The first important steps in this regard were taken in the South, where the new frontier population of Presbyterians and Baptists (and, for that matter, numerous nonbelievers) resented having to pay tithes to the official Anglican church. In 1776 the Anglican church was disestablished in Maryland, and in North Carolina the state constitution declared: "There shall be no establishment of any one religion, church or denomination in this State in preference to any other."

In terms of influence, the most important struggle for religious liberty took place in Virginia. The battle for separation of church and state was led by that state's great democrats, Madison and Jefferson, and lasted ten years before victory was achieved. It was, Jefferson said, "the severest contest in which I have ever been engaged." Jefferson's *Act for Establishing Religious Freedom,* which the Virginia Assembly finally passed under Madison's leadership in 1786, was a ringing declaration of intellectual liberty. Indeed, Jefferson regarded it as one of the three important achievements of his life. The *Act* may be considered the triumphant culmination of Roger Williams' lonely fight, begun more than a century before Jefferson was born. It read in part:

> Well aware that Almighty God hath created the mind free; that all attempts to influence it by temporal punishments or burdens, or by civil incapacitations, tend only to beget habits of hypocrisy and meanness . . . ; that our civil rights have no dependence on our religious opinions . . . ; *Be it therefore enacted* . . . , That no man shall be compelled to frequent or support any religious worship, place or ministry whatsoever, nor shall be enforced, restrained, molested, or burthened in his body or goods, nor shall otherwise suffer on account of his religious opinions or belief; but that all men shall be free to profess, and by argument to maintain, their opinions in matters of religion, and that the same shall in no wise diminish, enlarge, or affect their civil capacities.

Thus by the time the federal Constitution came into being a broad base for religious freedom already existed in America. The doctrine of church–state separation had penetrated so widely that the Constitutional Convention did not think it necessary to waste much time on the subject. The leading figures at the Convention—Franklin, Washington, Madison, Mason, among others—shared an eighteenth-century "tolerance" in the realm of religion and took it for granted that faith was a purely personal, rather than a political, affair. There was a certain amount of discussion on the question of the oath of office: Should a man swear by God or the Bible? But the requirement of a religious oath was rejected. Article VI provided for a simple oath or affirmation to support the Constitution, and nothing else: "no religious test shall ever be required as a qualification to any office or public trust under the United States." This basic idea was finally reinforced by the First Amendment to the Constitution, which stated tersely and without equivocation: "Congress shall make no law respecting an establishment of religion, or prohibiting the free exercise thereof."

The separation of church and state was more than a legal or constitutional provision. It was intended to create a secular civilization in all its aspects. Religious practices were to remain forever free and protected, but to operate outside governmental institutions and without political support. The founders of the United States were determined that government should be divorced from any ecclesiastical activity or program, in perpetuity. As early as 1797, a treaty between the United States and Tripoli stated: "The Government of the United States is not, in any sense, founded on the Christian religion." Jefferson, as President, refused to proclaim fasting and thanksgiving, considering any alliance between church and state a "loathsome combination." Madison, as President, in 1811 vetoed two bills involving churches (the incorporation of an Episcopal one in the District of Columbia and the relief of a Baptist one in the Mississippi Territory) on the ground that they violated the "essential distinction between civil and religious functions" and were thus "contrary to the . . . Constitution."

In this way, American society was secularized on all fronts, and the notion that religion was a private affair took deep root over the years. Generations of Americans came to accept without question the principle of separation of religion from politics. To leaders and nation alike, secularization became axiomatic; it entered the bone and sinew of America. Any institution supported by public moneys (notably education) was to have no sectarian control or meddling. An American could believe in God, and be an active member of his particular church, without feeling that government should have anything to do with the matter.

On the contrary: wherever government entered actively, as in the case of schools, there religion was to move out. In December 1875, President Ulysses S. Grant, in his seventh annual message to Congress on the need for universal public-school education in America, reflected the nation-wide acceptance of secularization when he recommended that

> No sectarian tenets shall ever be taught in any school supported in whole or in part by the State, nation, or by the proceeds of any tax levied upon any community.... Declare Church and State forever separate and distinct, but each free within their proper spheres; and that all church property shall bear its own proportion of taxation.

There have been breaches in the wall that separates religion and politics, but the principle of separation has remained steadfast. It has had the support of the courts and majority opinion and has been a commanding force in the shaping of the American political mind and outlook.

In the absence of an official religion, the ideal of liberty developed as a national commitment. Belief in liberty has been so pervasive that it may, in a deep sense, be considered the secular religion of the American people. The ideal of freedom has provided the American nation with both a fighting faith and a unifying force. Underlying the whole democratic philosophy, liberty has been identified with America itself. Freedom as an ideal has had no serious critics in America, with the possible exception of such eccentrics as Henry and Brooks Adams, those dour descendants of the crusty second President of the United States. But even such aloof men as the Adams brothers, whose type of pessimism has been relatively rare in America, seem to have been more skeptical about the nature of man than about the quality of the ideal of freedom.

Freedom as a pervasive ideal and goal has been incorporated in the great documents of American life. Foremost, of course, is the Declaration of Independence. It promulgated the "self-evident" truths that "all men are created equal, that they are endowed by the Creator with certain unalienable rights, that among these are life, liberty, and the pursuit of happiness." Although of no logical validity, the Declaration has remained an inexhaustible reservoir of American aspiration to freedom. Abraham Lincoln credited it with being his chief inspiration. Woodrow Wilson regarded it as an imperishable "whip for tyrants."

Similarly, one finds the ideal of liberty imbedded in the nation's basic legal charters and inspirational statements. The Northwest Ordinance of 1787, which laid down the rules of government for the territory north of the Ohio River, was designed to guarantee freedom in the newly emerging American West. Section 13 provided "for extending the fundamental principles of civil and religious liberty, which form the basis whereon these republics,* their laws, and constitutions are erected; to fix and establish those principles as the basis of all laws, constitutions, and governments, which forever hereafter shall be formed in the said territory."

The federal Constitution embodied these principles for the whole nation. The Preamble proclaimed that, among other things, the goal of the Constitution was to "secure the Blessings of Liberty to ourselves and our Posterity." Subsequent documents, both legal and nonlegal, have echoed those objectives. Lincoln's Gettysburg Address pointed to a "new birth of freedom." Woodrow Wilson's war message to Congress in 1917, involving the United States in the unprecedented step of mobilizing for war abroad, stressed that its aim was to fight "for democracy" and for a "concert of free peoples." Finally, Franklin D. Roosevelt in 1941 applied the national ideal of liberty on a global scale with his proclamation of the "Four Freedoms" as the essential basis for a new world, not as a "vision of a distant millennium" but as a goal "attainable in our own time and generation." This culmination of American libertarian idealism read:

> The first is freedom of speech and expression—everywhere in the world.
> The second is freedom of every person to worship God in his own way—everywhere in the world.
> The third is freedom from want . . . —everywhere in the world.
> The fourth is freedom from fear . . . —everywhere in the world.

Devotion to the ideal of liberty has pervaded America's political thinking and attitudes from the beginning of its history as a republic. It runs in a straight line, from Thomas Jefferson and John Marshall to Franklin D. Roosevelt and Earl Warren. Loyalty to liberty has been advocated by the political left as well as by the right, by liberals as well as conservatives, by intellectuals as well as businessmen. It has been preached by nineteenth-century Populists and by twentieth-century Socialists. It has been explicit in Walt Whitman and implicit in Henry George. It is implicit in the publications of the Chamber of Commerce and in the activities of the labor unions. Its philosophy underlies the opinions of the United States Supreme Court and the educational pro-

* The states of Ohio (1803), Indiana (1816), Illinois (1818), Michigan (1837), Wisconsin (1848), and part of Minnesota (1858) were carved out of the Northwest Territory.

gram of the American public schools. Liberty, in sum, is America's image of itself as a nation.

Given the pervasiveness of the ideal, the question may be asked whether it has any specific meaning. The answer is that, apart from the ideal of liberty as a national symbol, it has had in practice a dual interpretation. It has involved on the one hand the right of the individual to be unrestrained in his activities and expression, and on the other hand the conception of government as hardly anything else than a protector of those individual rights.

This individualization of politics has been one of the unique features of American civilization. Unlike other cultures, where emphasis has been on the state or the society, in the United States the stress has been on the individual. Beginning with the Bill of Rights, the significance of which transcends merely legal–constitutional aspects in the sense that it symbolizes a national attitude, Americans have placed the individual at the center of their political life. They have taken the position that government exists for freedom, and that freedom means individual freedom vis-à-vis government.

The emphasis here is on freedom *from*—mainly from government intervention. The individual, being at the core of the political structure, has considered it his sacred right and even his privilege as an American to be free from governmental curbs, domination, meddling, advice, and even assistance—except in times of dire crisis. For the individual to retain and enjoy his freedom—freedom to express himself, to educate himself, to achieve status, to acquire property, as and if he sees fit—government must be kept at arm's length. It must be neither helpful friend nor threatening enemy. It must leave man alone to take advantage of whatever opportunity offers and to enjoy the fruits of his personal effort.

The concept of freedom as personal expression uncoerced by government is found in varying forms in the thought of Americans of virtually every persuasion and political hue. One sees this absorbing individualism in the agrarianism of John Taylor, in the anarchism of Henry David Thoreau, in the Over-Soul of Ralph Waldo Emerson, in the Darwinism of William Graham Sumner, in the capitalism of Andrew Carnegie, in the industrialism of Henry Ford. Central to the whole idea is the notion of personal ambition and personal opportunity. Government and society exist for the sole purpose of giving the individual free rein in his strivings for the attainment of whatever it is he desires or is able to achieve.

This political philosophy has been formulated with particular cogency by Herbert Hoover, a wealthy engineer who became thirty-first President of the United States in 1931. For an understanding of the American concept of capitalism in its political sense, one can do no better than read Hoover's articles, speeches, and books, especially his *American Individualism* (1922). Hoover proclaimed the "great ideals" of America to be free opportunity and personal achievement. He hailed individualism, operating through the "emery wheel of competition," as the key to America's greatness. Despite his eminent position in politics, he had a deep-rooted distrust of government and intense dislike of bureaucrats. American life was to him a competitive personal race in which the track was clear of all obstacles.

"It is as if we set a race," Hoover said in a campaign speech in 1928. "We, through free and universal education, provide the training of the runners; we give to them an equal start; we provide in the government the umpire of fairness in the race. The winner is he who shows the most conscientious training, the greatest ability, and the greatest character."

But it has never been that simple. The notion that society was a race in which the individual winner, presumably because of superior ability, took all, was fraught with danger to the society. It has led to large-scale misery, as Henry George pointed out, and to social hypocrisy. In putting a premium on individualism, this philosophy institutionalized selfishness and intensified social irresponsibility. It has produced a species of political schizophrenia, wherein the promises of democracy came into continuing conflict with the practices of glorified individualism. The political system said—and promised—one thing; the economic structure did the opposite. It was not so much that the two, democracy and egocentric capitalism, contradicted each other; it was rather that the two engaged in a continuing struggle for mastery over America.

In a sense, this meant the existence of a double set of political institutions—one private and one public. The private system was that of successful businessmen and industrialists, whose influence over government was paramount. Directly or indirectly, they controlled officials and as a rule had the courts on their side. "Not an ambassador or foreign consul to any nation or part of the world," a historian of New York City's businessmen wrote in 1885, "can be appointed without the consent of the merchants of New York." The public system was that of the official democracy, with its machinery of government and paraphernalia of democratic procedures. It was designed to express the popular will, but real power was wielded elsewhere.

From the mid-nineteenth century on, American life has thus been characterized by extremes of individual power and social ruthlessness. By 1892, it was estimated that the country had between three and four thousand millionaires, forming, in effect, a state within a state. (Ida M. Tarbell, in *The Nationalizing of Business, 1878–1898* [1936], cites the New York *Tribune* to the effect that in 1892 there were 4047 millionaires in the United States; the New York *World* estimated the number as 3045. The majority of the *Tribune*'s list of millionaires made their fortunes in transportation [1752], merchandising [986], banking [294], railroads [186].) The accumulation of vast individual fortunes went hand in hand with callousness toward the general welfare. Unregulated economic power, wielded by bankers and industrialists through monopolistic trusts and interlocking directorships, dominated the politics as well as the economy of the nation. This militated against governmental assumption of responsibility in the realm of public welfare. Social legislation in matters such as child labor, old-age pensions, unemployment insurance, or sick benefits was virtually nonexistent on a national scale well into the first third of the twentieth century. The individualist philosophy insisted that each person, regardless of age or infirmity, must fend for himself. His troubles were not society's responsibility but his own. This helps to explain why the United States has been the only industrial country in the world without an effective socialist or radical movement. Since any variety of socialism, almost by definition, means a substantial measure of government controls, it has never been able to strike lasting roots in American soil. The American mind, bred in the concept of private freedom and accustomed to the idea of full personal reward for unchecked individual effort, has been hostile to anything that smacked of "governmental interference."

Given this emphasis on individualism, it was understandable that government would be kept within circumscribed limits and viewed with suspicion. But this institutionalized limitation, which Emerson hailed and Whitman echoed as "the less government we have the better," has created a continuing split in the American public mind and attitude. Whereas Americans have looked upon strong government as an evil, they have condoned irresponsible economic power by individuals. They have accepted the philosophy of democratic morality but have tolerated the practice of political corruption.

Limited government—that is, government shorn of power—became, particularly after the Civil War, a shabby and despised creature. The masters of economic power came to consider the public authority a personal instrument to be used for private purposes. They dominated both major political parties and spent millions on systematic bribery at all levels of government. Nearly everywhere politicians were for sale. An Ohio congressman said in 1873 that the "House of Representatives was like an auction room where more valuable considerations were disposed of under the speaker's hammer than in any other place on earth." Between 1875 and 1885 the Central Pacific spent some $500,000 annually on graft. In 1906 Theodore Roosevelt quoted Edward H. Harriman of the Union and Southern Pacific as saying that "he could buy a sufficient number of Senators and Congressmen or State legislators to protect his interests, and when necessary he could buy the judiciary."

Notorious political machines, "the worst in Christendom," according to Andrew D. White in 1890, dominated the big cities, including the "gas ring" in Philadelphia, the "gas-house gang" in Chicago, and the "real-estate ring" in Washington. Best known, and typical, was New York City's Tammany Hall, whose executive committee of twenty-seven, according to the New York *Evening Post* (April 3, 1890), consisted of two murderers (one convicted), one convicted felon, four professional gamblers, five dive-keepers, eight liquor dealers and their sons, three pugilists, four toughs. "Good municipal government," said Detroit's reform mayor, Hazen E. Pingree, "is an impossibility while valuable franchises are to be had and can be obtained by corrupt use of money in bribing public servants." The very word *politician* became a term of amused contempt, as Artemus Ward illustrated in his famous witticism: "I'm not a politician and my other habits are good."

The masters of the economy and their spokesmen defended their position on two main grounds. In the first place, they argued that their power and privilege were justified on the basis of their superior personal ability. In the second place, they proclaimed that their wealth entailed moral responsibility to their fellow men.

The argument of superior ability, given sociological form by such men as William Graham Sumner, drew sustenance from the Darwinian theory of the survival of the fittest. Again and again, the great magnates repeated this soothing idea. Russell Sage, the nineteenth-century financier who is best remembered for the foundation that bears his name, said: "To rail against the accumulation of wealth is to rail against the decrees of justice. . . . So long as some men have more sense and more self-control than others, just so long will such men be wealthy, while others will be poor." John D. Rockefeller, the richest man in America, said in a Sunday-school sermon: "The growth of a large business is merely a survival of the fittest. . . . The American Beauty rose can be produced in the splendor and fragrance which brings cheer to its beholder only by sacrificing the early buds.... This is not an evil tendency in business. It is merely the working out of a law of nature and a law of God." George Hearst, the millionaire father of publisher William Randolph Hearst, said of the United States Senate, the "Millionaire's Club" of which he was a member from 1886 to 1891: "I do not know much about books . . . ; but . . . I have made up my mind after all my experience that the members of the Senate are the survivors of the fittest."

John J. Ingalls, the Kansas senator who was for a time president pro tem of the Senate, put the "survival of the fittest" idea in blunt political terms when he said in 1890: "The purification of politics is an iridescent dream. Government is force. Politics is a battle for supremacy. Parties are the armies. The Decalog and the Golden Rule have no place in a political campaign.... In war it is lawful to deceive the adversary, to hire Hessians, to purchase mercenaries, to mutilate, to destroy. The commander who lost the battle through the activity of his moral nature would be the derision and jest of history. This modern cant about the corruption of politics is fatiguing in the extreme. It proceeds from tea-custard . . . dilettanteism and frivolous sentimentalism."

In truth, the ruthlessness of the plutocracy was mitigated by the other facet of its philosophy—moral obligation. The idea that great wealth involved personal responsibility became widespread in the latter half of the nineteenth century. Under the pressure of mounting public criticism, the magnates displayed extraordinary personal benevolence. They were unconscionable in the exploitation of the nation's human and natural resources, but they also became fantastically generous in their social beneficence. Wealth came to be considered an instrument Providence had created for man's ennoblement. "By the proper use of wealth," Daniel Seely Gregory wrote in his widely used college textbook, *Christian Ethics* (1875), "man may greatly elevate and extend his moral work. It is therefore his duty to seek to secure wealth for this high end. . . . The Moral Governor has placed the power of acquisitiveness in man for a good and noble purpose." This was echoed by Andrew Carnegie—who made a fortune of some $400,000,000 before he reached middle age—who wrote in his *The Gospel of Wealth:* "Surplus wealth is a sacred trust which its possessor is bound to administer in his lifetime for the good of the community."

Carnegie, in whose steel industry labor conditions were appalling, gave away the bulk of his fortune for a number of purposes, among them church bells, town libraries, teachers' pensions, education, and international peace. Similarly, John D. Rockefeller—whose practices in the setting up of Standard Oil were the scandal of the age—left a large part of his gigantic fortune for benevolent purposes. "The good Lord," he said simply, "gave me my money"; through various foundations his money has been distributed for the advancement of learning, science, and public health, not only in America but in many parts of the world.

Other magnates have followed these examples, confounding John Stuart Mill's remark about American materialism (in *Principles of Political Economy*) that in the United States "the life of one sex is devoted to dollar-hunting, and of the other to breeding dollar-hunters." The dollar-hunters have spent billions in the founding of institutions of higher learning (The University of Chicago, Stanford, Duke, Colgate, among others), libraries, museums, planetariums, scholarship funds, literary and scientific foundations. The American landscape is dotted with the works and gifts of the great capitalists.

But one effect of this titanic philanthropy has been to strengthen the idea that culture and higher education were mainly private matters, to be maintained by individual charity. It has discouraged government from assuming large-scale responsibility for the national welfare in fields (the arts, health, the sciences, higher education) that are usually prime public concerns in other lands. Another effect has been to perpetuate the influence of private economic power upon the nation's political life.

None of this has occurred without protest. In fact, dissent has become a well-established American tradition. Protest movements, "third parties" such as the National Grange and the Populists, and even some major party leaders like Grover Cleveland and Theodore Roosevelt, voiced opposition to the inequalities and injustices resulting from unregulated economic individualism.

President Cleveland's fourth annual message to Congress (1888) contains an indictment that is especially striking in view of his political conservatism. Cleveland, in words reminiscent of Walt Whitman and Henry George, said:

> Our cities are the abiding places of luxury; our manufactories yield fortunes never dreamed of by the fathers of the Republic; our business men are madly striving in the race for riches, and immense aggregations of capital outrun the imagination....
>
> ...We find the luxury of our cities mingled with wretchedness and unremunerative toil.... We discover that the fortunes realized by our manu-

facturers are no longer solely the reward of sturdy industry and enlightened foresight, but that they result from the discriminating favor of the Government. . . .

As we view the achievements of aggregated capital, we discover the existence of trusts, combinations, and monopolies, while the citizen is struggling far in the rear or is trampled to death beneath an iron heel. Corporations, which should be the carefully restrained creatures of the law and the servants of the people, are fast becoming the people's masters. . . . The existing situation is injurious to the health of our entire body politic.

The long-established tradition of impotent government was particularly troublesome in the twentieth century. Acute problems arising from extensive industrialization, widespread urbanization, far-flung world wars and continuing international crises could be solved only by central governmental authority. But government had not always been strong enough, or, as when it was headed by men like Herbert Hoover, willing enough, to use the political authority for the solution of public problems. American leadership has had to struggle not only to meet modern crises but also to overcome an ingrained national distrust of political power. Even so vigorous a leader as Theodore Roosevelt did not, as President, have sufficient authority to end a coal strike that threatened to paralyze the nation or to do anything effective about monopolies that had a stranglehold on the country's economic life. Government, he said, was "well-nigh impotent to deal with the great business combinations."

Woodrow Wilson, too, complained that the position of the national government vis-à-vis private economic power was "of a nature absolutely intolerable." In his book *The New Freedom,* Wilson, proposing a strengthening of government for the defense of human rights, had recourse to the spirit of Jefferson: "One of the interesting things that Mr. Jefferson said in those early days of simplicity . . . was that the best government consisted in as little governing as possible. And there is still a sense in which that is true. . . . But I feel confident that if Jefferson were living in our day he would see what we see: that the individual is caught in a great confused nexus of all sorts of complicated circumstances, and that to let him alone is to leave him helpless as against the obstacles with which he has to contend; and that, therefore, law in our day must come to the assistance of the individual. It must see . . . that he gets fair play. Without the watchful interference . . . of the government, there can be no fair play between individuals and such powerful institutions as the trusts."

President Wilson instituted a series of reforms that provided a certain amount of "watchful interference" by government, but his program, cut short by World War I, was hardly more than a precedent. The practice, if not the theory, of limited government did not fully come to an end until the 1930s, in the administration of Franklin D. Roosevelt, who had been in a significant sense a disciple (as well as Assistant Secretary of the Navy) of Wilson. The Roosevelt New Deal brought about a veritable revolution in the role of government in the United States. Designed for the relief of nationwide unemployment and economic bankruptcy, the New Deal went far beyond immediate goals and exigencies. It affected every aspect of the nation's life.

The unprecedented and far-flung New Deal program brought relief and protection to farmers, workers, bankers, investors, businessmen, youth, Indians, writers, artists, and actors. It created agencies for public housing, for rural electrification, for mortgages, for hydroelectric dams, for irrigation, for bank loans—for practically everything, including culture. It penetrated everywhere. One New Deal agency, the Public Works Administration [PWA], for example, went into every one of the nation's 3070 counties, where it spent billions of dollars constructing the astonishing number of 26,474 projects, among them schools, armories, libraries, airfields, hangars, hospitals, power plants, garbage-disposal plants, highways, courthouses, waterworks, and all types of municipal structures. The New Deal, in short, took government fully into the multifarious activities of the nation.

Thus ended the career of feeble government in the United States. The process was completed by World War II, which in the nature of things required massive governmental controls of the nation's economy and institutions. This assumption of governmental responsibility in numerous spheres of what had long been considered private domain has remained unchanged, despite criticism from powerful sources. Franklin D. Roosevelt's predecessor, Herbert Hoover, has continued to proclaim the philosophy that *any* kind of governmental economic regulation is "tyranny." His successor, Dwight D. Eisenhower, has denounced such New Deal monuments as the Tennessee Valley Authority [TVA] as "creeping Socialism." But in fact there has been no actual weakening of government or reversal of the New Deal reforms. Government, especially the national one, is today all-pervasive in its power and influence.

Americans are still ambivalent on the subject of government. They tolerate its bigness and demands as measures of national necessity but they distrust its power. They expect it to "do something" whenever a crisis occurs, but they resent its encroachments. Although this mistrust of political power has been to a large extent instrumental in preserving traditional freedoms in the United States, it may also turn out to be a serious liability in modern times. In an atomic age, when science and technology are shrinking the globe and creating unprecedented situations that require swift solutions on a vast scale, it is questionable whether America's intensive individualism and fear of government are superior virtues. To meet the onrushing challenges of the modern world, American government may have further to widen its functions and penetrate deeper into the everyday lives of the citizens—bringing national control into such hitherto private or locally administered areas as health, education, communication media, crime, and delinquency. This will involve major adjustments in thought and action. But a nation that produced William James and John Dewey and created pragmatism as an indigenous philosophy may be expected to adapt itself to unexpected contingencies.

The variety of adaptation that American political thought has undergone can be seen in the biographic studies that follow. These are not intended to be a comprehensive survey of the American political mind. They are designed rather to illustrate the richness and flexibility of the nation's political character and its special genius for the practicalities needed for the maintenance of a free and egalitarian society.

# 2

## *THE AMERICAN AS ARCHETYPE:* George Washington *(1732–1799)*

> *The head of Washington hangs in my dining-room for a few days past, and I cannot keep my eyes off it. It has a certain Appalachian strength, as if it were truly the first-fruits of America, and expressed the Country. The heavy, leaden eyes turn on you, as the eyes of an ox in a pasture. And the mouth has gravity and depth of quiet, as if this* MAN *had absorbed all the serenity of America, and left none for his restless, rickety, hysterical countrymen.*
>
> —*Ralph Waldo Emerson,* Diary (*July 6, 1852*)

For more than a century and a half the granite reputation of George Washington has withstood the attentions of his idolators. Few other national heroes have ever been a greater target of idolatry, hagiography, iconolatry, myth-making, and breathless patriotic oratory. Washington was made into a graven image for the nation to worship.

This sanctification has done a grave injustice to a good and great man. It has stripped him of the common humanity with which he was so abundantly endowed. A passionate, sensitive, earthy, deeply feeling human being was transformed into an idol that, presumably, had never experienced anything but the loftiest patriotic emotions.

The person and character of Washington did, of course, lend themselves easily to national deification. He was of the stuff of heroes. He even looked the way a hero should look—tall and handsome, powerfully built and graceful. Jefferson said of him: "His person . . . was fine, his stature exactly what one would wish, his deportment easy, erect and noble; the best horseman of his age, and the most graceful figure that could be seen on horseback."

His sheer presence impressed everybody. Abigail Adams thought he had more grace and dignity than King George III of England. John Page, a governor of Virginia, considered him greater than Cicero. Benjamin Franklin, bequeathing to him his gold-headed crabtree walking-stick, said: "If it were a sceptre, he has merited it and would become it." And his Negro servant, recalling the twenty-seven-year-old Washington's marriage to Martha Custis, exclaimed that there was nobody in that glittering wedding assemblage like the young Colonel: "So tall, so straight! and . . . with such an air! Ah, sir; he was like no one else! Many of the grandest gentlemen in their gold lace were at the wedding, but none looked like the man himself."

His dignity and self-esteem were such that to a superficial observer he appeared cold. Actually he was emotional, tender, and capable of outbursts of violence. An iron discipline, which he imposed upon himself all his life, kept a leash on his passions. "All the muscles of his face," Captain George Mercer, a fellow soldier, wrote of him, "[are] under perfect control, though flexible and expressive of deep feeling when moved by emotion." His infrequent outbursts of anger were legendary. On the occasions when his rigid self-control broke under stress, he was, according to a contemporary, "most tremendous in his wrath."

One such instance is recorded in Jefferson's diary. At an important cabinet meeting in August 1793, Secretary of War Knox referred to some particularly nasty abuse of the President that had just been printed in Freneau's hostile *National Gazette* and Bache's *General Advertiser*. The mention of these inimical newspapers so inflamed Washington's "irritable and high-toned" temper that it finally broke up the session. Jefferson relates: "The Presdt . . . got into one of those passions when he cannot command himself, ran on much on the personal abuse which had been bestowed on him, defied any man on earth to produce one single act of his since he had been in the govmt which was not done on the purest motives, that he had never repented but once the having slipped the moment of resigning his office, & that was every moment since, that *by god* he had rather be on his farm than to be made *emperor of the world* and yet they were charging him with wanting to be a king."

Washington had the aloofness of the very shy. He was a poor public speaker, slow in expression, halting in thought, unendowed with quips or glibness. Strangers were likely to embarrass him and to reduce him to a slightly awkward silence. Only among friends would he warm up and show the gentle and sometimes whimsical side of his nature. At best, however, he was a mediocre conversationalist, possessing, in the words of a contemporary, "neither copiousness of ideas nor fluency of words."

In person-to-person contact he was a gentleman of considerable charm, invariably courteous and attentive. His voice was pleasant and well modulated. In conversation he would look the interlocutor full in the face, weigh his words carefully, and show him an engaging deference. Ladies found him charming and he, in turn, could not easily resist them. His letters to women show him to be something of a romantic where they were concerned, curiously awkward in his faintly ursine attempts at badinage.

He was especially susceptible to the "fair ladies" in his youth. As an adolescent he was tormented by sex and sometimes poured out his sorrows in verse, which he either wrote himself or copied. Some of the preserved verses show that he had amorous troubles. Possibly he was too bashful. To his journal he occasionally confided the sorrows of what he called "my Poor Resistless Heart." One verse, written by young Washington, is perhaps characteristic:

> From your bright sparkling Eyes, I was undone;
> Rays, you have more transparent than the sun,
> Amidst its glory in the rising Day,
> None can you equal in your bright array....
> Ah! woe is me...

As a young officer serving on the lonely western frontier, he wrote to a friend that he was in love with someone far away, that he was unhappy and tormented by the "recollection of a thousand tender passages." "The hours at present," he concluded, "are melancholy dull.... I dare believe you are as happy as you say. I wish I was happy also."

A strong, masculine man, he was attracted to women all his life. "When once the woman has tempted us," he wrote to a lady at the age of fifty-one, "and we have tasted the forbidden fruit, there is no such thing as checking our appetites, whatever the consequences may be."

An emotional man at bottom, Washington, the seemingly frosty hero, was capable of the grand dramatic gesture. His farewell to his officers on December 4, 1783, at Fraunces Tavern in New York was a scene out of a play. Standing before the men he had commanded for eight perilous and finally triumphant years, his customary self-control deserted him. Tears filled his eyes as he stood up, filled a glass with a shaking hand, and said in a trembling voice: "I cannot come to each of you to take my leave, but shall be obliged if you will each come and shake me by the hand." Silently they lined up and shook his hand. Then he returned home to Mount Vernon, after an absence of eight years, journeying through communities that embarrassed him by their outpourings of homage, determined to retire from public life forever. He had started his military career more than thirty years back, and now that he had won independence for his country, the American Cincinnatus, as the newspapers and the orators called him, felt that he merited retirement to the plow. He was only fifty-one and, as he wrote to his friend Lafayette, his sole desire was to be a private citizen, to sit under his "own vine and fig-tree," and "move gently down the stream of life until I sleep with my fathers."

Retirement was a luxury that destiny did not permit him to enjoy.

What was there in George Washington that attracted so many diverse men and that made his country turn to him, almost as if by instinct, in any crisis? He was not a particularly great general; some of the more important battles of the Revolution were won by others. He was not, like Alexander Hamilton, a brilliant man; his mind was slow and methodical. Nor was he an educated man; in literary culture and knowledge he could in no way be compared to such colleagues and contemporaries as Adams, Jefferson, or Madison. In articulateness or wit he was nowhere near Franklin.

Washington had little formal education. A nonwealthy orphan, he had left school at about the age of fifteen, having acquired merely the rudiments of arithmetic, the art of reading, and a rather limited skill in spelling. It was only after he grew older, and by hard application, that he learned to write without doing too much violence to spelling or structure. As a lad his literary compositions left much to be desired, especially in his early diaries. An interesting example is taken from his diary of March 15, 1748, covering his first surveying trip at the age of sixteen: "We got our suppers & was Lighted into a Room & I not being so good a woodsman as ye rest of my company, striped myself very orderly and went into ye Bed, as they calld it, when to my surprize, I found it to be nothing but a little straw matted together without sheets or anything else, but only one thread bear blanket with double its weight of vermin, such as Lice, Fleas, &. I was glad to get up . . . I put on my cloths & lay as my companions."

What gives Washington his special distinction, what in fact accounts for his peculiar greatness and appeal, is not book learning but character. In the course of a busy and active life he found little time and had small inclination to read; what reading he did was confined mainly to books of history and agricultural reports. But his character and personality were molded by a different kind of education—the living world around him. Washington carefully observed the best examples of proper behavior and deliberately modeled himself after the well-bred, class-conscious, and almost feudally elegant Virginia gentry, particularly the aristocratic Fairfax family. In the virtually self-contained plantation world of eighteenth-century Virginia a man was in a position to learn values that form the basic ingredients of leadership. There was hardly a better school anywhere in which to acquire the habits of sane command, the importance of good manners and dignified behavior, and, above all, that special *noblesse oblige* which fortifies the sense of leadership, no matter how self-sacrificing, and of responsibility, no matter how onerous. Among members of his family and his neighbors young Washington chose models of manliness, ambition, self-respect, and practicality. He became an exquisitely constructed, firmly disciplined product of a society that was, in its day, steady of purpose and supremely self-confident.

He set himself gentlemanly standards of behavior quite early in life. At the age of thirteen he elaborately copied a set of 110 "Rules of Civility and Decent Behaviour in Company and Conversation." The rules are an amalgam of Calvinistic morals, Franklinian maxims, and Chesterfieldian manners. The significant thing about this handbook of behavior is not that Washington copied it as a schoolboy but that he seriously strove to live up to it as a man. A few examples will convey the flavor of the maxims:

Every Action done in Company, ought to be with some Sign of Respect, to those that are present.

Sleep not when others Speak, Sit not when others stand, Speak not when you should hold your Peace.

At Play and at Fire its Good manners to Give Place to the last Commer.

Come not near the Books or Writings of Another so as to read them unless desired or give your opinion of them unask'd.

Let your countenance be pleasant but in serious matters somewhat grave.

Reproach none for the Infirmaties of Nature.

Shew not yourself glad at the Misfortune of another though he were your enemy.

When you meet with one of Greater Quality than yourself, Stop, and... give way for him to Pass.

Let your Discourse with Men of Business be Short and Comprehensive.

In writing or Speaking, give to every Person his due Title according to his Degree & the Custom of the Place.

Strive not with your superiors in argument, but always submit your Judgment to others with Modesty.

Undertake not to teach your Equal in the Art himself professes; it savors Arrogancy.

In your Apparel be Modest and endeavour to accomodate Nature, rather than to procure Admiration.

Associate yourself with Men of good Quality if you Esteem your own reputation; for 'tis better to be alone than in bad Company.

Let your Conversation be without Malice or Envy . . . And in all Causes of Passion admit Reason to Govern.

Be not apt to relate News if you know not the truth thereof.

Undertake not what you cannot Perform but be Carefull to keep your Promise.

Speak not Evil of the Absent for it is unjust.

Be not tedious in Discourse.

When you Speak of God or his Attributes, let it be Seriously & with Reverence.

Let your Recreations be Manfull not Sinfull.

Labour to keep alive in your Breast that Little Spark of Celestial fire Called Conscience.

The virtues Washington adopted and made his own were an integral part of his massive character. His qualities were not those of a wild-eyed dreamer or frenetic patriot. They were, rather, those of a tough-minded man of the world, ambitious to acquire wealth and honor, practical and conservative in all his dealings, always accepting the world exactly as it was, and generally untroubled by illusions of human nobility. "We may," he would tell his impatient friends, "lament that things are not consonant with our wishes, but cannot change the nature of man." In all his dealings with people he acted on the assumption that follies and foibles are inherent in mankind. "We must," he said often, "take the passions of men as nature has given them."

It was imperative for a gentleman to recognize the limitations of human nature and to act so as not to be entrapped by the weakness or greed of others. The weak and unfortunate called for assistance, but not for personal involvement in their ill luck. Washington practiced charity, but lost no emotions over its recipients. It was out of his carefully developed sense of duty that he often helped the needy even when he could hardly afford it. In his relations with individuals he scrupulously calculated their characters and gave them the exact respect they deserved.

Typical of his practical attitude is the letter he wrote to his twenty-one-year-old nephew, Bushrod Washington, who went to Philadelphia to study law. Washington gave young Bushrod—later to become a justice of the United States Supreme Court (1798–1829)—advice worthy of Polonius:

Let the object, which carried you to Philadelphia, be always before your Eyes. Remember, that it is not the mere study of the Law, but to become eminent in the profession of it, which is to yield honor and profit. The first was your choice; let the second be your ambition.... Dissipation is incompatible with both; ... the Company, in which you will improve most, will be least expensive to you; and yet I am not such a Stoic as to suppose that you will, or to think it right that you should, always be in Company with senators and philosophers; but of the young and juvenile kind let me advise you to be choice. It is easy to make acquaintances, but very difficult to shake them off, however irksome and unprofitable they are found. ... The indiscretions and scrapes, which very often they involuntarily lead one into, prove equally distressing and disgraceful.

Be courteous to all, but intimate with few; and let those few be well tried before you give them your confidence. True friendship is a plant of slow growth, and must undergo and withstand the shocks of adversity before it is entitled to the appellation....

Do not conceive that fine clothes make fine men any more than fine feathers make fine Birds. A plain genteel dress is more admired, and obtains more credit than lace and embroidery....

The last thing, which I shall mention, is first in importance; and that is, to avoid Gaming. This is a vice which is productive of every possible evil; equally injurious to the morals and health of its votaries. It is the child of avarice, the brother of iniquity, and father of mischief. It has been the ruin of many worthy families, the loss of many a man's honor, and the cause of Suicide.... In a word, few gain by this abominable practice ... while thousands are injured.

If this sounds like mere moralizing, it should be kept in mind that Washington himself practiced his preachings. He was courteous, modest, moderate, and abstemious. He neither gambled nor drank immoderately. From early youth he imposed upon himself a severe code of conduct which formed a kind of frame into which he fitted himself. Instead of repressing his character, the strong discipline and conscious purpose of his life elevated it. Of him it could be said that he learned to command himself so that he could command others.

The towering character of the man—that compound of Calvinistic morality and aristocratic obligation—enabled him to play the vital role that he did in the early years of the United States. It is perhaps hazardous to speak of individual indispensability in history, but if there ever was an indispensable leader at a critical moment in history, it was George Washington. In the formative years of the American republic, roughly between 1776 and 1796, the man, the moment, and the crisis coincided.

The sheer personality of Washington was the decisive element in the three crucial events of early America—the Revolutionary War, the Constitutional Convention, and the first national administration. Hardly anything more than his steeled will power held together the ragged Revolutionary army in times of darkest despair; a weaker man would have given way to hopelessness as the troops kept on deserting, provisions were reduced to a famishing trickle, and funds dwindled to near-nothingness. The Commander in Chief complained furiously and bitterly, he wrote despairing letters of appeal for aid that were veritable cries of anguish, and he stuck to his guns. His iron sense of duty did not permit him the luxury of giving up what at times appeared to be a hopeless struggle.

Similarly, his presence held together the Constitutional Convention in 1787. Chairman of the Convention, he was a silent member, but the fact that he was there was a guarantee of the importance of the meeting and helped to cement disparate elements. Washington's immense prestige was also a major factor in the adoption of the bitterly assailed Constitution, especially in the Virginia legislature, where the instrument, eloquently battered by the formidable Patrick Henry, was adopted by a mere majority of 5 out of a total of 168 votes. Rejection of the Constitution by Virginia, Washington knew, would have been a fatal blow to national union, particularly since Virginia, in numbers and in influence, was the biggest state in America. Thus in June 1788 he helped save the union just before it began its operations.

Finally, it was Washington's personality—recognized so widely for integrity, courage, wisdom, and patriotism—that launched the Republic under the Constitution. His delicate sense of balance and steadying wisdom reconciled clashing interests and opposing sections, and gave the new nation the fundamental shape that it has retained.

An analysis of George Washington inescapably raises the question of the meaning of leadership. Washington was an almost classic type of leader, looked up to as such even by those who were his political opponents. What were the elements involved in his leadership?

I have already mentioned the obvious—the surface—traits: character, appearance, and self-discipline. But leadership is a two-way affair. It consists of the interplay between the leader and the led, between the person who symbolizes conspicuousness and those to whom it appeals. Washington's leadership, therefore, tells us a great deal about the America of his day. To the men and women of late-eighteenth-century America Washington was the embodiment of the qualities they were taught to revere or to which they aspired. Had he not possessed the characteristics which to them were admirable or desirable, he would have been just another soldier, merely another aristocratic planter, no better and no worse than a thousand others.

Washington had exactly what his contemporaries knew was important in life—an unflinching belief in principles and a stern devotion to virtue. The principles were held to be inherent in man, and the virtues eternal. Any compromise with principles or virtues was an offense to God and man. A person who aspired to a respected position in society or to leadership had to be conspicuous for his adherence to the values which the common people were taught to respect. An ordinary individual might violate the public virtues—he might get drunk, or beat his wife, or cheat at cards—but a leader, conscious of his position, could not and would not do so. The essential point is that a man like George Washington was expected to look and act like a gentleman, like a superior person, at all times and in all circumstances. Upon him and his kind devolved the social responsibility of living up to the high standards of personal and public behavior that the eighteenth century considered natural and immutable.

For in those days American society was, in David Riesman's term, "inner-directed." It had built-in standards of right and wrong and it looked to its leaders to maintain them. A great leader's role was to be completely himself, to live in such a way as to strengthen the existing virtues of the people and to set them a model that they could follow and imitate. It was not required of him to talk down to the people or to flatter the masses. He was not expected to seek popularity through appeals to crude or base emotions. Indeed, the leading figures of that period did not make any appeals at all. Neither Washington nor Jefferson, for example, waged any campaigns for the presidency. They did not promise or flatter or orate. Had a man like Washington been "other-directed"—concerned with the unstable stream of public sentiment—he would have lost both caste and position. His function was to be above immediate fluctuations of opinion, to pay no attention to the ever-changing momentary emotions of the majority. Deep inside himself he knew what was right and what was wrong, and he expected others, to a larger or lesser extent, to have the same moral mechanism that would make them respect the leader who had these steady and high moral virtues.

(It is perhaps ironic to reflect that in our own "other-directed" society George Washington would hardly be a successful leader, if, indeed, he would be considered a leader at all. A society whose main and overriding concern is with conformity would probably be disinclined to follow a man of severe moral conduct, a person who always knew right from wrong, and who was convinced that moral principles are the foundations of the universe and that they never change. It is difficult to see how Washington could receive many votes from the mid-twentieth-century American electorate. But all this is, of course, mere speculation.)

It is important to note that Washington himself was always conscious of his social position and, in later life, of his role as national leader. Although not a particularly religious individual or especially interested in theological questions, he became both vestryman and warden of his neighboring church, which he attended regularly and supported financially. His essential motive here was probably more social than ecclesiastical; he felt that a gentleman must set the proper example. This is not to suggest that Washington was an atheist or a deist; in point of fact he did not question the existence of God. His writings are full of references to the Deity, Providence, and the Divine Creator who watches over man's destinies, punishing evil and rewarding virtue.

Likewise Washington took extreme care in ordering his military uniform, paying minute attention to buckles, laces, buttons, and other paraphernalia. This was not so much a matter of vanity—Washington was not a vain man—as of policy. A commanding officer must at all times not only act like one but look like one. He was equally careful in being meticulously garbed when posing for a portrait painter, and even in purchasing a "chariot." When he ordered a carriage in London, he gave his agent every possible detail as to materials, colors, shape, and quality. This was done not for vulgar display but for the fitness of things. He expected the carriage to last him a lifetime and he wanted it to be of the best—so that a gentleman would not be ashamed to be seen in it even when it was old. "I would willingly," he wrote to his London agent, "have the chariot you may now send me made in the newest taste, handsome, genteel and light; . . . to be of the best seasoned wood, and by a celebrated workman. . . . Green being a color little apt . . . to fade, and grateful to the eye, I would give it the preference, unless any other color more in vogue and equally lasting is entitled to precedency. In that case I would be governed by fashion. A light gilding on the mouldings . . . and any other ornaments, that may not have a heavy and tawdry look . . . might be added. A lining of a handsome, lively colored leather of good quality I should also prefer, such as green, blue, &, as may best suit the color of the outside."

He went into similar details when ordering his clothes from his London tailor. Again we have here a gentleman's consciousness of his worth and appearance. The emphasis is always on good quality and good taste. His "superfine broad cloth" must be "handsomely chosen."

After the Revolution, when he was a national figure, he became doubly aware of his role in the country and of his position in the eyes of posterity. He did not know much history but he had enough familiarity with the names of the great men of the past to think of himself a little in comparison with them. Once more it is necessary to stress that we are not dealing here with a vain man but with a historically conscious one. Modest although not humble, Washington was not unaware of his historic stature. When America had grown secure and powerful —and he was convinced the United States would become a great "empire"—then, he felt, her writers and poets would do for him and for other important American leaders what bards had done in the past in other countries. Somehow he sensed that there was a connection between the hero and the poet, between the political figure and the literary one. In antiquity, he once said, the poets were "both the priests and door-keepers to the temple of fame." This he wished to be true in America also.

There is an unusual letter which Washington, one year before his election to the Presidency, wrote to his friend Lafayette in Paris. In it he recommended Joel Barlow, an American poet as widely known in his day as he is obscure today. In introducing Barlow, of whom Washington was proud as an American, he indulged in historical-literary reflections of the most rare variety. The letter throws a fascinating light into one corner of Washington's personality:

Men of real talents in arms have commonly approved themselves patrons of the liberals and friends to the poets, of their own as well as former times. In some instances by acting reciprocally, heroes have made poets, and poets heroes. Alexander the Great is said to have been enraptured with the poems of Homer, and to have lamented that he had not a rival muse to celebrate his actions. Julius Caesar is well known to have been a man of a highly cultivated understanding and taste. Augustus was the professed and magnificent rewarder of poetical merit—nor did he lose the return of having his achievements immortalized in song. The Augustan Age is proverbial for intellectual refinement and elegance in composition; in it the harvest of laurels and bays was wonderfully mingled together. The age of your Louis the Fourteenth, which produced a multitude of great poets and great captains, will never be forgotten; nor will that of Queen Ann in England, for the same cause, ever cease to reflect a lustre upon the kingdom. Although we are yet in our cradle, as a nation, I think the efforts of the human mind with us are sufficient to refute . . . the doctrines of those who have asserted that every thing degenerates in America. Perhaps we shall be found at this moment, not inferior to the rest of the world in the performances of our poets and painters; notwithstanding many of the incitements are wanting which operate powerfully among older nations.

Then he concluded, as if he were suddenly ashamed of this outburst, with its oblique reflections and hopes about himself: "I hardly know how it is that I am drawn thus far in observations on a subject so foreign from those in which we are mostly engaged, farming and politics, unless because I had little news to tell you."

Small wonder that so many of his countrymen began to deify him. The process of canonization started soon after his death. In 1800, a few months after he was buried in the family vault at Mount Vernon, the first eulogistic biography appeared; it was to set the pattern. The title is descriptive of the book—*A History of the Life and Death, Virtues and Exploits of General George Washington, with Curious Anecdotes Equally Honourable to Himself and Exemplary to his Young Countrymen.* The author, Mason Locke Weems, described himself on the title page as "Formerly Rector of Mount Vernon Parish," an identification with Washington's own church that undoubtedly had much to do with the book's fabulous success. Young America, in the second decade of its nationhood, was hungry for a hero, especially one as ready-made as George Washington, and devoured Weems' rhapsodic production. As edition succeeded edition—there were about seventy of them altogether—the good parson kept on inventing more "curious anecdotes" until the figure of Washington was smothered in a morass of sentimental and moralistic extravaganza. Weems even appealed to future generations to genuflect before the sacred idol he helped to create. On the title page he urged: "Lisp! lisp his name, ye children yet unborn!"—a bit of advice which, if carried out, would be the neatest trick of the century.

Probably the most famous Weemsey was the cherry-tree story. It is a gem of Americana that must not be permitted to lapse into oblivion:

> The following anecdote . . . is too valuable to be lost, and too true to be doubted; for it was communicated to me by the same excellent lady to whom I am indebted for the last.
>
> "When George," says she, "was about six years old, he was made the wealthy master of a hatchet! of which, like most little boys, he was immoderately fond, and was constantly going about chopping everything that came in his way. One day, in the garden, where he often amused himself hacking his mother's pea-sticks, he unluckily tried the edge of his hatchet on the body of a beautiful young English cherry-tree, which he barked so terribly, that I don't believe the tree ever got the better of it. The next morning the old gentleman, finding out what had befallen his tree, which, by the way, was a great favorite, came into the house; and with much warmth asked for the mischievous author, declaring at the same time, that he would not have taken five guineas for his tree. Nobody could tell him anything about it. Presently George and his hatchet made their appearance. 'George,' said his father, 'do you know who killed that beautiful little cherry tree yonder in the garden?' This was a tough question; and George staggered under it for a moment; but quickly recovered himself: and looking at his father, with the sweet face of youth brightened with the inexpressible charm of all-conquering truth, he bravely cried out, 'I can't tell a lie, Pa, you know I can't tell a lie. I did cut it with my hatchet.'—'Run to my arms, you dearest boy,' cried his father in transports, 'run to my arms; glad am I, George, that you killed my tree; for you have paid me for it a thousand fold. Such an act of heroism in my son is more worth than a thousand trees, though blossomed with silver, and their fruits of purest gold.' "

It is not easy to survive this kind of prose, and George Washington—as a human being—was immolated by it. If there is such a thing as a crime of herocide, Washington was its victim. To his countrymen he became an embalmed image, a figure of wood, a mindless icon. When this writer, in recent years, told friends and students that he was preparing a book on George Washington's political and social ideas, he was invariably asked the surprised and skeptical question: "Why, did Washington have any ideas?"

He had very definite ideas, especially about the kind of world he wished to see established in America. He was not a systematic thinker, nor did he take the trouble to formulate his ideas. "With me," he wrote in December 1797, "it has always been a maxim rather to let my designs appear from my works than by my expressions." But scattered through his letters, addresses, and public utterances there are strains of thought that show a basic pattern and that have fundamental consistency.

At bottom, George Washington was an eighteenth-century rationalist, a firm believer in the rule of reason and of justice, and a champion of republicanism. Despite his aristocratic habits and predilections, he detested the very idea of monarchical or autocratic government; the suggestion that he should become a king outraged and shamed him. Unlike some of his distinguished contemporaries, Washington was a genuine republican. "I am told," he wrote to John Jay a year before the Constitutional Convention, "that even respectable characters speak of a monarchical form of government without horror. From thinking proceeds speaking; thence to acting is often but a single step. What a triumph for our enemies to verify their predictions! What a triumph for the advocates of despotism to find that we are incapable of governing ourselves."

He was determined that, in so far as it was in his power and influence to do anything about it, America would not become an autocracy. He knew that there was no such thing as an ideal government, but he was convinced that a constitutional republic, run by responsible and honest men, was, as he told James Madison, "as near to perfection as any human institution ever approximated." He did share Madison's middle-of-the-road political philosophy, striving for a government that would be strong enough to protect property and maintain order but not too strong to endanger the rights and liberties of the citizens. He was properly suspicious of too much military domination in public life, and always insisted that the civilian authority must be paramount at all times.

"General Washington," Jefferson said of him, "sincerely wished the people to have as much self government as they were competent to exercise themselves. The only point on which he and I differed in opinion, was, that I had more confidence than he had in the natural integrity and discretion of the people, and in the safety and extent to which they might trust themselves with a control over their government. He has asseverated to me a thousand times his determination that the existing government should have a fair trial, and that in support of it he would spend the last drop of his blood."

Washington constructed America's first national government with the same durable courage, inflexible purpose, and prudence that he showed during the most hopeless days of the Revolution. He built from scratch, fully aware that he was laying the foundations of American liberty and that he was creating precedents that would determine the shape of the future. "Many things which appear of little importance in themselves and at the beginning," he wrote as President, "may have great durable consequences from their having been established at the commencement of a new . . . government. It will be much easier to commence the administration, upon a well adjusted system, built on tenable grounds, than to correct errors or alter inconveniences after they shall have been confirmed by habit." He was thus doubly careful as President to act in such a way that his successors would be able to continue in a sensible republican path. One precedent, incidentally, which he almost set was the official title of his office. He wanted to be called "His Mightiness, the President of the United States and Protector of their Liberties." Fortunately, a plainer title was adopted, and to this day the man who occupies the position of America's chief executive is simply "Mr. President."

Whether as planter, soldier, or statesman, Washington was an incomparable administrator. Basically, good administration meant to him sound business principles. It was a matter of systematic application to the job at hand, attention to details, mastery of facts in any given situation, a careful recording of every act, a patient listening to clashing opinions, and a final decision based upon a balancing of the known data and interests. As commander in chief, Washington—who served the Revolution without pay—kept such a careful record of his expenditures during the eight years of the conflict that when he finally submitted his accounts to Congress his figures were off by only a few cents. He administered the army during the Revolution as meticulously as if it were his own extensive plantation. He kept complete records, worked long hours, delegated authority with the utmost care, never shirked responsibility or painful decisions, and maintained stern discipline among officers and men alike. Careless, pompous, untidy, or otherwise erring officers, no matter how high their rank, would feel the lash of his wrath, for Washington did not believe in sparing the rod or concealing his opinions. Few officers or men dared brave his whiplike displeasure.

This is how he outlined his idea of military discipline in a letter to one of his officers: "The best general advice I can give . . . is to be strict in your discipline; that is, to require nothing unreasonable of your officers and men, but see that whatever is required be punctually complied with. Reward and punish every man according to his merit, without partiality or prejudice; hear his complaints; if well founded, redress them; if otherwise, discourage them, in order to prevent frivolous ones.

Discourage vice in every shape, and impress upon the mind of every man, from the first to the lowest, the importance of the cause, and what it is they are contending for" (to Colonel William Woodford, 1775).

As planter, too, Washington insisted that his managers stick to sound business practices and follow a system. He urged them to think before acting, to plan each step in advance, not to waste time or labor, and, above all, to keep records of all their doings. Once when an overseer failed to reply to some of his questions, Washington wrote him a letter in which he carefully and patiently instructed him in the common sense of good administration:

> Whenever I set down to write you, I read your letter, or letters carefully over, and as soon as I come to a part that requires to be noticed, I make a short note on the cover of a letter or piece of waste paper;—then read on the next, noting that in like manner;—and so on until I have got through the whole letter and reports. Then in writing my letters to you, as soon as I have finished what I have to say on one of these notes I draw my pen through it and proceed to another until the whole is done—crossing each as I go on, by which means if I am called off twenty times whilst I am writing, I can never with these notes before me finished or unfinished, omit anything I wanted to say; and they serve me also . . . as memorandums of what has been written if I should have occasion at any time to refer to them.

He brought to the presidency the gift of his administrative genius, which was enriched by thirty-five years of experience as a large-scale farmer and commanding officer. In the presidency he set the pattern of orderliness, promptness, and, above all, method. Upon assuming the duties of chief executive, he issued the following instructions to the cabinet and heads of departments: "Let me impress the following maxim upon the executive officers. In all important matters, deliberate maturely, but execute promptly and vigorously and do not put things off until tomorrow; which can be done and require to be done today. Without an adherence to these rules, business will never be done, or done in an easy manner, but will always be in the arrears, with one thing treading upon the heels of another."

As President, he made it a habit to listen to all sides of a question—"that I may extract all the good I can"—and then to make his own decision. When it came to appointments, he was secretive up to the last moment, in order to escape undue influences. In naming men to office, he was unmoved by political or social pressures, and impervious to the claims of special interests if he felt they ran counter to the national weal. He rigorously abstained from appointing relatives to office, lest he be accused of practicing nepotism. Consciously and systematically he strove, as President, to avoid even the slightest suspicion of partiality or bias and always to keep the interest of the whole United States in the forefront of his attention. Jefferson remarked that Washington's sense of integrity was so pure and inflexible that "no motives of interest or consanguinity, of friendship or hatred" were "able to bias his decision." His basic maxim of presidential conduct was that what was good for America was good for George Washington.

"In every act of my administration," he once wrote to a group of Boston citizens who were critical of his foreign policy, "I have sought the happiness of my fellow citizens. My system for the attainment of this object has uniformly been to overlook all personal, local, and partial considerations; to contemplate the United States as one great whole; ... and to consult only the substantial and permanent interests of our country."

In Washington's eyes the new federal government had to be a model of integrity and impartiality, so that it could command the respect of the community and the loyalty of future generations. He well knew that any political system, in order to be durable and successful, must be rooted in the affections and loyalties of the society.

America's experiment in self-government was important to Washington for two essential reasons, domestic and international. In his opinion, the American Constitution provided for a government based on what he called "the pure and immutable principles of private morality." As such a government, the American political structure must perforce bring happiness to the people, since it was to him axiomatic that virtue must be rewarded. The second reason for Washington's satisfaction with the launching of the new national government was that it would serve as an example to all mankind. If successful in America, a self-governing republic would be imitated he was sure, by other peoples. In common with many eighteenth-century minds, he took a world view. Indeed, Washington was a Freemason at a time when Masonry was reputed to be actively revolutionist, engaged in a fight for freedom in many lands. In Europe, and probably also in Latin America, Masons were in secret or open opposition to clericalism, autocracy, and tyranny. They seem to have played a vital role in the French Revolution. As an active Freemason, Washington was pleased, he said, to have "true Brothers in all parts of the world."

His view of the new America as a land of domestic virtue and international example was unequivocally expressed in his first inaugural address. He said—and these words are astonishing when one recalls that America was then a numerically small backwoods on the fringe of the Atlantic Ocean:

> There is no truth more thoroughly established, than that there exists in the economy and course of nature an indissoluble union between virtue and happiness, between duty and advantage, between the genuine maxims of an honest and magnanimous policy, and the solid rewards of public prosperity and felicity; . . . we ought to be no less persuaded that the propitious smiles of Heaven can never be expected on a nation that disregards the eternal rules of order and right, which Heaven itself has ordained; and . . . the preservation of the sacred fire of liberty, and the destiny of the republican model of government, are justly considered as *deeply,* perhaps as *finally* staked, on the experiment intrusted to the hands of the American people.

And to Thomas Paine, whose writings he greatly admired, he wrote in 1792: "No one can feel a greater interest in the happiness of mankind than I do. . . . It is the first wish of my heart, that the enlightened policy of the present age may diffuse to all men those blessings, to which they are entitled, and lay the foundation of happiness for future generations."

He had a definite philosophy of republican self-government. Republicanism, to him, meant a way of life that guaranteed personal freedom, the enjoyment of private property, and equal justice for all individuals. Although himself a southerner and a planter, Washington, unlike most of his neighbors, was no agrarian. He took a national view of the republic, convinced that there were other interests and honorable ways of making a living other than agriculture. He was pleased to observe the early growth of industry in Pennsylvania and New England; it meant a strengthening of the republic.

Paradoxical as it may seem, the owner of several hundred slaves was also opposed to the institution of slavery. Washington, like other liberals of the period (he did refer to himself as a liberal), found slavery abhorrent, but, as a southern landowner, he was trapped in its tragedy. There was simply no way to continue without slaves, since other labor was virtually impossible to obtain. But he detested the whole system of slavery. "There is not a man living," he told Robert Morris in 1786, "who wishes more sincerely than I do to see a plan adopted for the abolition of it." With Jefferson, he often felt that the existence of slavery was like a bell in the night—it would toll death and tragedy. He considered a number of plans for emancipation; but for economic and political reasons nothing came of them. In his will, however, he provided for the manumission of his slaves.

In matters of religion, too, Washington was a child of the eighteenth-century Enlightenment. With Jefferson, Madison, and the other liberals of his day he shared the idea of complete religious freedom. He was wholly free of the vulgarity of religious or racial bias. Once in trying to obtain some servants, he said that he did not care where they came from or what deity they worshipped or did not worship. "If they are good workmen," he wrote, "they may be from Asia, Africa, or Europe; they may be Mahometans, Jews, or Christians of any sect, or they may be Atheists."

He knew that, in the past, religious persecutions had caused great misery. "Of all the animosities which have existed among mankind," he wrote, "those which are caused by differences of sentiments in religion appear to be the most inveterate and distressing, and ought most to be deprecated." For himself, he did not particularly care which, if any, path a man took to get to heaven. Referring to the conflicting sects of Christians, he told Lafayette: "Being no bigot myself, I am disposed to indulge the professors of Christianity . . . with that road to heaven, which to them shall seem the most direct, plainest, easiest."

It was a matter of special pride to Washington that the American republic guaranteed full religious liberty to all, particularly to such persecuted groups as the Quakers and Jews. To the Phildelphia Quakers he wrote a characteristic letter: "The liberty enjoyed by the People of these States, of worshipping Almighty God agreeably to their conscience is not only among the choicest of their *blessings* but also of their *rights*. While men perform their social duties faithfully, they do all that Society or the State can with propriety demand or expect; and remain responsible only to their Maker for the religion or modes of faith which they may prefer to profess. . . . I assure you very explicitly that in my opinion the conscientious scruples of all men should be treated with delicacy and tenderness."

In a similar vein he wrote to the Hebrew Congregation at Newport, Rhode Island, whose service he once attended. In that famous letter he rejected the idea of mere toleration, stressing that in America freedom of religious worship was one of the "inherent natural rights." America, he said, did not require of its citizens spiritual conformity but only decent civic behavior. "For happily the Government of the United States . . . gives to bigotry no sanction, to persecution no assistance."

He was touchingly proud of America, proud that it was his country that was given the historic chance of serving as a model of republican freedom, which was the only way of attaining happiness. As he wrote to a French friend during the third year of his presidency: "The United States are making great progress towards national happiness; and, if it is not attained here in as high a degree as human nature will admit . . . I think we may conclude, that political happiness is unattainable."

In retrospect, it is now clear that the victorious American Revolution inspired not only the French Revolution of 1789 but also republican movements in many parts of the world, and most particularly throughout Latin America. George Washington's America started a worldwide chain reaction the end of which has not yet been reached. The republic, which he did so much to create, showed itself to be so enduring and successful that it became an example for many other nations to imitate. Hence it can be held that George Washington, the eighteenth-century Virginia planter, is more than a national figure. He may be truly regarded as a giant in the history of human freedom.

# 3

## *THE AMERICAN AS ARISTOCRAT:* John Adams *(1735–1826)*

> *I dined this day with Mr. Adams. . . . In the course of our conversation he said, that no republic could ever last which had not a Senate . . . strong enough to bear up against all popular storms & passions . . . ; that the only fault in our Senate was that it was not durable enough. . . . That as to trusting to a popular assembly for the preservation of our liberties it was the merest chimera imaginable, they never had any rule of decision but their own will . . . , that anarchy did more mischief in one night than tyranny in an age. . . .*
>
> —*Thomas Jefferson,* The Anas (*February 15, 1798*)

John Adams' reputation among the American people has been dimmer than his achievements. He lacked the aura that surrounded Washington, whom he succeeded in the presidency in 1797. Despite their agreement on political fundamentals, the two men differed in their personalities and methods. Washington was aloof and inarticulate, Adams sprightly and opinionated. Unlike Washington, the second President suffered from a tactlessness that produced unnecessary enmities.

Adams was unpopular during his tenure of office, and the subsequent years have not substantially changed the public image of him. That image has been one of a crusty, sharp-tongued, somewhat eccentric antidemocrat so capricious in his views that he fitted into no discernible political pattern. A Federalist, he was not in the camp of Hamilton, whom he detested; a republican, he did not cooperate with Jefferson, whom he admired. To confuse matters further, Adams began his political career as a revolutionary liberal (espousing the cause of American independence), an ardent defender of human rights, and ended it as a champion of aristocracy and property. No wonder later generations of increasingly democratic Americans found it difficult to understand a man who belonged to no clear-cut category.

Yet John Adams embodied many of the great virtues of his age and background. He was a tough-minded if crotchety New England realist, granitic in his integrity and eccentric to a point that made some contemporaries (Benjamin Franklin, for one) pronounce him "mad." He also suffered from what many considered "excessive vanity," a trait against which he struggled vainly. "Oh!" he exclaimed as a young man, "that I could . . . conquer my natural pride and self-conceit!" But these traits which so annoyed his contemporaries did not prevent Adams from becoming one of the most widely read and learned men of his time, particularly in the fields of humanistic studies and political philosophy. His long life, indeed, was passionately devoted to the problems of government and the art of politics. Even as a youth his mind dwelt on political matters and there were moments when he visualized himself as "some dictator at the head of a commonwealth."

Despite his later pro-aristocratic philosophy, Adams was of modest origin. A third-generation New Englander, he was a descendant of sturdy farmers and clergymen, respectable but poor. About a dozen years before his death—he lived to the age of ninety-one and died, as did Jefferson, on the fiftieth anniversary of the Declaration of Independence—he wrote a terse autobiography:

I was born October 1735 in Quincy then the North Parish in Braintree, my Father was John Adams in the same Parish, my grandfather was Joseph Adams Junior born in the same Parish. . . . My great great grandfather was Henry Adams who came from England. These all lived, died and were buried in this Parish as their grave-stones in the Congregational Church yard distinctly show to this day. My Mother was Suzanna Boylston a Daughter of Peter Boylston of Brookline. I was educated partly at the public grammar school and partly at a private Academy under Mr. Joseph Marsh, both in this Parish. In 1751 I entered Harvard Colledge in Cambridge. In 1755 took my Degree of Batchelor of Arts, and immediately undertook the care of the Public Grammar School in Worcester where I . . . studied law in the office of James Pittman till 1757 when I took my second Degree at Colledge and the Oath of an Attorney in Boston. In 1761 I was admitted a Barrister at Law in Boston. . . . In 1764 I married Abigail Smith, a daughter of the Reverend

William Smith, of Weymouth. In 1767 my son John Quincy Adams * was born in this Parish. . . .

In 1760 and 1761, upon the first appearance of the Design of Great Britain to deprive us of our Liberties by asserting the Sovereign Authority of Parliament over us, I took a decided Part against her, and have persevered for Fifty years in opposing and resisting to the utmost of my power every Instance of her Injustice, and arbitrary Power, toward us.

Adams spent more than a quarter of a century in public life, first in his home state and then in the service of the nation. Like his Boston cousin Samuel Adams, he took an active part in the movement for independence from Great Britain, sensing earlier than most of his contemporaries that a break with the mother country was unavoidable. "The Revolution," he said later, "was effected before the war commenced. The Revolution was in the hearts and minds of the people." As a delegate to the Continental Congress, he had the distinction of proposing George Washington as commander in chief of the Revolutionary forces and of serving—with Jefferson, Franklin, Livingston, and Sherman—on the committee that drafted the Declaration of Independence. For more than a decade during and after the Revolutionary War, he was on American diplomatic missions in Europe, negotiating important treaties and otherwise representing the interests of his countrymen at great trouble and financial cost to himself, as he explained in a letter to Secretary of the Treasury Hamilton in April 1791, asking for some reimbursement:

The frequent removals from one country to another, the continual change of servants and liveries, the wear [*sic*] and tear of baggage, and destruction of furniture, beside the perpetual plunder I was subjected to in my absence from my house in one country, while attending my duty in another, have wasted and consumed my salary in such a manner, that my family must be deprived of that reward for my time, trouble, risk, and services, which all of us were entitled to.

For eight years, from 1789 to 1797, Adams served as the first Vice-President of the United States, a position he described in a famous phrase as "the most insignificant . . . that ever the invention of man contrived, or his imagination conceived." He followed George Washington in the presidency, but was defeated by Jefferson in the election of 1800, when he tried to win a second term. His defeat, mainly as a result of the Alien and Sedition Acts which he had signed, and his per-

* Fifth President of the United States (1825–1829).

sonal unpopularity also ended the rule of his party, the Federalist. Thereafter he retired to Braintree, Massachusetts, and devoted the rest of his days to the life of the mind, primarily reading (philosophy, religion, political thought) and brilliant letter-writing. His correspondence with Jefferson, resumed (in 1812) through the intercession of their mutual friend Dr. Benjamin Rush of Philadelphia after a political estrangement of a dozen years, is one of the most delightful intellectual exchanges in history. Many of Adams' liveliest opinions were expressed in that robust correspondence.

Apart from letters, Adams' fundamental political ideas can be traced in his public writings, which are at the same time eloquent and prolix. Among his important published writings are: *A Dissertation on the Canon and the Feudal Law* (1765), in which he took a liberal position in regard to human rights ("I say RIGHTS, for such they [the people] have, undoubtedly, antecedent to all earthly government—*rights* that cannot be repealed or restrained by human laws—*rights* derived from the great Legislator of the universe"); *Novanglus: Or A History of the Dispute with America, From Its Origin in 1754, to the Present Time,* a series of learned legal-political articles published in the *Boston Gazette* between December 1774 and April 1775; *Thoughts on Government* (1776), an elaboration of a letter to Richard Henry Lee which was read by the delegates to the Continental Congress; *Defense of the Constitutions of Government of the United States of America* (1787), an erudite three-volume work on American political institutions (defending the system of the separation of powers that existed in the American states) which, despite its turgidity, impressed the members of the Constitutional Convention in 1787; and *Discourses on Davila,* a continuation of the same general ideas, published as a series of essays during the first years of his vice-presidency.

In terms of political philosophy, these works (as well as letters and polemical articles under the pen-name *Publicola*) reveal—despite contradictions and changes of mind—certain basic ideas. Like most of his educated contemporaries, Adams accepted the philosophy of natural law—the premise that men are born into society with certain inalienable rights, including the most important of all rights, that of setting up and administering their own government. At bottom Adams was a republican, though his occasionally hasty and intemperate antidemocratic utterances led his enemies to accuse him of being a monarchist. Actually, he rejected monarchy and any other kind of individual dictatorship, and gloried in the fact that the American political institutions were a model of republicanism for the world to imitate, as he pointed out in his *Defence of the Constitutions:* "The United States of America have exhibited, perhaps, the first example of governments erected on the simple principles of nature. . . . Thirteen governments thus founded on the natural authority of the people alone, without a pretence of miracle or mystery, and which are destined to spread over the northern part of that whole quarter of the globe, are a great point gained in favor of the rights of mankind."

Adams also favored a government of divided powers, opposing the centralized authority that then existed practically everywhere in the world and most strikingly in Bourbon France. His *Defence of the Constitutions* was inspired by the writings of Louis XVI's famous Physiocratic minister, Baron Turgot, who defended the idea of a highly centralized state. In the face of the great prestige Turgot enjoyed in the Western world, Adams nevertheless dared to challenge his fundamental political assumptions. Where Turgot assumed the desirability of concentrated governmental authority, Adams argued learnedly for its opposite—divided and balanced political powers. Turgot, Adams wrote, may use such high-sounding phrases as "authority of the nation" (which, in the case of France, meant the absolutist monarch who was supposed to embody all power within his person), but in reality effective political life necessitated a division of functions which are usually described as legislative, executive, and judicial. Such a functional separation, Adams argued, however it is labeled or not labeled, was moreover the most practical way to maintain public harmony and, in the last analysis, freedom. In the *Defence* he wrote:

> Mr. Turgot seems to be of a different opinion, and is for "collecting all authority into one centre, the nation." It is easily understood how all authority may be collected into "one centre" in a despot or monarch; but how it can be done when the centre is to be the nation is more difficult to comprehend. . . . When a number of men, women, and children are simply congregated together, there is no political authority among them. . . . Not one will have any authority over any other. The first "collection" of authority must be an unanimous agreement to form themselves into a *nation, people, community,* or *body politic,* and to be governed by the majority of suffrages. . . . But even in this case, . . . that centre is no longer the nation, but the majority of the nation.
>
> A simple and perfect democracy never yet existed among men. If a village of half a mile square, and one hundred families, is capable of exercising all the legislative, executive, and judicial powers, in public assemblies of the whole . . . , it is more than has ever yet been proved in theory or experience.

A government with divided powers, on the other hand, was not only the most practical but also in accord with nature. Governments constituted otherwise, Adams wrote, "will be found to be imperfect, unstable and so enslaved." Primarily, this was due to the fact that a division of powers created the kind of equilibrium that society needed to escape the perils of chaos or of tyranny. "All nations, under all government, must have parties," he said; "the great secret is to control them. There are but two ways, either by a monarchy and standing army, or by a balance in the constitution. Where the people have a choice, and there is no balance, there will be everlasting fluctuations, revolutions, and horrors, until a standing army, with a general at its head, commands the peace, or the necessity of an equilibrium is . . . adopted by all."

But this preference for a republican government with balanced and divided powers did not make Adams a democrat in the Jeffersonian or modern liberal sense. On the contrary, Adams specifically rejected democracy—if by democracy is meant universal suffrage and equal participation in government by all the citizens—in terms so blunt that he incurred almost universal disfavor in an age when democratic forces, unleashed by the American Revolution, were sweeping the young country. Instead of democracy, Adams favored republicanism, which he conceived as responsible government by a limited number of capable persons, representing the people and operating within a framework of law. He believed, he wrote in *Thoughts on Government,* that power should be delegated "from the many to a few of the most wise and good." To his cousin Samuel Adams he defined republican government as one "in which the people have collectively, or by representation, an essential share in the sovereignty." To which Samuel, a radical Jeffersonian democrat, retorted that "an essential share" was not enough: the people must have the whole sovereignty.

Adams' refusal to accept the philosophy of democracy, in theory or in practice, was based on a set of tenets about human nature which, he thought, underlay politics. He did in fact attempt to construct a science of politics—a "divine science," he called it—on what he regarded as the immutable laws of human behavior. "We have," he wrote to Samuel, "human nature, society and universal history to observe and study, and from these we may draw all the real principles" to guide us.

From his political and historical studies, Adams came to the conclusion that the frailties and passions of man—the ordinary or "average" man, not the aristocrat—made him incapable of responsible participation in government. The whole egalitarian philosophy of the eighteenth-century Enlightenment was, he felt, based upon a thoroughly false conception of human nature. Where Rousseau (and in the United States, Jefferson) assumed man to be essentially good and decent, Adams considered him inherently the opposite, corrupt and avaricious. By nature, Adams wrote, the human being is "so corrupt, so indolent, so selfish and jealous, that he is never good but through necessity." He held with Hobbes and Hamilton that human beings are naturally unprincipled and violent, impelled not by any noble motives or ideas but by lust and ambition, whether for power, gold, or material goods. These passions and traits were so integral a part of the human animal that there was no sense in either denying or deploring them. They existed, as nature intended them to exist, and had to be reckoned with soberly and realistically by statesmen and philosophers. Answering his own question, "What kind of beings men are," Adams thus explained human psychology in the *Defence:*

> It is weakness rather than wickedness which renders men unfit to be trusted with unlimited power. The passions are all unlimited; nature has left them so; if they could be bounded, they would be extinct; ... They certainly increase too, by exercise, like the body. The love of gold grows faster than the heap of acquisition; the love of praise increases by every gratification, till it stings like an adder, and bites like a serpent; till the man is miserable every moment when he does not snuff the incense. Ambition strengthens at every advance, and at last takes possession of the whole soul so absolutely that a man sees nothing in the world of importance ... but in his object.

Given these human "appetites, passions and propensities," how, Adams asked, was any orderly, civilized existence possible? His reply was that only government could keep man in leash. Curbing the passions of the human animal was indeed "the principal end of government ... which in its turn becomes a principal means of government. It is the only adequate instrument of order and subordination in society, and alone commands effectual obedience to laws, since without it neither human reason, nor standing armies, would ever produce that great effect."

But what is there in the human character that makes it respond to the efforts of government to restrain it? Nature, Adams explained, fortunately provided the possibilities for orderly government through the creation of two human traits. One was gregariousness, the other inequality. Men, he wrote, even the most primitive ones, were born with a desire to live with their kind rather than in isolation. The existence of this sense of gregariousness meant that nature intended men for organized living—"to render them useful to each other in their social connections." But gregariousness by itself, in view of human lusts, would only result in social chaos and strife. Hence nature produced that other human characteristic, inequality, which makes it possible for the stronger (better endowed, or richer, or more experienced) to impose social order and maintain public discipline—that is, government. "By the law of nature," he wrote, "all men are men and not angels—men and not lions—men and not whales—men and not eagles, that is, they are all of the same species. But man differs by nature from man almost as man from beast. . . . A physical inequality, an intellectual inequality of the most serious kind is established unchangeably by the Author of nature."

This is the crucial point on which Adams parted company with such democrats as Jefferson. While Adams admitted that all men were born with the same urges and desires—that is to say, "created equal" in their passions—they were not alike in regard to abilities or opportunities. This inequality, found throughout the whole human spectrum at all times, meant that only a limited number of persons could be in a position to gratify their aims and ambitions. Hence in every society or social grouping there always exist two distinct human categories, the rulers and the ruled, based upon gradations of property and power. "The people of all nations," Adams said, "are naturally divided into two sorts, the gentlemen and the simple men. . . . The poor are destined to labor, and the rich, by the advantage of education, independence and leisure, are qualified for superior stations." Far from deploring such inequality, Adams held it was actually desirable and necessary for the governance of society. If anything, inequality should be encouraged, for "society has a right to establish any other inequalities it may judge necessary and good."

Adams used the word *aristocrat* or *aristocracy* to describe those who wielded power and enjoyed a superior status everywhere as a result of natural inequality in the human species. In general, the aristocrat was one who, regardless of immediate origin, had some special talent or conspicuous virtue. This could be beauty, or stature, or elegance, or wisdom, or skill, or anything that makes a human being stand out. The true aristocrat, according to Adams, was not necessarily a person born to a title but one who was to be found in all human activities, among women ("female aristocrats are nearly as formidable as males") as well as men, in the arts as well as in the sciences. In politics, the aristocrat was the individual able to influence or lead in any given situation, by no matter what means; he (or she) was the person who always naturally emerged as outstanding wherever there were groups of people organized for any purpose. In a letter dated November 15, 1813, Adams retorted to Jefferson, who had insisted upon a distinction between a "natural" and an "artificial" aristocracy:

Fashion has introduced an indeterminate use of the word talents. Education, wealth, strength, beauty, stature, birth, marriage, graceful attitudes and motions, gait, air, complexion, physiognomy, are talents, as well as genius, science and learning. Any one of these talents that in fact commands or influences two votes in society, gives to the man who possesses it the character of an aristocrat, in my sense of the word. Pick up the first hundred men you meet, and make a republic. Every man will have an equal vote; but when deliberations and discussions are opened, it will be found that twenty-five, by their talents, virtues being equal, will be able to carry fifty votes. Every one of these twenty-five is an aristocrat in my sense of the word; whether he obtains one vote in addition to his own, by his birth, fortune, figure, eloquence, science, learning, craft, cunning, or even his character for good fellowship, and a *bon vivant.*

In his recognition of inequality and acceptance of the existence of differences among men, Adams did not mean to defend the titled nobility as it existed in Europe. He was, in fact, highly critical of the established aristocracies, the "old families" whose sole virtue was an escutcheon rather than a brain. An aristocracy born to privileges, but without particular intelligence or special endowment, was to be deplored as ethically undesirable and politically stupid. "When I consider," Adams wrote, "the weakness, the folly, the pride, the vanity, the selfishness, the artifice, the low craft and mean cunning, the want of principle . . . , the unfeeling cruelty of a majority of those (in all nations) who are allowed an aristocratical influence, and, on the other hand, the stupidity with which the more numerous multitude not only become their dupes, but even love to be taken in by their tricks, I feel a stronger disposition to weep at their destiny, than to laugh at their folly."

Nevertheless, Adams accepted *that* kind of aristocracy too, if for no other reason than as evidence of the existence of human inequality. Whether one liked it or not, and no matter which type of aristocracy one preferred, the fact was that aristocrats *did* exist everywhere and *did* wield influence—and, in consequence, always *would*—regardless of how they acquired their position, power, or property. In his famous letter to John Taylor (April 1814), replying to the latter's "attack upon me, by name, for the doctrines of aristocracy in my three volumes of *Defence*" which appeared in Taylor's *An Inquiry into the Principles and Policy of the Government of the United States,* Adams thus explained his ideas on the origins of aristocracy:

Paper wealth has been a source of aristocracy in this country, as well as landed wealth, with a vengeance. Witness the immense fortunes made *per saltum* by aristocratical speculations, both in land and paper.... But, sir, land and paper are not the only source of aristocracy. There are master shipwrights, housewrights, masons, etc., who have each of them from twenty to a hundred families in their employment, and can carry a posse to the polls when they will. These are not only aristocrats, but a species of feudal barons....

Should a planter in Virginia sell his *clarissimum et illustrissimum et celeberricum locum* with his thousand negroes, to a merchant, would not the merchant gain the aristocratical influence which the planter lost by his transfer? Run down, sir, through all the ranks of society . . . , from the first planter and the first merchant to the hog driver, the whiskey dram-seller, or the Scottish peddler, and consider, whether the alienation of lands, wharves, stores, pike stock, or even lottery tickets, does not transfer the aristocracy as well as the property.

Adams' belief in natural inequality among men made it, therefore, impossible for him ever to be a democrat or, despite his important political position, to understand the American people of his time. He was honestly and, being Adams, bluntly of the opinion that democracy meant "a nation . . . without any government at all," since the people at large were not capable of ruling themselves. He wrote in the *Defence:* "The proposition that the people are the best keepers of their own liberties is not true. They are the worst conceivable, they are no keepers at all; they can neither judge, act, think, or will, as a political body." Democracy, by definition, meant giving rein to popular turbulence, to a society guided by neither reason nor public interest but one that always culminated, through anarchy, in dictatorship. Such, Adams argued, had been the experience of history, and he would have none of it.

He would have frankly preferred a monarchical or aristocratic government but, even apart from the fact that it was impractical in democratic-minded America, he had a genuine dread of any autocratic powers and, as we have seen, he questioned the wisdom of a nobility based on "hereditary legal descent." Unlike Hamilton, Adams opposed *any* governmental system that had no restraints on it, convinced that an oligarchy, even of the rich and the well-born, could be as unprincipled as any uncurbed democracy. "The fundamental article of my political creed," he wrote to Jefferson in 1815, "is that despotism, or unlimited sovereignty, or absolute power, is the same in a majority of a popular assembly, an aristocratical council, an oligarchical junto, and a single emperor. Equally arbitrary, cruel, bloody, and in every respect diabolical."

The best that he finally hoped for was an aristocratically inclined republic, founded on an educated ruling group, with a powerful chief executive enjoying monarchical prestige, appointive officials with high titles, and a strict limitation of popular participation in the government. For the President, Adams, like Washington, favored a most high-sounding title, such as "His Highness, the President of the United States of America, and Protector of Her Liberties"—a title which the Senate approved and the House rejected in favor of plain "President of the United States," now abbreviated to "Mr. President."

Adams was critical of the federal Constitution, primarily because it provided for regular popular elections, which in his opinion meant a dangerous opening of the Pandora's box of democracy. When, as American minister in London, he received a copy of the Constitution, his characteristic reaction was one of disapproval. He wrote to Jefferson (December 1787), who was also critical of the Constitution, but mainly because it lacked a Bill of Rights:

> The project of a new constitution has objections against it, to which I find it difficult to reconcile myself. . . .
>
> You are afraid of the one, I, of the few. We agree perfectly that the many should have a full, fair, and perfect representation. You are apprehensive of monarchy, I, of aristocracy. I would, therefore, have given more power to the president, and less to the senate. The nomination and appointment to all offices, I would have given to the president, assisted only by a privy council of his own creation; but not a vote or voice would I have given to the senate or any senator unless he were of the privy council. Faction and distraction are the sure and certain consequences of giving to a senate a vote in the distribution of offices. You are apprehensive that the president, when once chosen, will be chosen again and again as long as he lives. So much the better, as it appears to me. You are apprehensive of foreign interference, intrigue, and influence. So am I. But as often as elections happen, the danger of foreign influence renews. The less frequently they happen, the less danger; and if the same man may be chosen again, it is possible he will be, and the danger of foreign influence will be less. . . . Elections, my dear sir, to offices which are a great object of ambition, I look at with terror. Experiments of this kind have been so often tried, and so universally found productive of horrors, that there is great reason to dread them.

Adams never did reconcile himself to the democratic features of the Constitution and even less so to the democratic institutions and practices that were rapidly spreading throughout the United States. For the rest of his life he remained a stout upholder of conservative republicanism, an enemy at the same time of democracy and of despotism. Despite his pessimism and gloomy prognosis about democracy, America's democratic political system has triumphantly survived storms and strains. If Adams had seen its success, he might have agreed that the American people were what Walter Bagehot has said about those of Massachusetts: "The men of Massachusetts could work *any* constitution."

# 4

## *THE AMERICAN AS DEMOCRAT:*
# Thomas Jefferson *(1743–1826)*

> *All honor to Jefferson—to the man, who, in the concrete pressure of a struggle for national independence . . . , had the coolness, forecast, and capacity to introduce into a merely revolutionary document an abstract truth, applicable to all men and all times, and so to embalm it there that today and in all coming days it shall be a rebuke and a stumbling-block to . . . tyranny and oppression.*
>
> —*Abraham Lincoln* (*April 6, 1859*)

No two men could be more dissimilar on the surface than Jefferson and John Adams, his immediate predecessor in the presidency. The volatile little New Englander was in sharp contrast to the tall and reserved Virginian. There were paradoxical differences between them: the son of New England farmers was a spokesman for aristocracy; the descendant of southern planters (at least on his mother's side) was a champion of democracy. But despite their differences, they had enough in common—belief in religious freedom and respect for books and ideas, for example—to enable them to entertain great esteem for one another, as can be seen in their remarkable correspondence.

To James Russell Lowell, Thomas Jefferson seemed the "first American man" and the best thinker of his day. Abraham Lincoln considered Jefferson's principles the "definitions and axioms of a free society." Woodrow Wilson thought him immortal because of his attitude toward mankind. The world at large has long regarded him as the embodiment of American democratic idealism.

Jefferson's personality was elusive and complex. The most wide-ranging intellect of his day, he was at the same time the champion of democratic rights. A landed gentleman, he was the leader of the common people. The most successful political figure of his generation, he never made a political speech. A party leader of matchless adroitness, he had practically no personal contact with the mass of his followers. He was at once a subtle political theorist and a wily politician, a philosopher and a strategist. Soft-spoken in manner, he was uncompromising in principle. Underneath the suppleness of the serene scholar was the iron will of the leader whose vision never faltered.

Thomas Jefferson was born on April 13, 1743, in Shadwell, western Virginia, on a farm which his father had personally cleared and built. The Jefferson homestead lay in the wilderness of the Blue Ridge mountains, a region that was then opening up for white settlement. The fact that Jefferson was a frontiersman and not a mansion-bred aristocrat (although his mother, a Randolph, was a member of a well-established Virginia family) had a lasting influence on his ideas and on American democracy. The frontier taught Jefferson the virtues of self-reliance, common sense, and above all an abiding respect for his fellow men. Indeed, the champion and theorist of democracy cannot be understood without reference to his frontier environment.

Next to the frontier, the two other major influences on Jefferson's development were his father and the eighteenth-century Enlightenment. Jefferson's father, Colonel Peter Jefferson, was an early American pioneer of the classic mold, one of those rugged and strong men whose endurance and courage broke the wilderness and opened it up to civilization. He was, it is important to keep in mind, of modest birth, self-made and self-educated. A giant in stature, Colonel Jefferson was widely respected. Even the neighboring Indians—who had no reason to like white men—admired Thomas Jefferson's father and often enjoyed his hospitality, a lesson in human brotherhood young Thomas never forgot.

Colonel Jefferson died when Thomas was fourteen, leaving him heir to an estate of about 1400 acres and, more precious, a fine name. From his father he had learned the arts and crafts of the pioneer—to ride, shoot, paddle a canoe; to manage a farm, plant, and build; to judge livestock and to size up men. He had also acquired a respect for truth and a love of knowledge as well as strict intellectual discipline and physical endurance.

The eighteenth-century Enlightenment, the Age of Reason, rounded out the influence that shaped the mind and personality of Thomas Jefferson. Beginning with his college days at William and Mary, he continued, through the rest of his long life, to read and to study, above all, the scholars and scientists of the seventeenth and eighteenth centuries. He had a lifelong passion for books; he accumulated what was in his day the largest private library in America. Jefferson, the inveterate reader, is graphically recalled by his Negro slave, Isaac; "Old master had abundance of books: sometimes would have twenty of 'em down on the floor at once: read fust one, then tother. Issac has often wondered how old master came to have such a mighty head: read so many of them books: & when they go to him to ax him anything, he go right straight to the book & tell you."

Like Sir Francis Bacon two centuries earlier, Jefferson took all knowledge for his province. His intellectual and scientific interests are astounding. He was a surveyor, mathematician, violinist, architect, botanist, geologist, ethnologist, astronomer, agronomist, horticulturist, jurist, furniture designer, inventor, and engineer. A glance through his letters shows that he occupied himself with (and often wrote learnedly about) gardening, gunnery, rice, olives, fortifications, medicine, weaving, foundries, Greek and Latin grammar, prosody, weights and measures, mathematics, musical instruments, education, distillation of sea water, Indian languages, religion, silk culture, spinning machines, steam engines, sulphur, tides, viticulture, speedometers, saw mills, sheep, meteors, tides, plows, coinage (he set up the dollar unit which is still the basis of the U.S. currency system), canals, chemistry, almanacs, and torpedoes. He knew something about everything, and about some things he knew a great deal.

Jefferson had deep reserves of moral strength and intellectual conviction. In all matters of human existence, whether personal or political, he said *Yes* to life. Neither personal bereavement nor public defeat long shook his poise or affected his confidence. He exerted influence by the quietly radiant force of his personality. Tall and lean, his eyes kind and quizzical, his jaw firm, the carrot-haired Virginian was an impressive figure, even in old slippers. At all times and under all conditions, he stood out as a leader of men. His mind and soul formed a perfect harmony. He combined a classical Greek sense of balance with a Renaissance curiosity about life and nature. His whole personality was illuminated by reason.

Jefferson towers in modern history because of his great vision. His life was dedicated to the ideal of freedom. His writings, notably his voluminous correspondence (some 18,000 letters), are replete with arguments in favor of self-government, liberty, the dignity of man, and the hatred of all kinds of tyranny. Jefferson simply stated fact when he said, during the presidential campaign of 1800, "I have sworn upon the altar of God, eternal hostility against every form of tyranny over the mind of man." Probably no other man in recorded history has ever provided humanity with so full and illuminating a complex of ideas which, in their totality, add up to the philosophy of democracy. Much of his writing is sparkling and aphoristic, and endlessly quotable.

Jefferson's whole systematic thought was based upon the foundation of natural rights and reason. A profound student of John Locke and the English jurists, as well as of the great galaxy of eighteenth-century *Philosophes* (especially Montesquieu and Helvetius), Jefferson accepted as a matter of scientific fact the guiding idea that men were born with certain rights which could never be taken away from them. These rights —to life, liberty, and the pursuit of happiness—were "natural" and "unalienable" and not open to question intellectually or to challenge politically. They were, he said, permanent rights because all men came into the world with them. Nearly half a century after the Declaration of Independence, which embodied the philosophy of natural rights, Jefferson wrote: "Nothing is unchangeable but the inherent and inalienable rights of man."

Closely connected with the idea of natural rights is his assumption of the existence of a moral instinct. This was conceived to be a built-in mechanism that enabled men to tell right from wrong and to guide them in all moral fields, including religion. Man, according to Jefferson and other contemporary rationalists and moralists, was born with such an instinct exactly as he was with arms and legs. Without such an inherent moral sense, man would be but a beast and civilization would be impossible. The fact that there were always some individuals in society who were unscrupulous and amoral—Napoleon Bonaparte was the prime example of this in Jefferson's eyes—only proved the rule by the glaringness of the exceptions. In a letter to Thomas Law in 1814, Jefferson wrote:

> Some men are born without the organs of sight, or of hearing, or without hands. Yet it would be wrong to say that man is born without these faculties, and sight, hearing, and hands may with truth enter into the general definition of man. The want or imperfection of the moral sense in some men, like the want or imperfection of the sense of sight and hearing in others, is no proof

that it is a general characteristic of the species. When it is wanting, we endeavor to supply the defect by education, by appeals to reason and calculation. . . .

Some have argued against the existence of a moral sense, by saying that if nature had given us such a sense . . . , then nature would also have designated, by some particular earmarks, the two sets of actions which are, in themselves, one virtuous and the other vicious. The answer is that nature has constituted *utility* to man the standard and test of virtue. Men living in different countries, under different circumstances, different habits and regimens, may have different utilities; the same act, therefore, may be useful, and consequently virtuous in one country which is injurious and vicious in another differently circumstanced. I sincerely, then, believe . . . in the general existence of a moral instinct. I think it the brightest gem with which the human character is studded, and the want of it as more degrading than the most hideous of the bodily deformities.

Next to man's inherent moral sense is his reason, which guides him in his practical activities. The rule of reason was the ultimate arbiter in human society, and was of special importance in a free society. But, to operate effectively for the benefit of man, reason requires two essential conditions: freedom and education. The human mind must not be hampered by any governmental organization or ecclesiastical body in its search for truth. At the same time, truth, once discovered, has no meaning unless it is utilized for the benefit of men. Such utilization calls for widespread popular education, since it is axiomatic that the ignorant could not possibly use or appreciate the actual and potential creations of the human mind, especially in the fields of science and scholarship. Consequently, Jefferson championed absolute freedom of the mind and advocated the establishment of a tax-supported school system for all children and higher education for the gifted ones. "The cultivation of science," he said, "is an act of religious duty."

Implied in the theory of natural rights was the idea of human equality. Since all men were born equal, in the sense that their natural rights and instincts were inherent, it meant that an aristocratic society or caste system was against nature and, in consequence, had to be rejected. Who, then, was to rule? Jefferson accepted the Aristotelian idea that there exists a "natural aristocracy" among men, consisting not of inherited titles but of superior ability. Nature, he said, scatters human talents among all types of people, rich as well as poor, and this reservoir of abilities, which has nothing to do with income or social condition, must be trained and used for the enrichment and leadership of society. Here was the core of true democracy. In a letter to John Adams on October 28, 1813, Jefferson expressed his idea of democratic leadership and spoke of the "pure selection" of leaders. This choice was to take place through a process of systematic schooling, beginning with a "general diffusion of knowledge" among the people at large and culminating with special training at the top. Such a process of education would be costly, but would be worth the effort and expense for the sake of preserving a free and elastic society. "Preach, my dear Sir," Jefferson wrote to his friend and teacher, the great Virginia jurist George Wythe, "a crusade against ignorance; establish and improve the law for educating the common people. . . . The tax which will be paid for this purpose, is not more than the thousandth part of what will be paid to kings, priests and nobles, who will rise up among us if we leave the people ignorant."

Widespread popular education was ever in Jefferson's thought, for the conviction never left him that the greatest enemy of man was ignorance and all the ills it breeds. "If a nation," he said, "expects to be ignorant and free, in a state of civilization, it expects what never was and never will be." His advocacy of education was strengthened by the prevailing conditions of Europe, where nine tenths of the people were poor, enslaved, and ignorant so that one tenth could live in liberty and luxury. Looking over the European scene, what did he see? England, where a corrupt nobility ruled through an unbalanced monarch. Prussia, dominated by a competent despot to be succeeded by an incompetent one. Russia, an enormous prison-house for serfs under the lash of semi-Oriental tyrants. Austria, half-feudal, struggling vainly to throw off aristocracy and clericalism. France, in an agony of misgovernment and poverty, sliding into the abyss of revolution and anarchy. Wherever Jefferson looked in Europe he saw nothing but examples of tyranny and despair.

"While in Europe," he relates, "I often amused myself with contemplating the characters of the then reigning sovereigns. . . . Louis XVI was a fool. . . . The King of Spain was a fool, and of Naples the same. They passed their lives in hunting. . . . The King of Sardinia was a fool. . . . The Queen of Portugal . . . was an idiot by nature. And so was the King of Denmark. . . . The King of Prussia, successor to the great Frederick, was a mere hog in body as well as in mind. Gustavus of Sweden and Joseph of Austria, were really crazy, and George of England . . . was in straight waistcoat. . . . These animals had become without mind and powerless."

This negative influence of Europe upon Jefferson's thinking and upon

American democracy cannot be too strongly emphasized. Europe was socially cruel and politically unjust, and Europe's children crossed thousands of miles of ocean in order to escape intolerable conditions. "Europe," Jefferson once said, "is a first idea, a crude production, before the maker knew his trade, or had made up his mind as to what he wanted." By implication, America must be an improvement upon the first rough model.

Jefferson's residence in France as American ambassador further deepened his aversion to caste and absolutism. The poverty and suffering in that country filled him with indignation. "Of twenty millions of people supposed to be in France," he wrote from Paris, "I am of opinion there are nineteen millions more wretched, more accursed in every circumstance of human existence than the most conspicuously wretched individual of the whole United States." He knew that the reason for this unnecessary wretchedness was a "bad form of government."

America must never tread this anguished European path, where, Jefferson wrote, the governments are those of "kites over pigeons." Only those who went abroad could fully appreciate the paradise that America really was. A trip to Europe, Jefferson wrote to James Monroe in 1785, "will make you adore your own country, its soil, its climate, its equality, liberty, laws, people, and manners." "My God!" he exclaimed, "how little do my countrymen know what precious blessings they are in possession of, and which no other people on earth enjoy."

Here in the Western Hemisphere was a new land and a citizenry not yet demoralized by hereditary inequality. With a population uncorrupted and unchained, and living for the most part on rich and uninfeudated soil, it was possible to build a new society that would not repeat the tragic experience of Europe.

The basic social fact in Jefferson's day, as it is now, was the problem of government. Almost every social ill derived ultimately from the nature and function of the state. There were few limits to the cruelties and degradations a bad government could inflict upon its subjects, who in Jefferson's time were largely without political rights and therefore helpless. To him it was axiomatic that where the citizens have no right to control the government the result is a society of wolves ruling over sheep. He could not see that there was even room for argument on this point. Even the worst popular government was preferable to the most glorious autocratic one; men, Jefferson held, have the natural privilege of committing errors, and if let alone their common sense would soon rectify mistakes. He regarded it as self-evident that the best government was the one in which the citizens had the most freedom, even to the point of reducing that government to semi-impotence. By the same token, a powerful government was inevitably bad, because sooner rather than later it ceased to be a servant and became master of the citizens who created it.

Jefferson had no illusions about the nature of government. As a realistic reader of history—like Voltaire, he read history for the lessons it taught rather than for entertainment—Jefferson looked at government in general with skeptical eyes. So, incidentally, did many of his American contemporaries, especially those who were active in the making of the Constitution. Jefferson feared government as a potential menace but accepted it as a necessary evil. Society, he realized, required some sort of regulation, and the individual needed a certain amount of freedom; since these two requirements appeared mutually exclusive, the conflict between order and liberty seemed irreconcilable. Historically, Jefferson well knew, governments always encroached upon individual freedom, sometimes by means of coercive laws and sometimes by means of naked violence. That few rulers ever exercised power for the genuine benefit of the ruled was an almost equally evident proposition. In one of his most revealing sentences, Jefferson once admitted that if he had to choose between despotism and anarchy he would prefer anarchy: "Were it made a question, whether no law, as among the savage Americans [Indians], or too much law, as among the civilized Europeans, submits man to the greatest evil, one who has seen both conditions of existence would pronounce it to the last." And he added a phrase that is still applicable to a large part of the world today: "The sheep are happier of themselves, than under the care of the wolves."

Since the inexorable tendency of governments was to deteriorate into tyrannies, the problem before men of Jefferson's generation was how to keep a necessary social servant from growing into a monster. How, in other words, could one prevent government from encroaching upon liberty?

"There are rights," Jefferson wrote in 1789, "which it is useless to surrender to the government, and which governments have yet always been found to invade. These are the rights of thinking, and publishing our thoughts by speaking or writing; the right of free commerce; the right of personal freedom."

To Jefferson, government was entirely subservient to life and liberty, and without the latter there could be no pursuit of happiness. A powerful state that would control men's thoughts and action, Jefferson wrote to James Monroe in 1782, would "annihilate the blessing of existence" and would make men feel "that it were better they had never been born."

The solution lay in self-government. Men must be guaranteed their right to elect and to control their public officials, not as a matter of expediency or favor but as a function endowed by nature. "Every man, and every body of men on earth," Jefferson explained to President Washington in 1790, "possess the right of self-government. They receive it with their being from the hand of nature. Individuals exercise it by their single will; collections of men by that of their majority; for the law of the majority is the natural law of every society of men."

Critics of democracy argued that men were not capable of governing themselves. Jefferson dismissed this argument against democracy in four brief sentences. "Sometimes it is said that man cannot be trusted with the government of himself. Can he, then, be trusted with the government of others? Or have we found angels in the forms of kings to govern him? Let history answer this question." Nor would Jefferson accept a half-hearted, partial democracy under the tutelage of some person or group. "No, my friend," he wrote to Joseph Cabell, "the way to have good and safe government, is not to trust it all to one, but to divide it among the many."

To his French friend Dupont de Nemours he said, "We both consider the people as our children. . . . But you love them as infants whom you are afraid to trust without nurses, and I as adults whom I freely leave to self-government." Professor Charles E. Merriam has called this one of the best statements of democratic principles.

Jefferson had confidence in human character and in the common sense of mankind. Men who rule themselves may commit mistakes, but they have a chance to correct them. But men who are ruled have no recourse except patient suffering or violence. "I have such reliance on the good sense of the body of the people and the honesty of their leaders," he said, "that I am not afraid of their letting things go wrong to any length in any case." The people may be misled or deceived for a time, but if the avenues of truth are open, they will learn to reject what is false and harmful. "Where the people are well informed they can be trusted with their own government; whenever things get so far wrong as to attract their notice, they may be relied on to set them to rights."

For the same reason Jefferson advocated an untrammeled press. If a democracy needed citizens who could read, it followed that they had to be free in their reading. Censorship of any kind would negate the very spirit of democracy by substituting tyranny over the mind for despotism over the body. Moreover, since the essence of democracy was the right of minorities to be heard, the principle of censorship would supply the majority with a tyrannical weapon. "Our liberty," Jefferson said, "depends on the freedom of the press, and that cannot be limited without being lost." And although he was the victim of unrestrained abuse on the part of the newspapers—most of them were venal—he felt that the press must be protected at all costs. During his first administration, he said of the rabid newspapers: "I shall protect them in the right of lying and calumniating."

The same principle applied also to books. Jefferson said that if the facts in a book were false they should be disproved, and if the reasoning were fallacious it should be refuted. "But, for God's sake, let us freely hear both sides." Unpopular ideas must be given a hearing and criticism encouraged. Without unhampered criticism of public figures and public policy, a democracy would soon deteriorate. "To demand the censors [critics] of public measures to be given up for punishment is to renew the demand of the wolves in the fable that the sheep should give up their dogs as hostages of the peace and confidence established between them."

A democracy where men were free to think and say what they pleased also implied freedom of conscience. To Jefferson, ecclesiastical tyranny was even more abhorrent than political despotism. Religious fanaticism, he was well aware, had caused bloodshed and suffering in the past. In his *Notes on Virginia* Jefferson wrote "Millions of innocent men, women and children, since the introduction of Christianity, have been burnt, tortured, fined, imprisoned; yet we have not advanced one inch towards uniformity."

Since religious uniformity was neither obtainable nor desirable, it was wise policy to give up the attempt altogether. Let each man worship as he please, or not worship as he please. Religion, Jefferson held, was a "matter between every man and his maker, in which no other, and far less the public, had a right to intermeddle." He himself was no churchman, and he disliked creeds, but he held fast to the moral principles enunciated by Jesus.

To give the state power to prescribe the religion of the citizens was as intolerable as the principle of punishing people for their beliefs. One of the lasting achievements of the American Revolution was religious toleration, and all his life Jefferson took pride in his epoch-making Act for Establishing Religious Freedom which the Virginia Assembly ratified in 1786. In his humanistic philosophy, religious toleration was a prime need not only for its own sake but for the preservation of democratic society. He knew the cruelty inherent in bigotry and the formidable tyranny exerted by a state that joined forces with a dominant church. Such a "loathsome combination of Church and State," as Jefferson called it, had in the past wrought havoc with human society, and it must not be permitted to do so in America. "In every country and in every age, the priest has been hostile to liberty. He is always in alliance with the despot, abetting his abuses in return for protection of his own."

In America men must be free in body as well as in mind, and no person or law should have the right to tell them what to believe. Jefferson stated this principle of toleration with striking bluntness when he said, "It does me no injury for my neighbor to say there are twenty gods, or no God. It neither picks my pocket nor breaks my leg."

Jefferson's devotion to American democracy brought him to the principle of uncompromising isolation in the sphere of international politics. His bitter experiences could lead to no other. It will be remembered that his most active years in politics coincided with one of Europe's periodic upheavals. When he was Secretary of State under President Washington, the French were decapitating their monarchs and thereby inviting foreign war. When he was Vice-President of the United States, Bonaparte was beginning to win those victories that were paving the way for his dictatorship of Europe. As President of the United States, he faced a world trampled by Napoleon on land and ravaged by the British at sea. For more than two decades, during most of which time Jefferson was in office, the world knew no peace. He viewed the international violence and bloodshed with something close to despair.

"In the whole animal kingdom," he wrote to his friend Madison, "I recollect no family but man, steadily and systematically employed in the destruction of itself." And he uttered a plaint that could with equal justice be spoken today, "The moral principles and conventional usages which have heretofore been the bond of civilized nations . . . have now given way to force, the law of Barbarians, and the nineteenth century dawns with the Vandalism of the fifth."

The European combatants ruthlessly violated American rights and American shipping. What was the United States to do? Go to war? Such a remedy, in Jefferson's view, was as bad as the disease. "I love peace," he wrote, "and I am anxious that we should give the world still another useful lesson, by showing to them other modes of punishing injuries than by war, which is as much a punishment to the punisher as to the sufferer."

This "other mode" was to cut off all communications with the belligerents, to have no commercial dealings with any aggressor, and not to permit their quarrels to disrupt America's free institutions. America's unique position in a chaotic world was stated by Jefferson in historic perspective:

> Our difficulties are indeed great, if we consider ourselves alone. But when viewed in comparison to those of Europe, they are the joys of Paradise.... The destinies have placed our portion of existence amidst such scenes of tumult and outrage, as no other period, within our knowledge, has presented.... A conqueror roaming over the earth with havoc and destruction.... Indeed..., ours is a bed of roses. And the system of government which shall keep us afloat amidst the wreck of the world, will be immortalized in history. We have, to be sure, our petty squabbles and heart burnings, and we have something of the blue devils at times.... But happily for us, the Mammoth cannot swim, nor the Leviathan move on dry land; and if we will keep out of their way, they cannot get at us.

Jefferson's policy was not only to keep out of the way of the European "lions and tigers" but, equally important, to keep them out of America's way. He hoped that some means could be found to establish a line of demarcation in midocean, in order to separate the two hemispheres forever. He saw the future of the American continent as a home of freedom and peace, and was anxious to keep wartorn Europe from infecting the Western Hemisphere with its madness. His correspondence with his disciple President Monroe shows how deeply he felt on this subject of isolation—perhaps *insulation* would be a better word—which came to be embodied in the Monroe Doctrine. One of Jefferson's letters to Monroe elucidates this doctrine:

> I have ever deemed it fundamental for the United States never to take active part in the quarrels of Europe. Their political interests are entirely distinct from ours. Their mutual jealousies, their balance of power, their complicated alliances, their forms and principles of government, are all foreign to us. They are nations of eternal war. All their energies are expended in the destruction of the labor, property and lives of their people. On our part, never had a people so favorable a chance of trying the opposite system, of peace and fraternity with mankind, and the direction of all our means and faculties to the purposes of improvement instead of destruction.... Of the brethren of our own hemisphere, none are yet, or for an age to come will be, in a shape, condition, or disposition to war against us. And the foothold which the nations of Europe had in either America, is slipping from under them, so that we shall soon be rid of their neighborhood.

The notion of isolation in the sphere of international politics also carried over into the realm of economic activity. A farmer and the son of a farmer, Jefferson had a distrust of cities and commercial classes. He could never overcome his bias against an urban economy and an urban civilization. Country people were preferable to city dwellers, he believed, essentially because land ownership gave them a sense of freedom and independence.

Fearing urbanization and the consequent deterioration of democratic virtue, he was anxious to see the United States remain an agricultural society, growing its own foodstuffs but not producing its own manufactured products. "For the general operations of manufacture, let our workshops remain in Europe." Let Europe keep its proletariat and its slum cities while America remained an agricultural democracy with open spaces. Contact with Europe should be limited to a mere exchange of agricultural commodities for manufactured articles.

Conditions have changed since Jefferson's time. Modern technology has begun to conquer space and the United States has become a global power deeply involved in world politics. It has also evolved into a mighty industrial nation with a population of over 180 million—compared to some 5 million when Jefferson was inaugurated. Most Americans today, unlike those of a century or two ago, live in cities, and, contrary to his expectations, they have shown themselves no less capable of the democratic life than were their ancestors in the eighteenth century.

Jefferson insisted that, except for natural rights, nothing human was permanent or immutable. This was particularly true of human institutions, which were always subject to change. He believed in the possibility of progress and in improvement of existing conditions. Man, in short, was a free agent, the sole architect of his own destiny. In 1816, Jefferson wrote:

> Some men look at constitutions with sanctimonious reverence and deem them like the ark of the covenant, too sacred to be touched. They ascribe to the men of the preceding age a wisdom more than human, and suppose what they did to be beyond amendment.... I am certainly not an advocate for frequent and untried changes in laws and constitutions.... But I know also that laws and constitutions must go hand in hand with the progress of the human mind.... As new discoveries are made, new truths disclosed, and manners and opinions change with the change of circumstances, institutions must advance also, and keep pace with the times. We might as well require a man to wear still the coat which fitted him when a boy, as civilized society to remain

ever under the regimen of their barbarous ancestors. . . . Each generation . . . has a right to choose for itself the form of government it believes the most promotive of its own happiness.

In sum, Jefferson was the master formulator of the ideas and ideals of democracy on the philosophical basis of inalienable natural rights and an inherent system of moral values. To him, the central idea of democracy was freedom—of mind, of spirit, of action, of the whole self. It is significant of Jefferson's set of values that he wanted posterity to remember him only for what he had done in the field of freedom and the mind. Although he spent more than half his life in the public service, occupying the foremost positions of trust within the gift of the American people—congressman, governor, minister, Secretary of State, Vice-President, and President of the United States—he asked only for the following inscription, "& not a word more," to be put on his tombstone:

*Here was Buried*
*Thomas Jefferson*
*Author of the Declaration of American Independence*
*Of the Statute of Virginia for Religious Freedom*
*& Father of the University of Virginia*

# 5

## *THE AMERICAN AS CONSERVATIVE:* Alexander Hamilton *(1755[57?]—1804)*

*By some he is considered as an ambitious man, and therefore a dangerous one. That he is ambitious, I shall readily grant, but it is of that laudable kind, which prompts a man to excel in whatever he takes in hand. He is enterprising, quick in his perceptions, and his judgment intuitively great.*

*—George Washington to John Adams (September 25, 1798)*

Of all the outstanding early American statesmen, Alexander Hamilton is probably the only one who has never been fully enshrined as a hero acceptable to all his countrymen. There are few divisions of opinion about Washington's towering character or Franklin's earthy wisdom or Jefferson's democratic philosophy; these are fully and widely accepted, although with varying degrees of admiration. But not so Hamilton. Admired for generations by conservatives, who have held him up as a paragon of all that is desirable in a well-ordered republic, Hamilton has been consistently assaulted by their opponents, who, incidentally, have always been influential in the country's intellectual life. As late as 1948, nearly a century and a half after Hamilton's death, the distinguished American historian, Charles A. Beard, found it necessary to complain that Hamilton's name "still arouses choking emotions in the bosoms of all 'right thinkers' who confine their knowledge and thinking to the Anti-federalist tradition." As he was during his short and stormy life, so Hamilton has remained since his tragic death—a figure of controversy and misunderstanding.

Much of the difficulty lies in Hamilton's character, which was, at bottom, his fate. There was something turbulent and explosive about him. Contemporaries who observed him, although not versed in the sophistications of modern psychology, were struck by his almost violent restlessness and lack of personal serenity. He gave the impression of a man who could not curb his feelings—or his tongue. "My heart," he once admitted to General Henry Knox, "has always been the master of my judgment." He could be sweet-tempered to some people and unbearably arrogant to others. On occasion he could be gentle and diplomatic, but more often he was ruthless and aggressive. The consistent pattern of Hamilton's character was one of outer unquiet and inner disharmony.

His life, although not his basic ideas, reflected this internal imbalance. Deeply attached to his wife and children, he was yet capable of an unsavory sexual adventure which he admitted publicly. Scrupulously honest himself, he winked at the peculations of friends. Under lasting obligation to Washington, he made insulting and slighting remarks about the General. A bitter enemy of Jefferson, he helped him decisively in the election to the presidency in 1801. A humble-born British colonial, he openly sang the praises of Britain's aristocracy. A life-long believer in monarchy as the best form of government, he fought heroically for the adoption of the federal Constitution. Filled with contempt for democracy, he gave the American republic loyal and probably invaluable support. Rejecting duelling as un-Christian and uncivilized, he permitted himself to be drawn into a duel that killed him. This by no means exhausts the list of contradictions.

The judgment of contemporaries, particularly political opponents, reflects awareness of Hamilton's inconsistencies and also of his great gifts. Jefferson's final evaluation of his enemy, written fourteen years after Hamilton's death, has the merit of fairness. "Hamilton was," he wrote in 1818, "indeed, a singular character. Of acute understanding, disinterested, honest, and honorable in all private transactions, amiable in society, and duly valuing virtue in private life, yet so bewitched and perverted by the British example, as to be under thorough conviction that corruption was essential to the government of a nation." James Madison, a milder critic, after paying tribute to Hamilton's "intellectual powers of the first order," made a similar point. "If," Madison said of his collaborator on *The Federalist,* "his theory of government deviated from the republican standard he had the candor to avow it, and the greater merit of cooperating faithfully in maturing and supporting a system which was not his choice." And John Quincy Adams, whose father was one of Hamilton's aversions, summarized the contradictory character of his parent's enemy in these terms:

> [Hamilton's] talents were of the highest order, his ambition transcendent, and his disposition to intrigue irrepressible. His consciousness of talent was greater than its reality.... His valor was deliberate and undaunted; his experience in war not inconsiderable; the powers and resources of his mind extraordinary; his eloquence, both of speaking and writing, in the very first style of excellence; he had within him to a great degree that which subdues the minds of other men, perhaps the first of all qualities for the commander of an army. But he was of that class of characters which cannot bear a rival—haughty, overbearing, jealous, bitter and violent in his personal enmities, and little scrupulous of the means which he used against those who stood in the way of his ambition.

Hamilton's background helps us understand his character. Psychologically, it is not too much to say that his birth and parentage must have left an ineradicable scar on his life. For, like William the Conqueror, Leonardo da Vinci, and many another famous man, Alexander Hamilton was illegitimate. Indeed, it is even doubtful whether, from a strictly legal point of view, he had a right to his father's name of Hamilton.

There has been much confusion about Hamilton's early dates and his parentage. Recent researches, however, especially in the Danish State Archives at Copenhagen, have helped to clear up some obscure points. We now know, for example, that Hamilton was probably two years older than he claimed or knew. His mother died on February 19, 1768, and in that year the court, when it settled her small estate, noted that she had a son, Alexander, who was "13 years of age." If he was thirteen in 1768, then his year of birth was 1755, instead of 1757, which is usually given in the history books.

Hamilton's early years are somewhat clouded. What is indisputable is that he was born in St. Nevis, the smallest (60 square miles) of the Leeward Islands in the British West Indies. Beyond that, the record is not satisfactory. His mother was Rachel Faucette—variously spelled as Faucitt, Fawcet, Fawcette, Fotzett—daughter of a poor island family. Some time about 1745, when Rachel was around sixteen, she married an older man named John Michael Levine—or Lawein or Leweine or Lavine or Lavien—said to be a Danish Jew. The marriage to Levine, who had a small business in St. Nevis and a little plantation in nearby St. Croix, lasted about five years; after giving birth to a son, Peter, Mrs. Levine, at the age of around twenty-one, left her husband.

Some time after abandoning her husband, Rachel Levine set up household with an itinerant Scotsman named James Hamilton, about whom not much is known, except that he seems to have been something of a drifter and a failure in life. Alexander and another boy two years younger were the products of that union, which, while without benefit of clergy, seems to have been respectable. In February 1759, about four years after Alexander was born, John Michael Levine sued Rachel for a divorce in the court of St. Croix. Levine charged that his wife had "absented herself from him for nine years and gone elsewhere, where she has begotten several illegitimate children." Rachel Levine—legally she was never Mrs. Hamilton—accused of desertion and adultery, did not contest the suit, and the court granted the divorce in June but, under Danish law, denied Rachel the right to remarry. Alexander, therefore, could not be made legitimate.

On the death of Rachel, James Hamilton abandoned his children and simply drifted away, and Alexander—to whom the much-provoked John Adams was later to refer as the "bastard son of a Scotch peddlar"—was never to see or have much to do with his father again. The thirteen-year-old Alexander was thrown on the mercy of his mother's relatives, but not for long. The proud and strong-willed boy entered the counting house of a local businessman named Nicholas Cruger, and by the time he was fifteen he was in charge of the business. But he was too ambitious to be satisfied with a clerkship in a colonial store. At the age of fourteen he wrote to his boyhood friend, Edward Stevens: "To confess my weakness, Ned, my ambition is prevalent, so that I contemn the grovelling condition of a clerk or the like, to which my fortune, etc., condemns me, and would willingly risk my life, though not my character, to exalt my station. I am confident, Ned, that my youth excludes me from any hopes of immediate preferment; nor do I desire it; but I mean to prepare the way for futurity. I'm no philosopher, you see, and may justly be said to build castles in the air; my folly makes me ashamed, and I beg you'll conceal it; yet, Neddy, we have seen such schemes successful when the projector is constant."

In this youthful letter we see the germ of the later Hamilton—pride, ambition, desire for place and prestige, determination to achieve his goal. While clerking, he read incessantly, taught himself the art of disciplined writing, and learned to speak French fluently. *"Il parle et écrit parfaitement bien la langue,"* a French traveler, the Marquis de Chastellux, said of him after he met him in the United States. This mastery of French was to be most useful to Hamilton when he had to deal with Lafayette and other French officers, as aide to General Washington, whose knowledge of that tongue was close to zero.

Soon young Hamilton was ready to break out of the narrow confines of his insular world. Some time in September or October 1772 he sailed from St. Croix to Boston, whence he went to New York. Apart from a little money given to him by his aunts on the island, his most precious material possessions were letters of introduction to influential Americans. Among the most important of them was one from his teacher Hugh Knox, a Presbyterian clergyman who had studied at Princeton, to William Livingston, member of a prominent New Jersey family, later governor of his state and a delegate (as was Hamilton) to the Constitutional Convention in 1787.

Hamilton was seventeen when he came to the mainland, a frail boy of small stature, reddish-haired and blue-eyed. He was full of fire, precocity, intense energy, and a burning desire to make his name and place in this new world. After a year at boarding school in New Jersey, he entered King's College (now Columbia University) in New York. King's was not much of a college in those days. It had a total faculty of three, one of whom (Myles Cooper) was the president, another (Samuel Clossy) taught in the medical school, and the third (John Vardill) taught nearly everything, including rhetoric, philosophy, theology, disputation, and what is known today as economics and sociology. The underlying ideas of the curriculum of King's College, as throughout the colonies, were natural law and Old Testament ethics. These were given as "self-evident truths." Central to this universe was the enshrinement of property and its institutions as virtually sacred to man in a civilized environment. There is no reason to assume that Hamilton, then or later, doubted for a moment the sacredness and the paramount rights of property.

King's College was but a steppingstone, for Hamilton did not require much intellectual guidance or help. He was, to say the least, as quick, as perceptive, as articulate as any of his elders at the college. Endowed with a mind of immense discipline and retentive power, he read voraciously and with a concentration oblivious to everything but the world of hard facts and logical construction. His brain stored everything away in an orderly fashion, ready for instant use when the time came. He was probably not consciously aware of it, but he was preparing himself for the building of a new nation—the "American empire," he later referred to it proudly—his mind an instrument of marvelous precision, his language lean, muscular, and persuasive, sometimes torrentially persuasive. In his type of mental structure there was, it seems, no room for originality or the exploration of new avenues of thought. Hamilton acquired his ideas early in life and he never changed them. Blunt, tough, and practical, he had no understanding whatever of dreamers, visionaries, or any kind of idealist.

Hamilton spent only a year at King's College. At nineteen his formal education was complete and he plunged into a life of action. This was 1774, the threshold of the great crisis that was, in the end, to lead to war and independence. When young Hamilton entered upon the public scene, the land was in a state of agitation and uncertainty. British imperial policy antagonized the colonists, but the leading men in the colonies were not yet sure what course to pursue. Few dared think of complete independence of Great Britain; yet many no longer thought of themselves as Englishmen. What, then, were they, and what were to be their future relations with the British crown?

As yet an American nation did not exist, but obviously there were undercurrents of nationalism. Many of the colonists wanted Great Britain to grant large concessions, even up to the point of independence, but many more seemed to be loyal to the crown. As the debate deepened, arguments were dredged up from history, from natural law, and, above all, from English jurisprudence, for there was an astonishingly large number of lawyers in the colonies; and many of them—John Adams and Thomas Jefferson come immediately to mind—were soon to be found on the side of those who wanted to cut the umbilical cord with the mother country. Hamilton, who, too, was preparing to become a lawyer, unhesitatingly joined what is known as the "popular cause," that is, the side that challenged the absolute authority of the British crown over the colonies.

He began to contribute political articles to Holt's *New York Journal, or General Advertiser* in 1774. Toward the end of the year, when he was not yet twenty, he published his first important work, a major contribution to the literature of the American Revolution. This consisted of two pamphlets, *A Full Vindication of the Measures of the Congress from the Calumnies of Their Enemies* (14,000 words) and *The Farmer Refuted* (35,000 words). Following the fashion of the times, they were written anonymously, as an answer to widely read articles by Samuel Seabury who, under the pen name of "A Westchester Farmer," eloquently defended the British colonial system. Hamilton's polemics against Seabury were so brilliantly conceived and maturely reasoned that contemporaries, when they learned the name of the author, could not believe that they had before them the work of a stripling just out of college. "There are displayed in these papers," says George Ticknor Curtis in his *Constitutional History of the United States,* "a power of reasoning and sarcasm, a knowledge of the principles of government and of the English constitution, and a grasp of the merits of the whole controversy, that would have done honor to any man at any age. To say that they evince precocity of intellect gives no idea of their main characteristics. They show great maturity—a more remarkable maturity than has ever been exhibited by any other person, at so early an age, in the same department of thought."

When hostilities broke out between the colonies and Great Britain, Hamilton enlisted and became a captain of artillery. He soon attracted the attention of Nathanael Greene, one of the ablest generals of the Revolutionary War, who in turn introduced him to George Washington, then having trouble with incompetent adjutants. As usual, Hamilton made a great impression, and in March 1777 the commander in chief of the American Revolutionary forces appointed him aide-de-camp with the rank of lieutenant colonel. Of General Washington's seven aides-de-camp, Hamilton was by far the best equipped—he wrote many of the General's important military papers and letters—and certainly the one most appreciated by the commander. Despite his icy reserve and aloofness, General Washington used to refer affectionately to the youthful Colonel Hamilton as "my boy."

It is a commentary on Hamilton's personality that he did not reciprocate Washington's affection or appreciation. Indeed, it may be said that Hamilton was one of the very few contemporaries and collaborators of the General who was unimpressed by his true greatness. Neither then nor later did Hamilton show any understanding of the paramount quality that made Washington so impressive a personality: his towering character, a mixture of unshakable strength, dignity, and fairness. Hamilton, the insecurely born, seems to have had an instinctive dislike of Washington, the big man who loomed as a father image to so many people. The two were in sharp contrast. The tall general was slow-minded, inarticulate in speech, modest, and without any sparkle; the little colonel was quick-witted, intellectually arrogant, overbearingly self-assured. Washington was apparently unaware that his young aide harbored anything but friendly feelings toward him; he continued to respect and admire him throughout his life.

After four years as aide-de-camp, Hamilton broke with Washington.

The decision to do so was not a sudden one; it had been in his mind for some time. Hamilton had long been fretting at what he considered his position as an underling. In view of his insatiable ambition, it is also possible that he was jealous and resentful of Washington's high military position and reputation. As a matter of fact, Hamilton, who fancied himself fit to command armies, secretly disparaged Washington's military abilities and his knowledge of the art of war. The twenty-six-year-old colonel, thirsting for martial glory which he could not achieve so long as he was chained to a desk at headquarters, soon found an opportunity abruptly to leave "the General's family," as he put it. The story, as related by Hamilton to his father-in-law, General Philip Schuyler,* is not without drama.

One day in February 1781, at headquarters in New Windsor, Connecticut, as Washington and Hamilton passed each other on the stairs, the General said that he wanted to see him. Hamilton replied that he would present himself immediately, as soon as he had delivered something to his fellow adjutant, Colonel Tench Tilghman. On his way to Washington's room, Hamilton was stopped by General Lafayette, and the two friendly young officers had a brief chat. Suddenly General Washington appeared at the upper landing and spoke angrily: "Colonel Hamilton, you have kept me waiting at the head of the stairs these ten minutes. I must tell you, Sir, you treat me with disrespect." Hamilton, sure that his conversation with Lafayette had lasted only about two minutes, snapped back: "I am not conscious of it, Sir, but since you have thought it necessary to tell me so, we part." "Very well, Sir," said Washington, "if it be your choice." An hour later, Colonel Tilghman came with a conciliatory message from General Washington, assuring Hamilton of his "great confidence" in him and explaining that the regrettable incident "could not have happened but in a moment of passion." Would Colonel Hamilton forget the whole thing and return to his duties? He adamantly refused. Not only would he not resume his post but also he would not see the General. The relationship, he said, was ended.

"Perhaps," he explained to his father-in-law, "you may think I was precipitate in rejecting the overture made by the General. . . . I assure you, my dear Sir, it was not the effect of resentment; it was the deliberate result of maxims I had long formed for the government of my own conduct." He then went on to say that he disliked the General, and that

* On December 14, 1780, Hamilton married Elizabeth Schuyler, daughter of the general, who belonged to one of the most distinguished families in New York state.

for the last three years he had neither felt nor professed any friendship for him. He considered Washington merely a connection that might be useful to him in his later career. "He was an Egis," Hamilton was to say cold-bloodedly after Washington's death in 1799, "very essential to me." "I always disliked the office of aide-de-camp," Hamilton continued his explanation, "as having in it a kind of personal dependence. I refused to serve in this capacity with two major-generals at an early period of the war. Infected, however, with the enthusiasm of the time, an idea of the General's character, *which experience taught me to be unfounded,* overcame my scruples, and induced me to accept his invitation to enter into his family. It was not long before I discovered he was neither remarkable for delicacy nor good temper . . . I was always determined, if there should ever happen a breach between us, never to consent to an accommodation."

Hamilton's petulance and dislike found no responsive echo in Washington. Although the younger man never showed the General any warmth or affection, Washington continued to be unfailingly generous toward him. Nine months after the breach between the two, in the autumn of 1781, Hamilton, yearning for a chance to distinguish himself on the field of battle, asked Washington to permit him to lead a small storming party during the siege of Yorktown. The General gave him his chance—and Hamilton had his brief moment of military glory, which he felt he needed for the record. After the Revolutionary War, when Hamilton was rising rapidly as a leading politician and lawyer in New York, he asked Washington in Mount Vernon to scotch the persistent rumor that he had "palmed" himself off on Washington during the war and had been dismissed from his service. Washington promptly gave him his clearance, saying, "I do . . . explicitly declare that both charges are entirely unfounded" and that "quitting was altogether . . . your own choice." As President, he appointed the still youthful Hamilton to the second highest position in his cabinet and gave him staunch support throughout a stormy administration. When the time came for Washington to retire from public life, it was to Hamilton that he turned, in 1796, for help in the drafting of the Farewell Address, a state paper for which both men deserve a share of immortality. And in 1798, when war with France seemed imminent and the country was mobilizing for it, Washington used his immense influence to have President John Adams appoint Hamilton major general and second in command, a post the latter hungrily coveted and clamored for, thereby bypassing and antagonizing older and more experienced officers. Truly, as Hamilton wrote to the widowed Martha Washington early in 1800, her husband had always been useful to him.

But the usefulness worked both ways. Just as Washington had been essential to Hamilton's career, so Hamilton was invaluable to the early history of the United States. His greatest services to the country covered only some eight years, from 1787 to January 1795, when he resigned the secretaryship of the Treasury, but they were of supreme importance. In that period of time, Hamilton was outstanding in his fight for the adoption of the federal Constitution, wrote the majority of the *Federalist* papers in its defense, and, finally, as the first Secretary of the Treasury, laid the durable foundations of American fiscal and economic policies. Although he lived almost another decade after he resigned from President Washington's cabinet, his important work may be said to have been over by the time he was forty.

What greatness there was in Hamilton came out in those years of the making of the Constitution and the first Washington administration. It was the period when the national structure was built, and Hamilton was, beyond doubt, one of its indispensable architects. Here, paradoxically enough, his foreign birth played a not inconsiderable role, for it gave him the kind of perspective most native Americans still lacked. The leading men of the day did not yet think of themselves as citizens of the United States. They were, rather, Virginians, Pennsylvanians, New Yorkers, Carolinians, and so forth; their roots and loyalties were in their native states, and only with some difficulty could they identify with a larger unit; when they finally moved from the native state to the union of states, they did so slowly, reluctantly, and with many grave reservations.

Not so Hamilton. He had no native roots in the new country. He was not emotionally attached to any single state. Indeed, he could not understand how anybody could have strong attachments to a comparatively small political unit like Rhode Island or Delaware or New Jersey or, for that matter, New York. To his severely logical mind it made no sense whatever to continue the existence of separate and independent states when, instead, they could combine and transform themselves into a powerfully united "American empire." He had the vision of such a union from the very beginning. As a young staff officer during the Revolution, he had firsthand experience with the shocking incompetence that prevailed under the loose government of the Articles of Confederation. His sense of order was outraged by the political weakness, the local intrigues, the administrative inefficiency of the existing confederation. Referring to the self-oriented states that operated as independent political entities, he wrote early in the Revolutionary War: "This pernicious mistake must be corrected."

Thus he became one of the prime agents in the movement for an effective federal union. He had two main objectives. The first was the creation of a united nation, which, he hoped, would abolish the individual states. The second was the establishment of a highly centralized government equipped with power to defend property and to maintain order against potentially turbulent radical forces. Both of these goals were more difficult of achievement than would appear to a twentieth-century observer. Hamilton was painfully aware that, in general, public opinion was against a strong national union, and that the Revolutionary War had unleashed popular forces outspokenly hostile to any rule by the rich and the aristocratic.

The delegates to the Constitutional Convention, which sat in Philadelphia from May to September 1787, shared Hamilton's awareness of the prevailing antiauthoritarian temper of the people. But they were not otherwise so sure of things as was their eminent colleague, the delegate from New York. Like Hamilton, the majority of them—only thirty-nine of the fifty-five chosen delegates attended the sessions more or less regularly—were conservative in their economics and politics. With rare exceptions, they distrusted the people. Hamilton, more blunt and articulate than most, may be said to have been the spokesman of the most extreme wing of this group.

A fellow delegate, William Pierce of Georgia, has left the following portrait of Hamilton at the Convention: "Colo. Hamilton is deservedly celebrated for his talents. He is . . . a finished Scholar. To a clear and strong judgment he unites the ornaments of fancy. . . . He is rather a convincing Speaker, than a blazing Orator. Colo. Hamilton requires time to think—he enquires into every part of his subject with the searchings of phylosophy, and when he comes forward he comes highly charged, with interesting matter, there is no skimming over the surface of a subject with him, he must sink to the bottom to see what foundation it rests on. . . . His eloquence is not so diffusive as to trifle with the senses, but he rambles just enough to strike and keep up the attention. He is . . . of small stature, and lean. His manners are tinctured with stiffness, and sometimes with a degree of vanity that is highly disagreeable."

During the first several days of the convention, Hamilton was a silent member. He listened to various proposals, including those that provided for a mere amendment of the Articles of Confederation. He was increasingly depressed as the delegates, still statebound, refused to face boldly the central problem that confronted them: the creation of a national union with a strong government. They could not bring themselves to the point of cutting down sharply the sovereignties of the individual states, and they were afraid of antagonizing public opinion by setting up a government ruled primarily by the upper classes. Hamilton finally lost patience with what he thought was mere shilly-shallying, and one day he rose and delivered a major speech in which he cut across all those currents of doubt and bluntly focused attention on the political realities as he saw them. James Madison, in his Journal of the Convention, thus briefly summarized Hamilton's long utterance:

> This view of the subject almost led [Hamilton] to despair that a republican government could be established over so great an extent [of American territory]. He was sensible, at the same time, that it would be unwise to propose one of any other form. In his private opinion, he had no scruple in declaring . . . that the British Government was the best in the world; and that he doubted much whether anything short of it would do in America. He hoped gentlemen of different opinions would bear with him in this, and begged them to recollect the change of opinion on this subject which had taken place, and was still going on. It was once thought that the power of Congress was amply sufficient to secure the ends of their institution. The error was now seen by everyone. The members most tenacious of republicanism . . . were as loud as any in declaiming against the vices of democracy. This progress of the public mind led him to anticipate the time when others . . . would join in the praise bestowed by Mr. Necker on the British Constitution, namely, that it is the only government in the world, "which unites public strength with individual security."

Much of Hamilton's reputation as a reactionary derives from this particular speech at the Convention. In the course of it, and secure in the feeling that he was protected by the secrecy which covered the proceedings and debates, he uttered many sentiments which, while familiar doctrine to his upper-class contemporaries, are shocking to American democratic ears today. It was in the Constitutional Convention that Hamilton used the expression: "Take mankind in general, they are vicious." He also remarked: "The voice of the people has been said to be the voice of God; and, however generally this maxim has been quoted and believed, it is not true to fact. The people are turbulent and changing; they seldom judge or determine right."

These are, indeed, extreme statements, uttered in the heat of debate. Martin Van Buren comments in his *Autobiography,* that Hamilton, "absorbed in the egotism and . . . vanity which have been the lot of great orators in all ages," blindly threw himself "headlong upon the Convention and recklessly proclaimed sentiments at variance with . . . . the riveted feeling of the American people."

Standing by themselves, Hamilton's statements in the Convention would condemn him as a hopelessly narrow, even unintelligent, politician, unworthy of consideration as a leader of men. But in proper context they merely underline a well-reasoned and consistently held political philosophy, although it was voiced without tact and without regard for public opinion in general. One may reject Hamilton's view of mankind and his theory of political society as needlessly myopic, but one must grant that he did have a clearly defined philosophy which had the merit of utter frankness and which, thereby, served to evoke and polarize opposite opinions. In a negative way, Hamilton may perhaps be given some credit for the fact that his outspoken antidemocratic views, by infuriating contemporaries who believed in democracy, stimulated them to a more vigorous and searching defense of their democratic faith. This can certainly be said of Jefferson, who was not infrequently angered by Hamilton's candidly and repeatedly uttered contempt for democracy. Jefferson could barely control his aversion when he heard Hamilton, at his own dinner table (as he relates in his diary for April 1791), proclaim that the British monarchical-aristocratic system, precisely *because it was corrupt,* was the "most perfect government which ever existed."

How did so superlatively intelligent a man as Hamilton justify such a view? He did so on the basis of psychology, or at least what he conceived to be psychology. His political philosophy, which also shaped his economic principles and policies, was based on a strongly held view of human nature. Indeed, it is not possible to understand his political beliefs without a knowledge of his psychological ones. Central to Hamilton's thought was a concept of man as a corrupt and selfish animal, always motivated by greed and self-interest. "The passions . . . of avarice, ambition, interest . . . ," he said at the Constitutional Convention, "govern most individuals, and all public bodies."

Here, of course, is the crucial idea on which Hamilton parted company with democrats, then and forever. Underlying the democratic belief is confidence in the virtue and potentialities of the human being, as well as, according to the Jeffersonians, in his perfectibility, through education and otherwise. Without such an assumption about human nature, democracy, or any other polity that calls for even a limited amount of self-government, becomes impossible and, indeed, a self-contradiction. For how can the corrupt and the selfish be expected to rule, with any prospect of success or stability, over others who are equally corrupt and selfish?

In rejecting the notion that man has in him the possibilities of decency and improvement, and hence is fit to participate fully in his own government, Hamilton may be said to have cut himself off spiritually from the main current of American history. Durably sound in his economics, he failed in his politics. The American experience, with its promises of a boundless and good life, has not borne out Hamilton's pessimism. From 1800, when the Jeffersonians triumphed over the Hamiltonians, the country's political life has moved, by and large, in the direction of enlarged, rather than limited, democracy. In general, we have witnessed the full acceptance of the philosophy of human improvability—as is shown, among other things, by our vast and expensive educational system—and of equal political rights and economic opportunities for all the people. In this sense Hamilton, as the symbol and voice of restriction, has met defeat at the hands of the American people, whose conspicuous national trait has been one of quite un-Hamiltonian optimism, with its accompanying dynamics of continuous expansion, experimentation, and improvement.

Hamilton, it must be said, was consistent and logical. Since human passions were a fact of nature and could not be altered, he proposed that they be recognized as such and harnessed for useful political ends. It was, he said, "a principle of human nature" that political institutions must be founded on "men's interests." He could see no other way to build a successful government than through an appeal to what he called "avarice and ambition." "Political writers," he argued, ". . . have established it as a maxim, that, in contriving any system of government, and fixing the several checks and controls of the constitution, every man ought to be supposed a knave; and to have no other end, in all his actions, but private interest. By this interest we must govern him; and, by means of it, make him co-operate to public good, notwithstanding his insatiable avarice and ambition. Without this, we shall in vain boast of the advantages of any constitution."

Although his generalizations about human nature and behavior applied to all men, Hamilton made a distinction between the many and the few, between the mass of the people and "the rich and well born." The many, he said, were "turbulent and uncontrollable," driven by nothing but blind passion, and hence too imprudent to be entrusted with governmental power. The few, on the other hand, while also motivated by greed and selfishness, had enough sense and education to judge matters, and, in consequence, could be depended upon to realize that their own best interests lay in using political power responsibly. It was not that he had any particular admiration for the wealthy—"I hate moneyed men," he once blurted out in an intimate letter to a friend—but that he thought they were a safer despository of power than the equally selfish common people. Having no illusions about what motivated the upper classes, he suggested that their loyalty to the new government be won through special privileges and economic advantages—through what he called "a dispensation of . . . regular honors and emoluments."

More than that. He proposed that the rich be given "a distinct, permanent share in the government," to serve as an unalterable check on whatever democratic institutions might develop in the future. To keep the "imprudence of democracy" in leash, he advocated the establishment of a permanent senate and an executive for life. Both were to be chosen indirectly, through electors or governors in the state, from the ranks of the economically privileged individuals in the community.

Would not such a lifelong executive, to all intents and purposes, be a monarch, another kind of George the Third? That, countered Hamilton, was a matter of definition; if, he said, you choose an executive for, say, seven years, what have you? You have a seven-year monarch, but still a monarch or whatever you care to call him. So what difference does it make, particularly if he be an excellent man and on his good behavior?

Again, was not a senate chosen for life too dangerous? If human nature was as depraved and avaricious as Hamilton said it was, how could a handful of senators be safely entrusted with unrestrained power? Precisely because they were assured of lifelong positions and conspicuous honors, argued Hamilton, the senators would have no motive for corruption or for radical changes. This was likewise true of the lifelong executive. Such, he said, had been the experience of the most ideal government on earth, that of Great Britain, with its Lords and hereditary crown. He told his fellow delegates at the Constitutional Convention in June 1787: "The British . . . House of Lords is a most noble institution. Having nothing to hope for by a change, and a sufficient interest by means of their property, in being faithful to the National interest, they form a permanent barrier against every pernicious innovation, whether . . . on the part of the Crown or of the Commons. No temporary Senate will have firmness enough to answer the purpose. . . . As to the Executive

. . . no good one could be established on republican principles. . . . The English model was the only good one on this subject. The Hereditary interest of the King was so interwoven with that of the Nation, and his personal emoluments so great, that he was placed above the danger of being corrupted."

But would the American people tolerate a class government? Public opinion, Hamilton admitted, was hostile to anything resembling hereditary rule or domination by the wealthy. He felt, however, that once the people realized that it was to their advantage to have the elite in power, their hostility would abate. Furthermore, he said, the mass of the people would not be completely powerless or disfranchised, since there was a general feeling—which he shared, although with reluctance—that, as a sop to the people, at least the lower legislative chamber should be popularly elected. The House of Representatives, with its periodic and frequent elections, would thus give the common people a certain amount of control over their rulers.

A popularly chosen lower chamber raised two questions. One was that the representatives might be dangerous and irresponsible democrats. The other was that the house might not properly represent all the "feelings and interests" of the various classes in the society. Hamilton argued that the chances were that even in the democratic lower chamber the representatives would come from the ranks of the well-to-do and the educated. Would such upper-class individuals truly be able to represent, and hence satisfy, the less-privileged people? Hamilton was sure that only the rich and the educated could know what was good for the others, and therefore could best represent them for their common interest. This is the way he stated it in *The Federalist* (No. 35):

> The representative body . . . will be composed of landholders, merchants, and men of the learned professions. But where is the danger that the interests and feelings of the different classes of citizens will not be understood or attended to by these three descriptions of men? Will not the landholder know and feel whatever will promote or insure the interest of landed property? And will he not, from his own interest in that species of property, be sufficiently prone to resist every attempt to prejudice or encumber it? Will not the merchant understand and be disposed to cultivate, as far as may be proper, the interests of the mechanic and manufacturing arts, to which his commerce is so nearly allied? Will not the man of the learned profession, who will feel a neutrality to rivalships between the different branches of industry, be likely to prove an impartial arbiter between them, ready to promote either, so far as it shall appear to him conducive to the general interests of the society?

Who, Hamilton asked, was in a better position to understand the problems and attitudes of the people as a whole than the individual who has had a chance to travel and to study? The uneducated and impecunious man, of necessity, did not possess an enlarged view and hence could not be expected to be as good a representative as the one who had opportunities to widen his intellectual and political horizon. Referring to national problems, Hamilton asked rhetorically: "Is the man whose situation leads to extensive inquiry and information less likely to be a competent judge of their nature, extent, and foundation than one whose observation does not travel beyond the circle of his neighbors and acquaintances? Is it not natural that a man who is a candidate for the favor of the people, and who is dependent on the suffrages of his fellow-citizens for the continuance of his public honors, should take care to inform himself of their dispositions and inclinations, and should be willing to allow them their proper degree of influence upon his conduct? This dependence, and the necessity of being bound . . . by the laws to which he gives his assent, are the true, and they are the strong chords of sympathy between the representative and the constituent."

Hamilton's basic proposals for the new government of the United States were not, in the last analysis, acceptable to the Constitutional Convention. While the majority of the delegates shared many of his views, virtually all of them being members of the wealthy and professional classes, they yet sensed that public opinion would reject a government from which the common people would be, as Hamilton desired, to a large extent excluded. Nearly all of them were native-born and, unlike Hamilton, had roots and relations in their home communities; and this enabled them almost instinctively to understand, without necessarily sharing, the outlooks and attitudes of their neighbors. The delegates knew that there were limits to American tolerance and patience, and that the Hamiltonian suggestions for the creation of what in effect would have amounted to a permanent ruling class went beyond anything that a fiercely individualistic people would tolerate. The convention, moreover, contained a small group of what today would be called liberals—among them such outstanding men as Benjamin Franklin, George Mason, James Wilson, and, to a lesser degree, James Madison—who warned their colleagues not to push things to an extreme. As Franklin once drily reminded the delegates, they should not permit themselves to forget that it was the common people who had fought and died in the Revolutionary War.

Fortunately for all concerned, Hamilton was not present during some of the most crucial debates at the Convention. For about two months, during July and August, he was absent from Philadelphia, returning only in September, when the Constitution was nearly completed and ready for signature. Sensing that he could not sway the Convention, he had left it in a mood of depression. "I own to you, Sir," he wrote to Washington on his way back to New York, "that I am seriously and deeply distressed at the aspect of counsels which prevailed when I left Philadelphia. I fear that we shall let slip the golden opportunity of rescuing the American empire from disunion, anarchy, and misery." In his absence the delegates abated their antidemocratic position and, despite doubts, agreed to a number of compromises that added up to the granting of a considerable share of potential power to the people. This was not to Hamilton's liking; in his eyes, the Constitution's democratic features—the periodic election of the President and the senators, for example—made it fundamentally defective. Nevertheless, as a practical man, he signed it. Not only was it better than nothing, but he hoped that in some future crisis, such as war, this "frail and worthless fabric," as he called it, might be transformed into a powerful instrument that would help the ruling classes contain the centrifugal and democratic forces then at large in the land.

At this point, in September 1787, when the Constitution was made public and submitted to the states for ratification, began Hamilton's great service to the United States. The document so painfully hammered out in Philadelphia immediately caused a storm of opposition throughout the country. Just as Hamilton did not like the Constitution because it was too democratic, so the people in general objected to it because it was not democratic enough. It was this widespread popular hostility to the Constitution that nerved and steeled Hamilton to an heroic effort in its defense: an instrument so detested by the masses must clearly have something good in it.

Hamilton threw himself into championship of the Constitution with characteristic vigor and unmatched brilliance. But a proper appreciation of his achievements in that struggle calls for an understanding of the currents of opinion that eddied around it.

Three main streams can be discerned. They may be described as conservative, popular, and liberal. The first supported the Constitution wholeheartedly. The second and third were either hostile or reserved. The conservative viewpoint, the position of Hamilton's rich and wellborn, was perhaps best stated by Washington, who said: "The Constitution . . . is not free from imperfections, but there are as few radical defects in it as could well be expected."

Popular opinion opposed the Constitution on two main grounds: first, by providing for a central government, it threatened the independence of the individual states; secondly, the proposed new system appeared to be an instrument of the rich for the oppression of the poor. Patrick Henry, in his eloquent, violent attack on the Constitution in the Virginia ratification convention, described it as "extremely pernicious, impolitic and dangerous." Others argued that it would "take away all we have—all our property," that it contained "no proper restriction of power," that it was "founded on the principles of monarchy," and that it was "like a mad horse" that would run away with its rider. As one opponent said in the New York State constitutional convention, anybody who trusted this new-fangled Constitution was like a man getting on a horse without a bridle; he would "justly be deemed a mad man, and deserve to have his neck broken."

Finally, there was the liberal opposition. This group, while granting that the Constitution contained a number of good features, objected to the absence of a bill of rights. The Constitution, the liberals said, contained safeguards for the protection of property but not for individual liberty (it was this oversight which aroused the widest hostility and in the end forced its defenders to promise a bill of rights at the first opportunity). The liberal viewpoint was most articulately voiced by Jefferson, who wrote, in a letter to his friend James Madison in December 1787:

> I like much the general idea of framing a government, which should go on of itself. . . . I like the organization of the government into legislative, judiciary and executive. I like the power given the legislature to levy taxes. . . . I approve the greater House being chosen by the people directly. . . . I am captivated by the compromise of the opposite claims of the great and little States. . . . There are other good things. . . . I will now add what I do not like. First, the omission of a bill of rights, providing clearly, and without the aid of sophism, for freedom of religion, freedom of the press, protection against standing armies, restriction of monopolies, the eternal and unremitting force of the habeas corpus laws, and trials by jury. . . . To say . . . that a bill of rights was not necessary, because all is reserved in the case of the general government which is not given . . . is surely a *gratis dictum*. . . . It would have been much more just and wise to have concluded the other way . . . and to have established general right instead of general wrong. Let me add that a bill of rights is what the people are entitled to against every government on earth . . . and what no just government should refuse, or rest on inferences.

Hamilton was aware of all these criticisms and, in one of the great *tours de force* in the history of political thought, he faced them head on. He lost no time in plunging into the national debate on the subject. About two weeks after the Constitution was signed in Philadelphia, he published in the New York *Independent Journal* for October 2, 1787, the first article in its defense. The series continued, in the *Journal* and in other New York publications, until April 1788, in which year all the articles, including those written by Hamilton's collaborators, John Jay and James Madison, were published in book form under the title of *The Federalist*. Of the eighty-five *Federalist* papers, Hamilton wrote fifty-one himself and three in collaboration with Madison. The authorship of twelve is uncertain: they were written either by Hamilton or by Madison. In any case, the bulk of the contributions was Hamilton's.*

This is not the place to expatiate on the virtues of *The Federalist*. It has been sufficiently and rightly praised by many others in the past. Written in the heat of the campaign for the ratification of the Constitution, and designed as a polemic against its critics, *The Federalist* has nevertheless become both an American classic and a major contribution to the world's literature of political science. In its searching and far-ranging analysis of the principles of free government, as well as of the mechanics of republicanism in general, *The Federalist* has probably no equal in any language. Chancellor James Kent said of it in his *Commentaries on American Law* (1826), "It is equally admirable in the depth of its wisdom, the comprehensiveness of its views, the sagacity of its reflections, and the fearlessness, patriotism, candor, simplicity, and elegance, with which its truths are uttered and recommended."

Considering Hamilton's deep-rooted prejudices against democracy and republicanism, it is ironic to reflect that in *The Federalist* he wrote what is probably still the best and most cogently reasoned defense of the institution of free government. His *Federalist* essays show unusual moderation and a profound grasp of republicanism, if not democracy, the latter of which, he argued, was fully embodied in the Constitution, since in the last analysis it derived its power from the people. In pleading that the Constitution be given a chance, he showed that he was capable of rising above personal bias to statesmanlike heights.

Hamilton threw himself wholeheartedly into the fight for the Consti-

* By Hamilton: Numbers 1, 6–9, 11–13, 15–17, 21–36, 59–61, 65–85. By Hamilton and Madison: Numbers 18–20. By Hamilton or Madison: Numbers 49–58, 62, 63. Of the remaining nineteen papers, Madison wrote fourteen (Numbers 10, 14, 37–48) and Jay five (Numbers 2–5, 64).

tution not because he loved republicanism but because he hated anarchy. He was revolted by the prevailing disunity and by the to him senseless pretensions to independence of the thirteen individual states. Rejection of the Constitution, he was convinced, would lead not to a better Constitution but to chaos and possibly a military dictatorship. Thus the great opportunity to create a free and powerful nation, which was, he said, America's destiny, would be forever lost. Pleading for the adoption of the Constitution and citing David Hume on the desirability of reasonableness and moderation in political affairs, Hamilton wrote in the concluding paragraph of the last *Federalist* paper (Number 85):

> These judicious reflections contain a lesson of moderation to all the sincere lovers of the Union, and ought to put them upon their guard against hazarding anarchy, civil war, a perpetual alienation of the States from each other, and perhaps the military despotism of a victorious demagogue.... It may be in me a defect of political fortitude, but I acknowledge that I cannot entertain an equal tranquillity with those who affect to treat the dangers of a longer continuance in our present situation as imaginary. A nation without a national government, is, in my view, an awful spectacle. The establishment of a Constitution, in time of profound peace, by the voluntary consent of a whole people, is a prodigy, to the completion of which I look forward with trembling anxiety.... I dread the more the consequences of new attempts, because I know that powerful individuals, in this and in other States, are enemies to a general national government in every possible shape.

While the *Federalist* papers were coming out, friends of the Constitution, probably strengthened and inspired by their arguments, won ratification victories in seven states. Delaware, Pennsylvania, and New Jersey ratified in December 1787, Georgia and Connecticut in January 1788, and Massachusetts and Maryland in February and April.* Two more states were needed to make up the nine required to put the Constitution into effect. Of the remaining six states, some, like the Carolinas, had too sparse a population to be politically important, and others, like Rhode Island, were hostile to the Constitution; the latter, indeed, did not ratify until long after the federal government was established.** Everything, therefore, now depended upon the two most populous and in-

* Delaware, December 7 (unanimously). Pennsylvania, December 12 (46 to 23). New Jersey, December 18 (unanimously). Georgia, January 2, 1788 (unanimously). Connecticut, January 9 (128 to 40). Massachusetts, February 6 (187 to 168). Maryland, April 26 (63 to 11).

** Rhode Island, May 29, 1790 (34 to 32). South Carolina, May 23 (149 to 73). New Hampshire, June 21 (57 to 47). North Carolina, November 21 (195 to 77).

fluential states, Virginia and New York. Rejection of the Constitution there would have been a disaster.

For a while it looked as if both pivotal states, where the ratification conventions met in June 1788, would turn down the Constitution. Hamilton kept in communication with Madison in Virginia and was filled with anxiety at the outcome of the contest. There was a sharp struggle, but on June 25, largely because of the eloquence of Madison and the prestige of Washington, the Constitution squeezed through the Virginia convention by the narrow vote of 89 to 79. Now it was up to New York —and to Alexander Hamilton.

The situation in New York was bad, and Hamilton girded himself for what was, beyond a doubt, the most important battle of his political career. New York opinion was inimical to the Constitution, and the state's ratification convention, which met at Poughkeepsie, reflected this hostility. "The anti-federal party," Hamilton informed Madison in unhappy pessimism, "have a majority of two thirds in the convention, and . . . about four sevenths in the community." Of the sixty-five delegates, only nineteen were known to be willing to vote for the Constitution; forty-six were opposed. Dreading that nonadoption would lead to "disunion and chaos," Hamilton took on the seemingly hopeless task of winning over the hostile delegates. For seven days, between June 20 and June 28, he poured himself out in a torrent of oratory, logic, and political analysis so formidable that his audience was dazzled. It was not a vain effort. In the end, nearly a dozen reluctant delegates were won over by Hamilton's forensic preformance—just enough to give victory to the Constitution. The final vote—by far the slimmest of all the important states—stood 30 for and 27 against. It was the triumph of one lone individual, a man of only thirty-three who was truly, in Jefferson's words, "a host unto himself."

Thus the Constitution went into effect, and on April 30 in the following year George Washington was inaugurated first President of the new union. For the post of Secretary of the Treasury, which turned out to be the most important position in the cabinet, he selected his former aide-de-camp, the brilliant Alexander Hamilton. It was in some ways an extraordinary choice, for Hamilton, whose reputation was primarily that of a lawyer-politician and orator, had no special experience in finance or economics. As it turned out, Hamilton needed no previous experience. A careful student of Adam Smith, he grasped the situation with his usual acuteness and by applying his disciplined mind and energies to unaccustomed problems, came up with sharply defined conclusions and decisive recommendations. For more than five years (September 1789 to January 1795) Hamilton served as Secretary of the Treasury, and in that crucial period he laid the foundations of economic and fiscal policies that have remained substantially the same ever since. In this respect his contributions to the durable construction of the American republic may be said to have been exceeded only by those of George Washington himself.

His services were especially remarkable in view of the fact that the new federal union had inherited economic chaos. In the absence of a central government, there was no national currency. Trade and the ordinary transactions of daily life were paralyzed by a welter of currencies whose exact value could be neither calculated nor compared. Everything circulated—Spanish doubloons and pistoles, Arabian chequins, English and French guineas, German and Dutch ducats, Portuguese moidores, Brazilian gold johanneses. Even worse than the currency chaos was an actual shortage of pieces of money. People had to resort to barter. In Virginia so-called "tobacco notes" circulated in place of coinage. In Kentucky and Tennessee cows and horses and oxen and acres of land constituted the exchange used for ordinary transactions. In western Pennsylvania the circulating medium was whiskey. Elsewhere, coin-starved people cut silver dollars into halves and quarters, known as "sharp-shins." Nothing could be done about this anarchy because the Congress of the Confederation, while it had the authority to coin money, did not possess the funds to build a mint or buy the necessary metal.

Compounding the economic disorder was the practice of the individual states of levying tariffs on their neighbors. Duties were imposed, not merely on foreign commerce but also on American. Connecticut taxed the goods coming in from Massachusetts. New York levied duties on New Jersey's agricultural products. New Jersey taxed New York's Sandy Hook lighthouse. Each sovereign state was arrayed against every other sovereign state.

Hamilton, with a ruthless disregard for prevailing local prejudices, set about to solve financial evils and to eradicate economic absurdities. His program, which had the solid backing of President Washington, was imaginative, integrated, and thorough. It also aroused bitter and lasting hatreds.

To bring order into the currency chaos, Hamilton had Congress enact a law providing for the coinage of gold and silver at the ratio of 15 to 1 (changed to 16 to 1 in 1834). Any person having gold or silver bullion could take it to the mint in Philadelphia and have it turned into coin, free of charge. The coinage act created the dollar as the monetary unit, the gold dollar containing 2.5 grams of gold and the silver one fifteen times that amount of silver (37¼ grams). The mint struck eagles, half and quarter eagles of gold; and dollars, half dollars, quarters, dimes, and half dimes of silver. For small exchanges, 150 tons of copper was coined into cents and half cents.

To establish the new government as a good credit risk, Hamilton proposed to Congress that it undertake to pay the debts of the individual states as well as of the nation, amounting to a total of around $75,000,000. In his famous financial report to Congress (January 14, 1790) he argued that every dollar to this debt must be paid, whether owed to foreigners or to Americans, in order to create faith in the United States government. "States, like individuals," he said, "who observe their engagements are respected and trusted." Despite fierce opposition, Congress gave him the authority to assume the state debts at face value. As the Secretary of the Treasury had foreseen, this underwriting of a debt that had seemed worthless brought to the new government the loyal support of the monied classes.

Hamilton's next step in his drive for national economic centralization and stability was the establishment of a national bank for the depositing of government funds and for borrowing. In the face of violent opposition from Jeffersonians and others, who felt that such a bank was monopolistic and unconstitutional, Hamilton was again victorious. In 1791, the first Bank of the United States was established, with a capital stock of $10,000,000. Within an hour of the opening of this bank in Philadelphia, its stock was sold out. The Bank's notes circulated at face value, paying 8 per cent. For twenty years, until 1811 when the charter of the United States Bank expired, it served as a stabilizing force in the rapidly growing American economy, as Hamilton had expected it would.

His revenue program was equally controversial—and successful. In his celebrated *Report on Manufactures* (December 5, 1791) he proposed a tariff, not merely for income but also for the protection of infant American industries, for he was convinced that the "American empire" whose greatness he visualized, could not be powerful or secure except on an industrial base. His tariff and excise policies aroused bitter hatreds and, as in the case of the tax on whiskey (7 cents on a gallon), armed revolt. But Hamilton's total program succeeded in its fundamental objectives: to give the new country unshakable financial stability and an opportunity for indefinite economic expansion. When he finally left the

Treasury, at the age of forty, he could have done so with the satisfaction that the United States, which he had done so much to create, was well launched on its destiny. But he felt no happiness.

Hamilton returned to New York to the practice of the law, but despite occasional plunges into local and state politics, he felt increasingly left out of the main stream of national life. This helped to bring out his unhappy gift for making enemies. As he attacked others and was attacked in turn, he tended to consider himself a victim of persecution. It was galling to him to have his fellow Federalist, President John Adams, all but ignore him. Hamilton, after secretly meddling with and needling Adams' cabinet, branded the President as "very unfit and incapable," a man who was "excessively vain and jealous and ignobly attached to place," and one whose administration had "very materially disgraced and sunk the government." And President Adams lost no love for Hamilton either.

Politically, the final straw for Hamilton was Jefferson. The two men had clashed angrily when they served together in President Washington's cabinet. Their enmity was primarily political, but it also had personal undertones. They were in sharp contrast, and their disagreement was as old as history—the conflict between the city man and the country man, between the individual who lives by trade and the one who earns his bread from the soil. Hamilton had no affection for farmers, and Jefferson none for bankers. In addition, Hamilton, small of stature and illegitimate, probably felt a secret resentment of Jefferson, who was tall and moved with the serenity of one with a securely established social and family position. Nor could Hamilton find consolation in intellectual superiority to Jefferson, as he did vis-à-vis Washington, for he knew that his agrarian opponent was at least as well educated and mentally gifted as himself. Jefferson, in turn, while respecting Hamilton's conspicuous abilities, found his politics most objectionable.

The painful moment for Hamilton came during the presidential election of 1800, which resulted in a tie between Aaron Burr and Jefferson. In the House of Representatives, which met to break the tie, Hamilton's Federalists were tempted to avenge themselves on Jefferson by voting for Burr. And once again Hamilton rose to a moment of greatness—above his personal dislike. He had been in political conflict with Burr in New York, and he considered him an "unprincipled and dangerous" man, who, once in power, would make himself dictator and destroy the republic. Hamilton, despite his detestation of Jefferson, exerted all his influence to prevent Burr's election by the House of Representatives. "I trust," he wrote to an important Federalist leader, "New England, at least, will not so far lose its head as to fall into this snare. There is no doubt that, upon every virtuous and prudent calculation, Jefferson is to be preferred. He is by far not so dangerous a man; and he has pretensions to character. As to Burr, there is nothing in his favor. . . . He is truly the Catiline of America."

And so Jefferson was elected President, but the victory was no triumph for Hamilton. Jeffersonianism, in Hamilton's eyes, meant the further spread of the "poison" of democracy. He was despondent over Jefferson's "visionary" administration, with its "pernicious dreams." What increasingly depressed him was Jefferson's growing popularity and the prospect that Jeffersonianism was on the increase. "Amidst the triumphant reign of democracy," Hamilton, with a touch of bitterness, wrote to his friend General Charles C. Pinckney at the end of the second year of Jefferson's administration, "do you retain sufficient interest in public affairs to feel any curiosity about what is going on? In my opinion, the follies and vices of the Administration have as yet made no material impression to their disadvantage. On the contrary, I think the malady is rather progressive than upon the decline. . . . The last *lullaby* message [Jefferson's message to Congress], instead of inspiring contempt, attracts praise. Mankind are for ever destined to be the dupes of bold and cunning imposture."

With "bold and cunning imposture" triumphantly enthroned in the President's House in Washington, the "American world" seemed to Hamilton to have become an alien environment. Politically frustrated and isolated, he wondered whether he understood his country. Or was there a deep difference between him and other Americans, especially those "who drew their first breath on American ground"? After some thirty years of living in and fighting for the United States, he finally questioned whether he really belonged here. One of his last letters on the subject is a veritable cry of pain: "Mine is an odd destiny," he wrote to Gouverneur Morris, in February 1802. "Perhaps no man in the United States has sacrificed or done more for the present Constitution than myself; and contrary to all my anticipations of its fate . . . I am still laboring to prop up the frail and worthless fabric. Yet I have the murmurs of its friends no less than the curses of its foes for my reward. What can I do better than withdraw from the scene? Every day proves to me more and more, that this American world was not made for me."

In July 1804, two and a half years after that letter was written, the increasingly troubled Hamilton permitted himself to be maneuvered into a duel with his old enemy, Aaron Burr. Hamilton, distressed at the thought that he might have done Burr an injustice in the past, did not fire. Burr did, and killed Hamilton in his forty-ninth year.

Woodrow Wilson, analyzing Hamilton's career, concluded, "A very great man, but not a great American." A case might be made, however, for the reverse. In his magnificent contributions to the building of the United States, Hamilton was a very great American. That he was a great man—in the universal sense that Washington and Jefferson are recognized as great men—is more doubtful.

# 6

## *THE AMERICAN AS REPUBLICAN:* James Madison *(1751–1836)*

> *...He acquired a habit of self-possession which placed at ready command the rich resources of his luminous and discriminating mind, & of his extensive information, and rendered him the first of every assembly ... of which he became a member. Never wandering from his subject into vain declamation, but pursuing it closely in language pure, classical, and copious, soothing always the feelings of his adversaries by civilities and softness of expression.... With these consummate powers were united a pure and spotless virtue which no calumny has ever attempted to sully.*
>
> —*Thomas Jefferson,* Autobiography (*1821*)

For whatever reasons Hamilton is remembered by posterity, he is well remembered. But not so James Madison. Except among scholars, Madison is one of the obscure leaders in American history. Many a person in the United States could no doubt identify him as an early President of the republic (the fourth); others may remember him as Jefferson's Secretary of State or as the husband of the "buxom" Dolly or as the man whose name graces a shop-lined Manhattan avenue. But not many people are familiar enough with Madison's thought to classify him, as he should be, among the Western world's important and influential political thinkers.

Madison was, first of all, a child of the eighteenth-century Enlightenment, brought up in its libertarian ideals and nurtured, as were his great contemporaries, in the classics. He was born March 16, 1751, at Port Conway, Virginia, and was raised on his father's plantation in Orange County. The Madisons were people of "independent and comfortable circumstances," and, like so many other slaveowners of the period, were refined and cultured. James, the eldest of ten children, was bookish and shunned sports. It was said of him that he "never was a boy." Tutored at home, the frail young man studied Greek, Latin, French, Spanish, and mathematics. At eighteen, in 1769, he was sent to the College of New Jersey, now Princeton, and received his B.A. degree in October 1771. He remained another year, studying Hebrew and ethics under the Scottish-born divine, Dr. John Witherspoon, president of the college.

At the age of twenty-one Madison returned to Virginia full of melancholy and depression. He did not, he said, "expect a long or healthy life," and therefore would not prepare for a profession or take any steps that would lead to an accumulation of earthly goods.

After three years of brooding, reading, and inner conflict, Madison was stirred into political action. This was the period of struggle with Great Britain, when the colonies were preparing to assert themselves against the mother country. In 1775, at twenty-four, Madison became chairman of the Committee of Public Safety of his own county and in the following year was chosen delegate to the Williamsburg convention that drafted Virginia's first constitution. At Williamsburg Madison first met Jefferson.

At long last he had found a profession, that of public servant, which satisfied him and gave full scope to his singular abilities. He did not think of his political activities as a profession. Indeed, at one period in his life he took up the study of law, in order, he wrote to Edmund Randolph (July 26, 1785), "to provide a decent and independent subsistence" for himself and "to depend as little as possible on the labour of slaves." But as President Franklin D. Roosevelt pointed out, Madison never became a lawyer or a member of the bar.*

From 1776 Madison was almost continuously in public life until his retirement from the presidency in 1817. From the Virginia House of Delegates he went to the Continental Congress, from there to the Con-

* "The Constitution of the United States was a layman's document, not a lawyer's contract. That cannot be stressed too often. Madison, most responsible for it, was not a lawyer—nor was Washington or Franklin, whose sense of the give and take of life had kept the Convention together." (Cited in New York *Herald Tribune,* September 18, 1937).

stitutional Convention, from the convention to the United States House of Representatives, and thence to the secretaryship of state and the presidency. In all positions, whether elective or appointive, Madison was an intellectual leader, sometimes *the* leader.

His leadership derived from solid merit, for Madison was a man of formidable mental equipment. He continued to study a variety of subjects, including natural history, at one time confessing to Jefferson "a little itch to gain a smattering of chymistry." For the great tasks of his life, such as the Constitutional Convention and the crucial first eight years of the United States Congress, Madison prepared himself with overwhelming and sometimes health-breaking thoroughness.

He read the most important and authoritative works in the fields of politics, history, jurisprudence, international law, and comparative institutions, particularly accounts of ancient and modern confederacies. He bought as many books as opportunity permitted. When Jefferson was American minister in Paris he served, among other things, as Madison's book-buyer.

In terms of American history, Madison lived and was active in a heroic period. Among his friends, colleagues, and collaborators were a number of remarkable men who struck a spark in him. Mention of George Washington, George Mason, John Adams, Alexander Hamilton, James Wilson, Benjamin Franklin, and Thomas Jefferson shows Madison's environment. Most important of all these contemporaries, so far as Madison's public and intellectual life is concerned, was Jefferson.

No two men could have been closer, both as intimate friends and as trusted collaborators. History records no comparable friendship of similar duration and esteem. For a full half-century the two were warm friends and ardent admirers of one another. "The soul of Jonathan was knit with the soul of David, and Jonathan loved him as his own soul." Jefferson even gave Madison a "throne," as did Jonathan to David. Madison's senior by eight years, Jefferson could not have been more devoted to the younger man had he been his own son; Madison reciprocated the admiration and affection of his "Tutelary Genius" with filial devotion and unbounded respect.

Despite their intimacy, it would be misleading to assume that Madison was a carbon copy of Jefferson. Madison was not only a great personality in his own right; he also differed from Jefferson in a number of significant and subtle ways. The first and most obvious difference was physical. Jefferson was tall—about six feet two inches—rangy, and vigorous; Madison was tiny, frail, and hypochondriac. Washington Irving said that "poor Jemmy Madison" was "but a withered little apple-john." The slouching Jefferson was inclined to be casual in appearance and often dressed for comfort rather than looks. Madison, on the other hand, was always neat and precise. As if to underline his conservatism, he never dressed in anything but black. This was, among other things, a matter of economy. He was not wealthy, and his wardrobe was severely limited. "He never had but one suit at a time," his servant wrote. "He had some poor relatives that he had to help, and wished to set them an example of economy in the matter of dress." Where Jefferson often looked what in many ways he was—a western pioneer on horseback—Madison gave the impression of a sober and studious ecclesiastic. "He has," Senator Mills of Massachusetts said of President Madison in 1815, "much more the appearance of what I imagined a Roman cardinal to be."

Perhaps the main difference between Madison and Jefferson lay in temperament. Where Jefferson had a sweeping vision and lively imagination, Madison was cool and balanced. Jefferson loved to theorize about men and nature, and to let his fancy soar; Madison was judicious and almost passionless. It is hard to conceive Madison writing or speaking such Jeffersonian sentences as "The tree of liberty must be refreshed from time to time with the blood of patriots and tyrants. It is its natural manure." Madison might—possibly did—share these sentiments; he might even have expressed them privately, but he would have stated them with less color and more qualification.

Madison was always temperate. Moderation and balance permeated his whole thought. At the Constitutional Convention he took a middle position between what would be called today the right and the left, between men like Hamilton who distrusted the people and those like Wilson who had confidence in them. In Madison's view, people were neither inherently good nor naturally bad; they were, he argued, what society had made them. If shown confidence, they would be likely to reciprocate it; if degraded by their rulers, they would become depraved. The American colonial experience, he pointed out, had shown that wherever a certain amount of freedom is entrusted to the common people they learn to appreciate it. "A sufficient portion of liberty," he wrote, "had been everywhere enjoyed to inspire both a sense of its worth and a zeal for its proper enlargement."

On the other hand, as a student of history, he was not an optimist concerning human nature. He never permitted himself to forget that the whole human record was full of tales of evil, viciousness, cruelty, and folly. Mankind's political history, especially the record of conferences and assemblies, he wrote in *The Federalist* (Number 37), was hardly anything more than a story of "factions, contentions, and disappointments, and may be classed among the most dark and degraded pictures which display the infirmities and depravities of the human character." His sober appraisal of human nature was, at bottom, Calvinistic rather than Jeffersonian, but he was enough a child of the Enlightenment to balance his gloom with a streak of hopefulness. Although he did not share Jefferson's optimistic faith in progress and human perfectibility, Madison nevertheless rejected the Hamiltonian concept of total human depravity. Man, he said, is both good and evil, with the latter perhaps predominating. The problem for the statesman is to find means of preventing the bad qualities in human nature from taking possession of the whole society.

"As there is a degree of depravity in mankind," he wrote in *The Federalist* (Number 55), "which requires a certain degree of circumspection and distrust, so there are other qualities in human nature which justify a certain portion of esteem and confidence. Republican government presupposes the existence of these qualities in a higher degree than any other form."

Madison recognized that the idea of complete human depravity implied the impossibility of self-government. Clearly, people who were permanently greedy, vicious, stupid, and cruel could not be entrusted with the task of administering affairs, whether private or public. Such an assumption about human nature meant the abandonment of any attempt at setting up a republic—a dilemma that the Hamiltonians never resolved but one that Madison faced quite squarely. But he would not go so far as did Jefferson, who always insisted that only the people—the whole adult population, regardless of status or income—had the right, the power, and the essential wisdom to rule themselves.

Despite his pessimism, Madison reluctantly accepted the Jeffersonian logic that if one man was good enough to govern others, then all, or most, men had the same capacity to rule themselves. Cautiously he granted that there was "sufficient virtue" in the human character to justify the institution of self-government. Any other interpretation of the human psychology would lead, he said, to the conclusion that "nothing less than the chains of despotism can restrain [men] from destroying and devouring one another."

Assuming thus that man was at best imperfect, and always potentially a danger to himself and to his fellows, Madison conceived of government, particularly the kind of self-governing republic that he helped establish in the United States, as nothing but a necessary evil. Government was needed for simple self-protection. Although Madison did not phrase it in these terms, it is clear from his writings that he conceived of government as a kind of jailkeeper whose function was to see to it that the prisoners did not maim or kill one another. At the same time he felt that the jailkeeper must not have too much power, for being himself an imperfect human being with all the normal passions and potentialities for evil, he would be likely to abuse it.

To prevent such abuse, Madison advocated and worked for a governmental system that consisted of a series of intricate contrivances known as checks and balances. Both inside and outside the governmental structure there were to be a number of delicately balanced wheels and cogs, each moving within its own delimited sphere of interest and activity but checking the others. Citizens were to be protected from one another, the government from citizens, citizens from the government, governmental departments from other governmental departments, states from the central government, the central government from the states, and individuals inside governmental offices from other individuals in potentially rival offices. Madison and his contemporaries plainly trusted neither man nor government.

This Swiss watch concept of government, which is the underlying political philosophy of the American Constitution, was most clearly formulated in a memorable passage in *The Federalist* (Number 51):

> But the great security against a gradual concentration of the several powers in the same department, consists in giving to those who administer each department the necessary constitutional means and personal motives to resist encroachments of the others. The provision for defense must in this, as in all other cases, be made commensurate to the danger of attack. It may be a reflection on human nature, that such devices should be necessary to control the abuses of government. But what is government itself, but the greatest of all reflections on human nature? If men were angels, no government would be necessary. If angels were to govern men, neither external nor internal controls on government would be necessary. In framing a government which is to be administered by men over men, the great difficulty lies in this: you must first enable the government to control the governed; and in the next place oblige it to control itself. A dependence on the people is, no doubt, the primary control on the government; but experience has taught mankind the necessity of auxiliary precautions.
>
> This policy of supplying, by opposite and rival interests, the defect of better motives, might be traced through the whole system of human affairs, private as well as public. We see it particularly displayed in all the subordinate

distributions of power, where the constant aim is to divide and arrange the several offices in such a manner as that each may be a check on the other—that the private interest of each individual may be a sentinel over the public rights. These inventions of prudence cannot be less requisite in the distribution of the supreme powers of the State.

These "inventions of prudence" were necessary not merely as a corrective of human defects but also as a safeguard of economic and group interests. Madison, unlike some of his more romantic contemporaries, had a theory of society which certain modern socialists and Marxists have claimed as akin to their own. He conceived of society as a body of men divided along lines of special interest, mainly but not exclusively economic in origin. Historically, he pointed out, such special-interest groups have tended to organize into factions, which he defined as "a number of citizens . . . who are united and actuated by some common impulse of passion, or of interest, adverse to the rights of other citizens, or to the permanent and aggregate interests of the community."

In Number 10 of *The Federalist* Madison specifically formulated his concept of the economic basis of social–political action in terms that are almost Marxist:

But the most common and durable source of factions had been the various and unequal distribution of property. Those who hold and those who are without property have ever formed distinct interests in society. Those who are creditors, and those who are debtors, fall under a like discrimination. A landed interest, a manufacturing interest, a mercantile interest, a moneyed interest, with many lesser interests, grow up of necessity in civilised nations, and divide them into different classes, actuated by different sentiments and views. The regulation of these various and interfering interests forms the principal task of modern legislation, and involves the spirit of party and faction in the necessary and ordinary operations of the government.

This sober recognition of the "class" divisions of society led Madison to an additional conclusion: that there exists also an inescapable division of opinions. He wrote:

As long as the reason of man continues fallible, and he is at liberty to exercise it, different opinions will be formed. As long as the connection subsists between his reason and his self-love, his opinions and his passions will be objects to which the latter will attach themselves. The diversity in the faculties of men, from which the rights of property originate, is not less an insuperable obstacle to a uniformity of interests. The protection of these faculties is the first object of government. From the protection of different and unequal faculties of acquiring property, the possession of different degrees and kinds of property immediately results; and from the influence of these on the sentiments and views of the respective proprietors, ensues a division of the society into different interests and parties.

Here we have the core of Madison's political thought. It is interesting to note how, assuming more or less the same premises as those of the Marxists, he came to different conclusions. Where the orthodox Marxists embrace the idea of class conflict following the recognized class divisions, Madison, likewise accepting class divisions as basic to society, concluded that the only way to alleviate such strife is to attempt to harmonize all interests through the use of government. His reasoning here was tight and logical. How, he asked, do you cure the "mischiefs of faction?" There are, he answered, two possible ways of doing it. One is to remove the causes, and the other is to change the effects. How do you remove the causes? Again, he replied, there are two methods: first, to make every person uniform in his passions, ideas, and interests; second, to destroy the freedom of action and thought that permits diversity and conflict. The first way, that of uniformity, is clearly an impossibility. The second is a remedy "worse than the disease," since freedom is a prime necessity to civilized society. "Liberty is to faction what air is to fire, an aliment without which it instantly expires," he wrote. "But it could not be less folly to abolish liberty, which is essential to political life, because it nourishes faction, than it would be to wish the annihilation of air, which is essential to animal life, because it imparts to fire its destructive agency."

What, then, does one do in this case? To begin with, he proposed, you openly recognize and accept the existence of human diversity, whether in opinion or in property. Then you control the effects of such diversity (conflicts) by making government protect each interest or "faction." Government can best do so by preventing any one group or party from invading the rights of any other. That, according to Madison, is the primary object of government.

To play this role of umpire, government must itself remain neutral. It must be circumscribed by a clear definition of its powers, and balanced by a sharp separation of functions. "No political truth," he wrote in *The Federalist* (Number 47), "is . . . of greater intrinsic value . . . than that . . . the accumulation of all powers, legislative, executive and judiciary, in the same hands, whether of one, a few, or many, and whether hereditary, self-appointed, or elective, may justly be pronounced the very definition of tyranny." Government must never be too strong or too weak. "It is a melancholy reflection," he wrote to Jefferson, "that liberty should be equally exposed to danger whether the Government have too much or too little power, and that the line which divides these extremes should be so inaccurately defined by experience."

Madison's own experience and enormous reading convinced him that the answer lay in this concept of the finely balanced middle. Government must have enough power—but just enough—to carry out its main task, the protection of liberty and property. He pointed out during the bitter debate at the Virginia constitutional convention (June 1788), when he had to defend the federal Constitution against such brilliant but erratic men as Patrick Henry: "That the laws of every country ought to be executed, cannot be denied. That force must be used if necessary, cannot be denied. Can any government be established, that will answer any purpose whatever, unless force be provided for executing its laws?" But government must not have so much force as to threaten the rights and possessions of the citizens. That, Madison said, was the main purpose of the federal Constitution, or of any good republican constitution—to defend "liberty against power, and power against licentiousness, and . . . [to keep] every portion of power within its proper limits."

On another fundamental question, one that disturbed many of his contemporaries, especially at the Constitutional Convention, Madison was equally clear-eyed. This was the problem of majority versus minority rule. At the convention there were a number of delegates who shared, though they did not express themselves with the same brutal frankness, Hamilton's distrust of and contempt for men. Such an assumption of human viciousness and dishonesty militated against the establishment of any republic and against the granting of the suffrage to most of the people in the country. Madison struggled, and with considerable success, against this image of hopelessness.

First of all, he insisted, only a republican form of government is worthy of civilized man. Second, such a government must be based, not on any one faction or group, but on the majority of the people. And finally, the danger of majority tyranny or viciousness, while it is always potentially or actually present, can be checked through proper governmental mechanisms. "We may define a republic," Madison wrote in *The Federalist* (Number 39), ". . . [as] a government which derives all its powers directly or indirectly from the great body of the people, and is administered by persons holding their offices during pleasure, for a limited period, or during good behaviour. It is essential to such a government that it be derived from the great body of the society, not from an inconsiderable proportion, or a favoured class of it. . . . It is sufficient for such a government that the persons administering it be appointed, either directly or indirectly, by the people."

That being the case, how did he propose to protect the society—especially the supreme values of liberty and property—from the encroachments of a potentially ignorant majority which could be swayed by some demagogue? Madison knew from history that such a peril exists; he admitted that liberty had often been lost through what he called the "licentiousness" of turbulent majorities, and that often in the past the "majority trampled on the rights of the minority" and thereby produced despotism. But the answer, he argued, lies not in depriving the people at large of any voice in the government, but in increasing group interest and participation. Here again his concept of balance came into play. In essence, he said, the more you divide interests and spread powers, the safer you are. Large numbers of special interests, whether deriving from property or from opinion, will not easily combine into a majority that will threaten the minority.

Directly or indirectly, many of these Madisonian ideas were incorporated into the federal Constitution, in the formation of which he played a preponderant role. As Professor Edward S. Corwin has remarked, insofar as paternity can be applied to the Constitution, Madison can claim to be its father. He attended every session of the convention, participated in all the important debates, and contributed sagely from his vast store of learning in the field of constitutional history and law. Above all, he kept a meticulous record of the convention, which is still the primary source of our knowledge of what happened there.

"In pursuance of the task I had assumed," Madison wrote later in life, "I chose a seat in front of the presiding member, with the other members on my right and left hands. In this favorable position for hearing all that passed, I noted, in terms legible and in abbreviations and marks intelligible to myself, what was read from the Chair or spoken by the members; and, losing not a moment unnecessarily between the adjournment and reassembling of the Convention, I was enabled to write out my daily notes during the session. . . . In the labor and correctness of this I was not a little aided by . . . a familiarity with the style and the train of observation and reasoning which characterized the principal speakers. It happened, also, that I was not absent a single day, not more than a casual fraction of an hour in any day, so that I could not have lost a single speech, unless a very short one. . . ."

In a brilliant speech at the Constitutional Convention, on June 6, 1787, Madison most clearly summarized his whole philosophy of federal republicanism, with its widest possible distribution of powers and the scattering of sovereignties. He said:

All civilized societies would be divided into different sects, factions, and interests, as they happened to consist of rich and poor, debtors and creditors, the landed, the manufacturing, the commercial interests, the inhabitants of this district, or that district, the followers of this political leader or that political leader, the disciples of this religious sect or that religious sect. In all cases where a majority are united by a common interest or passion, the rights of the minority are in danger. What motives are to restrain them? A prudent regard to the maxim that honesty is the best policy is found by experience to be as little regarded by bodies of men as by individuals. Respect for character is always diminished in proportion to the number among whom the blame or praise is to be divided. Conscience, the only remaining tie, is known to be inadequate in individuals: In large numbers, little is to be expected from it. Besides, religion itself may become a motive to persecution and oppression. These observations are verified by the histories of every country ancient and modern. In Greece and Rome the rich and poor, the creditors and debtors, as well as the patricians and plebeians alternately oppressed each other with equal unmercifulness. . . . We have seen the mere distinction of color made in the most enlightened period of time, a ground of the most oppressive dominion ever exercised by man over man. . . . The lesson we are to draw from the whole is that where a majority are united by a common sentiment and have an opportunity, the rights of the minor party become insecure. In a republican government the majority if united have always an opportunity. The only remedy is to enlarge the sphere, and thereby divide the community into so great a number of interests and parties, that in the first place a majority will not be likely at the same moment to have a common interest separate from that of the whole or of the minority; and in the second place, that in case they should have such an interest, they may not be apt to unite in the pursuit of it.

This idea of the need and desirability of a large number of divided and balancing interests, whether material or mental, also underlay Madison's attitude toward religion and property. He shared with Jefferson a lifelong passion for religious freedom and distrust of any and every kind of clericalism. History taught him that established churches, relying on the power of the state, created "ignorance and corruption." The exercise of religion, he insisted, should be completely separated from government, so that every person is free to worship, or not to worship, where, how, and what he pleases. Man, he said, "is accountable to his God alone," and not to any hierarchy. Complete religious liberty for every individual and every sect, he argued, not only would free the human mind from that "religious bondage [that] shackles and debilitates it, and unfits it for every noble enterprise," but also would lead to harmony in society. Instead of any one church, he therefore favored a multiplicity of sects, because the existence of a number of religions would, among other things, prevent any one from dominating the others.

Madison was to a great extent instrumental in establishing "freedom of religious opinions & worship" in the United States. In the first Virginia Constitution, which he helped to draw up, he inserted the provision for the "free exercise of religion according to the dictates of conscience." In 1785, when an attempt was made in the Virginia legislature to impose a tax on the people for the support of "teachers of the Christian religion," Madison led a successful attack on the bill. During the course of that conflict he wrote *A Memorial and Remonstrance Against Religious Assessments,* which still remains a classic statement of religious freedom. In this work he said:

> We remonstrate against the said bill because we hold it for a fundamental and undeniable truth "that religion, or the duty which we owe to our Creator, and the manner of discharging it, can be directed only by reason and conviction, not by force or violence." The religion, then, of every man must be left to the conviction and conscience of every man; and it is the right of every man to exercise it as these may dictate. . . .
>
> Because, finally, "the equal right of every citizen to the free exercise of his religion, according to the dictates of conscience," is held by the same tenure with all our other rights. If we recur to its origin, it is equally the gift of nature; if we weigh its importance, it cannot be less dear to us. . . . Either, then, we must say that the will of the legislature is the only measure of their authority, and that in the plenitude of that authority they may sweep away all our fundamental rights, or that they are bound to leave this particular right untouched and sacred. Either we must say that they may control the freedom of the press, may abolish the trial by jury, may swallow up the executive and judiciary powers of the state . . . ; or we must say that they have no authority to enact into law the bill under consideration.
>
> We, the subscribers, say that the General Assembly of this commonwealth have no such authority. And in order that no effort may be omitted on our part against so dangerous an usurpation, we oppose to it this remonstrance; earnestly praying . . . that the Supreme Lawgiver of the Universe . . . may

... guide them ... [to] establish more firmly the liberties, the prosperity, and the happiness of the commonwealth.

A few years later, in 1789, it was Madison, as a member of the first Congress of the United States, who led the movement for the passage of the Bill of Rights, which was to guarantee forever the basic liberties, including religion, of all Americans. It should be added that in introducing the first draft of the Bill of Rights he formulated certain basic principles of freedom which were considered somewhat too radical: "That all power is originally vested in, and consequently derived from, the people, that government is instituted and ought to be exercised for the benefit of the people ... ; that the people have an indisputable, inalienable and indefeasible right to reform their government, whenever it be found adverse or inadequate to the purposes of its institution."

Madison's views of religious liberty formed an integral part of his whole philosophy of freedom, which embraced both material and spiritual objects. He argued that the possession of property could not and should not be separated from the possession of opinions, intellectual or religious. A human being, as a member of civilized society, he insisted, must have a right to property and a property in rights. No just society can deprive a citizen of his material property; it cannot take away his freedom of expression, which Madison regarded as a fundamental property right. He conceived of property not merely as merchandise or money, but as a totality of possessions which "embraces every thing to which a man may attach a value and have a right." In a remarkable essay on property and liberty, Madison formulated his theory in these words: "A man has property in his opinions and the free communication of them. He has a property of peculiar value in his religious opinions, and in the profession and practice dictated by them. He has property very dear to him in the safety and liberty of his person. ... In a word, as a man is said to have a right to his property, he may be equally said to have a property in his rights."

Madison must thus be described as a striking historic figure, deserving to rank among the wisest men who created the American republic. He was a man of almost classic virtues—a statesman, a selfless patriot, and a political philosopher who was in the fortunate position of being able to translate his thoughts into living institutions. He was indeed one of the major architects of the American democracy and "Father of the Constitution."

# 7

## *THE AMERICAN AS AGRARIAN:* John Taylor *(1753–1824)*

*Colonel Taylor and myself have rarely, if ever, differed in any political principle of importance.*
—*Thomas Jefferson to Thomas Ritchie (December 25, 1820)*

A Virginian of the Revolutionary period and theorist of the Jeffersonian camp, John Taylor of Caroline * has been called "the philosopher and statesman of agrarianism." He was a radical democrat who supplied a theoretical framework for the agrarians in their prolonged struggle with the Hamiltonian northern capitalists. But as a systematic thinker who integrated politics with economics, showing how institutional roots were intertwined, and drawing universal moral–democratic conclusions from his studies, Taylor transcends the limits of regionalism. His neglect by posterity may have been due largely to a writing style that was forbiddingly dull and persistently repetitive; his "endless verbiage" was described even by an admirer, Professor William E. Dodd, as "tiresome beyond endurance." Nevertheless, so cogent was Taylor's thought that contemporaries, especially in the agrarian South, read him with admiration. This was particularly true of his chief work, *An Inquiry into the Principles and Tendency of Certain Public Measures* (1814), which

* Caroline was the name of Taylor's estate in Virginia. He is referred to as John Taylor of Caroline in order to distinguish him from such namesakes as John Taylor (1580–1653), the English pamphleteer known as the "Water-Poet"; John Taylor (1704–1766), the English classicist who deciphered Greek inscriptions; John Taylor (1808–1887), the Anglo-American Mormon collaborator of Joseph Smith and Brigham Young, who championed polygamy.

had a deep influence on his time as well as on the Jacksonian era. A century after the *Inquiry* was published, Charles A. Beard, the leading American student of the period, ranked it, in his *Economic Origins of Jeffersonian Democracy* (1915), "among the two or three really historic contributions to political science which have been produced in the United States."

By origin and background, Taylor belonged to the Virginia gentry, the small but remarkable group that did so much to shape the republic. He was born in Orange County, near the home of James Madison. Orphaned at the age of ten, Taylor was adopted by his mother's brother, Edmund Pendleton (1721–1803), one of Virginia's foremost jurists who, among other things, collaborated with young Thomas Jefferson in the radical revision of the laws of that state. Like Jefferson, John Marshall, and James Monroe, Taylor attended William and Mary College (1770–72); like them, he studied law under Pendleton and served intermittently in the Virginia legislature. But unlike his more famous contemporaries, Taylor was not politically ambitious. He neither sought nor gained high public office, although he was appointed United States senator on three different occasions for short periods of time. Such appointments he accepted, as did Cincinnatus, a Roman prototype to whom Taylor's classic-oriented contemporaries often compared him, as a matter of duty and patriotism.

Taylor's personal preferences were farming and reading. He was a bookish farmer who carried out agricultural experiments, among them rotation of crops, and wrote about them. His book, *Arator,* a "Series of Agricultural Essays," has been a classic in the field since its publication in Georgetown in 1813. Taylor regarded himself a plain farmer, wore simple clothes of "London brown," and consciously practiced republican virtue. Those who knew him were impressed by his sturdy simplicity. Thomas Hart Benton, Missouri's durable (1821–51) senator—who knew Taylor in the Senate—thus described him in his autobiographical *Thirty Years' View* (1854–56): "I can hardly figure to myself the ideal of a republican statesman more perfect and complete than he was . . . : —plain and solid, a wise counsellor, a ready and vigorous debater, acute and comprehensive, ripe in all historical and political knowledge, innately republican—modest, courteous, benevolent, hospitable."

Taylor's thought can best be understood in terms of what he opposed and what he preferred. He opposed the prevailing idea of a natural aristocracy, then sedulously advocated by such New England Federalists as John Adams and Fisher Ames (1758–1808), and he fought against the growth of a moneyed aristocracy championed by Alexander Hamilton and other northerners. Taylor advocated, instead, a democratic polity based on the idea of human equality (but not for Negroes) and a "productive" (noncapitalist) economic system.

Underlying Taylor's political philosophy was the theory of society that goes by the name *Physiocratic,* then widely prevalent in influential circles in Europe and accepted by certain Americans. The Physiocratic school of economists and philosophers was founded by a group of Frenchmen, led by the physician François Quesnay (1694–1774), the economist Jean Claude Marie Vincent de Gournay (1712–59), the philosopher Pierre Samuel Dupont de Nemours (1739–1817), as well as the economists Anne-Robert Jacques Turgot (1727–81) and Destutt de Tracy (1754–1836). Their contact with and influence on Taylor and other American agrarians was largely through Jefferson who, among other things, secretly revised the English translation of de Tracy's *A Treatise on Political Economy* and encouraged his friend, "the enlightened, philanthropic, and venerable" Dupont de Nemours, to settle in the United States (where he founded the American dynasty of that name). It was Dupont, in fact, who named the group *Physiocrats,* deriving it from the Greek words for "nature" and "rule."

The Physiocratic economists, who so impressed Taylor and others, based their economic analysis on a distinction between "productive" and "sterile" wealth. The former was supposed to derive from the soil, which produced agriculture and minerals; the latter was regarded to be the result of commerce, which presumably produced nothing but merely transferred already-existing wealth (food, metals, etc.) from one person to another. Despite Adam Smith, who showed up the falsity of the notion that trading and manufacturing added nothing of "value" to the material stock of society, Taylor did not question the Physiocratic theory regarding the two types of wealth, the productive (socially good) and the parasitic (morally evil).

"A love of wealth," he wrote in his *Construction Construed, and Construction Vindicated* (1820), "fostered by honest industry, is an ally both of moral rectitude, and national happiness, because it can only be gratified by increasing the fund for national subsistence, comfort, strength and prosperity; but a love of wealth, fostered by partial laws for enriching corporations and individuals, is allied to immorality and oppression, because it is gratified at the expense of industry, and diminishes its ability to work out national blessings."

To Taylor, Physiocratic economics, on which he constructed his political theory, was acceptable because it was supported by personal experience and observation. Even if the French Physiocrats had never existed, it may be assumed that Americans in Taylor's position would have interpreted society through the eyes of men whose lives and livelihoods were rooted in the soil, and to whom urban ways were remote and alien. As a farmer, Taylor was sure that all history proved the existence of exploitation—of the productive farmers and workers by the nonproductive political rulers.

He wrote in *Arator:* "We farmers and mechanics [i.e., working people] have been political slaves in all countries, because we are political fools. We know how to convert a wilderness into a paradise, and a forest into palaces and elegant furniture; but we have been taught by those whose object is to monopolize the sweets of life, which we sweat for, that politics are without our province, and in us a ridiculous affectation.... Sometimes, after one of these marauding families have pillaged for a thousand years, we detect the cheat, rise in the majesty of our strength, drive away the thief, and sink again into a lethargy of intellect so gross, as to receive him next day in a new coat, as an accomplished and patriotic stranger, come to cover us with benefits.—Thus we got rid of tythes, and now we clasp banks, patronage, and protecting duties to our bosoms.... This legal faction of capitalists, created by protecting duties, bankers and contractors,... will, in the case of the mechanics, soon appropriate the whole of their labour to its use, beyond a bare subsistence..."

America's capitalist economy, as it was developing with the help of the federal government and as a result of Alexander Hamilton's fiscal and economic policies, proved to Taylor that the United States was in danger of becoming a moneyed oligarchy. The "moneyites," as his fellow Virginian Richard Henry Lee wrote in an earlier period (*Letters from the Federal Farmer to the Republican* [1787]), were "dangerous men" who "avariciously grasp at all power and property" and showed "an evident dislike to free and equal government." Taylor was convinced, as were his fellow agrarians, that the new financial interests were determined to build up a powerfully entrenched American aristocracy and to keep the producing classes—farmers and "mechanics"—in a state of permanent dependence and exploitation. This, as he saw it, the moneyed people did through such politically created devices as trusts, banks, tariffs, credit control, strict limitation of suffrage, cruel debt laws, and, above all, a stranglehold on the sources of power, namely government. If this process continued, Taylor felt, it would end with an institutionalized perpetuation of the Old World's feudal wrongs and inequalities in the New World. Hence he undertook a searching analysis of the whole existing political system from the point of view of its economic origins, in order to expose what he regarded as its dangerously false theoretical basis.

Apart from the agricultural *Arator* and such early pamphlets as *An Enquiry into the Principles and Tendency of Certain Public Measures,* which he published in 1792 as a criticism of Hamilton's funding policies, Taylor formulated his ideas in four main works. The first and most ambitious was *An Inquiry into the Principles and Policy of the Government of the United States,* in 1814. The second, published in Richmond six years later, was *Construction Construed, and Constitutions Vindicated.* The third, which appeared in Washington two years afterward, was *Tyranny Unmasked* (1822). The fourth was *New Views of the Constitution of the United States,* published in Washington in 1823, one year before his death.

Each of Taylor's works was a repetition of and elaboration on its predecessor, but always maintaining the fundamental views of the democratic, anticapitalist agrarian advocate of strictly limited government. Thus his *Inquiry* was an assault on Hamilton's economic policies and John Adams' aristocratic theories; *Construction Construed* was an attack on John Marshall's judicial decisions; *Tyranny Unmasked* challenged the tariff as an instrument of special privilege; *New Views* was a general interpretation of the federal Constitution from the point of view of states' rights—a theoretical formulation which had a profound impact on John C. Calhoun.

From all of these writings, verbose and loosely formulated though they are, one can construct Taylor's general political philosophy and its rationale. To begin with, he accepted (as did Jefferson and the other democrats of the day) the theory of the social compact with its accompaniment of "inalienable" rights—rights to life, liberty, property, and self-government. These rights were given to man by the law of nature. Hence they were built on a universal moral sanction that could not be altered by any government or ruling class. From such inherent rights flowed the greatest one of all, that of free and equal participation in the government by all the people.

Second, and this springs from the theory of natural rights, the claims to aristocracy (to justify economic inequality and exploitation of the producing classes) made by the Federalists had no validity either in nature or in current experience. Taylor argued that aristocracy was not only undesirable but artificial. It was undesirable because it perpetuated injustice by favoring the few at the expense of the many. It was artificial because it was not based on real superiority, such as greater knowledge or virtue, but on institutionalized political privileges and claims. Neither knowledge nor virtue, Taylor wrote, was inheritable; there was no such thing as a "natural aristocracy" in nature. Aristocracy was merely the product of government, and government was nothing but a human creation. "I am unable to discern any natural political state," Taylor wrote to Jefferson in June 1798; "... a political state [is] in the antithesis to a state of nature."

Of all aristocratic claims that had been made throughout history, Taylor insisted, the worst were those in the United States, mainly because there was no visible justification for them. Those who in America now demanded privileges on the ground that they were "natural aristocrats" were, in fact, neither more educated nor more opulent, in the sense of productive capacity, than the rest of their fellow citizens. In other lands, aristocrats maintained their privileged positions so long as the people in general were kept ignorant. But "an opposition to aristocratical power seems to have been constantly coeval with an advance of national information," Taylor wrote. This was true in America, where education was relatively widespread, at least as compared to the Old World, and there was no need for a ruling class because the people possessed qualities which elsewhere were considered to be an aristocratic monopoly.

"Talents and virtue," Taylor wrote in *An Inquiry,* "are now so widely distributed, as to have rendered a monopoly of either, equivalent to that of antiquity, impracticable; and if an aristocracy ought to have existed whilst it possessed such a monopoly, it ought not also to exist, because this monopoly is irretrievably lost."

The new American rich, with their aristocratic pretensions, were particularly offensive to Taylor because of their crass materialism and secret manipulation of government. Without special virtue or abilities, they based their claims only on money and political favors—on what he called "paper and patronage." Such a moneyed aristocracy, he wrote, was "the most formidable" that mankind had ever had to contend with.

"As the aristocracies of priestcraft and conquest decayed," to quote again from *An Inquiry,* "that of patronage and paper stock grew ... ; without rank or title; regardless of honor; of insatiable avarice. ... It is ... inimical to public good. ... Let us moderns cease to boast of our victory over superstition and the feudal system, and our advancement in knowledge. Let us neither pity, ridicule or despise the ancients, as dupes of frauds and tricks, which we can so easily discern; lest some ancient sage should rise from his grave and answer, 'You moderns are duped by arts more obviously fraudulent, than those which deceived us.' "

Having established the position that aristocracy was artificial and not in the natural order of things, Taylor proceeded to show that political structures founded on privileged classes were equally false. For one thing, it was a law of nature that talents and virtues were not hereditary but were distributed equally among all classes of people. For another, human nature was not a fixed entity but one that changed constantly throughout history. Each historic epoch developed its own inner morality, ways of behavior, ethical values, and community organization. To understand government, therefore, one must study it in the context of the particular epoch in which it grew and operated. Government was not something fixed for all time, any more than was human nature. "If man is not always the same," Taylor observed in *An Inquiry*, "it is not true that he requires the same political regiment." The key to an understanding of politics was diversity, both of human nature and of social organization.

"Out of this intellectual variety," he wrote, "arises the impossibility of contriving one form of government, suitable for every nation; and also the fact that human nature, instead of begetting one form constantly, demonstrates its moral capacity, in the vast variety of its political productions."

The concept of diversity was elaborated by Taylor into a political philosophy that rejected both the theory and the practice of centralized government. Given his belief in inalienable individual rights, especially to political liberty and property, and his dread of a national government run by urban moneyed men, it followed, at least in his reasoning, that the individual must not be subjected to undue governmental coercions or controls. Centralized power, he said, was "fatal to civil liberty." The way to prevent such a danger was through splitting governmental powers and spreading them out thinly, as was intended by the framers of the national Constitution when they set up the federal system in 1787–89.

"Power," Taylor stated in *An Inquiry,* "is divided by our policy that the people may maintain their sovereignty.... Our principle of division is used to reduce power to that degree of temperature which may make it a blessing and not a curse, its nature resembling fire, which uncontrolled consumes, in moderation, warms."

This is the key to Taylor's political philosophy—fear of power. Political power, he knew, was needed in civilized society but it was too dangerous to be permitted to accumulate in the hands of a few. Hence the necessity for its distribution among the separate states; and even there, keeping it within prescribed limits. A states' righter par excellence, Taylor drew up the Virginia Resolutions (1798) which, together with the Kentucky Resolutions (drafted secretly by Jefferson), were the first historic declarations that certain acts of the national Congress were unconstitutional.

Taylor also fought a prolonged battle against John Marshall's Supreme Court decisions that were designed to strengthen the federal government, especially in the economic sphere. In writings such as *Construction Construed,* Taylor vehemently denied Justice Marshall's assertion that there existed a single United States, insisting that "the people" were not one but several in the individual states, and that in 1787 they had not formed a national union but an association of states. To Taylor, the claim of federal supremacy was unconstitutional and illegal—a position that John C. Calhoun and other southerners were to carry to its extreme limits a generation later.

In the last analysis, Taylor disliked government altogether. It was, he knew, a necessary evil but he wanted it to be confined to hardly anything more than police functions. In political matters, he desired civil liberty. In economic affairs, he wished *laissez faire* to reign supreme. The government was not to interfere in any way with economic activities but was to leave the whole field to the individual. Governmental control in property matters he regarded as tyranny. "To define the nature of a government truly," he stated in *Construction Construed,* "I would say, that a power of distributing property, able to gratify the avarice and monopoly, designated a bad one; and that the absence of such power, designated a good one."

He carried his peasantlike distrust of government so far that he even opposed regulation of such presumably vital economic functions as banking, tariffs, and money. In *An Inquiry* he wrote, "Money (like prices, trades, and manufactures), regulates itself better than it can be regulated by doctors, despotism, monopoly or banking. A regulation of money, is always a regulation of prices, and an interposition by law, in the economy of individuals. . . . Such an interposition with [even] a single article of industry, has invariably terminated in mischief."

In all other matters, too, he wanted government to keep hands off. He was a complete individualist even in such fields as slavery, religion, and education. While he deplored slavery as a misfortune to agriculture, he did not think that it was the government's business either to change or abolish it. This, incidentally, was the only major area in which he and Jefferson were in some disagreement; Taylor gently criticized Jefferson for his "impassioned censure of slave holders." In religion, as in so many other spheres, Taylor was a true Jeffersonian in that he believed in absolute separation of church and state, saying "God needs no champion to assert his honour or to avenge his quarrels," and "When a government usurps a power of legislating between God and man, it proves itself to be an atheist."

Even in education he believed that government was to play no role. A school system supported by government meant political meddling by "parties of interest"—political parties, the existence of which he deplored as potential instruments of the economically powerful. A schoolmaster paid by government, he said, would in effect be its servant and would no more be able to educate the people against tyranny than was a priest able to keep them out of purgatory. Everything was to be left to the individual: "Our policy is founded upon the idea . . . to leave the distribution of property to industry and talents; that what they acquire is all their own." He wrote in *Arator*, "The utmost favour which it is possible for a government to do for us farmers and mechanics, is neither help nor hurt us."

Thus did John Taylor draw the battle lines in the political and economic spheres that were to divide Americans for a long time. Despite his faulty economics and misconceived politics, he foreshadowed and outlined the ongoing conflict between those who put their faith in unrestrained personal enterprise and those who believe in the duty of government to regulate the public welfare. Taylor, the agrarian democrat, sided with what later came to be known in the popular vernacular as the rugged individualists.

# 8

## *THE AMERICAN AS FEDERALIST:* John Marshall *(1755–1835)*

> *John Marshall died at Philadelphia last Monday. He was one of the most eminent men that this country has produced—a Federalist of the Washington school. . . . Marshall, by the ascendancy of his genius, by the amenity of his deportment, and by the imperturbable command of his temper, has given a permanent and systematic character to the decisions of the Court. . . . Marshall has cemented the Union which the crafty and quixotic democracy of Jefferson had a perpetual tendency to dissolve.*
>
> —*John Quincy Adams,* Diary (*July 10, 1835*)

John Marshall's reputation is legendary among lawyers and students of the Constitution. Enshrined in American memory as the greatest chief justice of the United States Supreme Court and as a jurist of matchless accomplishment, he is rarely ranked among political thinkers. Nevertheless, because of his unprecedented influence on American law, nationalism, legislation, and the whole federal system, it is illuminating to analyze his political ideas, particularly those explicit and implicit notions on which he based his judicial decisions.

His eminence and achievements have had an overawing quality about them. Oliver Wendell Holmes, speaking in Boston on the centenary of Marshall's appointment to the Supreme Court, said of his famous predecessor: "A great man represents a great ganglion in the nerves of society . . . , a strategic point in the campaign of history, and part of his greatness consists in his being there." Marshall was in the historic position, at the historic moment, of firmly establishing the "Oneness of the nation and the supremacy of the national Constitution." In his *Rise of American Civilization,* Charles A. Beard described Marshall, whose conservative politics he did not share, as "an ornament to the humble democracy which brought him forth." The reasons for these eulogies are perhaps best summarized by a leading constitutional scholar, Professor Edward S. Corwin, in *John Marshall and the Constitution* (1920): "Marshall established judicial review; he imparted to an ancient legal tradition a new significance; he made his Court one of the great political forces of the country; he founded American Constitutional Law; he formulated . . . the principles on which the integrity and ordered growth . . . have depended. . . . His judicial statesmanship finds no parallel . . . outside our own annals."

Marshall's background hardly explains the role he played or the ideas in which he believed. By environment and experience one would have expected him to follow the pattern of the other famous Virginians of his time—to be a democrat like Jefferson, a states' righter like Madison, or an agrarian like Taylor. But Marshall, despite his rural southern origin, was nothing of the kind. Like all notable historic figures, he had unique traits. He did not fit into the customary political categories of his time.

One of the ironies of American history is the fact that Marshall and Jefferson, lifelong archenemies representing antithetical political philosophies, had almost identical backgrounds. Both were born and raised on the same frontier; both were of humble paternal origin; they were strongly influenced by their pioneer, poorly educated fathers, attended the same college (Marshall only briefly), and studied law under the same jurist, George Wythe (1726–1806). Other parallels could be added, including the fact that Marshall and Jefferson were related by blood. Marshall's mother, Mary Isham Keith, was a Randolph, as was Jefferson's (and Robert E. Lee's), both descendants of William Randolph of Turkey Island and his wife, Mary Isham.

Marshall was born in a log cabin on the Virginia frontier in what is now Fauquier (then Prince William) County. He grew up, as did Jefferson, near the Blue Ridge wilderness and did not leave the region until his twentieth year. His early education was supervised by his father, Thomas Marshall (1732–1806), sometime sheriff and clerk of Shenandoah (then Dunmore) County, a man who, John Marshall recalled, possessed scarcely any fortune, and had received a very limited education. The elder Marshall inspired his son with a love of history and poetry, although they had few books.

Apart from the dictionary, the book that had the deepest influence on young Marshall was Pope's *Essay on Man* (1733), which he transcribed and memorized. Pope's philosophic poem contained political and moral aphorisms which, in different expressions, can be traced in the later Marshall:

> . . . this scene of man;
> A mighty maze! but not without plan.
>
> One truth is clear. What is, is right.
>
> Know then thyself, presume not God to scan;
> The proper study of mankind is man.
>
> Learn of the little nautilus to sail
> Spread the thin oar, and catch the driving gale.
>
> For forms of government let fools contest;
> Whate'er is best administer'd is best.
>
> For modes of faith let graceless zealots fight;
> His can't be wrong whose life is in the right.
>
> An honest man is the noblest work of God.

Marshall's formal education was rudimentary. With the classics, which then formed the backbone of a gentleman's curriculum, he was barely acquainted, a gap in his education he apparently regretted in later years. "Proficiency in Greek and Latin," he once wrote to his grandson, "is indispensable to an accomplished scholar, and may be of great real advantage in our progress through human life." He felt the same way about history, which he considered "among the most essential departments of knowledge." But he had little of either in his youth, where the environment was rough, his uncultivated playmates given to "hardy athletic exercises," and his father, he said, "my only intellectual companion."

His lack of scholarly training is shown in his most ambitious literary production, the *Life of George Washington,* published in three volumes between 1805 and 1807. This work, which enjoyed considerable success in its day and added to the author's reputation, has not stood the test of time. In the light of modern criticism, the biography emerges as a condensation of other people's works. In the words of a recent historian, Marshall "borrowed extensively and flagrantly" from the *Annual Regis-*

*ter* and other sources, and reproduced his materials without acknowledging his authorities. This clearly indicated an unawareness of the methods and obligations of scholarship.

During his few months at William and Mary College and while preparing for the law in Wythe's office, Marshall became familiar with some of the standard authors, among them Sir William Blackstone, Edmund Burke and Adam Smith, but he was never a widely educated or broadly read man, as were so many of his eminent contemporaries, colleagues, and opponents. One finds him, already famous as the Chief Justice, reading novels. Among his favorites were those of Jane Austen, of whose writings he said: "Her flights are not lofty, she does not soar on eagle's wings, but she is pleasing, interesting, equable, and yet amusing." In his own field, the law, he was no scholar either, but relied for his opinions on native intelligence, shrewd common sense, and remarkable logical agility. In technical legal matters he would sometimes consult colleagues, notably the erudite Justice Joseph Story (1779–1845), author of the classic *Commentaries on the Constitution of the United States* (1833), with whom he maintained an intimate correspondence that contains such passages as: "I wish to consult you on a case which to me who am not versed in admiralty proceedings has some difficulty."

According to Marshall's own recollections, the decisive event that shaped his outlook was his experience during the Revolutionary War. He enlisted at the age of eighteen, became a lieutenant at twenty and a captain at twenty-two. He fought in the battles of Brandywine, Germantown, and Monmouth, and underwent the ordeal of Valley Forge. In 1781, at twenty-six, he resigned his commission because the Revolutionary army had "more officers than soldiers" and in a short time entered the practice of law and politics. He was too young and unimportant to represent Virginia at the Philadelphia convention of 1787, but was a delegate to the state's ratification convention, where he distinguished himself alongside those who fought the critical battle for the adoption of the Constitution.

At that point young Marshall had reached his political maturity and arrived at a conviction that was to remain fixed for the rest of his life —unswerving nationalism. The memories of Valley Forge were sharp in his mind; he had seen fellow soldiers freeze and starve while the Continental Congress, operating under the Articles of Confederation, remained a "symbol of futility." So he learned to detest loose government. During the Revolution, he had fought and suffered in the company of fellow Americans from other parts of the country and had discovered that they shared common feelings and outlooks. Thus Marshall the Virginian lost his parochialism and became Marshall the American. These two experiences—awareness of the impotence of barely confederated government, and identification with men from other parts of America—blended to create in Marshall the fundamental political outlook that was thereafter to guide his public life and judicial decisions. That outlook was starkly simple: a dedication to the ideal of American nationalism (as against states' rightism) based on a vigorous and authoritative national government. In embracing the new Nationalism, Marshall once and for all abandoned the "wild democracy" of his frontier youth and became the powerful spokesman of centralized governmental power.

In an autobiographical letter to Justice Story, he explained his radical change of mind:

> When I recollect the wild and enthusiastic democracy with which my political opinions of that day were tinctured, I am disposed to ascribe my devotion to the union, and to a government competent to its preservation, at least as much to casual circumstances as to judgment. I had grown up at a time when a love of union and resistance to the claims of Great Britain were the inseparable inmates of the same bosom;—when patriotism and a strong fellow feeling with our suffering fellow citizens of Boston were identical;—when the maxim, "united we stand, divided we fall" was the maxim of every orthodox American; and I had imbibed these sentiments so thoroughly that they constituted a part of my being. I carried them with me into the army . . . , where I was confirmed in the habit of considering America as my country, and congress as my government. I partook largely of the sufferings and feelings of the army, and brought with me into civil life an ardent devotion to its interests. . . . In the state legislatures . . . everything was afloat, and . . . we had no safe anchorage ground, [which] gave a high value in my estimation to that article in the [federal] Constitution which imposes restrictions on the states. I was consequently a determined advocate for its adoption.

Young Marshall distinguished himself at the Virginia ratification convention by joining the embattled defenders of the federal Constitution against the onslaughts of such distinguished Virginians as the formidable Patrick Henry and the aristocratic George Mason. Henry, a Virginia-first man who absolutely saw no need for a real national government, passionately attacked the Constitution from every point of view, including the charge that the delegates to the Philadelphia convention had exceeded their authority and had prepared an antidemocratic instrument of tyranny.

"Sir," Henry cried at one point, "give me leave to demand, What right had they to say, *We, the people?* ... Who authorized them to speak the language of, *We, the people,* instead of *We, the States?* ... The people gave them no power to use their name.... The Federal Convention ought to have amended the old system; for this purpose they were solely delegated.... The principles of this system [the Constitution] are extremely pernicious, impolitic, and dangerous.... It is not a democracy, wherein the people retain all their rights securely.... The rights of conscience, trial by jury, liberty of the press, all your immunities and franchises, all pretensions to human rights and privileges, are rendered insecure, if not lost, by this change [of government]...."

Marshall's defense against such criticism was insistence that the new Constitution was actually the best guarantee of the kind of liberty for which Henry pleaded. It provided security against despotism. It assured stability and the rights of the people.

"We, Sir," Marshall argued, "idolize democracy. Those who oppose it [the Constitution] have bestowed eulogisms on monarchy. We prefer this system to any monarchy, because we are convinced that it has a greater tendency to secure our liberty and promote our happiness. We admire it, because we think it a well regulated democracy...."

Marshall believed himself to be a democrat. The question is, what kind of a democrat? He was certainly no democrat in the Jeffersonian or Jacksonian sense. But neither was he the black reactionary depicted by liberal scholars—as by Vernon L. Parrington in his monumental *Main Currents in American Thought.* As a matter of fact, Marshall was too lacking in fanaticism to be a hidebound rightist. Flexible and simple, he disliked any kind of extreme—both extreme democracy and extreme reaction. Neither in social matters nor in religious affairs did he have the usual earmarks of the reactionary. He was easygoing and humane in his general attitudes. He had, for example, genuine compassion for women, whose underprivileged position aroused in him "a deep sense of their social injuries" and sympathy for "their cause." He expressed indignation at what he called "our disreputable conduct" toward the Indians, writing to Justice Story that "every oppression now exercised on a helpless people ... impresses a deep stain on the American character." In the matter of religion, too, Marshall was as liberal as Jefferson, whom he feared, and Madison, whom he admired, disliking sectarian fanatics and believing strongly in the separation of church and state. An established church, he once told the English writer Harriet Martineau (*A Retrospect of Western Travel:* 1837), was "an institution which, after a long study of it, he considered so monstrous in principle and so injurious to true religion in practice that he could not imagine that it could be upheld for anything but political purposes." All this does not, by any stretch of the imagination, constitute the portrait of a reactionary.

Actually, Marshall was a conservative in questions relating to property and a republican in his fundamental political views. A follower of Hamilton in economic matters, he did not share the latter's aversion for democracy. A Federalist, he did not go so far as his northern colleagues (John Adams and Fisher Ames, for example) in accepting the idea of aristocratic rule. Marshall did not question the desirability of self-government and participation of the people in their own rule—within certain limits. Where he differed from the Jeffersonian democrats was in his lack of confidence in the wisdom or goodness of the people at large. Unlike Jefferson, Marshall feared that unrestrained popular majorities would tend to destroy public order and endanger private property. He believed, in the words of his definitive biographer, Albert Beveridge (*The Life of John Marshall;* 4 vols., 1916–19), that the more the people "directly controlled public affairs the worse the business of government would be conducted. He feared that sheer majorities would be unjust, intolerant, tyrannical . . . untrustworthy and freakishly changeable."

Marshall distrusted political reformers and what he considered visionary democrats, but did not question the right of the people to their own rule. "Nothing you can find in his career," Professor Henry Steele Commager has said (in a letter to the author in June 1959), "can make him a real democrat." It is, nevertheless, interesting to note that in the Virginia constitutional convention of 1829–30, the Chief Justice presented a "Memorial of the Non-Freeholders of Richmond" in favor of manhood suffrage. Although Marshall did not write the "Memorial" which he introduced, it is such a cogently reasoned defense of what is the essential foundation of democracy that it merits analysis here, particularly since the suffrage was then opposed by leading conservatives.

The "Memorial of the Non-Freeholders" denied that the possession of land as such determined one's suffrage or bestowed special political privilege. Limitation on the suffrage, where it existed, was but an arrogation on the part of propertyowners, without legal validity or rational justification:

"Nothing is more reasonable than that those whose purses contribute to maintain, whose lives are pledged to defend the country, should participate in all the privileges of citizenship.... Whence did the freeholders derive it [the exclusive right to vote] ... ? Will they arrogantly tell us that they own the country, because they hold the land? The right by which they hold their land is not itself a natural right, and by consequence, nothing claimed is incidental to it. Whence then did they derive this privilege? From grant or conquest? Not from the latter. No war has ever been waged to assert it. If from the former, by whom was it conferred?"

The "Memorial" went on to say that the right to suffrage was a "natural right" belonging to all the citizens. It was not bestowed by anybody. It was inherent. More specifically, it did not depend upon or derive from ownership of property. Such a natural right to vote, moreover, underlay all republican government. To pretend otherwise, it said bluntly, was hypocritical and a denial of the very principles on which the American government was founded: "If we are sincerely republican, we must give our confidence to the principles we profess. We have been taught by our fathers, that all power is vested in, and derived from the people; not the freeholders: that the majority of the community, in whom abides the physical force, have also the political right of creating and remoulding at will their civil institutions. Nor can this right be anywhere more safely deposited."

Both republican principle and common sense required that political power and opportunity be open to all. In that way social cleavages, class or regional divisions, and oppressive political combinations would be mitigated.

"No community can exist," to quote again from the "Memorial," "no representative body be formed, in which some one division of persons or section of country, or some two or more combined, may not preponderate and oppress the rest. The east may be more powerful than the west, the lowlanders than the highlanders, the agricultural than the commercial or manufacturing classes. To give all power, or an undue share, to one, is obviously not to remedy but to ensure the evil. Its safest check, its best corrective, is found in a general admission of all upon a footing of equality. So intimately are the interests of each class in society blended and interwoven, so indispensable is justice to all, that oppression in that case becomes less probable from anyone, however powerful...."

There still remained the argument of corruption and ignorance. The ultraconservatives insisted that the people, especially in the industrial centers, could not be entrusted with the franchise, because, being ignorant, they would abuse it by lending themselves to the demagogic uses of corrupt bosses. This reasoning was insincere, merely another time-worn device used by oppressors of the people: "The alarm is sounded too of danger from large manufacturing institutions, where one corrupt individual may sway the corrupt votes of thousands. It were a vain task to attempt to meet all the flimsy pretexts urged, to allay all the apprehensions felt or feigned by the enemies of a just and liberal policy. The danger of abuse is a dangerous plea. Like *necessity,* the detested plea of the tyrant, or the still more detestable plea of the Jesuit, *expediency;* it serves as an ever-ready apology for all oppression."

As for the argument that property would be endangered once the populace was enfranchised, the "Memorial" dismissed it on two grounds as making no sense. First, it was not realistic to assume that the people at large were naturally motivated by a base wish for the destruction of possessions; actually, they wished to own property and, once given the opportunity to do so, it would be to their advantage to join in its lawful defense. Thus, they would become a mainstay of property and public order rather than an enemy: "The generality of mankind, doubtless, desire to become owners of property: left free to reap the fruit of their labours, they will seek to acquire it honestly. It can never be their interest to overburthen, or render precarious, what they themselves desire to enjoy in peace."

Secondly, if it were really true that the people were inherently inimical to possessions and orderly government, then any constitutional system was doomed. Since constitutional government required popular consent in order to exist at all, the absence of such acquiescence meant that only force could be the final arbiter. This was a manifestly untenable position to take in a republic; "But should they [the people] ever prove as base as the argument supposes, force alone; arms, not votes, could effect their designs; and when that shall be attempted, what virtue is there in Constitutional restrictions, in mere wax and paper, to withstand it?"

In his fundamental ideas Marshall was a conservative republican. He believed in the natural right to self-government; he rejected rule by an aristocracy. But he added several dimensions to republican practice and these, after his thirty-five years on the Supreme bench as chief justice, became engrafted as the constitutional and political principles of the American nation. By the time he ended his life work, the American federal structure had been in many ways transformed; the simple republicanism of the founders, with its explicit distrust of strong government and implicit faith in the separation of powers as a safeguard of liberty, had given way to the doctrines and (increasingly) the practices of a national state. This was, almost single-handedly, the achievement of John Marshall.

The Chief Justice, in appearance a deceptively simple frontiersman, dominated the Court by sheer force of personality. Considering his historic role in the Supreme Court, to which he was appointed on January 31, 1801, it is surprising how fortuitous his appointment was. Positions on the Court were not greatly sought after. At one time or another, such eminent persons as Patrick Henry, William Cushing, and Alexander Hamilton had turned down the chief justiceship. The first chief justice, John Jay (1745–1829), resigned in 1795; his successor, Oliver Ellsworth (1745–1807), did the same in 1800. Upon Ellsworth's resignation, John Marshall, then Adams' secretary of state, suggested William Paterson (1744–1806), but the President decided to renominate Jay. When Adams received Jay's letter of refusal, he said to Marshall: "Who [sic] shall I nominate now?" Marshall again proposed Paterson (he spelled it *Patteson*), but Adams, after some hesitation, said to him: "I believe I must nominate you." Marshall commented: "I had never before heard myself named for the office and had not even thought of it. I was pleased as well as surprised, and bowed in silence. Next day I was nominated."

Prior to Marshall's term, the Supreme Court was considered so unimportant that when the federal government moved to Washington in 1800, the architect of the Capitol had not even provided a special room for it. The Court had to sit in the basement of the Old Senate Chamber, in a room so obscure that the sardonic John Randolph dubbed it the "cave of Trophonius," in reference to the legendary Greek architect who delivered his dour oracles from a subterranean nook in ancient Lebadea. It was from the "cave of Trophonius" that some of Marshall's greatest decisions emanated.

"They were an innocent lot," Oliver Wendell Holmes once said of Marshall and his colleagues, "and didn't need caviar for luncheon." Quietly, Marshall imposed on the Court not only his will but, more important, his guiding ideas and assumptions. He personally wrote more decisions than any of his colleagues on the bench, and in one area—constitutional law—more than all of the justices combined.

Of the 1215 cases that appeared before the Court during Marshall's tenure of office, the Chief Justice wrote 519 (43 per cent) of the decisions. If one takes into consideration the fact that of the 1215 cases, 94 required no opinion and 15 were "by the Court," the percentage of the decisions written by Marshall was actually higher—about 47. In cases involving international law, Marshall wrote 80 out of the 196 opinions; the next highest number were by Justices Story (37) and William Johnson (28). Marshall's percentage is even greater when one considers constitutional cases alone: of the 62 decisions involving questions relating to the Constitution, no less than 36 (58 per cent) came from the pen of the Chief Justice. Clearly, this was Marshall's court.

His decisions show the consistency of a man guided by inflexible convictions and a clear philosophy of law and politics. Three main ideas underlie Marshall's judicial opinions. First, at least chronologically, was the assertion of the supremacy of the judiciary over the legislature. The classic case involving this principle of judicial review is *Marbury v. Madison* (1803). Second, there is the doctrine of the irrevocability of contract as the basic defense of property. Here the important decisions deal with the Yazoo Land Fraud case in *Fletcher v. Peck* (1810) and the Dartmouth College case in *Trustees of Dartmouth College v. Woodward* (1819). And third, the sweeping assertion of the supremacy of the federal Constitution over all other political entities, including state constitutions and legislatures. Among the historic decisions in which Marshall gave a "loose construction" to the Constitution and formulated the idea that the nation was supreme, the most explicit and famous are *McCulloch v. Maryland* (1819), *Cohens v. Virginia* (1821), and *Gibbons v. Ogden* (1824).

The power of judicial review, by which the federal Court assumed the right to pass on the constitutionality of acts of Congress, had not been specifically granted in the federal Constitution. Nor was it even discussed at the convention. The closest that the framers of the Constitution came to any mention of a possible check on the legislative branch was the eighth article of the Virginia Plan (May 29, 1787), providing for a "council of revision with authority to examine every act of the National Legislature," but this actually called for an executive, rather than judiciary, veto. At any rate, the plan was defeated and the matter dropped. The Constitution left the subject open, which was obviously no solution.

Even before Marshall, the political-legal realities required authoritative decisions about what was clearly lawful. Given a written national Constitution, it followed that all legislative acts had to be passed within that constitution's framework. But *who* was to decide what was in accord with the letter or spirit of the written constitution? This question was particularly complicated because of the existence of an interlocking system of written state constitutions and a tripartite federal structure in which each of the branches, while "co-ordinate," was nevertheless equal to and independent of the other, at least in theory. Manifestly, in such a situation conflicts of interest and clashing interpretations were bound to occur. To avoid chaos, somebody had to assume the responsibility for ultimate arbitration. As Justice Learned Hand put it (1958):

"It was probable, if indeed it was not certain, that without some arbiter whose decision should be final, the whole system would have collapsed, for it was extremely unlikely that the Executive or the Legislature, having once decided, would yield to the contrary holding of another 'Department.' ... The courts were undoubtedly the best 'Department' in which to vest such a power, since by the independence of their tenure they were least likely to be influenced by pressure. It was not a lawless act to import into the Constitution such a grant of power."

Actually, even before Marshall made formal the "import into the Constitution" of the power of judicial review, the lower courts were feeling their way in this direction. Between 1789 and 1803, state courts held ten legislative acts unconstitutional, on the general ground (best expressed by Judge Spencer Roane of Virginia in 1793) that the "judiciary may and ought to adjudge a law unconstitutional and void, if it be plainly repugnant to the letter of the Constitution, or the fundamental principles thereof." In the same period, five state laws were declared contrary to the Constitution by the federal circuit courts, but since decisions were then not published, the reasoning behind them can only be surmised. One of the few opinions that did survive was that of Justice William Paterson in the case of *Vanhorne's Lessee v. Dorrance* (1795), which is worth quoting because it clearly foreshadows the later decisions of his colleague Marshall.

"The Constitution," Justice Paterson (who had been a New Jersey delegate to the federal convention of 1787) wrote in the *Vanhorne* case, "is certain and fixed; it contains the permanent will of the people, and is the supreme law of the land; it is paramount to the power of the legislature, and can be revoked or altered only by the authority that made it.... I take it to be a clear position; that if a legislative act oppugns a constitutional principle, the former must give way, and be rejected on the score of repugnance. I hold it to be a position equally clear and sound, that, in such a case, it will be the duty of the Court to adhere to the Constitution, and to declare the act null and void."

This was in essence the position that Marshall took in *Marbury v. Madison.* The case itself was of no importance, but Marshall, by his decision, made it so. It involved William Marbury, who had been appointed to a minor federal judicial post in one of John Adams' "midnight appointments." This term was used by Jefferson to denote Adams' last-minute appointments of Federalists in order to embarrass Jefferson's incoming republican-democratic administration.

Years later, in a letter to William Johnson (June, 1823), Jefferson gave this version of the background of the *Marbury v. Madison* case: "Among the midnight appointments of Mr. Adams, were commissions to some federal justices of the peace for Alexandria. These were signed and sealed by him, but not delivered. I found them on the table of the department of State, on my entrance into office, and I forbade their delivery. Marbury, named in one of them, applied to the Supreme Court for a mandamus to the Secretary of State, to deliver the commission intended for him. The court determined at once, that being an original process, they had no cognizance of it; and therefore the question before them was ended. But the Chief Justice went on to lay down what the law would be, had they jurisdiction of the case, to wit: that they should command the delivery. The object was clearly to instruct any other court having the jurisdiction, what they should do if Marbury should apply to them. Besides the impropriety of this gratuitous interference, could anything exceed the perversion of law? For if there is any principle of law never yet contradicted, it is that delivery is one of the essentials to the validity of the deed. . . . Yet this case of Marbury and Madison is continually cited by bench and bar, as if it were settled law, without any animadversion on its being merely an *obiter* dissertation of the Chief Justice."

Marbury asked the Supreme Court for a writ of mandamus to compel Secretary of State Madison to give him his commission. He based his case on Article 13 of the Judiciary Act of 1789, which authorized the Court to issue "writs of mandamus, in cases warranted by the principles and usages of law, to any courts appointed, or persons holding office, under the authority of the United States."

The Chief Justice, sensing the potential political implication of the case, was in a quandry. If he decided in favor of Marbury, Madison and Jefferson would ignore his decision and thereby further undermine the position of the Supreme Court, which was already under severe attack by the victorious Jeffersonians. If he ruled in favor of Madison, it would signify the Court's sanction of an administration whose leader and principles he hated. "To Mr. Jefferson," he told Alexander Hamilton in January 1801, ". . . I have felt almost insuperable objections. His foreign prejudices seem to me totally to unfit him for the Chief Magistracy. . . . He will . . . sap the fundamental principles of government." And two months later, on the morning of the day when he had to administer the oath of office to Jefferson (as he was also to do to Madison, Monroe, and Jackson), he wrote with heavy heart to a fellow Federalist: ". . . Today the new political year commences—. The new order of things begins. . . . The democrats are divided into speculative theorists & absolute terrorists. With the latter I am not disposed to class Mr. Jefferson. If he arranges himself with them it is not difficult to foresee that much calamity is in store for our country. . . ." Clearly, feeling so strongly about his cousin, Marshall was not disposed to give any aid or comfort to Jefferson.

The Chief Justice solved his dilemma with an ingeniousness that, for years afterward, left his opponents in a state of impotent anger. He took up three points in the Marbury case: did the applicant have a right to his commission; if he did, and if the law was violated, what was his remedy; if there was a remedy in the law, was it the writ of mandamus? Marshall easily disposed of the first two questions, ruling in favor of Marbury on the ground that his commission was a "vested legal right" which nobody could take from him, not even the President, who, like everybody else, "is amenable to the laws for his conduct; and cannot at his discretion sport away the vested rights of others."

But this did not mean that Marbury could get his commission, for he had sued under the "writ of mandamus" article of the 1789 Judiciary Act, the constitutionality of which Marshall invalidated. It was this third point on which Marshall made history. His reasoning here was brilliant. The Constitution, he pointed out, had conferred both original and appellate jurisdiction to the Supreme Court, but the former was explicit, limited to cases "affecting ambassadors, other public ministers and consuls, and those in which a State shall be a party." All other jurisdiction was appellate, left to be determined by future laws of the Congress. Now the question under consideration was under which head did the granting of a mandamus belong—the original or the appellate? Marshall answered that a mandamus was in its nature an "original jurisdiction." But Congress *did* incorporate Article 13 (writ of mandamus) in its Judiciary Act of 1789. That, concluded the Chief Justice, was precisely the issue. The Congress had no right to do so under the Constitution. Article 13, he said, was not "warranted by the Constitution." Hence it was void. Hence it was unconstitutional!

That was not the end of his process of reasoning. Having declared an act of Congress unconstitutional, the question remained: Whence did the Supreme Court derive its authority to do so? The Constitution gave no such specific grant of power. Here Marshall fell back on Hamilton's *Federalist* paper Number 78, which, in essence, reasoned that the supremacy of a written constitution required that the courts be left to interpret the law.

Hamilton had written:

"... Every act of a delegated authority, contrary to the tenor of the commission under which it is exercised, is void. No legislative act, therefore, contrary to the Constitution, can be valid.... It is far more rational to suppose, that the courts were designed to be an intermediate body between the people and the legislature, in order, among other things, to keep the latter within the limits assigned to their authority. The interpretation of the laws is the proper and peculiar province of the courts. A constitution is, in fact, and must be regarded by the judges, as a fundamental law. It therefore belongs to them to ascertain its meaning, as well as the meaning of any particular act proceeding from the legislative body...."

Marshall argued that the Constitution was the supreme guiding instrument of the nation and the fact that it was *written* meant that it mentioned *limits* on power and jurisdiction. Who, if not the courts, under their sworn obligation to the Constitution, may pass judgment on when constitutional limits have been passed?

The powers of the legislature [Marshall stated in *Marbury v. Madison*] are defined and limited; and that these limits may not be mistaken or forgotten, the constitution is written. To what purpose are powers limited, and to what purpose is that limitation committed to writing, if these limits may, at any time, be passed by those intended to be restrained?... It is a proposition too plain to be contested, that the constitution controls any legislative act repugnant to it; or, that the legislature may alter the constitution by an ordinary act....

Certainly all those who have framed written constitutions contemplate them as forming the fundamental and paramount law of the nation, and consequently the theory of every such government must be that an act of the legislative repugnant to the Constitution is void....

It is emphatically the province and duty of the judicial department to say what the law is.... If two laws conflict with each other, the courts must decide on the operation of each....

The judicial power of the United States is extended to all cases arising under the Constitution. Could it be the intention of those who gave this power to say that in using it the constitution should not be looked into? That a case arising under the constitution should be decided without examining the instrument under which it arises? This is too extravagant to be maintained.

In some cases, then, the constitution must be looked into by the judges. And if they can open it at all, what part of it are they forbidden to read or to obey?

Therefore, he concluded:

It is also not entirely unworthy of observation, that in declaring what shall be the *supreme* law of the land, the constitution itself is first mentioned, and not the laws of the United States generally but those only which shall be made in *pursuance* of the constitution have that rank.

Thus, the particular phraseology of the constitution of the United States confirms and strengthens the principle, supposed to be essential to all written constitutions, that a law repugnant to the constitution is void, and that courts, as well as other departments, are bound by that instrument.

Marshall thus achieved a number of objectives. At one and the same time he vindicated Marbury's right to his commission but denied him the mandamus; he condemned President Jefferson (who criticized the *Marbury v. Madison* decision as "very irregular and very censurable"); and he laid the basis for a claim to power over the legislature, which, despite the caution with which it was used by Marshall himself and his immediate successors, the Supreme Court has retained to the present.

But not until the Dred Scott decision of 1857, that is, more than half a century after *Marbury v. Madison,* did the Court declare any federal law unconstitutional. In the period of Marshall's tenure, the Court did set aside thirteen *state* laws as being contrary to the Constitution. Altogether, there has been a total of some seventy-eight federal statutes which the Court ruled in whole or in part unconstitutional—all except *Marbury v. Madison* taking place after 1857 (twenty-three between 1860 and 1900; thirty-five between 1900 and 1930; eighteen between 1930 and 1950).

The principle of judicial review, which Marshall initiated and brillantly justified in *Marbury v. Madison,* remains a major contribution to the science of law and politics, regardless of one's political evaluation of it.

Similarly, Marshall affirmed the doctrine of the inviolability of property in his judicial interpretations of the contract clause. His basic position, which he developed particularly in *Fletcher v. Peck,* involving land sales in Georgia which one state legislature approved and another annulled, and the Dartmouth College case, involving that school's charter, was that private property was so fundamental a bulwark of society that the laws could not alienate or adversely affect it. A right in property, once vested by contract or otherwise, remained, in effect, sacred. Thus the Georgia lands, even if sold fraudulently, could not be alienated from their buyers by any act of the succeeding legislature; and the old charter of Dartmouth could not be set aside by the new trustees, because a charter was a contract, and a contract was perpetually binding. No legislature, Marshall held, could deprive an owner of his vested property. In this respect, Marshall put property rights above all others, including the will of the people as expressed by their elected representatives. Where property was concerned, he ruled, there must be a fence around the legislature and a limit to its authority to pass laws.

"If an act be done under a law" he held in *Fletcher v. Peck,* "a succeeding legislature cannot undo it. The past cannot be recalled by the most absolute power.... When, then, a law is in its nature a contract, when absolute rights have been vested under that contract, a repeal of the law cannot divest those rights.... It may well be doubted whether the nature of society and of the government does not prescribe some limits to the legislative power; and if any be prescribed, where are they to be found, if the property of an individual, fairly and honestly acquired, may be seized without compensation.... The validity of this rescinding act, then, might well be doubted, [even] were Georgia a single sovereign power...."

Finally, there was Marshall's continuing assertion of national supremacy over all states. In every decision in which federal–state relations were in any way involved, the Chief Justice adamantly maintained that, at all times and on all issues, the federal Constitution took precedence as the supreme law of the land. It is not without irony to contemplate that while Marshall insisted upon the principle of limitation where state legislatures were concerned, he proclaimed the reverse (always excepting property rights) in the case of the national Congress. It was his self-dedicated task on the supreme bench to interpret the Constitution with such astonishing flexibility and suppleness as always to give the Congress the benefit of the decision in jurisdictional clashes between the states and the federal government. If there was no specific mandate in the Constitution, Marshall created one by his so-called "loose construction," justified on the ground that what was not specifically forbidden was generally allowed—especially where the supreme needs of the nation, as he interpreted them, were concerned.

As in *Marbury v. Madison,* the justice was guided by Hamilton's reasoning in still another case. Hamilton had stated in his *Opinion on the Constitution of the Bank of the United States* (1791): "Every power vested in a government is in its nature sovereign and includes, by force of the term, a right to employ all the means requisite and fairly applicable to the attainment of the ends of such power, and which are not precluded by restrictions and exceptions specified in the Constitution. . . . If the end be clearly comprehended within any of the specified powers, and if the measure have an obvious relation to that end, and is not forbidden by any particular provision of the Constitution, it may safely be deemed to come within the compass of national authority."

Two decades later Marshall followed the famous reasoning, and sometimes almost the very words, of Hamilton's *Opinion* in the *McCulloch v. Maryland* case (1819). Marshall's decision laid down the following broad interpretation of the Constitution:

"... We think the sound construction must allow to the national legislature that discretion, with respect to the means by which the powers it confers are to be carried into execution, which will enable that body to perform the high duties assigned to it, in the manner most beneficial to the people. *Let the end be legitimate, let it be within the scope of the constitution, and all means which are appropriate, which are plainly adapted to that end, which are not prohibited, but consistent with the letter and spirit of the constitution, are constitutional.*" [Italics supplied.]

Thus, interpreting the Constitution in the broadest possible terms in order to empower the national government with all the requisite authority, Marshall repeatedly indicated to individual states that they were subordinate to the nation at large. He made it bluntly clear that to him there was no sovereign Maryland (in the McCulloch case) or sovereign New Hampshire (in the Dartmouth case) or sovereign Georgia—as he stated sharply in *Fletcher v. Peck:*

"But Georgia cannot be viewed as a single, unconnected, sovereign power, on whose legislature no other restrictions are imposed than may be found in its constitution. She is part of a large empire; she is a member of the American union; and that union has a constitution, the supremacy of which all acknowledge, and which imposes limits to the legislatures of the several states."

There was only one sovereign—the United States, whose Constitution, Marshall wrote again and again, was the "superior paramount law," "fundamental," "supreme," "irresistible," "untrammelled," its powers "illimitable." This idea of a sovereign central government he developed with particular explicitness in *Cohens v. Virginia* (1821).

This case involved the sale of lottery tickets by P. J. and M. J. Cohen in Virginia in violation of a state statute. Fined for doing so, the Cohens, in their appeal to the Supreme Court, claimed the protection of a Congressional act of 1802 which had established a lottery. Marshall, in the *Cohens v. Virginia* decision, while reaffirming federal supremacy over state laws, nevertheless ruled against the Cohens on the technical ground that the 1802 lottery act was confined to the District of Columbia and did not apply to Virginia.

The importance of this case rests on Marshall's written decision, which not only reaffirmed federal supremacy but insisted that there was but one "single nation"—the American:

"That the United States form . . . a single nation, has not yet been denied. In war we are one people. In all commercial regulations we are one and the same people. In many other respects the American people are one, and the government which is alone capable of controlling and managing their interests in all these respects, is the government of the Union. It is their government, and in that character they have no other. America has chosen to be . . . a nation; . . . her government is complete. . . . It is supreme. It can, then, in effecting these objects, legitimately control all individuals or governments within the American territory. The constitution and laws of a State, so far as they are repugnant to the constitution and laws of the United States, are absolutely void."

Marshall's opinion in *Cohens v. Virginia,* a direct challenge to his powerful native state, stirred the states' rights advocates to special anger. It brought to a focus the Chief Justice's fundamental ideas. It further sharpened the clash between those, notably in the South, who increasingly dreaded a strong central government, and those, like the Chief Justice and the Federalists, who felt that America's destiny lay in a strong union. In his native Virginia, Marshall was bitterly attacked in such books as John Taylor's *New Views of the Constitution* (1823), articles such as those by Judge Spencer Roane (writing under the pseudonym Algernon Sidney), and letters such as those by Jefferson, who wrote that Marshall and his Court were the "subtle corps of sappers and miners constantly working under ground to undermine the foundations of our confederated fabric." They considered Marshall a deadly enemy, not primarily because of his threat to states' rights but because of their conviction that centralized government, as espoused by the Chief Justice, was a standing danger to individual freedom. In their view, a concentration of federal office-holders in Washington, withdrawn from the eyes of the people, would, as Jefferson said, end by being "secretly bought and sold as at market"; and liberty would thus be at an end. Marshall, of course, rejected this philosophy.

The conflict of views seemed irreconcilable. Marshall, laboring to reduce the centrifugal forces of America which were ultimately to culminate in the tragedy of the Civil War, felt that the logical result of the states' rights philosophy was "dismemberment," as he wrote forebodingly to Justice Story in June 1821, and "destruction of the government." He devoted his life to an effective national union, an ideal which many of his countrymen and neighbors did not then share—and still do not accept in certain areas. The violent southern reaction against the 1955 Supreme Court decision on segregation of Negro and white school children shows that the tradition of opposition to national authority is still very much alive in parts of the United States. Governor Orval E. Faubus of Arkansas expressed a widely held southern opinion when he said in an interview that the Eisenhower administration asked him to declare "that I believed that the Supreme Court was the law of the land, which I don't." (*The New York Times,* September 1, 1958)

Despite the conservatism of his views, notably in the matter of private property rights, the result of his political convictions and judicial opinions was, in the ultimate sense, a triumph for liberalism—if by that word is meant an enlargement, rather than a restriction, of the world of thought and the world of action. By his remarkable judicial decisions Marshall conferred upon the national Congress a wide range of "implied powers" that enabled it, then as now, to deal with the economic and social welfare needs of a growing nation—needs which in no way could have been, or can possibly be, met by the states individually. Those were his imperishable contributions to the United States. In the words of Professor Edmund Cahn of the New York University Law School, John Marshall, in his thought and work, "represented the future."

# 9

## *THE AMERICAN AS STATES' RIGHTER:*
# John C. Calhoun *(1782–1850)*

> *Mr. Calhoun, the cast-iron man, who looks as if he had never been born and never could be extinguished.... His speech abounds in figures, truly illustrative. But his theories of government (almost the only subject on which his thoughts are employed), the squarest and compactest that ever were made, are composed out of limited elements, and are not, therefore, likely to stand service very well.*
>
> —*Harriet Martineau,* A Retrospect of Western Travel (*1838*)

In contrast to John Marshall, whose life was dedicated to the ideal of a strong national union, his fellow southerner John Caldwell Calhoun devoted the most fruitful years of his career to undoing it. Calhoun built his position of power and constructed his theory of politics on two fundamental premises: human inequality (including Negro slavery) and the supremacy of the individual states within the federal union.

For a generation Calhoun stood, a dour and dedicated figure of a "cast-iron man," as Harriet Martineau described him, against the dominant currents of his time and his country—against the expanding stream of democracy and the widening forces of nationalism. In terms more powerful and harshly logical than those used by any other American (the thrusts of his logic, Woodrow Wilson said, were "as sharp as those of cold steel"), Calhoun rejected the basic assumptions on which American democracy operated. Wrapped in the mantle of a South Carolina slaveowner and panoplied in the armor of the senator of a "sovereign" state, he refused to accept the existence of a united American nation that, in his eyes, threatened to impose egalitarianism upon the whole people. "I never use the word 'nation' in speaking of the United States," he wrote to Oliver Dyer in January 1849, a year before his death; "I always use the word 'union' or 'confederacy.' We are not a nation, but a *union,* a confederacy of equal and sovereign states."

Calhoun's political career spanned nearly half a century of American history, from the administration of President Jefferson to that of Zachary Taylor. Born five years before the drafting of the federal Constitution—which his father, Irish-born Patrick Calhoun, refused to support in the South Carolina ratification convention—John C. Calhoun entered public life at twenty-six and spent forty-two years in and out of office, mostly in. Throughout a major portion of his career he was a dominant national figure, attracting glory, sharing attention and competing for position with such illustrious men of his time as James Madison, James Monroe, John Quincy Adams, Andrew Jackson, Martin Van Buren, Henry Clay, and Daniel Webster. Calhoun was an influential member of the House of Representatives for six years, a member of the cabinet (Monroe's Secretary of War and John Tyler's Secretary of State) for ten years, Vice-President of the United States (Andrew Jackson's) for nearly eight years, and a United States senator for fifteen. Only the ardently sought presidency eluded him, as it did his equally ambitious colleagues Clay and Webster, and for the same overriding reason—conspicuousness and brilliance.

In *The American Commonwealth* (1888), Lord Bryce discusses "Why Great Men Are Not Chosen Presidents." He writes: "Europeans often ask . . . how it happens that this great office, the greatest in the world, unless we except the Papacy, to which any one can rise by his own merits, is not more frequently filled by great and striking men. . . . Since the heroes of the Revolution died . . . , no President except Abraham Lincoln has displayed rare or striking qualities in the chair."

One of the main reasons, Bryce explains, is the kind of eminence possessed by men like Calhoun: "Eminent men make more enemies, and give those enemies more assailable points, than obscure men do. They are, therefore, in so far less desirable candidates. It is true that the eminent man has also made more friends, that his name is more widely known, and may be greeted with louder cheers. Other things being equal, the famous man is preferable. But other things are never equal. The famous man has probably attacked some leaders in his own party, has supplanted others, has expressed his dislike to the crotchet of some active section, has perhaps committed errors which are capable of being magnified into offences. No man stands long before the public and bears a part in great affairs without giving openings to censorious criticism. Fiercer far than the light which beats upon a throne is the light which beats upon a presidential candidate. . . . Hence, when the choice lies between a brilliant man and a safe man, the safe man is preferred."

Had Calhoun been nothing more than an office-holder, he would rate no more or less attention than such similarly successful politicians as, say, Martin Van Buren. But Calhoun is remembered for reasons other than the political offices he filled, high though those were. His importance lies in the fact that, apart from being a distinguished politician, he was eminently a man of intellect, a logician, an eloquent speaker whose utterances had literary grace, and a thinker who—alone among his contemporaries—had the courage to reexamine and reject the major premises of American life. As August O. Spain points out in his admirable study, *The Political Theory of John C. Calhoun* (1951): "he is the only one in the American stream of thought of the period properly to be deemed a political philosopher." It is a pity that such superb gifts and moral fervor, with which Calhoun was abundantly endowed, should have been devoted to so wretched a cause as the preservation of slavery.

In point of fact, there were chronologically two Calhouns. The first was an American nationalist, the second a South Carolina plantation owner. During the first part of his career, roughly up to 1825 when he ended his services in Monroe's cabinet, Calhoun was a staunch supporter of American nationalism and Hamiltonian (centralized) capitalism. In Congress, he had been, with Clay, one of the "war hawks" who forced the United States into war with Great Britain in 1812. He had then voted for military establishments, supported a high tariff (because, he said, it would "bind together more closely our widely spread republic"), renounced *laissez faire* in favor of The American System, advocated internal improvements to strengthen the republic, and in general worked for all means that would advance national unity, integration, and prosperity.

In proposing a nationwide transportation network, he said in a speech in the House of Representatives (February 1817), "Let us, then, bind the republic together with a perfect system of roads and canals. Let us conquer space. . . . If . . . we permit a low, sordid, selfish and sectional spirit to take possession of this House, this happy scene will vanish. We will divide—and in its consequences will follow, misery and despotism."

The change in Calhoun—it is this second Calhoun who is of concern to us as a political thinker—took place sometime after he left the cabinet and returned to South Carolina, where he bought Fort Hill, a plantation at Pendleton. He was then in his early forties, vigorous and politically ambitious. He found, after living in Washington for fourteen years, that the South had not changed. While the North was increasing its population, building cities, bustling with industry, growing rich through trade and commerce and free enterprise, the South had remained unaltered, still basically rural, still dependent upon agriculture (and slavery) for its livelihood. In South Carolina, Calhoun found resentment against the North's economic policies, especially the tariff, which, the agrarian people felt, worked for the enrichment of the northern capitalists at the expense of the southern planters and farmers. What was developing, Calhoun sensed, was an ominous and, as it turned out, ultimately unbridgeable, gap between the two principal sections of the country, steadily moving in the direction of what he later called "two nations." And Calhoun, the erstwhile champion of American national unity and enemy of sectionalism, threw in his lot with his native state and region, and in the process rationalized his parochial position into a general philosophy.

Calhoun's first literary effort in this direction was his *South Carolina Exposition*, an essay he wrote secretly (while Vice-President of the United States) in 1828, in protest against the so-called "Tariff of Abominations," which the South considered grossly discriminatory. The *Exposition*, adopted by the legislature of South Carolina and three other southern states, introduced a number of ideas and procedures that were to become staples in the South's political arsenal. One of these ideas was "nullification" and another "interposition."

Following the reasoning of John Taylor of Caroline and the precedent set by the Virginia and Kentucky resolutions of 1798, Calhoun attacked the Tariff of 1828 as unconstitutional on the basis of the federal compact theory. According to this theory the federal union, as set up in 1787–89, was a voluntary partnership; whenever it legislated contrary to the interests of its component partners it violated the compact by acting unconstitutionally. Decision as to what was unconstitutional was to be in the hands of state conventions. Whenever such a special convention found a federal law to be void, it should recommend that the state legislature nullify it—declare that, having no legal validity, it would not be enforced within the state's borders. A law thus nullified in any particular state should not be enforced by the federal government anywhere else, unless three fourths of the states approved it by constitutional amendment. This was Calhoun's principle of interposition by the states.

South Carolina followed Calhoun's suggestions. In November 1832, the legislature of that state (by a vote of 136 to 26) adopted the Ordinance of Nullification, declaring that the Tariffs of 1828 (May 29) and of 1832 (July 14) were "unauthorized by the Constitution of the United States, and violate the true meaning and intent thereof, and are null and void and no law," and, as such, not "binding upon this State, its officers or citizens." Furthermore, should the federal government attempt to enforce the acts, the state of South Carolina would secede from the Union. Thus Calhoun sowed the first dragon's tooth.

The threat to the existence of the national union was met strongly by President Jackson, who sent a private message to Vice-President Calhoun's nullifying friends in South Carolina, telling them that they were at liberty to threaten "to their hearts' content." But, the formidable Jackson warned,* "if one drop of blood be shed there in defiance of the laws of the United States, I will hang the first man of them I can get my hands on to the first tree I can find."

To make sure his warning would be heeded, the President issued his famous proclamation of December 10, 1832. In it he pointed out that the Union would have been "dissolved in its infancy" if a state were permitted to veto the laws of the country—a doctrine of "impracticable absurdity," he called it. In effect, he directly challenged Calhoun when he stated flatly, "I consider, then, the power to annul a law of the United States, assumed by one State, *incompatible with the existence of the Union, contradicted expressly by the letter of the Constitution, unauthorized by its spirit, inconsistent with every principle on which it was founded, and destructive of the great object for which it was formed.*"

The battle that was to rend the United States within a generation was thus joined. Calhoun resigned as Vice-President and a few days later, on January 4, 1833, returned to the Senate, where he joined Clay and Webster in working out a compromise that was to delay South Carolina's secession from the Union for another twenty-seven years. Thenceforth

* Harriet Martineau described the President as he appeared to her in 1834: "General Jackson is extremely tall and thin, with a slight stoop, betokening more weakness than naturally belongs to his years. He has a profusion of stiff gray hair. . . . His countenance bears commonly an expression of melancholy gravity; though, when roused, the fire of passion flashes from his eyes, and his whole person looks then formidable. . . . His mode of speech is slow and quiet, and his phraseology sufficiently betokens that his time has not been passed among books."

Calhoun, steadily in opposition to the egalitarian drift of American life, became the most articulate spokesman of the extreme southern, sectional, pro-slavery point of view. The lean, harsh-faced, fierce-eyed, austere senator grimly and implacably pursued his course, intellectually isolated, increasingly unable to communicate with his fellow men on any level but his own, incapable of compromise, torrential in his harsh eloquence, a living symbol of doom for the Union.

Harriet Martineau, who visited Washington in 1834, found him to be "a volcano in full force," his talk about nullification filling her with forebodings about the future of the United States. Her picture of him is unforgettable: "It is at first extremely interesting to hear Mr. Calhoun talk; and there is a never-failing evidence of power in all he says and does which commands intellectual reverence; but the admiration is soon turned into regret, into absolute melancholy. It is impossible to resist the conviction that all this force can be at best but useless, and is but too likely to be very mischievous. . . . I know of no man who lives in such utter intellectual solitude. He meets men, and harangues them by the fireside as in the Senate; he is wrought like a piece of machinery, set agoing vehemently by a weight . . . ; he either passes by what you say or twists it into a suitability with what is in his head, and begins to lecture again. . . . a mind like this . . . , its influence at home is to be dreaded . . . ; there is every danger that it will break up all that it can."

What were the theories of government that gave Calhoun such a commanding position in his day? They were tied up with a course of political action, designed to provide the South with a formidable strategy in its resistance to northern expansion. Calhoun's theories were based on a logical and rigid system of politics and society that all but destroyed the assumptions of Jeffersonian democracy. Calhoun was sure that his theories, the most sweeping attack on democratic foundations ever made by a prominent American, were based on immutable scientific laws. "I hold them [politics and legislation] to be subject to laws as fixed as matter itself, and to be as fit a subject for the application of the highest intellectual power," he said in the Senate in 1833.

Calhoun's political strategy for the South was founded on at least four major premises. These, as he finally worked them out in his main work on politics, *A Disquisition on Government* and *A Discourse on the Constitution and Government of the United States* (both written in 1849–50 and published posthumously in 1851), underlie his fundamental political theory. These premises were:

(1) Northern society, based on the exploitation of free labor, was dangerously unstable; the South, built around docile slaves, was stable and durable. Moreover, humanly and morally, a better case could be made for slavery than for the capitalist system that exploited white labor in the North.

(2) The economically and socially stable South was the balance wheel of the Union; without this core of solidity it would dissolve in a welter of conflicting interests.

(3) Northern agitators and abolitionists were a menace to both the capitalist system in the North and the plantation society in the South. If those troublemakers succeeded in the North, they would then turn on the planters, and the result would be social disaster and civil war.

(4) Capitalist and planter, although antipathetic to each other and in conflict over many issues (such as the tariff), nevertheless had an overriding common interest: the preservation of the conservative classes against the inroads of radicals.

Behind these general premises lay Calhoun's theory of politics. In the main, the theory contained three elements: (1) the assumption of inherent human inequality; (2) the existence of permanent human conflict because of the existence of greed and self-interest (an idea Calhoun shared with such predecessors as John Adams and Alexander Hamilton); (3) the role of government as the sole keeper of order and protector of minority, particularly economic minority, interests. The first assumption enabled him to defend slavery as a "natural" state of things. The second gave a powerful rationale to his class theory of government. The third led him to the idea of the "concurrent majorities," which he proposed as a practical instrument for the defense of the South and its slave system.

Calhoun flatly denied the Jeffersonian theory that human beings are born equal. Such a theory was a myth, he said, unconfirmed by experience and indefensible in reason. Human beings, he argued, come into the world with no rights or special perquisites. They are merely born infants, and nothing else: "Nor is it less false that they were born 'equal.' They are not so in any sense in which it can be regarded; and thus . . . there is not a word of truth in the whole proposition as expressed and generally understood."

Just as human beings do not come into the world as equals, so also are they not born with any inherent or inalienable right to freedom. It was preposterous, Calhoun wrote, to apply this right to an infant, since by definition, freedom meant the "capacity of thinking and acting." A child obviously has no such capacity. Freedom is therefore a concept applicable only to grown human beings. But not all adults could enjoy it alike, since it had to be earned by those "growing to be men" under conditions applicable to their particular position in society. In other words, freedom (including suffrage) was not an automatic right which men possessed by virtue of the mere fact of their being born.

"It follows . . . that it is a great and dangerous error to suppose that all people are equally entitled to liberty," Calhoun said. "It [liberty] is a reward to be earned, not a blessing to be gratuitously lavished on all alike; a reward reserved for the intelligent, the patriotic, the virtuous and the deserving; and not a boon to be bestowed on a people too ignorant, degraded, and vicious, to be capable of either appreciating or of enjoying it."

Since men were not born either free or equal but had to earn both as adults within the context of their surroundings, it was clear to Calhoun that the idea of equality and freedom was totally inapplicable to Negro slaves. If inequality was the natural state of free whites at birth, it was much more so among Negroes. Apart from natural inequality, Negroes were considered morally inferior and mentally incapable of rising to higher status. But Calhoun's defense of slavery went beyond this widely held concept of Negro inferiority. Like his mentor John Taylor, who gave seven reasons in defense of slavery, Calhoun similarly justified it but on two main grounds: it was good for the country, and it was good for the slaves.*

Slavery was a positive good because it served as a force for stability and a foundation for culture. "We see it now," Calhoun wrote in 1838, "in its true light, and regard it as the most safe and stable basis for free institutions in the world." The labor of slaves released the aristocrats from the necessity of work and provided them with the leisure required to produce the refinements of civilization. Slavery was a necessary and normal institution found throughout human history, as Calhoun reminded his hearers in a Senate speech in 1837:

"I hold that in the present state of civilization, where two races of

* In *Arator,* Taylor listed the following reasons for justifying slavery: (1) Ancient Greece and Rome, which had more slaves than the United States, produced the greatest civilizations ever known; (2) in the United States, the slave states produced many men of distinction, such as Jefferson and Washington; (3) slaves excite our benevolence, as do horses, and if well treated they can be made to like their condition; (4) the low qualities of slaves (viciousness, servility) excite the opposite traits in the masters, and hence increase the latter's virtues; (5) slaves are morally degraded and mentally inferior; (6) slavery engenders restrained and humanitarian attitudes in whites; (7) slavery cannot be abolished by law.

different origin, and distinguished by color and other physical differences, as well as intellectual, are brought together, the relation now existing in the slavehold states between the two, is, instead of an evil, a good—a positive good. . . . I hold, then, that there never has yet existed a wealthy and civilized society in which one portion of the community did not, in point of fact, live on the labor of the other. Broad and general as is this assertion, it is fully borne out by history."

Furthermore, slavery was best for the Negroes themselves. Calhoun considered it a more humane system than that found in the industrial North, where free white workers were ruthlessly exploited in sweatshops and unsanitary factories, having none of the security of the black slaves on the plantation. To Calhoun, the relationship between slave and master was much more normal than that which existed between the wretched white worker and his profit-obsessed capitalist employer in the North. In the South, the master was benevolent, interested in the welfare of the slaves who—like children—could not manage on their own. The master cared for the slave when he was sick and provided for him when he was old. To change the slavery system and to give Negroes their freedom as the northern abolitionists advocated was, Calhoun wrote, "neither wise nor humane." Negroes, left to themselves, sink into sloth and degradation. Only under white masters do Negroes have a chance to live comfortably and to improve their characters.

"The census and other authentic documents," Calhoun wrote in a letter to Pakenham, the British Minister to the United States, in April 1844, "show that, in all instances in which the States have changed the former relation between the two races, the condition of the Africans, instead of being improved, has become worse. They have been invariably sunk into vice and pauperism, accompanied by the bodily and mental inflictions incident thereto—deafness, blindness, insanity, and idiocy—to a degree without example; while, in all other states which have retained the ancient relation between them, they have improved greatly in every respect—in number, comfort, intelligence, and morals."

The second aspect of Calhoun's political theory dealt with the question of human nature, "in which government originates." Like John Locke, Calhoun began with the premise that man was a social animal and that, in fact, he could not survive in any other state of existence except in association with his fellows.

"I assume as an incontestable fact," Calhoun wrote in *A Disquisition on Government,* "that man is so constituted as to be a social being. His inclinations and wants, physical and moral, irresistibly impel him to associate with his kind; and he has, accordingly, never been found, in any age or country, in any state other than the social. In no other, indeed, could he exist; and in no other—were it possible for him to exist—could he attain to a full development of his moral and intellectual faculties, or raise himself, in the scale of being, much above the level of the brute creation."

Having established this assumption, he proceeded to the "not less incontestable" premise that man's need for association with his fellow requires the establishment of political institutions to make it effective. The social state, Calhoun wrote, "cannot exist without government," as can be seen from the universal experience of mankind. "In no age or country," he pointed out, "has any society or community ever been found, whether enlightened or savage, without government of some description."

He then posited the "primary and important" question: "What is that constitution of our nature, which, while it impels man to associate with his kind, renders it impossible for society to exist without government?"

In answering this question, Calhoun formulated a political psychology not unlike that of Hobbes and Hamilton. Man, he explained, has a dual nature, moved by two separate sets of feelings. One was the "direct or individual" and the other the "sympathetic or social" feeling. The former stimulated man to satisfy his direct *personal* desires, and the latter directed him toward the *group* needs, which are more remote and indirect.

Calhoun made it clear that he was not expressing preferences, but only stating the facts of human nature as they existed. Each—the personal and the group need—had its proper place in the fixed psychological universe. To emphasize the scientific objectivity of his position, he even refused to use emotionally loaded words, such as *selfish*. For example: "I intentionally avoid the expression, *selfish* feelings, as applicable to the former [personal]; because, as commonly used, it implies an unusual excess of the individual over the social feelings, in the person to whom it is applied; and, consequently, something depraved and vicious. My object is, to exclude such inference, and to restrict the inquiry exclusively to facts in their bearings on the subject under consideration, viewed as mere phenomena appertaining to our nature—constituted as it is; and which are as unquestionable as is that of gravitation, or any other phenomenon of the material world."

Of the two sets of feelings that make up the human character, he felt, the direct or personal ones are by far the stronger. They predominate over the sympathetic or social affections, primarily because they are more directly connected with self-preservation. The needs and impulses of the individual are always immediate and, therefore, uppermost in motivation. This is true not only of man, but of the whole animal kingdom, and for the same reason—the urge to survive: "I . . . assert this to be a phenomenon, not of our nature only, but of all animated existence, throughout its entire range. . . . It would, indeed, seem to be essentially connected with the great law of self-preservation which pervades all that feels, from man down to the lowest and most insignificant reptile or insect. In none is it stronger than in man."

Occasionally, Calhoun admitted, social feelings have the upper hand, but then only briefly under the rarest conditions of material security and spiritual elevation. The universal rule is the individual, and not the social, urge. Only rarely are social feelings forceful enough to overcome the "essential law of animated existence."

The consequence of this psychological duality in man is constant social conflict. Since each person feels intensely what affects him directly, he is at war with other individuals, who have exactly the same emotions and motivations and urges as he does. A man's sympathetic or social feelings being always secondary to his immediate ones, he strives to achieve his personal safety and happiness at the expense of others, whom he is ready to sacrifice for his own desires.

"And hence, the tendency to a universal state of conflict, between individual and individual; accompanied by the connected passions of suspicion, jealousy, anger and revenge—followed by insolence, fraud and cruelty;—and, if not prevented by some controlling power, ending in a state of universal discord and confusion, destructive of the social state and the ends for which it is ordained."

This controlling power, "wherever vested, or by whomsoever exercised," that prevents the clashing individual interests and desires from producing permanent chaos, is "GOVERNMENT."

Here, however, was an age-old dilemma—men against men. The ancient Romans had asked the question: *Quis custodiet ipsos custodes?* —Who will watch the rulers? In *The Federalist* (Number 51), Madison raised the same question when he asked, "What is government itself, but the greatest of all reflections on human nature?" No government would be needed "if men were angels." But men are not.

Calhoun, too, faced this dilemma. The trouble with government, he pointed out, was the human element. Government was not an automatic mechanism; it was not self-executing. It depended on human beings to create it, to shape it, to direct it, to run it. But government office does not change human nature. A man in a political position retains the same feelings and emotions—individual interests overriding the social ones—as other human beings in society. Hence the normal tendency of men in power was to be oppressive, to use the instrument of government for their own individual purposes at the expense of the community as a whole. That was only natural.

Calhoun put it: "But government, although intended to protect and preserve society, has itself a strong tendency to disorder and abuse of its powers, as all experience and almost every page of history testify. The cause is to be found in the same constitution of our nature which makes government indispensable. The powers which it is necessary for government to possess, in order to repress violence and preserve order, cannot execute themselves. They must be administered by men in whom, like others, the individual feelings are stronger than the social ones. And hence, the powers vested in them to prevent injustice and oppression on the part of others, will, if left unguarded, be by them converted into instruments to oppress the rest of the community."

What, then, was the solution for this universal tendency toward governmental oppression? "How," Calhoun asked, "can those who are invested with the powers of government be prevented from employing them, as the means of aggrandizing themselves, instead of using them to protect and preserve society?"

In searching for a solution, he made a drastic reevaluation of the federal constitutional system and rejected the basic democratic idea of rule by numerical majority. Instead, he proposed his celebrated concept (first used in a letter to James Hamilton, August 23, 1832) of the "concurrent majority."

The steps by which Calhoun reached this theory are as illuminating as the proposition itself. As a general idea, he stated that abuse of political power and the defense of the minority against oppression by the majority were facilitated by the existence of a constitution, using the word "in its most comprehensive sense." There was, he pointed out, a fundamental difference between *constitution* and *government,* although each needed the other in order truly to achieve its ends. The difference lay in their origins: "Constitution is the contrivance of man, while government is of Divine ordination." Ordained by God "as necessary to preserve the race," government is an integral part of human existence, beyond man's will. "There is no difficulty in forming government. It is not even a matter of choice, whether there shall be one or not. Like breathing, it is not permitted to depend on our volition. Necessity will force it on all communities in some one form or another."

But the same was not true of a constitution. That is always and altogether the work of man. It is a purely human contrivance, and its workability, not to speak of its perfection, depends upon man's own ingenuity and wisdom: ". . . it is one of the most difficult tasks imposed on man to form a constitution worthy of the name; while, to form a perfect one, one that would completely counteract the tendency of government to oppression and abuse, and hold it strictly to the great ends for which it is ordained, has thus far exceeded human wisdom, and possibly ever will."

How does one contrive a constitution that would establish a government able successfully to achieve its "great ends" of defending human rights, especially of preventing the abuse of the minority by the majority? There were, Calhoun wrote, three possibilities—to give the government too much power, too little power, or "concurrent" power. Calhoun preferred the third.

The first alternative, that of clothing government with dictatorial authority—what Calhoun called "higher power"—was unacceptable because it solved nothing. Under it, there would still be human beings in office, driven by the usual self-interest and hence unavoidably abusing their positions, if anything, more grossly than those operating under a limited system of checks and balances. It would, Calhoun reasoned, "make this higher power, in reality, the government; with the same tendency, on the part of those who might control its powers, to pervert them into instruments of aggrandizement."

The second prospect, that of too little power, was not desirable either. A weak government might, to be sure, be too feeble to do damage, but by the same token it would lack the means to do the job for which government is instituted, "to protect and preserve society." An ineffectual government, moreover, would fail in another respect: it would not have the requisite power "to repel assaults from abroad." For, Calhoun pointed out, since human nature is universal, conflict existed throughout the world, not merely inside communities but also between communities and among nations. This was because social feelings were, if anything, even weaker among communities than inside them. Hence, he explained, the "almost incessant wars . . . for plunder and conquest" with which the annals of mankind are filled. In sheer self-defense, therefore, government must always have sufficient power to mobilize the community for survival. A weak government would never do.

"So long as this state of things continues," expounded Calhoun, "exigencies will occur, in which the entire powers and resources of the community will be needed to defend its existence. When this is at stake, every other consideration must yield to it. Self-preservation is the supreme law, as well with communities as with individuals. And hence the danger of withholding from government the full command of the power and resources of the state."

There remained only the third course, that of so organizing government that it would be strong enough to carry out its functions but would be prevented from abusing the interest of minorities. This was the idea of the "concurrent majority," Calhoun's most original single contribution to political theory.

As he conceived it, this concept had nothing to do with numbers as such. Rather, it rejected mere head-counting in favor of a consensus of organized interests. Calhoun challenged the democratic assumption that each vote is equal and that the largest number of them must always prevail. He denied that mere numbers spell wisdom or right decision. In effect, he saw no sense in the universal democratic belief that, say, fifty-one individuals were automatically right and forty-nine automatically wrong for no other reason than that numerically the one outweighs the other. Such a reliance upon mere numbers was hardly anything more than an invitation to anarchy, since the majority rarely had the requisite knowledge or disinterested judgment for wise decision.

Calhoun did not deny the right to vote. He merely questioned the effectiveness of majority rule as it operated in the United States. The voter, he wrote, is not entitled to make important decisions by the mere fact of being a voter. All that he was expected to do was to cast his ballot for "true and faithful representatives" and then keep an eye on their conduct to see that they acted in the true interests of the community. "The right of suffrage, of itself, can do no more than give complete control to those who elect, over the conduct of those they have elected. In doing this, it accomplishes all it possibly can accomplish. This is its aim—and when this is attained, its end is fulfilled. It can do no more."

On what basis, then, were the "true and faithful representatives" to make *their* decisions? They were to do so in the context of the total interest of the community, rather than that of the individual. In line with his theory of human behavior, Calhoun viewed society as a congeries of interests, primarily but not exclusively economic, in perpetual conflict with each other. These interests always strive for supremacy, and in the process of so doing tend to combine with others like them for the aggrandizement of their own group. Such combinations result in two hostile parties, each determined to seize "control of the powers of the government, and, thereby, of its honors and emoluments."

The only way to resolve this ongoing clash of interests, particularly as it was sharpening between the South and the North, was to work out a political-constitutional organism that would give weight to combined units of comparable interests within each region. Rather than treat the community (or geographic section) as a single unit and base its representation on mere numbers, Calhoun proposed representation by great and permanent interests, whether they be two or three or more. The voting unit, in other words, should be the economic group in a community and not the individual citizen-voter. Only by such a system would the South be able to overcome the North's steadily growing numerical preponderance in Congress and retain its political influence in the federal government.

Calhoun put it, ". . . in a word, instead of considering the community of twenty-four a single community, having a common interest, and to be governed by a single will of an entire majority, . . . the thirteen against the eleven, [we should] take the will, not of the twenty-four as a unit, but of the thirteen and eleven separately—the majority of each governing the parts, and where they concur governing the whole—and where they disagree, arresting the action of the government."

Calhoun is said to have explained his complicated theory of the concurrent majority to a farmer in the following illustration: If you have an association of seven equal partners, four shoemakers and three tanners, the majority would end up by exploiting the minority, because such is human nature. But this danger would be eliminated if you make a legal provision that the association could take action only when a majority of its constituent members—in this instance, a majority of the shoemakers and a majority of the tanners—agreed to it. Each would then speak with one voice for all the shoemakers and all the tanners through its own particular organ.

Calhoun believed that of the two modes of expressing community will and sentiment (numerical majority and concurrent majority) the latter was by far the most representative and hence the more equitable. It provided firm protection for every minority and, in reflecting true economic interests, it reflected the real sense of the community.

"[The] one regards numbers only," he wrote, "and considers the whole community as a unit, having but one common interest throughout. . . . The other, on the contrary, regards interests as well as numbers, considering the community as made up of different and conflicting interests, as far as the action of the government is concerned; and takes the sense of each through its majority or appropriate organ, and the united sense of all, as the sense of the entire community. The former of these I shall call the numerical or absolute majority; and the latter, the concurrent, or constitutional majority. I call it the constitutional majority, because it is an essential element in every constitutional government, be its form what it may."

Calhoun proposed that this idea of the concurrent majority be grafted into the United States constitutional system so that it could accomplish at least two major objectives. The first, in his eyes the most important, was that of giving the South an instrument for the perpetuation of its power inside the federal government; the second, which interlocked with the first at some points, was to provide the propertied classes with a constitutional protection against the excesses of democracy. Under a concurrent majority system, the South, acting as a bloc (made up of constituent but united economic parts), would always be in a position of controlling national legislation, even when the North had superior numbers in Congress. It would, in fact, destroy the value of numerical preponderance which the North possessed by virtue of its rapidly growing population.

Thus the South, acting on the principle of state sovereignty and rejecting the idea that a majority of the people of the nation had the right to impose its will upon a reluctant minority (or state), could always in effect veto national laws that it (or its ruling class) considered inimical —tariffs and antislavery acts, for example. "The government of the concurrent majority . . . excludes the possibility of oppression, by giving to each interest . . . —where there are established classes, the means of protecting itself, by its negative [veto], against all measures calculated to advance the peculiar interests of others at its expense."

In addition, once adopted, the principle of the concurrent majority would serve as a powerful check on northern democratic radicals and thereby protect the threatened interests of the capitalists there. Calhoun was convinced that planter and capitalist, despite the existing antagonism between them, had a common goal in defending property and class rule. As far back as 1828, more than twenty years before he wrote *A Disquisition,* he had observed in his *South Carolina Exposition* how the northern-based capitalist system was paralleling that of Europe by making the rich richer and the poor poorer, thereby unavoidably generating ultimate class war.

"The contest will be between the capitalists and operatives [workers]," he had stated; "for into these two classes it must, ultimately, divide society. The issue of the struggle here must be the same as it has been in Europe. Under the operation of the system, wages must sink more rapidly than the prices of the necessaries of life, till the operatives will be reduced to the lowest point, when the portion of the products of their labor left to them, will be barely sufficient to preserve existence."

As the North increased its population and enlarged its industrial centers, the class struggle was bound to grow more acute until it would end with demagogues, acting in the name of democracy, being voted into power by a numerical majority of propertyless whites. There was, Calhoun thought, more to fear from that white proletariat than "from our own slaves," for (he pointed out in *A Disquisition*) they would soon be numerous enough to take advantage of "governments of the numerical majority" and "obtain control" of the whole society.

Calhoun viewed the northern economic and political system with strong alarm. Capitalist exploitation of labor—"leaving," he told Arthur Brisbane, "the laborer to shift for himself in age and disease"—was bad enough, but unchecked democracy was far worse. Calhoun even disliked the label *democrat*. He wrote to R. B. Rhett (September 13, 1838): "The word democrat better applies to the North than the South, and as usually understood means those who are in favour of the government of the absolute numerical majority to which I am utterly opposed and the prevalence of which would destroy our system and destroy the South."

By putting a limit on democracy as well as on the national authority of the federal government, through his constitutional device of the concurrent majority, Calhoun hoped to maintain the status quo—to preserve the social-economic system of the South, prevent "social dissolution" in the North, and save the Union from disintegration. These were his irreducible terms. They were in vain.

He had constructed his political theory on too narrow a base. A sharply realistic observer of social forces, he nevertheless ignored them in his political calculations and expectations. His vision of human destiny was too restricted, and the system he proposed did not take into consideration the hopes and aspirations of people other than the ruling class to which he belonged. It is ironic that Calhoun, the harsh realist, failed precisely where Jefferson, the "utopian" idealist, succeeded—in the intangible realm of the human heart and spirit, the stuff of politics as of life in general.

In the end, planter and capitalist did not join forces in defense of class rule, as Calhoun had hoped. The nation did not embrace his theory of the concurrent majority. The people did not accept the idea of human inequality. The country did not tolerate the principle of nullification that he advocated.

Calhoun's last great speech—made in the Senate shortly before his death on March 31, 1850—in a sense summed up his life work. In it he delivered what amounted to an ultimatum to the rest of the nation: Unless the North stopped agitating against slavery, the South would leave the federal union; "the responsibility of saving the Union rests on the North, and not on the South." Symbolically, the American nation gave its answer through Lincoln's warning: "A house divided against itself cannot stand."

On April 12, 1861, eleven years after Calhoun's death, his native state, speaking through the cannon of Fort Sumter, gave irrevocable voice to his ultimate commitments. Calhoun's cause died in a welter of fratricidal blood, but his personality lives as a monumental reminder that the ideal of equality and democracy needs constant defense against grim and sincere critics—such as the formidable senator from South Carolina.

# 10

## *THE AMERICAN:* Abraham Lincoln *(1809–1865)*

*You have in him the type and flower of our growth. It is as if Nature had made a typical American, and then had added with liberal hand the royal quality of genius.... Lincoln owed nothing to his birth, everything to his growth.... Lincoln could understand men of all sorts and from every region of the land: seemed himself, indeed, to be all men by turns, as mood succeeded mood in his strange nature. He never ceased to stand, in his bony angles, the express image of the ungainly frontiersman. His mind never lost the vein of coarseness that had marked him grossly when a youth. And yet how he grew and strengthened in the real stuff of dignity and greatness.... He kept always the shrewd and seeing eye of the woodsman and the hunter, and the flavor of wild life never left him: and yet how easily his view widened to great affairs; how surely he perceived the value and the significance of whatever touched him.*

—*Woodrow Wilson, speech* (*Newark, N.J., May 16, 1895*)

History's answer to Calhoun was Lincoln. The severest challenge to the democratic ideal ever made by an American was taken up and refuted by another, greater American.

Of books about Lincoln and the Civil War, in which he was the central figure, there is no end. And with good reason. Lincoln remains a man of unplumbed depths. Next to Jefferson, whom he admired, he is the spiritual fountainhead of the philosophy of American democracy and the symbol of freedom.

Lincoln's life is a story stunning in its simplicity. Born in log-cabin poverty, he painfully educated himself, rose from comparative obscurity to national leadership in a nearly-fatal crisis, saved the United States from dissolution, and, at the moment of victory, was slain by an assassin. From humble birth in 1809 to martyr's death in 1865, the life of Lincoln follows the classic lines of tragic greatness.

Lincoln occupied the center stage of history for less than half a dozen years. At the time of his nomination for the Presidency he was so little known as a national figure that people were not even certain how to spell his name. On June 4, 1860, Lincoln wrote to George Ashmun, Chairman of the Republican Party: "It seems as if the question whether my first name is 'Abraham' or 'Abram' will never be settled. It is 'Abraham.'" But from his first emergence out of the Illinois prairie into public view —in 1858, when he met the powerful Senator Stephen A. Douglas in a debate about slavery—Lincoln began to fascinate certain observers. He both attracted and repelled, often simultaneously. "He was," Sherwood Anderson said, "like a tree, having its roots in black mire, its upper branches reaching toward the sky." Nathaniel Hawthorne, when he first saw the loose-jointed and uncouth figure, thought him to be "about the homeliest man I ever saw, yet by no means repulsive or disagreeable."

His physical appearance was bizarre. Inordinately tall, bony, stoop-shouldered, his dark hair was too coarse, his skin too sallow, his neck too scrawny, his arms too long, his hands too furrowed, his feet too big. He was awkward in his movements. His big, rail-splitter's hands and his ill-fitting, countrified clothes exaggerated the angularity of his thin body. In a letter to J. W. Fell (December 1859) he described his person in three lines: "I am, in height, six feet, four inches, nearly; lean in flesh, weighing, on an average, one hundred and eighty pounds; dark complexion, with coarse black hair, and grey eyes." The gauntness of his clean-shaven face was so naked that, during the campaign of 1860, it moved eleven-year-old Grace Bedell to write him: "if you will let your whiskers grow . . . you would look a great deal better for your face is so thin." To which Lincoln, with his usual gentleness, replied (October 19, 1860): "As to the whiskers, having never worn any, do you not think people would call it a piece of silly affectation if I were to begin now?" But begin he did soon after. And so the image of the historic Lincoln, on postage stamps and on five-dollar bills among others, has come down with whiskers.

His appearance seemed decidedly odd to such observes as Carl Schurz, the German-American Republican leader, who describes in his *Reminiscences* his first meeting with Lincoln. It was on the way to Quincy,

Illinois, October 15, 1858, as "Old Abe" got on the train, going to debate with Douglas: "I must confess that I was somewhat startled by his appearance. There he stood, overtopping by several inches all those surrounding him. Although measuring something over six feet myself, I had, standing quite near to him, to throw my head backward in order to look into his eyes. . . . On his head he wore a somewhat battered 'stovepipe' hat. His neck emerged, long and sinewy, from a white collar turned down over a thin black necktie. His lank, ungainly body was clad in a rusty black dress coat with sleeves that should have been longer; but his arms appeared so long that the sleeves of a 'store' coat could hardly be expected to cover them all the way down to the wrists. His black trousers, too, permitted a very full view of his large feet. On his left arm he carried a gray woolen shawl, which evidently served him for an overcoat in chilly weather. His left hand held a cotton umbrella of the bulging kind, and also a black satchel. . . . His right he had kept free for hand shaking, of which there was no end. . . . I had seen, in Washington, and in the West, several public men of rough appearance; but none whose looks seemed quite so uncouth, not to say grotesque, as Lincoln's."

When Lincoln spoke, the black-ringed eyes, set deep in his melancholy face, lighted up with flashes of animation and humor. Observers were surprised at the rapidity with which his mobile face could be transformed from brooding sadness to infectious radiance. His voice was not rich, nothing remotely comparable to the golden tones of the most famous contemporary champion of the larynx, Edward Everett—who held the audience spellbound with his oratorical marathon at Gettysburg, where Lincoln's few and simple words were all but ignored by the press. Lincoln's voice, according to his friend and law partner William Henry Herndon, was "shrill, squeaking, piping, unpleasant." But there was power behind the man and his words, stark simplicity, and a sweep of relentless logic and cool earnestness that commanded attention without recourse to oratorical embroidery. At his best, he had a genius for shaping simple sentences into the music of poetry.

No portrait of Lincoln can be complete without reference to his humor and story-telling. His irrepressible penchant for telling jokes, even in moments of crisis, and his habit of prefacing serious comments with a "That reminds me . . . ," infuriated earnest souls but were a source of pleasure to friends (and voters). The jokes were earthy, corny, and often very funny. There is no doubt that Lincoln was a natural humorist, a born "funny man," who told amusing stories for the sheer joy of it.

Ralph Waldo Emerson, who was not addicted to jokes, was struck on his visit to the White House in 1862 by the "boyish cheerfulness" of the President who, after he told his joke, "looks up at you with great satisfaction, and shows all his white teeth, and laughs."

But there was more to it than the personal pleasure of jesting. Lincoln found in story-telling an effective method of communication, particularly with untutored and unsophisticated country audiences. For a gifted raconteur like Lincoln, what better way was there to adorn a tale and point a moral? In addition, the funny stories served as a shield for a personality that was, despite surface coarseness, profoundly sensitive.

One reaction to Lincoln's jests can be seen in this comment which appeared in the Springfield (Illinois) *Register* on November 18, 1863, the day before the Gettysburg Address: "Nothing could have been more inappropriate than to have invited that prince of jokers, Old Abe, to be present at the consecration of the Gettysburg cemetery. But having been invited, it was hoped by his apologists that he would at least refrain from his clownish jokes while standing over the new-made graves of the thousands who had been slain in the recent battle."

As history has shown, the newspapers' fears were entirely unjustified. Nothing could have been more moving, more suitable to the occasion than the Gettysburg Address. But for Lincoln humor was sometimes a cover for misfortunes, both personal and political. To a Congressman who, reporting a disastrous event and getting in reply Lincoln's customary "That reminds me . . . ," jumped up in a rage, the President said gently: "Now, you sit down! If I couldn't tell these stories I would die."

The Lincoln stories, now part of America's folklore, are particularly memorable because political humor is a rare commodity. Men of politics are, as a rule, a humorless lot. For every Disraeli there are dozens of Gladstones; for every Lincoln or Alben Barkley, scores of Adamses. Apart from Lincoln, only two or three other Presidents, among them Franklin D. Roosevelt, had political humor, and they were generally inclined to make their jokes in private (as did James Madison). In the case of Lincoln, his amusing stories, told in public, added to the store of political wisdom and thereby enriched the American mind.

A few stories will illustrate the Lincoln touch, which could, on occasion be rapier-sharp but was customarily gentle–funny. During a discussion in Congress that proposed to raise funds for more public works by imposing duties on unbuilt canals, Lincoln remarked: "The idea . . . involves the same absurdity as the Irish bull about the new boots. 'I shall nivir get 'em on,' says Patrick, 'till I wear 'em a day or two, and stretch 'em a little.' " Of the Mexican War, which Lincoln, like so many others, including Ulysses S. Grant,* opposed as an act of unprovoked aggression by the United States, he said that it reminded him of the Illinois farmer who used to say: "I ain't greedy 'bout land. I only want what jines mine."

At one of the debates with Douglas, the senator amused the audience by recalling that when he first knew Lincoln the latter was a grocery-keeper who, among other things, sold whiskey and was "a very good bartender." The nondrinking Lincoln turned the laugh on his opponent by admitting the truth of what Douglas said: "But I remember in those days that Mr. Douglas was one of my best customers. Many a time have I stood on one side of the counter and sold whiskey to Mr. Douglas on the other side, but the difference between us now is this: I have left my side of the counter, but Mr. Douglas still sticks to his as tenaciously as ever."

What were the influences that went into the making of Lincoln and that shaped his thought? Of prime importance was the impact of the frontier, with its harsh realities and day-to-day struggle for existence. Neither the Kentucky frontier, where Lincoln was born, nor the Indiana and Illinois settlements, where he spent his childhood and youth, suffered from urban stratification or caste. Life was rude and simple. There was little wealth, and position depended primarily on personal effort and character. Frontiersmen lived in mud, drank whiskey, chewed tobacco and spat where they sat or stood. They smelled of horses, stables, and sweat. In the summer they were bathed in perspiration, and in the winter they froze—young Lincoln's hands and feet were always cold. But there was a pervasive air of freedom, an instinctive democracy, and a sham-hating sense of equality, blunt-spoken and earthy. Old Abe—even in early life his bony face inspired the appellation—was the full product of this rough and redolent democratic environment.

And there were certain books, limited in number but lasting in influence, which young Lincoln hungrily read, digested, and made an integral part of himself. Foremost among these was the Bible, which left an indelible imprint on his writing and speaking style. In his boyhood he also read the Arabian Nights, Parson Weems' fabulous life of George Washington, Aesop's fables and Bunyan's *Pilgrim's Progress*. These and

* In his *Memoirs,* Grant, who served in the Mexican War, said of it: "To this day [I] regard the war . . . as one of the most unjust ever waged by a stronger against a weaker nation."

a few other books, including Isaac Watts' *Hymns* and some elementary American histories, he read by himself, for he had virtually no schooling. He did not begin to learn grammar until he was twenty-two years old, in New Salem, Illinois.

In "A Little Sketch," a terse autobiography he wrote on December 20, 1859, when the Republicans began to consider his possibilities as a presidential candidate, he wrote:

"My father, at the death of his father, was but six years of age; and he grew up, litterally [*sic*] without education. He removed from Kentucky to what is now Spencer county, Indiana, in my eighth year. We reached our new home about the time the State came into the Union [1816]. It was a wild region, with many bears and other wild animals, still in the woods. There I grew up. There were some schools, so called; but no qualification was ever required of a teacher beyond 'readin, writin, and cipherin' to the Rule of Three. . . . There was absolutely nothing to excite ambition for education. . . . I have not been to school since. The little advance I now have upon this store of education, I have picked up from time to time under the pressure of necessity."

In his profession, that of law, Lincoln was also self-taught. The law being a ladder to personal advancement and political office, the ambitious young Lincoln prepared himself for the bar, which he passed in 1836 at twenty-seven, unaided by teachers. Referring to this self-training, he wrote (to Isham Reavis, late in 1855), "It is but a small matter whether you read *with* anybody or not. I did not read with anyone. Get the books, and read and study them till you understand them in their principal features; and that is the main thing. It is of no consequence to be in a large town while you are reading. . . . The *books,* and your capacity for understanding them, are just the same in all places."

The first law book he read was the statutes of Indiana (which included the Declaration of Independence and the federal Constitution), but his professional training was rooted in Sir William Blackstone's celebrated *Commentaries on the Laws of England* (1765–68), a four-volume work which for generations nourished America's lawyers, including Thomas Jefferson and John Marshall. Lincoln studied legal propositions (without challenging Blackstone's dubious philosophical assumptions in matters such as the "right of things" and the scientific nature of legal principles) with single-minded tenacity. He took up unaccustomed words and phrases, dug into their meaning, turned them this way and that, searched for their inner logic, and worried each concept until it made sense to his practical mind.

"In the course of my law reading," he explained to the Reverend J. P. Gulliver who, on a train in 1860, asked him how he had acquired his rare talent for lucid expression, "I constantly came upon the word *demonstrate*. I thought, at first, that I understood its meaning, but soon became satisfied that I did not. I said to myself, 'What do I mean when I *demonstrate* more than when I *reason* or prove? How does *demonstration* differ from any other proof? I consulted Webster's dictionary. That told of 'certain proof,' 'proof beyond the possibility of doubt'; but I could form no sort of idea what sort of proof that was. I thought that a great many things were proved beyond the possibility of a doubt, without recourse to any such extraordinary process of reasoning as I understood *demonstration* to be. I consulted all the dictionaries and books of reference I could find, but with no better results. You might as well have defined *blue* to a blind man. At last, I said, 'Lincoln, you can never make a lawyer if you do not understand what *demonstrate* means'; and I left my situation in Springfield, went home to my father's house, and stayed there until I could give any proposition in the six books of Euclid at sight. I then found out what *demonstrate* means, and went back to my law studies."

The need for definition became a kind of passion with him. It saved him from the ballast of verbiage that was the affliction of so many public figures and writers of his day. He was not satisfied until the words and ideas that he used were shaped clearly in his mind. In handling a thought, he said in later life, he was never easy until he had "bounded it north, and bounded it south, and bounded it east, and bounded it west."

Lincoln was never a great reader or book collector, although he had a reverence for learning. "This is not," he said, "because I am not an educated man. I feel the need of reading. It is a loss to a man not to have grown up among books." While reading for the law, he borrowed some books from friends, among them the works of Thomas Paine, Voltaire, Burns, and Shakespeare, the latter two of which he loved to read aloud and to memorize. During his presidency, he drew from the Library of Congress some 125 books, among them the writings of Thomas Jefferson in four volumes, General Henry Wager Halleck's *Elements of Military Art and Science,* Emerson's *Representative Men,* Plutarch's *Lives,* David Hume's *History of England,* and John Henry Walsh's *The Shot-Gun and Sporting Rifle*. He did not care much for history, distrusted biography as misleading, and had scant use for novels, although he seems to have read those of Mrs. Caroline Lee Whiting Hentz, the Massachusetts author of *Aunt Patty's Scrap-Bag* (1846) and *The Mob Cap* (1848). In general, Lincoln was not a bookish man, preferring to rely for his ideas upon his own shrewd sense and experience. "The truth about the whole matter is," said Herndon, who knew him as intimately as anyone, "that Mr. Lincoln read less and thought more than any man in his sphere in America."

What did his thought consist of and what contribution did he make to American political ideas? In studying a man like Lincoln, who was not a professional philosopher (any more than was Jefferson or Madison) but a man of action, it is necessary to summarize and refine his numerous utterances, addresses, conversations, letters, and basic policies in order to get a residue of fundamental views. Giving due allowance to human contradictions and political exigencies, one finds that Lincoln's basic position had a straight-line consistency and essential simplicity. He was, from first to last, a believer in human rights, individual dignity, personal liberty, and civil justice. His political ideas derived directly from the principles of the Declaration of Independence, which he often quoted, and from Jefferson, whom he considered "the most distinguished politician of our history." In the profoundest sense, therefore, Lincoln —moderate, just, undoctrinaire, and practical—was a liberal democrat. Where he differed from other democrats was in his genius for stating familiar ideas in a striking and symbolic form.

The essential Lincoln cannot be understood, or his contribution properly appreciated, without reference to the issue of Negro slavery, which tempered his soul and gave direction to his life. The institution of slavery, with its political and emotional complications, was the overriding reality of Lincoln's time. From the Missouri Compromise, which was passed when he was eleven, to the firing on Fort Sumter, which took place five weeks after he was inaugurated President at fifty-two, the issue of slavery directly or indirectly influenced the lives of Lincoln's generation. There was no escaping it. It was the American national tragedy.

Negro slavery began with the opening of American history, but it did not become a paramount issue until the nineteenth century. In 1619, a Dutch sea captain sold twenty "negars" as servants to Jamestown planters. This handful of unfree servants became the seed of the institution of slavery, which expanded steadily throughout the South. By 1760, the southern colonies had some 300,000 Negroes, with the supply constantly increased by English and Dutch traders. By the time of the Constitutional Convention of 1787, where the importation of slaves and the problem of the ratio of their representation in the new Congress were gravely debated and settled by compromise, there were about half a million Negroes in the country. This number increased sixfold in the succeeding decades, so that on the eve of the Civil War, of a total southern population of approximately eleven million, some three million were Negro slaves.

The existence of slavery in a country that was dedicated to democracy and to the ideal of freedom was a gigantic anomaly. It mocked the Declaration of Independence and the very foundations of the republic. Long before Lincoln was born, Jefferson said that slavery braved the wrath of God: "I tremble for my country when I reflect that God is just; that his justice cannot sleep forever." It troubled his conscience, as it did those of other leading slaveowners, such as George Washington, and disturbed his nights "like the gong of a fire bell." On every level of experience—economic, political and moral—slavery affected the whole country, permeating it like a miasma.

Economically, slavery contributed to an ever-widening gap between the two main sections of the nation. Two different, sharply contrasting, civilizations were developing under the same flag—one dynamic, industrial, and liberal; the other, rigid, agricultural, and feudal. While the northern states grew strong and prosperous on a venturesome business and individual-farm economy, both sustained by free labor that was constantly replenished by vigorous European immigration, the South remained stagnant and poor in its rural framework and its one- or two-crop agriculture. As the southern economist Hinton R. Helper wrote bitterly (and vainly) in his *Impending Crisis of the South* (1860), "It is a fact well known to every intelligent Southerner that we are compelled to go to the North for almost every article of utility and adornment, from matches, shoepegs and paintings up to cotton-mills, steamships and statuary; that we have no foreign trade, no princely merchants, nor respectable artists; that, in comparison with the free states, we contribute nothing to the literature, polite arts and inventions of the age."

This condition of nearly total cultural sterility, the result of the plantation economy, was to persist for generations after the Civil War. In 1920, H. L. Mencken could write, with exaggeration but with a core of solid truth: "There are single acres in Europe that house more first-rate men than all the states south of the Potomac. . . . It would be impossible in all history to match so complete a drying-up of a civilization. . . . In all that gargantuan paradise of the fourth-rate there is not a single picture gallery worth going into, or a single opera-house, or a single theater devoted to decent plays, or a single public monument (built since the [Civil] War) that is worth looking at, or a single workshop devoted to the making of beautiful things. . . . When you come to critics, musical composers, painters, sculptors, architects, and the like, you will have to give up, for there is not even a bad one between the Potomac mud-flats and the Gulf. Nor an historian. Nor a sociologist. Nor a philosopher. Nor a theologian. Nor a scientist. In all these fields the South is an awe-inspiring blank—a brother of Portugal, Serbia and Esthonia."

The southern economy, and hence the region's social system and political structure, revolved around a plantation system that was feudal in practice and narrowly aristocratic in outlook. The life of the South was dominated by a planter aristocracy consisting of about 2500 families, each of which had one hundred slaves or more. Next to this "conceited and tyrannical" minority, as Helper called it, there was another group of about 300,000 men who owned ten or fewer slaves each. Most of the white population—at least three fourths—had no slaves at all and no direct interest in the slavery system. But for a variety of reasons—emotional, racial, cultural, political—this large majority of truly poor whites, sunk in "galling poverty and ignorance" (to quote Helper again), was under the influence of the planters whom they supported unto death.

In Lincoln's day, new states were opening up in the Louisiana Territory of the North and West, where under the Missouri Compromise of 1820 slavery was forbidden, and the southern planters felt themselves doomed thereby. If this process continued, it was mathematically certain that the new senators from the free states would outvote the planters in the Senate, where the South had maintained the balance of power for decades. Politically skilled and audacious, brilliantly led by such men as John C. Calhoun, the planters were determined to do all in their power—through influence and pressure on the federal judiciary, the White House, and the Congress—to block developments that menaced their existence as a privileged minority. They achieved a temporary triumph in 1854, with the passing of the Kansas–Nebraska Act. This act, which declared the principle of "popular sovereignty" in the territories to be admitted into the Union, in effect repealed the Missouri Compromise by establishing the doctrine of congressional nonintervention in regard to slavery. It gave the planters a chance to foist the slave system on the new states.

The Kansas–Nebraska Act, followed three years later by the Dred Scott decision (1857) which declared the Missouri Compromise unconstitutional, was a Pyrrhic victory for the South. It reopened the whole question of slavery as an institution, and refocused the eyes of the rest of the nation on the tremendous political power wielded by the southern minority. It supplied new fuel to the northern abolitionist movement and further inflamed those who felt that slavery not only threatened the political foundations of American democracy but was also a moral outrage that should not be tolerated by a civilized country. It stimulated the emergence of a new political party—the National Republican Party—with strong antislavery planks. And, finally, it brought out Abraham Lincoln and catapulted him to national attention through his speeches and debates on the flaming issue of slavery. "I was losing interest in politics," he said in his autobiographical sketch, "when the repeal of the Missouri Compromise aroused me again."

The Republican party platform of 1860, on which Lincoln ran, declared among other things that the recent constitutional interpretation of the right to carry slavery into the territories was "dangerous political heresy"; that the normal condition of all U.S. Territories was "that of freedom"; that the opening of the slave trade was a "crime against humanity, and a burning shame to our country and age"; and that Kansas should be admitted as a free state.

Lincoln himself was not an abolitionist, at least not in principle. He had not joined any movement against slavery. He had none of the passionate hatred of slavery that burned in the hearts of martyrs like Elijah Parish Lovejoy and John Brown, or abolitionists like William Lloyd Garrison and John Hossack.

Garrison's "Statement of Principles," printed in his abolitionist Journal, *The Liberator* (January 1, 1831), echoed through the conscience of America for decades: "I am aware, that many object to the severity of my language; but is there not cause for severity? I will be as harsh as truth, and as uncompromising as justice. On this subject, I do not wish to think, or speak, or write, with moderation. . . . I am in earnest—I will not equivocate—I will not excuse—I will not retreat a single inch—AND I WILL BE HEARD."

Scottish-born Hossack, convicted in a Chicago federal court in 1860 for helping to rescue a Negro fugitive, said to the judge: "I came, Sir, from the tyranny of the Old World, when but a lad, landed upon American shores, having left my kindred and native land in pursuit of some place where men of toil would not be crushed by the property-holding class. Sir, I place myself upon the Constitution in the presence of a nation who have the Declaration of Independence read to them every Fourth of July, and profess to believe it. . . . The parties who prostitute the Constitution to the support of slavery are traitors—traitors not only to the liberties of millions of enslaved countrymen, but traitors to the Constitution itself.... Sir, the world never has furnished so great a congregation of hypocrites as those that formed the Constitution, if they designed to make it the greatest slaveholder, slave-breeder, and slave-catcher on earth."

Unlike such men as Garrison and Hossack, Lincoln was temperamentally incapable of *any* hatred or immoderation. Even during the bitterest moments of the Civil War, he had "malice toward none" and favored, he said, "short statutes of limitation" on hatreds. Nor did he particularly like—or dislike—Negroes as such. To him, Negroes were people in an unfortunate position, to be treated as human beings. Lincoln did not pretend that Negroes in their present state of existence were his social equals, but he was not patronizing toward them. During the Civil War, he invited Frederick Douglass, the Negro writer and abolitionist orator who had been born a slave, to the White House for a "cup of tea"—the first such honor for a colored man. "Mr. Lincoln," Douglass said later, "is one of the few white men I ever passed an hour with, who failed to remind me in some way before the interview terminated, that I was a Negro."

In his *Lectures on American Slavery* (1851), Douglass, born on a Maryland plantation around 1817, had thus described the system: "I grew up... as a SLAVE.... I feel that I have a right to speak, and to speak *strongly*.... The law gives the master absolute power over the slave. He may work him, flog him, hire him out, sell him, and in certain contingencies, *kill* him, with perfect impunity. The slave is... divested of all rights—reduced to the level of a brute...—placed beyond the circle of human brotherhood...—his name... is inserted in a *master's ledger,* with horses, sheep and swine. In law, the slave has no wife, no children, no country, and no home. He can own nothing, possess nothing, acquire nothing.... He toils that another may reap.... To ensure good behavior, the slaveholder relies on *the whip*...; to bind down the spirit of the slave, to imbrute and destroy his manhood, he relies on *the whip,* the chain, the gag, the thumb-screw, the pillory, the bowie-knife, the pistol, and the blood-hound.... The physical cruelties are... sufficiently... revolting; but they are as a few grains of sand... compared with the stupendous wrongs which it inflicts on the mental, moral and religious nature of its... victims."

Lincoln's political attitude toward slavery evolved gradually. In purely human terms, he had always disliked the degradation that it involved. The cruelties of the slave system, which, as a native southerner, he could not avoid witnessing, tormented him, as he reminded his friend Joshua F. Speed, in a letter dated August 24, 1855:

"In 1841 you and I had together a tedious low-water trip on a Steam Boat from Louisville to St. Louis. You may remember, as I well do, that from Louisville to the mouth of the Ohio there were on board, ten or a dozen slaves, shackled together with irons. That sight was a continual torment to me; and I see something like it every time I touch the Ohio, or any other slave-border. It is hardly fair for you to assume, that I have no interest in a thing which has, and continually exercises, the power of making me miserable."

But for a long time Lincoln closed his eyes to the evil. In this, he said he was like the great body of northern people who "crucify their feelings," keeping silent in order not to endanger the frail federal union. He had hoped that slavery, if not interfered with, might somehow die "a natural death." At any rate, he did not honestly know how to solve the terrible problem without violence, which, to the very last, he hoped could be avoided. Even as late as October 1854, in a speech at Peoria, Illinois, Lincoln frankly admitted that the slavery issue, involving the deepest human passions and politics, as well as questions of economics and social equality, was almost beyond him.

"If all earthly power were given me," he said, "I should not know what to do, as to the existing institution [of slavery]. My first impulse would be to free all the slaves, and send them to Liberia,*—to their own native land. But a moment's reflection would convince me that . . . its sudden execution is impossible. If they were all landed there in a day, they would all perish in the next ten days. . . . What then? Free them all, and keep them among us as underlings? Is it quite certain that this betters their condition? . . . What next? Free them, and make them politically and socially our equals? My own feelings will not admit of this; and if mine would, we well know that those of the great mass of white people will not. . . . A universal feeling, whether well or ill-founded, can not be safely disregarded. We can not, then, make them equals. It does seem to me that systems of gradual emancipation might be adopted. . . ."

* Founded in 1822 by American Negro freemen and colonization societies for the purpose of solving the United States' slavery problem, Liberia never fulfilled the expectation of its founders. Some of the reasons for the failure were mentioned by Lincoln. Today, Liberia, on the southwest coast of Africa, is a republic (since July 1847), the constitution of which is modeled after that of the United States, but the population (estimated at nearly three million) is almost entirely African Negro.

Under the pressures of the intensifying crisis in the 1850s, Lincoln was driven, step by step, to think through the harsh realities of the slavery problem. This he did laboriously, but with the relentless logic that marked his mature utterances. An example of this inner struggle to achieve honest clarity is his undated fragment on the logic of slavery, which he jotted down for himself—probably sometime in 1854:

> If A can prove, however conclusively, that he may, of right, enslave B,—why may not B snatch the same argument, and prove equally that he may enslave A?
>
> You say A is white, and B is black. It is *color*, then; the lighter, having the right to enslave the darker? Take care. By this rule, you are to be the slave of the first man you meet, with a fairer skin than your own.
>
> You do not mean *color* exactly?—You mean the whites are *intellectually* the superiors of the blacks, and to therefore have the right to enslave them? Take care again. By this rule, you are to be the slave to the first man you meet with an intellect superior to your own.
>
> But, say you, it is a question of *interest;* and, if you can make it your *interest,* you have the right to enslave another. Very well. And if he can make it his interest, he has the right to enslave you.

First in his own mind, then in public speeches and debates, Lincoln proceeded to demolish the rationale of slavery with merciless logic. To those, like John C. Calhoun, who argued that slavery was a desirable state of existence, Lincoln's answer was drily devastating: "Although volume upon volume is written to prove slavery a very good thing, we never hear of the man who wishes to take the good of it *by being a slave himself.*" The standard and widely current charge that equal rights for Negroes would lead to racial mixture, Lincoln contemptuously rejected as a fraudulent argument. "I protest, now and forever," he said in Chicago in 1858, "against that counterfeit logic which presumes that because I do not want a Negro woman for a slave, I do necessarily want her for a wife. My understanding is that I need not have her for either; but, as God made us separate, we can leave one another alone, and do one another much good thereby."

Lincoln's position on slavery finally crystallized around two fundamental and intertwined ideas. One was that slavery, even apart from being morally abhorrent, was a continuing threat to American democracy; and that unless it was in some way eradicated it would end by wrecking freedom altogether. The other principle was that the solution of the slavery problem must not be such as to lead to the destruction of the national union. In the process of working his way toward a solution of the looming national crisis, he refined and formulated conceptions about justice and freedom that have not only enriched the American heritage, but the whole philosophy of democracy as well.

First, he asked himself, what is government? What purpose does it serve? In view of the fact that, historically, government had nearly always been onerous and tyrannical. "*Most governments* have been based, practically, on the denial of the equal rights of men"—why did it exist? "Why, then," he wrote in 1854, "should we have government? Why not each individual take to himself the whole fruit of his labor, without having any of it taxed away, in services, corn, or money? Why not take just so much land as he can cultivate with his own hands, without buying it of anyone?"

He answered that government was needed in civilized society because individual effort was not enough to accomplish basic social objectives. He defined government as "a combination of the people of a country to effect certain objects by joint efforts." Those legitimate objects were, in the main, three: services, security, and freedom.

Among the vital services performed by government, he cited "making and maintaining roads, bridges, and the like; providing for the helpless young and afflicted; common schools; and disposing of deceased men's property." As for the security function of government, it embraced both military action and police powers. So long as men "will make war upon one another," government must of necessity organize itself for self-defense. In regard to police powers, including courts and jails and the whole paraphernalia of the law, those were needed because some individuals in society were always prone to violence: "If some men will kill, or beat, or constrain others, or despoil them of property, by force, fraud, or non compliance with contracts, it is a common object with peaceful and just men to prevent it."

But the most important of the legitimate objects of government was the maintenance of freedom, which embraced both the idea of justice and of equality. This was at the core of Lincoln's political thought. To him democratic government, particularly that of America as it derived from the promises of the Declaration of Independence, was inconceivable without freedom. Take away freedom, Lincoln asked, and what do you have? You may still have government, but it would not be an *American* government; it would be akin to a Czarist autocracy, or a southern slavocracy dominated by "a small, odious, and detested class" of "slave-breeders and slave-traders."

Lincoln's opinion of Czarist Russia is seen in the August 24, 1855, letter to Joshua F. Speed. On the subject of the Know-nothings, whose racist, antialien and anti-Catholic views troubled and disgusted him, he said: "You inquire where I now stand. . . . I am not a Know-nothing; that is certain. How could I be? How can any one who abhors the oppression of Negroes be in favor of degrading classes of white people? Our progress in degeneracy appears to me to be pretty rapid. As a nation we began by declaring that 'all men are created equal.' We now practically read it 'all men are created equal except Negroes.' When the Know-nothings get control, it will read 'all men are created equal except Negroes and foreigners and Catholics.' When it comes to this, I shall prefer emigrating to some country where they make no pretense of loving liberty,—to Russia, for instance, where despotism can be taken pure, and without the base alloy of hypocrisy."

What did Lincoln mean by *freedom?* He admitted that the word was difficult to define and that it had, in fact, never been really defined. The confusion existing around the term *freedom* (or *liberty*) was due to the fact that it was widely used to convey conflicting interests. The slaveholder, for example, insisted that under the federal Constitution he had absolute freedom to use and consume the labor of other (black) men. Those who challenged him were regarded by the planters as enemies of freedom. As Lincoln put it in a speech at Baltimore (April 1864): "The shepherd drives the wolf from the sheep's throat, for which the sheep thanks the shepherd as a *liberator,* while the wolf denounces him for the same act as the destroyer of liberty, especially as the sheep was a black one. Plainly the sheep and the wolf are not agreed upon a definition of the word liberty; and precisely the same difference prevails today among us human creatures, even in the North, and all professing to love liberty."

Freedom should not mean the exclusive right of the wolf over the sheep. The "wolf's dictionary," Lincoln said, should be repudiated in favor of a *general* equality of human rights, including the fundamental one of choosing one's means of livelihood and consuming the produce of one's labor. This conception of freedom, basic to the whole democratic idea, obviously contained no room for the institution of slavery. In a fragment, written around 1858, Lincoln formulated it pithily: "As I would not be a *slave,* so I would not be a *master.* This expresses my idea of democracy. Whatever differs from this, to the extent of the difference, is no democracy."

Freedom, Lincoln argued, is indivisible. You cannot, he pointed out, long deprive one particular group of people of their basic human rights without ultimately imperiling the rights of all. Toleration of even partial injustice slowly corrodes the whole spirit of the community; a worm deep inside a beautiful apple gradually rots it outward from within. In a remarkable speech at Edwardsville, Illinois, in 1858, Lincoln thus developed the theme of the integrity of freedom:

> When ... you have succeeded in dehumanizing the negro; when you have put him down, and made it forever impossible for him to be but as the beasts of the field; when you have extinguished his soul and placed him where the ray of hope is blown out in darkness like that which broods over the spirits of the damned; are you quite sure that the demon you have roused will not turn and rend you? What constitutes the bulwark of our own liberty and independence? It is not our frowning battlements or bristling sea coasts. ... These are not our reliance against a resumption of tyranny. ... Our reliance is in the love of liberty which God has planted in our bosoms. Our defence is in the preservation of the spirit which prized liberty as the heritage of all men, in all lands everywhere. Destroy this spirit and you have planted the seeds of despotism at your own doors. Familiarize yourselves with the chains of bondage and you prepare your own limbs to wear them. Accustomed to trample on the rights of others, you have lost the genius of your own independence and become the fit subjects of the first cunning tyrant who rises among you.

His conception of freedom was mingled with his ideas on economics and on equality. These were not complicated notions. In common with the Free-soil western Whigs, Lincoln was a believer in simple "small capitalism," based on open opportunity and deriving from reward for personal effort. The emphasis here is on "smallness" and "individualism." For large-scale capitalism, with its enthronement of the profit motive as the goal of life and its ramified financial-economic operations, Lincoln had as little sympathy as Jefferson or John Taylor. It was not that he was an agrarian, but he was a westerner who may not have altogether understood the intricacies of the capitalist system, as it was developing in the eastern states and was even then beginning to transform the country. To a product of the agrarian West like Lincoln, capitalist enterprise, permeating the nation's political life and depending on the functional use of labor as an impersonal force, was something alien. Lincoln, insofar as he understood capitalism, rejected its attitude toward labor as being nothing but a dependency of capital, as a fundamentally "false" assumption. His economic ideas seem not to have been enriched by any reading of Ricardo, Malthus, or Mill (or Marx, who in the 1850s was the London correspondent of the *New York Tribune*).

"Labor is prior to, and independent of capital," Lincoln said in his first annual message to Congress (December 3, 1861). "Capital is only the fruit of labor, and could never have existed if labor had not first existed. Labor is the superior of capital, and deserves much the higher consideration. Capital has its rights, which are as worthy of protection as any other rights. Nor is it denied that there is, and probably always will be, a relation between labor and capital producing mutual benefits. The error is in assuming that the whole labor of the community exists within that relation. . . . A large majority belong to neither class—neither work for others, nor have others working for them. . . ."

Lincoln spoke for this "large majority" of Americans, "average" men who were neither rich nor poor, who worked to support themselves and to improve their economic position; if they became wealthy, that was their right and good luck. Lincoln accepted it as axiomatic that men should be rewarded for their legitimate effort and skill and, like John Taylor, believed that there should be no institutional or governmental hindrance to individual economic activity or enterprise.

"I take it," he said in New Haven on March 6, 1860, "that it is best for all to leave each man free to acquire property as fast as he can. Some will get wealthy. I don't believe in a law to prevent a man from getting rich; it would do more harm than good. So while we do not propose any war upon capital, we do wish to allow the humblest man an equal chance to get rich with anybody else."

Open opportunity to acquire property or obtain reward for personal effort implied the idea of equality. Again the question arose: What was equality?

Was the Negro, for example, the equal of the white man? Lincoln did not pretend that, under the existing conditions of moral degradation and illiteracy, the Negro was in a position of equality with whites. What Lincoln argued for was equality of rights and opportunities.

He accepted and defended Jefferson's statement that "all men are created equal" (an assertion then being contemptuously dismissed by slaveholders as a "self-evident lie") on two grounds. First, the idea of equality, as stated in the Declaration of Independence, asserted general *rights* applicable to all men. Second, the concept was a formulation of standards that would serve as a guide to democratic conduct and a shield against potential despots—a "hard nut to crack," Lincoln said, for some future tyrant. Speaking at Springfield, Illinois, on June 26, 1857, he explained the Declaration of Independence:

I think the authors of that notable instrument intended to include *all* men, but they did not intend to declare all men equal *in all respects*. They did not mean to say all were equal in color, size, intellect, moral developments, or social capacity. They defined with tolerable distinctness in what respects they did consider all men created equal—equal in "certain inalienable rights, among which are life, liberty, and the pursuit of happiness." . . . They did not mean to assert the obvious untruth, that all were then actually enjoying that equality, nor yet that they were about to confer it immediately upon them. In fact, they had no power to confer such a boon. They meant simply to declare the right, so that enforcement of it might follow as fast as circumstances should permit. They meant to set up a standard maxim for free society, which should be familiar to all, and revered by all; constantly . . . spreading . . . and augmenting the happiness and value of life to all people of all colors everywhere.

As Lincoln interpreted the deeper meaning of the Declaration of Independence, the equality of rights and opportunities was basic to American democracy. It applied to Negro and white alike. "I want every man to have a chance," he said repeatedly. The American system of government, he believed, was set up for that purpose. "We proposed to give all a chance; and we expected the weak to grow stronger, the ignorant wiser, and all better and happier together." In his first debate with Douglas, at Ottawa, Illinois, on August 21, 1858, he stated bluntly that the struggle that was rending America was not over *social* equality but over *democratic* equality.

"There is no reason in the world why the negro is not entitled to all the natural rights enumerated in the Declaration of Independence," he said, "the right to life, liberty, and the pursuit of happiness. I hold that he is as much entitled to these as the white man. I agree with Judge Douglas he is not my equal in many respects—certainly not in color, perhaps not in moral or intellectual endowment. But in the right to eat the bread, without leave of anybody else, which his own hand earns, *he is my equal and the equal of Judge Douglas, and the equal of every living man.*"

The words of the humble and homely lawyer from Illinois struck an echo beyond the borders of his state. In a period of terrible national crisis, Lincoln's ideas, uttered on public platforms and clarified in debate, spoke to the heart of America and helped to crystallize opinion on the issues of slavery and union. He became symbolic of the fears, urgencies and hopes of the time. "Not often in the story of mankind," Carl Sandburg told a hushed joint session of Congress on the occasion of the 150th anniversary of Lincoln's birth, "does a man arrive on earth who is both steel and velvet, who is as hard as rock and soft as drifting fog." Nominated for the presidency by the antislavery Republican Party in 1860, Lincoln was elected by a minority of the national vote. As a result of a three-way split in the Democratic Party, he won 59 per cent of the electoral college, although his popular vote was only 39 per cent.*

With his election to the presidency, Lincoln faced the terrifying and unprecedented situation of a breakup of the federal union. Despite his known moderation and avowed intention not to interfere with slavery where it already existed, the South began to secede. "The people," wrote Alexander A. Stephens, the Georgia congressman who became Vice-President of the Confederacy, "are run mad. They are wild with passion and frenzy, doing they know not what." Reason fled from the political arena. South Carolina set the example of secession. On December 20 it declared in convention that its union with the "other States under the name of The United States of America is hereby dissolved." Others followed quickly. By the time Lincoln was inaugurated, seven states of the deep South * had seceded and formed their own Confederacy,** which was soon joined by the six remaining southern states. And so, as Lincoln took the customary oath of office to "preserve, protect, and defend the Constitution of the United States," the federal union had fallen apart.

Here was the ultimate test of Lincoln's character and statesmanship. Should he accept the advice of such influential Republicans as Horace Greeley of the *New York Tribune* and let the "wayward sisters depart in peace"? [But Greeley himself was not consistent. On December 22, 1860, he wrote to Lincoln: "Let the Union slide—it may be reconstructed; let Presidents be assassinated—we can elect more; let the

* The popular vote was 1,866,352 for Lincoln, and 2,841,519 combined for the three Democratic candidates (1,375,157 for Stephen A. Douglas, 849,781 for John C. Breckinridge, and 589,581 for John Bell). In the electoral college, out of a total of 303 votes, Lincoln got 180 (Douglas 12, Breckinridge 72, Bell 39). Lincoln did not win a single southern vote in the electoral college, but he carried all the northern ones, except New Jersey, which gave three of its four votes to Douglas. This clean North–South split in the electoral college made Lincoln a *northern-elected* President, an ominous sign for the nation.

* In addition to South Carolina, they were: Alabama [January 11], Florida [January 10], Georgia [January 19], Louisiana [January 26], Mississippi [January 9], and Texas [February 11].

** The Confederacy was set up at Montgomery, Alabama, on February 8, framed its own constitution [modeled after the federal one], and on February 9 elected Jefferson Davis President.

Republicans be defeated and crushed—we shall rise again; but another nasty compromise whereby everything is conceded and nothing secured will so thoroughly disgrace and humiliate us that we can never again raise our heads, and this country becomes a second edition of the Barbary States as they were sixty years ago]."

Could Lincoln in good conscience permit secession after having sworn to "protect" and "defend" the union? Was it politically possible to accept it without endangering the whole national fabric? Was it desirable from the point of view of freedom in general?

To all of these questions Lincoln gave an agonizingly painful *No*. He recoiled from the thought of fratricidal war, but if it had to come, he must, like a character in a Greek tragedy, accept it unflinchingly. As General William Tecumseh Sherman once remarked, when he refused to endorse the sentiment that "the pen is mightier than the sword": "Lincoln, who wielded a powerful and prolific pen, yet had to call to his assistance a million flaming swords." In his special message to Congress (July 4, 1861), delivered after the guns of the Civil War had already begun to bark,* Lincoln clarified the tragic situation by making three main points, each crucial to the idea of federal union and human freedom.

First, the United States was sovereign, and not the separate states. There was no legal or constitutional right to secession. With the possible exception of Texas, and even Texas, Lincoln argued, gave up its sovereignty "on coming into the Union," none of the states had ever been genuinely independent or possessed sovereignty. "Having never been [independent] States, either in substance or in name, *outside* of the Union, whence this magical omnipotence of 'State rights,' asserting a claim of power to lawfully destroy the Union itself?" Before the federal union, the states had not been sovereign but only colonies of Great Britain. Never having possessed any sovereignty, Lincoln said, the states had "no other *legal status*" except as members of the Union. If they break away, "they can only do so against law, and by revolution."

Second, no sovereign nation could permit the secession of any of its component members without facing total dissolution. Once the precedent is set, it would be followed by others, until no union was left. "If one State may secede, so may another . . ." Lincoln said. "If we now recognize this doctrine by allowing the seceders to go in peace, it is difficult

* The beginning of the Civil War is dated April 12, 1861, when the shore batteries of General Pierre G. T. Beauregard opened fire on the federal Fort Sumter, off Charleston, S.C.

to see what we can do, if others choose to go, or to extort terms upon which they will promise to remain."

Third, popular government is based on consent and free elections, the results of which cannot be challenged by the use of violence. To allow resort to force, after the votes have been freely cast, would be to destroy the very foundations of democracy: "When ballots have fairly and constitutionally decided, there can be no successful appeal back to bullets."

The southern "appeal to bullets" changed the whole character of the conflict between the North and South—from the problem of slavery to the question of national survival. Slavery became a secondary consideration. Lincoln's overriding concern was to save the Union. He told Horace Greeley in a letter dated August 22, 1862: "My paramount object in this struggle is to save the Union, and is *not* either to save or destroy slavery. If I could save the Union without freeing *any* slave, I would do it, and if I could save it by freeing all the slaves I would do it, and if I could save it by freeing some and leaving others alone, I would also do that."

In the end, the preservation of the Union and the freeing of the slaves were found to be inextricable goals. If the first objective succeeded, the second would follow. And when, on January 1, 1863, Lincoln signed the final Emancipation Proclamation,* which put a legal end to the institution of slavery, he said, "If my name ever goes into history, it will be for this act, and my whole soul is in it."

He was also aware that the fratricidal conflict, which was to cost more than 600,000 lives before it was over,* had significance beyond the frontiers of America. The Civil War was a war for human freedom everywhere.

He told Congress: "This is essentially a People's contest. On the side of the Union, it is a struggle for maintaining in the world, that form and substance of government, whose leading object is, to elevate the condition of men—to lift artificial weights from all shoulders—to clear the paths of laudable pursuit for all—to afford all, an unfettered start, and a fair chance, in the race of life."

* Now, therefore, I, Abraham Lincoln . . . , do order and declare that all persons held as slaves within said designated States . . . are, and henceforward shall be, free; and that the Executive government of the United States, including the military and naval authorities thereof, will recognize and maintain the freedom of said persons.

* Union casualties: 360,000 (including 110,000 deaths in battle). Confederate casualties: 258,000 (including 94,000 deaths in battle).

And so Abraham Lincoln, murdered at the age of fifty-six for his successful struggle to preserve the United States and the freedom of men, now towers beyond American history. By his words he deepened the meaning of democracy, and by his actions he widened the horizons of human dignity, giving his life to a universal ideal—"that government of the people, by the people, for the people, shall not perish from the earth."

# 11

## *THE AMERICAN AS PHILOSOPHER:*
# Ralph Waldo Emerson *(1803–1882)*

*Emerson is not only a philosopher, but . . . the Philosopher of Democracy . . . even if Emerson has no system, none the less he is the prophet and herald of any system which democracy may henceforth construct and hold by, and when democracy has articulated itself, it will have no difficulty in finding itself proposed in Emerson.*

—*John Dewey in* International Journal of Ethics (*July 1903*)

At first glance it may seem incongruous to include Ralph Waldo Emerson among political thinkers. He was essentially a poet and essayist, a man of letters in the classic sense, a professional writer and lecturer who deliberately eschewed politics and strove to remain above the battle. But the flavor of his personality and the influence of his teachings were such that he left an ineradicable imprint on the leaders and thinkers of his age. No account of American thought—whether its emphasis is on philosophy or theology or society or politics—can be complete without reference to Emerson.

Emerson bestrode his time, intellectually and morally, as no other American poet before him or since. In a rough age of materialism and violence, his life personified the triumph of the contemplative, sometimes even rarefied, mind. From 1837, when he delivered in Boston the Phi Beta Kappa address, "The American Scholar," to the end of the Civil War, when his faculties began to fail him, Emerson's was the voice that echoed throughout the land proclaiming the values of the spirit. In articles and books and—above all—in lectures, the gentle poet–philosopher reached unprecedented audiences in every part of the expanding country. Everywhere, in teeming cities, and uncouth frontier settlements, he appealed to what was highest and noblest in the human character. He thus achieved the unique career of being, in the words of literary critic Alfred Kazin, "the teacher of the nation." He had to an extraordinary degree what Oliver Wendell Holmes called "the gift of imparting a ferment."

Born in Boston in 1803, during the third year of Jefferson's administration, Emerson was the product of nearly two centuries of New England Puritanism. Seven of his ancestors were preachers, among them Samuel Moody of Maine who pursued sinners even into the alehouse, Joseph Emerson of Malden who prayed nightly that no descendant of his should ever be rich, and William Emerson of Concord who died while serving in the Revolutionary Army. Emerson's father, the Reverend William Emerson, was minister of the First Church (Unitarian) in Boston; his son followed family tradition by becoming, in 1829, pastor of the Second Church (Unitarian) in the same city.

It was the powerful Puritan tradition that molded Emerson into a psychologically sensitive and mentally tough instrument of self-expression. His background was one of proverbial high thinking and frugal living, with emphasis on the virtues of self-reliance, sobriety, and morality. But the Calvinistic virtues, although they steel character, tend to crush emotional life. Rigid Puritanism all too frequently led to ugly self-repression, self-righteousness, and hypocrisy. But in the case of Emerson, who in his childhood suffered from the terrors of theology, the conflict between Calvinistic sternness and normal human emotions resulted in spiritual elevation and heightened introspection. It was this self-searching that led Emerson to keep a diary, which he began while he was still a youth at Harvard; it has remained to this day a multivolume treasury of his innermost thoughts as well as a matchless record of American culture in the nineteenth century.

From his earliest days, in keeping with family tradition, Emerson was a reader of books. He was brought up on the Greek and Roman classics and the Bible as well as the best in English literature, particularly Shakespeare, Bacon, and Milton. He rarely read novels and had a special dislike for his contemporaries Jane Austen, Walter Scott, and Charles Dickens. Emerson's readings were confined mainly to poets, philosophers, and biographers, among them Dante and Goethe, Plato and Swedenborg, Plutarch and Saint-Simon. He read not for imitation but for inspiration, saying of books: "I value them to make my top spin."

The author who had the deepest impact upon him was Michel de Montaigne, whose *Essays* he read at the age of twenty-two in Charles Cotton's translation (1685–86). To the young divinity student in nineteenth-century Boston, the French skeptic of the sixteenth century came as a revelation. "It seemed to me," Emerson said of Montaigne, "as if I had written the book myself in some former life, so sincerely it spoke my thought and experience. No book before or since was ever so much to me as that."

Montaigne's exquisite introspection struck a responsive chord in Emerson. In his essay "Of Presumption," Montaigne had written, "The world looks always opposite; I turn my sight inwards, there fix and employ it. Every one looks before him, I look into myself. I have no other business but myself; I am eternally meditating upon myself, control and taste myself. . . . I circulate in myself."

Emerson constantly searched his own self, holding his mirror with a steady hand and looking into it with an unsparing eye. In his personal microcosm, nature yielded him truths which he knew to have a larger relevance.

An early entry in his diary, dated May 13, 1822, is characteristic of his self-criticism. "In twelve days I shall be nineteen years old . . . my heart [is] a blank. I have not the kind affections of a pigeon. Ungenerous and selfish, cautious and cold, I yet wish to be romantic; have not sufficient feeling to speak a natural, hearty welcome to a friend or stranger. . . . There is not in the whole wide Universe of God (my relations to Himself I do not understand) one being to whom I am attached with warm and entire devotion. . . . Perhaps at the distance of a score of years . . . , these will appear frightful confessions;— . . . it is a true picture of a barren and desolate soul."

A mind as searching and wide-ranging as Emerson's soon found itself uneasy in the pulpit. Although Unitarianism is a liberal creed, it was insufficient to provide him with the spiritual sustenance for which he searched. He began to distrust all religious sects. As early as June 1831, the third year of his pastorate, he wrote in his journal: "I suppose it not wise, not being natural, to belong to any religious party. In the Bible you are not directed to be a Unitarian, or a Calvinist or an Episcopalian. Now if a man is wise . . . , he will say to himself, I am not a member of . . . any party. I am God's child, a disciple of Christ. . . . As fast as we use our own eyes, we quit these parties or Unthinking Corporations, and join ourselves to God in an unpartaken relation. A sect or party is an elegant incognito devised to save a man from the vexation of thinking."

Gradually the pulpit became intolerable. His independent spirit rebelled against the rituals, and the prescribed requirements of institutionalized religion. "It is the best part of the man, I sometimes think," he wrote in his journal, January 10, 1832, "that revolts most against his being a minister. His good revolts from official goodness. . . . The difficulty is that we do not make a world of our own, but fall into institutions already made, and have to accommodate ourselves to them to be useful at all, and this accommodation is, I say, a loss of so much integrity and, of course, of so much power."

In June 1832 he informed his congregation that he was unwilling to administer the Lord's Supper, because Jesus "did not intend to establish an institution for perpetual observance when he ate the Passover with his disciples." He no longer believed in the usefulness of the pulpit, concluding that to be a good minister it was necessary to leave the ministry. In a diary entry, June 2, 1832, he called the profession antiquated, adding, "In an altered age, we worship in the dead forms of our forefathers. Were not a Socratic paganism better than an effete, superannuated Christianity?"

In September 1832 Emerson resigned the ministry—"this icehouse of Unitarianism"—and at the end of the year sailed for Europe. Like Roger Williams, another New England Puritan clergyman who left the ministry almost two centuries earlier, Emerson henceforth cut all connection with established churches, which he regarded as contrary to the real spirit of God and Christ. "You can never come to any peace or power until you put your whole reliance in the moral constitution of man, and not at all in a historical Christianity," he wrote in his diary in March. "The Belief in Christianity that now prevails is the Unbelief of men. They will have Christ for a Lord and not for a brother. Christ preaches the greatness of man, but we hear only the greatness of Christ."

Despite his declaration of independence from organized Christianity, Emerson remained a profoundly religious man all his life. But his conception of God was remote from that embodied in institutionalized religion. He objected to a divinity that was enshrined in edifices of brick and stone and in whose name man was relegated to comparative insignificance. Emerson proclaimed God to be an all-pervasive force, immortal life abiding in the deathless spirit of man. In an ultimate sense, this was a democratic conception of religion; by proclaiming God-in-man he elevated man to a central position of dignity in the scheme of the universe. His essential religious philosophy is perhaps best summed up in these words from his diary (September 8, 1833): "The purpose of life seems to be to acquaint a man with himself. . . . The highest revelation is that God is in every man."

Emerson's nine-month trip to Europe, made in 1833 at the age of thirty, widened his horizons and in a sense completed his education. For the first time in his life, he came in contact with cultural monuments and personalities not available to a young clergyman in America. In Italy, he saw the striking remains of ancient civilizations about which he had only hitherto read in books. In England he met eminent poets and writers, to whose talk he listened with sensitive appreciation but not awe. In Scotland, he visited Thomas Carlyle in his farmhouse at Craigenputtock. They formed a friendship that was to last the rest of their lives, though no two men could have been more dissimilar. Where Emerson was tranquil, poised, and quietly spiritual, Carlyle was tempestuous, dogmatic, and strident, his utterances so bristling with exclamation points that Walt Whitman once referred to *Heroes and Hero-Worship* as written in a "rapt weird [grotesque?] style." But there was a moral force in Carlyle, an inner sweetness and a devotion to the general ideal of democracy, that the young American was quick to recognize. The political-minded Carlyle was to serve Emerson as a stimulant in areas—public affairs, for example—which were not his primary preoccupation.

Emerson's over-all evaluation of his European experience was a characteristic blend of generous appreciation and skepticism. At Liverpool on his way home in September 1833, he wrote in his journal: "I thank the Great God who has led me through this European scene, this last schoolroom in which he has pleased to instruct me, from Malta's Isle, through Sicily, through Italy, through Switzerland . . . He has shown me the men I wished to see—Landor, Coleridge, Carlyle, Wordsworth; he has thereby comforted and confirmed me in my convictions. Many things I owe to the sight of these men. I shall judge more justly, less timidly, of wise men forevermore. To be sure not one of these is a mind of the very first class, but what the intercourse with each of these suggests is true of intercourse with better men, that they never *fill the ear*—fill the mind. . . . They [are] all deficient, all these four, . . . in insight into religious truth. They have no idea of that species of moral truth which I call the first philosophy. . . . But Carlyle—Carlyle is so amiable that I love him."

Upon his return from Europe, Emerson moved to Concord, where he was to spend the rest of his life and whence his voice, in speech and in print, was to radiate throughout the land. At first he lectured regularly in Boston and then, as his fame grew, his circuit widened until he went as far as California. He became a master of the art of lecturing, charming varied audiences with his wisdom and wit, his choice of diction that was poetic without being precious, and his learned allusions that were devoid of pedantry. An Emerson lecture was what he called "a panharmonicon," an instrument that combined the poetry of the soul with the truth of science, homely humor with monitory anecdote. Even those who did not always understand, or could not later paraphrase the words into prosaic language, were drawn into the "enchanting meshes" of the speaker's words.

James Russell Lowell (1819–91), himself a poet and essayist, thus described Emerson's performance as a speaker: "I have heard some great speakers and some accomplished orators, but never any that so moved and persuaded men as he. There is a kind of undertow in that rich baritone of his that sweeps our minds from their foothold into deeper waters with a drift we cannot and would not resist. And how artfully (for Emerson is a long-studied artist in these things) does the deliberate utterance, that seems waiting for the fit word, appear to admit us partners in the labor of thought and make us feel as if the glance of humor were a sudden suggestion, as if the perfect phrase lying written there on the desk were as unexpected to him as to us!"

George William Curtis (1824–92), journalist and editor (*Putnam's Monthly, Harper's Weekly, New York Tribune*), who heard Emerson lecture in Boston, was also impressed by the speaker's "simplicity of manner that could be called rustic if it were not of a shy, scholarly elegance; perfect composure; clear, clean, crisp sentences; maxims as full of glittering truth as a winter night of stars; an incessant spray of fine fancies like the November shower of meteors; and . . . intellectual and moral exaltation."

What did Emerson talk about? Better to ask, What didn't he talk about? Insofar as he had a "message," it was the ultimate meaning of life and nature. He proclaimed the divine spirit of man and all living things. His subject matter embraced the totality of sensed and observed experience. Within the range of his often epigrammatic discourses came

Napoleon and pickerel-weed, Empedocles and soft mushrooms, Pythagoras and wild geese, Swedenborg and cotton mills. He was particularly striking as a verbal painter of portraits of great men. For instance, this sketch of Daniel Webster: "His noble and majestic frame, his breadth and projection of brows, his coal-black hair, his great cinderous eyes, his perfect self-possession, and the rich and well-modulated thunder of his voice (to which I used to listen, sometimes, abstracting myself from his sense merely for the luxury of such noble explosions of sound) distinguish him above all other men."

After meeting Abraham Lincoln in the White House in 1862, he wrote: "The President impressed me more favourably than I had hoped. A frank, sincere, well-meaning man, with a lawyer's habit of mind, good clear statement of his fact; correct enough, not vulgar, as described, but with a sort of boyish cheerfulness, or that kind of sincerity and jolly good meaning that our class meetings on Commencement Days show, in telling our old stories over."

Emerson did not construct a consistent philosophy of man or nature. He did, indeed, distrust the rounded and logical structures so beloved of metaphysicians and philosophers. His ideas are scattered in his speeches, essays, and above all his diary, but a strain of unity runs through all his utterances. Despite his famous gibe that foolish consistency was the "hobgoblin of little minds," a remarkable harmony underlies his thought.

At the risk of oversimplification, one may say that Emerson's philosophy is characterized by one-ness, universality, and morality. To him, there was no distinction between man and nature. Both were part of the cosmic spirit. "To the dull mind all nature is leaden. To the illuminated mind the whole world burns and sparkles with light." He said that man was "made of the same atoms as the world is." The overpowering reality of nature-in-man he called the Over-Soul, in which every individual's "particular being is contained and made one with all other." This oneness is immortal and universal. It embraces the totality of thought and energy, always incarnating the individual in the general. "There is one mind common to all individual men," and each human being is the incarnation of the "universal mind."

The core of this universal spirit, incarnated, is the moral law, the substance of which is the ideal of freedom and man's struggle to rise upward. "The moral law," he wrote, "lies at the centre of nature and radiates to the circumference. It is the pitch and marrow of every substance, every relation, and every process." To break the moral law meant to lose the central reality of life, for thought and morals were an inseparable unity. "The high intellect is absolutely at one with moral nature."

Emerson's philosophy of universalism or the Over-Soul, although couched in terms that appeared at first glance mystifyingly metaphysical, nevertheless did not shut out political realities. On the contrary, it provided a powerful rationale for democracy and a base for eloquent attacks on existing evils, among them slavery (in his ode to Channing he spoke of "The jackals of the Negro-holder"), political corruption, and harsh materialism. Where certain influential Americans—Calhoun, for example—advocated a restriction on liberty as necessary for social stability, Emerson proclaimed man's freedom as divinely inherent in the system of the universe:

> For he that ruleth high and wise,
> Nor pauseth in His plan,
> Will take the sun out of the skies,
> Ere freedom out of man.

The existence of evil, Emerson said, only showed man's better nature. He explained the paradox by pointing out that the very act of recognition of depravity implied awareness of it, which in itself suggested possibilities of amelioration. Referring to the meanness of human life, he asked: "How did we find that it was mean?" Obviously, only the moral sense could indicate goodness and badness. And this sense, Emerson said, being part of the totality of nature, was undergoing cosmic stages of evolution toward higher levels of morality and betterment, including the establishment of freedom in America.

"The civic history of men," he wrote, "might be traced by successive ameliorations as marked in higher moral generalizations;—virtue meaning physical courage, then chastity and temperance, then justice and love;—bargains of kings with peoples of certain rights to certain classes, then of rights to the masses,—then at last came the day when . . . the nerves of the world were electrified by the proclamation that all men are born free and equal."

In giving utterance to the divine spirit that encompassed all and transcended all, Emerson became the most eloquent and most widely known spokesman of the idealistic movement known as Transcendentalism, which flourished from about 1820 to the Civil War. Centering around Concord, Transcendentalism combined spiritual uplift with revolutionary utopianism and attracted reformers, abolitionists, anarchists, and idealistic socialists. Among the outstanding members of the movement were reformer Amos Bronson Alcott (1799–1888), Unitarian minister William Ellery Channing (1780–1842), writer Margaret Fuller (1810–50), novelist Nathaniel Hawthorne (1804–64), abolitionist Theodore Parker (1810–60), critic George Ripley (1802–80), and philosopher Henry David Thoreau (1817–62), who in 1841 moved into Emerson's house, where he lived for two years. The group brought out a Transcendentalist journal, *The Dial,* the editorship of which Emerson took over from Margaret Fuller between 1842 and 1844.

In social and political matters, the Transcendentalists tended to be reformers, in sympathy with the pre-Marxist socialist and utopian movements which were then spreading in America. The utopian movement had started at about the time Emerson entered divinity school. In 1824, an English industrialist and reformer, Robert Owen (1771–1858), arrived in America and proclaimed: "I have come to this country to introduce an entire new state of society; to change it from an ignorant, selfish system to an enlightened social system." He set up the first experimental "communistic" society at Harmony, renamed New Harmony, Indiana. Although New Harmony did not live up to its name and dissolved within three years, the experiments continued elsewhere. Owen's disciple, Etienne Cabet, established a colony on the Red River in Texas and, this having failed, he moved to Illinois, where he founded another in the village of Nauvoo, which had been deserted by the Mormons. Other utopian "Associations," following the teachings of the French Socialist, François Fourier (1772–1837), as propagated by the wealthy Arthur Brisbane in the columns of Horace Greeley's *New York Tribune,* were established throughout the country, as far west as California. Between 1840 and 1850, there were no less than forty such colonies in the United States. Ultimately none of them, including the Transcendentalists' Brook Farm, was viable enough to survive the overwhelming pressures of a surging individualist economy.

While Emerson's heart was with the utopians, his head said *no.* Despite his sympathies for their aims, he found their approach uncongenial and could not bring himself to join them. He too believed in reform but of a deeper kind. For, like many idealists of the period, he was shocked by the excesses of the rising capitalism, the cruel disregard for the rights of labor, the cheapness of morals and the corrupting political influence of the new rich. The "new moneyed feudalism" bribed legislatures and, in general, debased the spirit of the country. "In America,"

Emerson wrote in *The Conduct of Life,* "the geography is sublime, but the men are not: the inventions are excellent, but the inventors one is sometimes ashamed of."

Criticism of the prevailing social misery, attacks on Wall Street, and demands for reform were particularly widespread after the panic of 1837. An example of such criticism is to be found in *Letters from New York* (1843) by the abolitionist and reformer, Mrs. Lydia Maria Frances Child (1802–80): "In Wall-Street, and elsewhere, Mammon, as usual, coolly calculates his chance of extracting a penny from war, pestilence, and famine; and Commerce, with her loaded drays, and jaded skeletons of horse, is busy as ever fulfilling the 'World's contract with the Devil.' . . . I have often anathemized the spirit of Trade, which reigns triumphant, not only on 'Change, but in our halls of legislation, and even in our churches. Thought is sold under the hammer, and sentiment, in its holiest forms, stands labelled for the market. Love is offered to the highest bidder, and sixpences are given to purchase religion for starving souls. In view of these things, I sometimes ask whether the Age of Commerce is better than the Age of War? Whether our 'merchant princes' are a great advance upon feudal chieftains. Whether it is better for the many to be prostrated by force, or devoured by cunning?"

The materialism and cynicism of his time offended Emerson. In one respect he agreed with Calhoun—the northern industrial entrepreneur also bought his slaves. Emerson's diary contains entries showing his condemnation of the prevailing conditions, for example (March 14, 1854): "The lesson of these days is the vulgarity of wealth. We know that wealth will vote for the same thing which the worst and meanest of the people vote for. Wealth will vote for rum, will vote for tyranny, will vote for slavery, will vote against the ballot, will vote against international copyright, will vote against schools, colleges, or any high direction of public money."

He knew the age was ripe for reform, and he admired the contemporary reformers and socialists who advocated programs for human betterment. Such men as Owen and Fourier seemed to him "the inspired men of their time." But much of what passed for political reform in his day was, he said, meaningless superficiality. "The salvation of America and of the human race," he noted ironically in his diary in 1848, "depends on the next election, if we believe the newspapers. But so it was last year, and so it was the year before, and our fathers believed the same thing forty years ago." The general run of reformers wanted merely to change existing institutions or to improve the material conditions of the poor. For Emerson, physical betterment without moral improvement had no significance. "Alas, that I must hint," he wrote in his journal (August 1841), "that poverty is not an unmixed good; that labor may easily exceed.... The Irish population in our towns is the most laborious, but neither the most moral nor the most intelligent." Something much more than improving labor conditions was necessary if reform was to be meaningful.

Looking beyond organized system, which, he knew, perpetuated evil and debased the human character, Emerson wanted a reform in the very nature of man. He wished to raise the moral character of the human being to make him capable of true brotherhood, to elevate his soul to a level where selfishness and materialism would be replaced by the ideals of love and sharing. Human love, once established as a guiding principle of society, would, he said, constitute a veritable political and social revolution—it would, in fact, be *the* revolution—in human affairs.

This idea of reform Emerson developed in a lecture, "Man the Reformer," delivered before the Boston Mechanics' Apprentices' Library Association in January 1841. Acutely critical and, at the same time, spiritually elevated, the lecture marks a high point in the history of American idealism.

"Our age and history, for these thousand years," Emerson stated, "has not been the history of kindness, but of selfishness. Our distrust is very expensive. The money we spend for courts and prisons is very ill laid out. We make, by distrust, the thief, and burglar, and incendiary, and by our court and jail we keep him so. An acceptance of the sentiment of love throughout Christendom for a season would bring felon and the outcast to our side in tears, with the devotion of his faculties to our service. See this wide society of laboring men and women. We allow ourselves to be served by them, we live apart from them, and meet them without a salute in the streets. We do not greet their talents, nor rejoice in their good fortune, nor foster their hopes.... We complain that the politics of masses of the people are controlled by designing men.... But the people do not wish to be represented or ruled by the ignorant and base. They only vote for these, because they were asked with the voice and semblance of kindness.... Let our affection flow out to our fellows; it would operate in a day the greatest of all revolutions. It is better to work on institutions by the sun than by the wind. The state must consider the poor man, and all voices must speak for him. Every child that is born must have a just chance for his bread. Let the amelioration in our laws of property proceed from the concession of the rich, not from the grasping of the poor. Let us begin by habitual imparting. Let us understand that the equitable rule is that no one should take more than his share. . . ."

Emerson had small enthusiasm for Brook Farm, the two hundred acres of dairy land where his Transcendentalist friends hoped to establish an ideal community based on "brotherly cooperation." Brook Farm aimed "to secure for our children and to those who may be trusted to our care, the benefits of the highest physical, intellectual, and moral education, which . . . the resources at our command will permit; to institute an attractive, efficient, and productive system of industry; to prevent the exercise of worldly anxiety by the competent supply of our necessary wants; to diminish the desire for excessive accumulation by making the acquisition of individual property subservient to upright and disinterested uses; to guarantee to each other the means of physical support and of spiritual progress, and thus to impart a greater freedom, simplicity, truthfulness, refinement and moral dignity to our mode of life."

To Emerson the whole scheme looked like a glorified jail. He felt that the proposed utopia, even if it were successful, could stifle all ideas and imagination—an opinion to be confirmed later when, after the farm's dissolution, its members unanimously told him: "We have no thoughts." Moreover, he was temperamentally averse to schemes based on euphoria. The holy fire in the eyes of his friends, when they discussed their projected millennium, left him embarrassed and uneasy, precisely because they were so enthusiastic. He relates in his diary (October 17, 1840), "Yesterday George and Sophia Ripley, Margaret Fuller and Alcott discussed here the Social Plans [Brook Farm]. I wished to be convinced, to be thawed, to be made nobly mad by the kindlings before my eye of a new dawn of human piety. But this scheme was arithmetic and comfort. . . . And not once could I be inflamed, but sat aloof and thoughtless; my voice faltered and fell. It was not the cave of persecution which is the palace of spiritual power, but only a room in the Astor House hired for the Transcendentalists. I do not wish to remove from my present prison to a prison a little larger. I wish to break all prisons."

Here we have the essence of Emerson in his capacity as a citizen reacting to practical challenges. A physical utopia on a tiny scale troubled his sense of proportion, and its fixed intellectual assumptions were a denial of his philosophy of the moving and energizing spirit throughout the universe. On a personal level, he was so finely balanced that he could not accept anything extreme, in the sense of being sharply and patently out of tune with the harmony of things. He had personally tried a number of small experimental departures from daily routines—being in all outward manifestations a quietly solid citizen, paying his taxes and obeying the laws—and found them uncompensating. For a short time, he was a vegetarian, but soon saw that eschewing animal flesh did him no particular good. To illustrate human equality, he tried to have his two servants sit at the table with the family, but the domestics were clearly inconvenienced by the arrangement. To test the theory that a scholar should give part of his time to physical labor, he attempted to work in the field—only to discover that it took away precious energy from writing, and he thus concluded sensibly: "The writer shall not dig."

Emerson would not bind himself to anything that would confine him or the free flow of his ideas. He conceived his function to be that of a transmitter of thought, which he considered the transcendent reality, the universal mind that energized the world. He was at one with it, giving expression to its continuing and ever-changing flow. This is what he meant when he said of himself: "I unsettle all things. No facts to me are sacred; none are profane; I simply experiment, an endless seeker, with no Past at my back. . . . Nothing is secure but life, transition, the energizing spirit. . . . No truth so sublime but it may be trivial tomorrow in the light of new thoughts."

If this sounded mystical and imprecise, Emerson had an answer for it. "I am," he said, "in all my theory, ethics, and politics a poet." He formulated his ideas in poetic language, only because that was the best way he knew to speak about things that could not be pinned down but were of ultimate significance. When one takes the trouble to read his phrases carefully, one finds, even in his comments on politics, a hard core of practical sense and humane wisdom.

His essay "Politics," written in 1842, is a fine illustration of the poet as political thinker. It is a departure from the traditional writings on the subject, emphasizing not power but morality, not property but character, not the state but the individual above the state. The echoes of these ideas can be found reverberating in Thoreau.

To begin with, Emerson established the proposition that government is neither sacred nor fixed. It is purely man-made and hence subject to change. "In dealing with the State," he said, "we ought to remember that its institutions are not aboriginal, though they existed before we were born: that they are not superior to the citizen: that every one of them was once the act of a single man: every law and usage was a man's expedient to meet a particular case: that they all are imitable, all alterable; we may make as good; we may make better."

From this it followed that the state was not an abstraction or an arbitrary ruler. "The State is our neighbor; our neighbors are the State." Politics, then, resolved itself to a question of the relationship between neighbor and neighbor. "My right and my wrong, is their right and their wrong." So long as the individual does what is fit and abstains from what is unfit, there is agreement and harmony in society.

"But whenever I find my dominion over myself not sufficient for me, and undertake the direction of him also [my neighbor], I overstep the truth, and come into false relations to him." This establishes a false relationship; it is a lie and "hurts like a lie both him and me." It can only be executed through "a practical lie, namely by force." Emerson found force revolting. "I do not," he said, "like to see a sword at a man's side. If it threaten man, it threatens me. A company of soldiers is an offensive spectacle." Force was the ultimate blunder, a "colossal ugliness" that marked all "the governments of the world."

"We live in a very low state of the world," he declared, "and pay unwilling tribute to governments founded on force. There is not, among the most religious and civil nations, a reliance on the moral sentiment and sufficient belief in the unity of things, to persuade them that society can be maintained without artificial restraints, as well as the solar system; or that the private citizen might be reasonable and a good neighbor, without the hint of a jail or a confiscation. What is strange too, there never was in any man sufficient faith in the power of rectitude to inspire him with the broad design of renovating the State on the principle of right and love. All those who have pretended this design have been partial reformers, and have admitted in some manner the supremacy of the bad State. I do not call to mind a single human being who has steadily denied the authority of the laws, on the simple ground of his own moral nature."

The solution for the bad political situation was the same as the one Emerson suggested in his lecture "Man the Reformer"—an improvement in human character through love and wisdom. "A man has a right to be employed, to be trusted, to be loved, to be revered. The power of love, as the basis of a State, has never been tried." Once tried, by men of moral stature and wisdom, it would ultimately abolish the state itself. "To educate the wise man the State exists, and with the appearance of the wise man the State expires. The appearance of character makes the

States unnecessary. The wise man is the State. He needs no army, fort, or navy—he loves men too well; no bribe, or feast, or palace, to draw friends to him. . . ."

Until man was morally elevated, government should remain as weak as possible. Power was too dangerous to be permitted in the hands of men of immature character. "Don't trust children with edge tools," Emerson wrote in his diary (January 20, 1832). "Don't trust man, great God, with more power than he has, until he has learned to use that little better. What a hell should we make of the world if we could do what we would! Put a button on the foil till the young fencers have learned not to put each other's eyes out."

Emerson thus believed in a strictly limited state. ". . . . The less government . . . the better,—the fewer laws, and the less confided power," he wrote in "Politics." This dislike of strong government, really a distrust of politicians of low moral character, was in the prevailing liberal tradition. When Emerson said, "The root and seed of democracy is the doctrine, Judge for yourself," he expressed the essence of Jeffersonian individualism. In his belief that government should be as weak as possible and should, above all, stay out of all economic affairs, he was at one with such *laissez-faire* democrats as John Taylor and Martin Van Buren. "The basis of political economy," Emerson wrote, "is non-interference. The only safe rule is found in the self-adjusting meter of demand and supply. . . . Do not legislate. Meddle, and you snap the sinews. . . ."

His thinking about government was unquestionably colored by the struggle over slavery that convulsed his age. His general distrust of government, deriving from his ethical philosophy, was reinforced by the fact that the southern slaveholders, for whom he had boundless contempt, wielded immense political influence in Washington. Until the Civil War—throughout most of Emerson's active life—the southern slaveowners either dominated or held the balance of power in the Senate and, in addition, they often occupied key positions in the federal structure. That in itself, in Emerson's eyes, demeaned government. "I confess," he said, "I do not wish to live in a nation where slavery exists."

The southern slaveocrats, who kept God's creatures in bondage and triumphantly lived on the labor of slaves, filled Emerson with horror. He viewed them as a breed of men alien to God's higher purposes, worshipping at the cult of violence. "I have not," he said, "a syllable of all the language I have learned, to utter for the planter." When Emerson, the preacher of human brotherhood, referred to the type, he lost all his gentleness.

His unsparing portrait of a typical southerner, etched in his journal (October 8, 1837), is memorable for the light it casts on the abolitionist fire that was ultimately to consume the Old South. "The young Southerner comes here a spoiled child, with graceful manners, excellent self-command, very good to be spoiled more, but good for nothing else—a mere parader. He has conversed so much with rifles, horses and dogs that he has become himself a rifle, a horse and a dog, and in civil, educated company, where anything human is going forward, he is dumb and unhappy, like an Indian in a church. Treat them with great deference, as we often do, and they accept it all as their due without misgiving. Give them an inch, and they take a mile. They are mere bladders of conceit. Each snipper-snapper of them all undertakes to speak for the entire Southern States. 'At the South, the reputation of Cambridge,' etc. etc., which being interpreted, is, In my negro village of Tuscaloosa, or Cheraw, or St. Mark's, I supposed so and so. 'We, at the South,' forsooth. They are more civilized than the Seminoles, however, in my opinion, a little more. Their question respecting any man is like a Seminole's— How can he fight? In this country, we ask, What can he do? His pugnacity is all they prize in man, dog, or turkey."

Emerson felt so strongly about slavery that, despite his habitual reluctance to participate in public causes and his avowed skepticism of reformers, he was an open abolitionist. "It is impossible," he wrote, "to be a gentleman, and not be an abolitionist," because a gentleman is "the natural defender . . . of the weak and oppressed." He opposed the annexation of Texas (a slave state) and the Fugitive Slave Act (1850), which he called "this filthy enactment," moved him to a defiance of the government itself. "I will not obey it, by God," he said.

As the crisis over slavery deepened, Emerson's customary philosophical serenity began slowly to desert him. "This calamity," he noted in his diary in 1851, "darkens my days." The evil of slavery moved him to abandon his pacifism. "Root it out," he said, "burn it up, pay for the damage, and let us have done with it. It costs a hundred millions. Twice so much were cheap. . . . I would pay a little of my estate with joy." When the Civil War, which he had foreseen, finally broke out, he said, "Sometimes gunpowder smells good." But the fratricidal conflict, continuing for four desperate years and costing nearly a million lives, horrified him. In one of his poems, "Terminus," he cried out: "No more!"

Emerson never quite recovered from the holocaust. The Civil War and its consequences shattered his fastidious world of serene optimism and loving-kindness. But by then his creative work was done. Material, and indeed revolutionary, changes in American society in no way negated Emerson's essential philosophy. He had, in the midst of crass materialism, proclaimed the all-pervasive value of human intelligence. By his emphasis on the universal spirit of morality, he had enriched the democratic mind with his vision of human nobility. He may well be considered the moral "Philosopher of Democracy," its "prophet and herald."

# 12

## *THE AMERICAN AS ANARCHIST:*
## Henry David Thoreau *(1817–1862)*

*Thoreau was a surprising fellow—he is not easily grasped—is elusive: yet he is one of the native forces—stands for a fact, a movement, an upheaval: Thoreau belongs to America, to the transcendental, to the protesters: then he is an outdoor man: all oudoor men, everything being equal, appeal to me. Thoreau was not so precious, tender, a personality as Emerson: but he was a force—he looms up bigger and bigger . . . : every year has added to his fame. One thing about Thoreau keeps him very near to me: I refer to his lawlessness—his dissent—his going down his absolute road, let hell blaze all it chooses.*

—*Walt Whitman*
(*December 24, 1888*)

In the context of American political thought, Thoreau is unique on at least two counts. His generalizations about society were based altogether on personal experience and on nothing else, for he refused to move out of the circle of his own self. He wrote only about what he saw and felt. As he said in the opening words of *Walden:* "I should not talk so much about myself if there were anybody else I knew as well." This was not irony.

Too, Thoreau was the only major figure among American writers to espouse wholly the idea of philosophical anarchy. Except for his passionate hatred of slavery, his participation in public affairs was as limited as his friend Emerson's. Primarily a naturalist, Thoreau was not interested in politics as such. Political writings do not loom large in his total output. But what he did write on the subject, either directly (in *On the Duty of Civil Disobedience*) or indirectly (for example, in the "Economy" chapter in *Walden*), was exceptional and unconventional, as was his character and mode of life.

No other important American literary man had ever written about the state so contemptuously or rejected government so uncompromisingly as did this New England individualist. There is a harsh but curiously poetic quality in his condemnation of government and the economic-social structure on which it rests. Whether or not one respects Thoreau's position—"I can't see why they seem to take the author of *Walden* (I forgot the name) so seriously," Oliver Wendell Holmes once remarked—it was so arresting in its approach and conclusions that it cannot be ignored in any account of American thought. Extreme though they were, his ideas were as uniquely American as the Yankee clipper ships.

Thoreau was born in Concord, Massachusetts, in 1817. His father, John Thoreau, a pencil-maker, was of French–Jersey Island and Scottish ancestry; his mother was the daughter of a New England minister. The Thoreaus were a simple family of artisans. Henry himself showed no outstanding qualities in his youth except an almost pagan delight in nature. At twelve, he was enrolled at Concord Academy, for the quarter ending February 1829, where, he said, "I was fitted, or rather made unfit for college." He went to Harvard, then a small college. Except for the Greek poets, he was not especially interested in book learning.

After he graduated from Harvard in 1837, at twenty, he supported himself by teaching school for a while, then by surveying, and finally by manual labor. For two years, between twenty-four and twenty-six, he lived in Emerson's home, doing household chores but being treated as a member of the family. He was an occasional member of the Transcendentalist circle, but in an aloof way—always nursing his own thoughts, unimpressed by those of others. In the latter years of his life, he was a general handyman in Concord village, needing and asking for little to live on. "He lived extempore from hour to hour . . . ," Emerson said of him; "the only man of leisure in his town; and his independence made all others look like slaves."

Thoreau was outwardly undistinguished. A true eccentric, he was nevertheless respected by the villagers as a self-sufficient recluse who cared little about what the neighbors thought of him. Angular, long-legged and short-bodied, with the narrow shoulders of a tubercular, he carried an umbrella even in the woods. Despite his unprosperous appearance, he was cheerful and, in fact, looked upon his social environment with the mockery of one who had sloughed off material values and risen beyond the picayune ambitions of his neighbors. Compared with the beauty of nature—the shape of a leaf or the grace of a flying bird—man's work was mean and his strivings ignoble. Immersed in and enchanted by the natural world, which he learned to read as other men read print, Thoreau would chuckle with merriment as he observed the behavior of his fellow townsmen. To him, *they* were the real freaks, whose lives made no sense at all. "There," said Emerson of Thoreau, "is an optimist for you."

Emerson, who occasionally accompanied his young friend on walks, was alternately baffled and elated by him. A serene and balanced philosopher, Emerson was troubled by Thoreau's appetite for intellectual aggression, his seeming need always to challenge and reject society. Not that Emerson disagreed with many of Thoreau's ideas. Quite the contrary, as he remarked with dry humor in his diary (September 1841): "I am very familiar with all [Thoreau's] thoughts—they are my own quite originally drest." It was the younger man's temperament that seemed discordant. "Henry," Emerson said of Thoreau, who claimed to be a pacifist, "is military." He meant that Thoreau was at his best fighting something, a stubborn and implacable critic who delighted in exposing fallacies and pillorying human blunders. Manly and wise, he was "rarely sweet." On the other hand, Emerson was impressed by the magnificent qualities of his protégé, who possessed a moral rectitude and a purity of character unmatched in his day. In addition, the clarity of his intellect was such that it penetrated the inner core of meaning and illuminated whatever it touched.

"My good Henry," Emerson wrote after a visit with him in February 1838, "made this solitary afternoon sunny with his simplicity in this double-dealing, quacking world. Everything that boy says makes merry with society, though nothing can be graver than his meaning."

On the surface, what Thoreau said and wrote seemed comic or ironic. He turned the world upside down. He praised snow for its warmth, the wilderness for its urbanity, woodchoppers for their culture, the outdoors for its domesticity. Merrily he argued that the less one possessed the richer one was and that the more one worked the poorer he became. He proposed that the order of the week be reversed—there should be one day of labor and six days of rest. About two weeks' work in every year, he thought, should suffice to provide for a man's essential needs. The rest of the time could be used for the enjoyment of life rather than for the accumulation of money, property, or power.

As it was, Thoreau asked, what did all these bustling Americans achieve by their incessant toil? Rich or poor, they were chained to their material wants, their lives enslaved in a round of chores that had no ultimate meaning. "But men labor under a mistake," he wrote in *Walden*. "The better part of the man is soon plowed into the soil for compost. By a seeming fate, commonly called necessity, they are employed, as it says in an old book, laying up treasures which moth and rust will corrupt and thieves break through and steal. It is a fool's life, as they will find when they get to the end of it."

Do labor and possessions make a man better and nobler and happier while he is alive? Not at all, said Thoreau, with almost an undertone of mockery. The farmer, despite his toil, rarely owns his own land in New England; most of the farms are mortgaged to bankers. And if he does own his farm, what good does it do him? He hardly ever rises above the level of his self-imposed drudgery: "Look at the teamster on the highway, wending to market by day or night; does any divinity stir within him? His highest duty to fodder and water his horses! . . . How godlike, how immortal, is he? See how he cowers and sneaks, how vaguely all the day he fears, not being immortal nor divine, but the slave and prisoner of his own opinion of himself."

The toiling farmer is not only a slave to himself but is also "tied to an ox, or horse, or cow, or pig." He has so little independence within himself that he needs animals to labor for him, and they in turn make demands upon him. A good portion of a farmer's land and much of his time have to be devoted to feeding and tending his beasts. Thus man's dependence on animals leads to the paradoxical situation that the beast becomes master of the man. "I am wont to think that men are not so much the keepers of herds as herds are the keepers of men," he said, "the former are so much the freer. . . . Man thus not only works for the animal within him . . . , he works for the animal without him."

If the man leaves the farm and hires himself out as a worker in one of the factories in Lowell and Lawrence, Thoreau said, he is not better off either. His toil in the shop does not raise the level of his own well-being. The product of his labor is not for him to enjoy. He simply exchanges one form of slavery for another. As the farmer works to support his animals, so the worker labors to enrich the factory owners: "I cannot believe that our factory system is the best mode by which men may get clothing. The condition of the operatives is becoming every day more like that of the English; and it cannot be wondered at, since as I have heard or observed, the principal object is, not that mankind may be well and honestly clad, but . . . that the corporations may be enriched."

Nor are the rich to be envied. What, Thoreau asked, does their wealth bring them? Certainly not spiritual elevation or ennoblement of character, the only values worth striving for. Dedication to wealth is merely another form of self-enslavement, no more desirable than the farmers' and workers' enchainment to toil. "I also have in mind that seemingly wealthy, but most terribly impoverished class of all, who have accumulated dross, but know not how to use it, or get rid of it, and thus have forged their own golden or silver fetters."

Thus, Thoreau held, material objectives and the institutions based upon them impoverish and degrade mankind. Worst of all, they bring neither peace of mind nor happiness. Both in the country and in the city, men have lost the pleasure of life. They cannot enjoy play because, Thoreau said, an "unconscious despair is concealed even under what are called the games and amusements of mankind." And, he concluded, "the mass of men lead lives of quiet desperation."

To test his theory that men could be independent and happy by living in utmost simplicity close to nature, Thoreau undertook his Walden experiment. A practical illustration, he felt, would give concrete confirmation—at least to his own satisfaction, since he did not believe in reforming others—of his unorthodox views. His conception of himself as a philosopher meant not merely to have subtle thoughts or even to found a school but to love wisdom and "to live according to its dictates, a life of simplicity, independence, magnanimity, and trust." To be a philosopher, involved the solution of some of the problems of life, "not only theoretically, but practically."

At Walden, Thoreau set out to demonstrate two propositions. One was that it was possible to be happy with a minimum of possessions. Since he valued his freedom above all else, he did not want to spend his time "in earning rich carpets or other fine furniture, or delicate cookery, or a house in the Grecian or the Gothic style."

The second proposition was a corollary to the first: that a man needed only a minimum of simple labor to maintain himself in well-being and freedom. "It is not necessary," he said with sardonic humor, "that a man should earn his living by the sweat of his brow, unless he sweats easier than I do." Life could be pleasant with only a little bit of work.

For two years, from July 1845 to 1847, Thoreau lived at Walden

Pond, in Concord, in a hut he built himself with a borrowed axe. "I have . . . a tight shingled and plastered house, ten feet wide by fifteen long, and eight-feet posts, with a garret and a closet, a large window on each side, two trap-doors, one door at the end, and a brick fireplace." Total cost, all for materials, was $28.12. Some of the furniture—a desk, a table, three chairs, a mirror—he made himself; the rest, together with a skillet, frying pan, wash bowl, two knives and forks, three plates, one cup, one spoon, one oil jug and lamp, he picked up for nothing. The village garrets were full of things, he said, "to be had for taking them away."

He planted two and a half of his eleven sandy acres (valued at about $89 and, in the words of one farmer, "good for nothing but to raise cheeping squirrels on") with potatoes, corn, peas, and turnips. This he supplemented with purchases of rice, molasses, meal, pork, flour, sugar, lard—at a total cost of $8.74 for the first eight months; clothing, oil, and some household utensils cost another $10.40, and the yearly rental of the farm was $14.72. Thus his total expenditure (not counting the building cost) amounted to $33.86. During the same period, he earned $13.34 by doing odd jobs ("for I have as many trades as fingers") and $23.34 by selling some of the produce he grew. His total income was, therefore, $36.68—$2.82 more than he spent. Here, he thought, was a personal triumph over the American capitalist economy!

"I maintained myself thus solely by the labor of my hands," he reported, "and I found that, by working about six weeks in a year, I could meet all the expenses of living. The whole of my winters, as well as most of my summers, I had free and clear for study."

Out of this experience came *Walden, or Life in The Woods* (1854), the masterpiece for which—next to his remarkable journal, published posthumously in fourteen volumes—he is best remembered. Like *A Week on the Concord and Merrimack Rivers* (1849), the only other book Thoreau published during his life, *Walden* was not a commercial success. It barely paid for the cost of printing. But it did slightly better than *A Week on the Concord*—this book sold so little that out of an edition of 1000 copies he got back 706, which led him to remark: "I have now a library of nine hundred volumes, over seven hundred of which I wrote myself."

*Walden,* the quintessence of Thoreau, by its revelation of his relationship to nature, paradoxically illuminates his political and social philosophy. It was Thoreau's very intimacy with the nonhuman environment around him that deepened his alienation from the human world. He had established a special rapport with living creatures; birds came when he called; wild animals nuzzled him; fish in the lake glided through his hands. The wind sang to him and the storm played "Aeolian music" to his ears. The pine needles befriended him and the loon laughed especially for him. He became as one with nature: "I am no more lonely than a single mullein or dandelion in a pasture, or a fern leaf, or sorrel, or a horse-fly, or a bumblebee. I am no more lonely than the Mill Brook, or a weathercock, or the north star, or the south wind, or an April shower, or a January thaw, or the first spider in a new house."

Absorbed in the contemplation of nature, Thoreau became insulated from humanity. He loved mankind, but had no sympathy for man. Basically detached from human beings, he never married and rarely participated in civic action. But his critical faculties, where human institutions and foibles were concerned, were abnormally sharp. He felt increasingly apart from his neighbors. For years he would not pay the existing poll tax and, in 1845, he spent one night in jail for his refusal to do so. The tax was small, but the principle—the money being ultimately spent to support a government that condoned slavery and waged war—loomed large. Going to jail was a moral vindication. "Under a government which imprisons any unjustly," Thoreau said, "the true place for a just man is also a prison"—a statement that was to be echoed by the Socialist leader Eugene Debs three quarters of a century later.*

Thoreau's brief imprisonment only confirmed his contempt for the whole existing machinery of justice, with its paraphernalia of constables, jailers, and judges. He was particularly disdainful of what he considered the preposterous assumption, on which the judicial system was based, that ideas could be imprisoned or punished as if they were mere physical objects.

Out of his meditation in jail came the essay *On the Duty of Civil Disobedience* (1849). This, together with his antislavery speeches—"Slavery in Massachusetts" (1854), "A Plea for Captain John Brown" (1859)—constitute Thoreau's main direct contributions to political thought. *Civil Disobedience* is a coherent statement of his philosophy of government and the speeches are elaborations on the fundamental theme.

* In September 1918, Debs, convicted for being a conscientious objector during World War I, told the court: "Your Honor, years ago I recognized my kinship with all living beings, and I made up my mind that I was not one bit better than the meanest of earth. I said, I say now, that while there is a lower class, I am in it; while there is a criminal element, I am of it; while there is a soul in prison, I am not free."

The theme consisted of two parts. One was contempt for the existing governmental structure and institutions. The other was an emphasis on the supremacy of moral values, as exemplified in the individual, over government and its laws. For existing government, including the American federal system, Thoreau had only disdain. It was, he insisted, without morality and without courage. In *Civil Disobedience,* he referred to it in a brief verse as:

> A drab of State, a cloth-o'-silver slut,
> To have her train borne up, and her soul trail in the dirt.

Government served no useful function. From jail, Thoreau had gone picking huckleberries and, he remarked sardonically, he could find "no State among the berry bushes." Why did men need something that even berries could do without? After observing the existing political institutions, Thoreau concluded that they were unworthy of any esteem. "I saw that the State was half-witted, that it was timid as a lone woman with her silver spoons, and that it did not know its friends from its foes, and I lost all my remaining respect for it, and pitied it."

Thoreau granted the necessity of a certain amount of government, but only on condition that it be severely limited and based on individual morality and justice. He had for a long time, he said, heartily accepted the motto that that government was best which governed least, but his final conclusion, as he explained in *Civil Disobedience,* was—"That government is best which governs not at all."

Thoreau argued that the fundamental law of life and society was morality, as interpreted by the individual conscience. Existing government was founded not on morality but on expediency. Insofar as the two coincided, and to the extent that they did, government was bearable and defensible. A certain amount of expediency, for example, protecting persons from others—"letting one another alone"—Thoreau conceded as a necessity. But wherever government overstepped the line and began to coerce the individual, it violated the moral law and had to be disobeyed. In any clash between what the government considered expediency and the individual regarded as morality, his duty was to follow the higher moral law and passively refuse obedience. Thoreau insisted that no government had a "pure right over my person or property but what I concede to it."

The machinery of existing government, the whole system of balloting, majority rule, political campaigning, left Thoreau unmoved. To him, it had no inner meaning. What he was concerned with was the soul of democracy, he said, not its paraphernalia. The important thing was to think right, rather than to vote right. A majority in itself meant nothing, if moral considerations were absent. As things stood in America, Thoreau said in 1849, "all voting is a sort of gaming, like checkers or backgammon . . . , a playing with right and wrong." The impersonal machinery of politics could not safeguard the soul of the nation. Something higher was needed.

"What is wanted," he said in his speech on slavery in Massachusetts, "is men, not of policy, but of probity,—who recognize a higher law than the Constitution, or the decision of the majority. The fate of the country does not depend on how you vote at the polls,—the worst man is as strong as the best at that game; it does not depend on what kind of paper you drop into the ballot-box once a year, but on what kind of man you drop from your chamber into the street every morning."

Thus Thoreau proclaimed, in the whole range of politics, the higher moral law as interpreted by the individual conscience against the dictates of government. In practice, this meant individual nullification of any act or law which a person might disapprove and, when necessary, a dissociation from the government altogether. As he wrote in *Civil Disobedience:* "How does it become a man to behave toward this American government today? I answer, that he cannot without disgrace be associated with it. I cannot for an instant recognize that political organization as *my* government which is the *slave*'s government also."

Law in itself, even if approved by the majority, had no validity if it was contrary to morality. This was the case, for example, with the Fugitive Slave Act (1850), requiring state authorities to extradite escaping southern Negroes, which Thoreau considered "dirt," to be thoroughly resisted even if it was necessary to destroy the government itself in the process. "My thoughts," he said in reference to the Fugitive Slave Act, "are murder to the State." Similarly, in his impassioned plea for Captain John Brown in 1859, Thoreau absolutely denied the validity of the laws that condemned the famous abolitionist. In Thoreau's eyes, Brown did not violate any law, even if all the lawyers and judges said that he did, because the existing statutes regarding slavery were contrary to the moral code that was superior to anything man-made.

"Is it not possible that an individual may be right and a government wrong?" he asked in the plea for John Brown. "Are laws to be enforced simply because they were made? or declared by any number of men to be good, if they are *not* good? . . . Are judges to interpret the law according to the letter, and not the spirit? What right have *you* to enter into a compact with yourself that you *will* do thus or so, against the light within you? . . . I do not believe in lawyers . . . , because . . . , in cases of the highest importance, it is of no consequence whether a man breaks a human law or not. Let lawyers decide trivial cases. . . . If they were the interpreters of the everlasting laws which rightfully bind man, that would be another thing. A counterfeiting law-factory, standing half in a slave land and half in a free! What kind of laws for free men can you expect from that?"

Thus Henry David Thoreau, who died at Concord in 1862 at forty-five, spoke to America with the voice of conscience and ethics. Alienated from the social world of material strivings and status, he uttered thoughts that seemed to have no practicality but did survive through the generations and across the world. Thoreau's teachings exerted a strong influence abroad—in India, for example, where Mahatma Gandhi adapted civil disobedience to his struggle for Indian independence. Thoreau's writings still have the freshness of ultimate truth, or perhaps of innocence. He spoke to the political heart, and not the head. He lived, in the words of Emerson, "like the birds and angels. . . ."

# 13

## *THE AMERICAN AS POET:*
# Walt Whitman *(1819–1892)*

*Perhaps his [Thoreau's] fancy for Walt Whitman grew out of his taste for wild nature, for an otter, a woodchuck, or a loon.*

—*Ralph Waldo Emerson,* Journal (*February 1862*)

Walt Whitman loved America and understood it as deeply and as mystically as did Lincoln ("O Captain! my Captain!"). Each in his own way symbolized the spirit and expressed the inner meaning of that triumphant experiment in self-government known as the United States. Whitman, identifying America with the mystique of freedom, in effect wrote one continuous song about democracy. "I shall," he said in *Democratic Vistas* (1871), "use the words America and democracy as convertible terms." Both in his poetry and prose, Whitman was dithyrambic, wild and disconnected, and yet the words were beautiful, with a deep underlying vision and consistency. "People have hesitated to call Whitman's poems poetry"; Lewis Mumford said in *The Golden Day* (1926), "it is useless to deny that they belong to sacred literature."

Whitman, the "Good Grey Poet," sang about America with an abandon and a mystical inclusiveness that sometimes bordered on the incoherent. His prose, if anything, was even more untamed than his poetry. Often they fused. Whitman's words and sentences deliberately broke all bounds.

I celebrate myself;
And what I assume you shall assume;
For every atom belonging to me, as good as belongs to you.

He was a triumphant Everyman:

Walt Whitman, a kosmos, of Manhattan the son,
Turbulent, fleshy, sensual, eating, drinking and breeding,
No sentimentalist, no stander above men and women or apart
from them,
No more modest than immodest.

Not only all men but all of America was his *kosmos*. He wanted to smash the conventions, open what was closed, and let in the spirit of life and love:

Unscrew the locks from the doors!
Unscrew the doors themselves from their jambs!

Whitman sang about his countrymen in the totality of their lives and doings. Unlike the poets of the past, who wrote about the rare, the romantic, or the heroic, Whitman celebrated the commonplace and the earthy. To him, the whole *kosmos* was beautiful and made of the stuff of poetry. So he "caroled" the life of everyday Americans, their fields and their follies, their leaders and their lusts, their politics and their *politesses* (Whitman loved foreign-sounding words), their lunatics and their *literats* (another Whitmanism), their sports and, yes, their spittoons:

I hear America singing, the varied carols I hear,
Those of mechanics . . . ,
The carpenter singing his as he measures his plank or beam,
The mason singing . . . ,
The boatman singing . . . , the deckhand singing. . . .

He was, indeed, so permeated with the sense of the fullness of American life that he developed an addiction for itemizing every detail, place and name that came to mind:

Land of coal and iron! land of gold! land of cotton, sugar, rice!
Land of wheat, beef, pork! land of wool and hemp! land of apple and the grape!
Land of the pastoral plans . . . !
Land of the herd, the garden . . . !
Land of the eastern Chesapeake! land of the Delaware!
Land of Ontario, Erie, Huron, Michigan! . . .

The richness of the American scene was overwhelming to Whitman. Contemplating it, he could barely control the rush of his words. "Have you learn'd the physiology, phrenology, politics, geography, pride, freedom, friendship of the land?" His passion for enumerating details, nouns, names, places, big words and little words led Ralph Waldo Emerson, bemused and bedazzled by *Leaves of Grass,* to ask wrily whether Whitman was writing poetry or "an auctioneer's inventory of a warehouse."

But through the seeming chaos of his literary outpourings, Whitman expressed the inner spirit of America and its freedom as nobody had ever done before or since. He was *the* poet of the American democracy. He had no other theme than democracy in all its human applications and universal implications. He did, indeed, identify democracy with poetry and art, conceiving them to be but different expressions of the unhampered life of a free people, deriving strength from the totality of nature and vigor from the outdoors, all interacting to form a whole.

"Democracy," he wrote in a remarkable passage in *Specimen Days* (1882), "most of all affiliates with the open air, is sunny and hardy and sane only with Nature—just as much as Art is. . . . American Democracy, in its myriad personalities, in factories, work-shops, stores, offices—through the dense streets and cities, and all their manifold sophisticated life—must either be fibred, vitalized by regular contact with out-door light and air and growths, farm-scenes, animals, fields, trees, birds, sun-warmth and free skies, or it will certainly dwindle and pale. We cannot have grand races of mechanics, work people, and commonalty (the only specific purpose of America), on any less terms."

This singularly American poet Walter Whitman—he changed his name to Walt in 1855, the year *Leaves of Grass* was published—was born on May 31, 1819, in West Hills, Long Island. He was one of nine children of Walter Whitman, a carpenter who read Tom Paine and occasionally listened to the sermons of the Quaker Elias Hicks, and Louise Van Velsor, a nonliterate woman of Dutch descent. The Whitmans and Van Velsors had lived on Long Island since the middle of the seventeenth century; they were country people so inbred that they developed strains of marked mental decay. One of Walt's brothers died young, of alcoholism and tuberculosis; another was an epileptic imbecile. One sister became an eccentric drunk; another died of syphilis in an insane asylum. Walt himself was stricken with paralysis at fifty-four and remained partially disabled until his death at seventy-three (March 26, 1892). Walt loved his sturdy mother rather than his morose father, with whom he worked as a carpenter. She held the somewhat squalid and shiftless family together.

Walt had little formal education. He went to school in Brooklyn, then a town of about ten thousand, for a few years and then quit. "From 1824 to '28," Whitman wrote in *Specimen Days,* "our family lived in

Brooklyn on Front, Cranberry and Johnson streets. In the latter my father built a nice house for a home, and afterwards another in Tillary Street. We occupied them, one after the other, but they were mortgaged, and we lost them. . . . Most of these years I went to the public schools."

Although Walt disliked school, he loved books. "A big, good-natured lad," one of his teachers remembered him, "clumsy and slovenly in appearance, but not otherwise remarkable." His character was shaped not by the classroom but by the outdoors. Summers he spent with haymakers and fishermen, and on the beaches. "I loved, after bathing, to race up and down the hard sand, and declaim Homer or Shakespeare to the surf and sea-gulls by the hour." Boy and young man, he roamed the length of Long Island, "from Brooklyn to Montauk Point," feeling about it as if he had "incorporated" it in himself.

After leaving school at the age of about eleven, he became an office boy for two years, then a printer's devil on the *Long Island Patriot* and afterward on the *Long Island Star*. Always he read books, especially poetry and novels, those of Sir Walter Scott and James Fenimore Cooper among others. "A most omnivorous novel-reader, these and later years, devour'd everything I could get." He learned the printing trade, for a while taught country school in Long Island, contributed to local weeklies, worked on papers in New York City and Brooklyn, including the *Brooklyn Daily Eagle* as editor, published occasional small newspapers of his own, and wandered for thousands of miles through the country as far west as the Mississippi River. Absorbing the sights and smells of an earthy and lusty America, Whitman kept notes and diaries in preparation for his career as a poet, which he considered the highest national expression. "By its popular poets," he wrote in later life (January 1880), "the calibers of an age, the weak spots of its embankments, its subcurrents (often more significant than the biggest surface ones), are unerringly indicated." Insofar as Whitman had a steady trade, it was that of a newspaperman.

In 1855, at thirty-six, Whitman put together a small number of his poems, polished them a little ("I had great trouble in leaving out the stock 'poetical' touches, but succeeded at last"), set up type in the shop of a friend ("the brothers Rome, in Brooklyn"), and printed some 1000 copies under the title *Leaves of Grass*. No respectable New York bookseller would handle the amateurish book by an unknown poet; it was distributed by a "phrenological depot" on Broadway. It did not sell. The press generally ignored it. The few notices it received were contemptuous. The *Boston Intelligencer* reviewed *Leaves of Grass* as "a heterogeneous mass of bombast, egotism, vulgarity, and nonsense.... The beastliness of the author is set forth in his own description of himself, and we can conceive of no better reward than the lash for such a violation of decency. The author should be kicked from all decent society as below the level of the brute. He must be some escaped lunatic raving in pitiable delirium."

Nearly all established men of letters to whom Whitman sent copies of *Leaves of Grass* paid no attention to it—all but one, Emerson, for whom he had a boundless admiration and whom he addressed as "Master." To Emerson, this book by "a journeyman printer in Brooklyn, New York, named Walter Whitman," came as a shock and at the same time, so sensitive and honest were his perceptions, as an agreeable surprise. Despite the coarseness of its language, Emerson, like his fellow Brahmin, Professor Charles Eliot Norton of Harvard, found the book full of tremendous power and originality. In his review of *Leaves of Grass* in *Putnam's Monthly,* September 1855, Professor Norton thought that it might have been written by a "fireman or omnibus driver," calling it a "mixture of Yankee transcendentalism and New York rowdyism," but granted "an original perception of nature, a manly brawn, and an epic directness in our new poet."

Emerson confided to his friend Carlyle that *Leaves of Grass* was "a nondescript monster which yet had terrible eyes and buffalo strength, and was indisputably American." A truly original poet, breaking into print in a country that had hitherto known only imitators of European literature and was widely regarded as a cultural wasteland, was someone for Emerson to hail. No doubt he was aware of the famous comment on American cultural sterility made by the English clergyman and wit, Sydney Smith (1771–1845). Writing in the *Edinburgh Review,* of which he was one of the founders, Smith had said: "During the thirty or forty years of their independence, they [the Americans] have done absolutely nothing for the Sciences, for the Arts, for Literature, or even for the statesman-like studies of Politics or Political Economy.... In the four quarters of the globe, who reads an American book? or goes to an American play? or looks at an American picture or statue? What does the world yet owe to American physicians or surgeons? What new substances have their chemists discovered? or what old ones have they analyzed? What new constellations have they discovered by the telescopes of Americans?—what have they done in mathematics ... ? Finally, under which of the tyrannical governments of Europe is every sixth man a Slave ... ?"

Despite his misgivings at Whitman's crudity and formlessness, Emerson wrote to the young poet from Brooklyn (July 21, 1855): "Dear Sir, —I am not blind to the worth of the wonderful gift of *Leaves of Grass*. I find it the most extraordinary piece of wit and wisdom that America has yet contributed . . . I give you joy of your free and brave thought. I have great joy in it. I find incomparable things said incomparably well, as they must be. . . . *I greet you at the beginning of a new career.*"

To his chagrin, Emerson, who took it for granted that his letter was a private communication, found that Whitman printed it in his next edition of *Leaves of Grass* (June 1856) and, in addition, stamped in gold the words *"I greet you . . ."* on the back of the book. The endorsement of America's foremost literary figure, even without permission to publish it, was to Whitman a veritable passport to fame. "I supposed," he said, "the letter was meant to be blazoned; I regarded it as the chart of an emperor."

Although Whitman despised the "supercilious" and culturally pretentious Bostonians, he continued to hold Emerson in the highest esteem. In 1871, when John Burroughs reported that Emerson told him: "Tell Walt I am not satisfied" with his poems, which are like "inventories," Whitman laughed, saying: "I know what I am about better than Emerson does. Yet I love to hear what the gods have to say." Later, when Whitman was sixty-nine, he said to his biographer Horace Traubel (October 19, 1888): "Emerson had the cutest, justest, brain of all our world: saw everything, literally everything, in right perspective—things personal, things general."

Writers like Emerson and Thoreau (who said that Whitman was "exhilarating . . . , a great fellow") might approve, but the American public in general either ignored or despised the author of *Leaves of Grass*. His relentlessly uncompromising unconventionality and bohemianism—in words, appearance, and attitudes—shocked a nation that was determinedly middle-class and Victorian. During the Civil War, Whitman could not get a job in Washington because he was considered "one of the roughs." As Secretary of the Treasury Salmon P. Chase said to a friend who interceded for Whitman, "his writings have given him a bad repute, and I should not know what sort of a place to give to such a man." When Walt heard about that, he laughed with sardonic good nature, saying: "He is right in preserving his saints from contamination by a man like me!" After serving in hospitals as a nurse to Civil War wounded, Whitman obtained a modest position in the Department of the

Interior, but when President Andrew Johnson's Secretary of the Interior, James Harlan of Iowa, heard that the clerk Walt Whitman was the fellow who had written the notorious *Leaves of Grass,* he fired him.

Whitman, once he embarked upon his literary career with the publication of his first volume of poetry, remained undaunted for the rest of his days. No rebuff could discourage him, no neglect could slow, let alone affect, the overriding aim of his life—to give utterance to the inner voice of America's people, to sing their songs and write their poetry. "I much enjoy making poems," he said in 1856. "Other work I have set for myself to do, to meet people and The States face to face, to confront them with an American rude tongue; but the work of my life is making poems."

He ranged among books uncritically but widely and hungrily. One of his less well-known activities as editor of the *Brooklyn Eagle* was that of book reviewer, a task which, although probably unappreciated by the subscribers of the newspaper, he cherished personally. Publishers sent him about one hundred review copies a year. Some of these he noticed briefly; others he reviewed at some length or mentioned more than once. There were books on history, poetry, literature, philosophy, astronomy, the classics, and geography. Among the historians, Whitman read and reviewed François Guizot, Henry Hallam, Washington Irving, Alphonse de Lamartine, Jules Michelet, and William H. Prescott. Among the poets were William Cullen Bryant, Samuel Taylor Coleridge, Goethe in translation, John Keats, Henry Wadsworth Longfellow, and John Milton.

Whitman's literary opinions, as a reviewer of books, were a mixture of the conventional and the unorthodox. He rarely challenged great and well-established literary reputations. Of Coleridge's *Biographia Literaria,* he said that it "stands above all poets." Bryant, he wrote, was "one of the best poets in the world." Longfellow's poems were "beautiful thoughts in beautiful words." Milton's were "heavenly high, and profoundly deep." Of histories, Whitman considered Guizot's work on the English revolution of 1640 "one of the really valuable books of the age"; Michelet's multivolume history of France the "best"; Lamartine's history of the Girondists "the most dramatic work we ever read." As for Irving's *History of the Life and Voyages of Christopher Columbus* in four volumes, Whitman was quite overwhelmed: "Our poor commendaation is not needed for any writing of such a man as Irving."

But Walt could also be unconventionally critical, especially when he wrote about men whose politics he opposed or distrusted. He liked Carlyle, but considered *Heroes and Hero Worship* written in a "grotesque" style. He was particularly contemptuous of Samuel Johnson, whom he regarded as an enemy of democracy. Reviewing Boswell's noted *Life of Samuel Johnson,* Whitman challenged the prevailing admiration for the snarling (and anti-American) Tory by writing (December 1846): "We are no admirer of such characters as Dr. Johnson. He was a sour, malicious, egotistical man. He was a sycophant of power and rank, withal; his biographer narrates that he 'always spoke with rough contempt of popular liberty.' His head was educated to the point *plus,* but for his heart, might still more unquestionably stand the sign *minus.* Nor were the freaks of this man the mere eccentricities of genius: they were probably the faults of a vile low nature. His soul was a bad one."

In his *Brooklyn Eagle* editorials, Whitman showed himself to be a radical democrat, taking positions that were characteristic of the American left-wing liberals of the time. He was influenced by William Leggett (1802–39), the aggressively reformist editor of the *New York Evening Post,* whom historian Allan Nevins has described as "the most potent force in shaping the ideas of democracy" at the period. When Leggett challenged the Tammany-dominated Democratic Party, Whitman was one of the *loco-focos*—a radical wing of that Party which advocated equal rights, direct popular vote, abolition of monopolies and special privilege. The name derived from the then-new friction matches, known as loco-focos, which were used by the dissident radicals to light candles when the Tammany stalwarts turned off the gas lights on them.

Whitman also espoused other radical causes—free trade, universal suffrage, prison reform, women's rights, paper money, and a single tax. By the same token, he was opposed to temperance laws ("The Intemperance of Temperance," was the title of one of his editorials), economic monopolies, political corruption, exploitation of workers, hard money, and whatever else was current among liberals as a public evil that required reform.

Whitman did not think about politics systematically. His conception of the function of government was limited. In the main, he was in the tradition of American liberalism—the tradition of Jefferson, Taylor, and Emerson. "Sensible men," Whitman echoed Emerson in one of his editorials, "have long seen that the best government is that which governs least." In common with other liberals of his time, Whitman could not see that the state had a creative role to perform in society. "Although government," he wrote in 1847, "can do little *positive* good to the people, it may do an *immense deal of harm.*"

Whitman distrusted on three main grounds the kind of federal, state, and city politics practiced in his day. First, such government meddled outrageously in the lives of the people. Second, it hampered freedom by protecting special privilege. Third, it undermined real democracy by operating through dishonest politicians whose systematic business was to mislead the people.

Whitman vehemently opposed what he called the "excessive management" and the "officiousness of the law-making powers" in moral behavior. He detested sumptuary legislation, Sabbath-closing ordinances, antidrinking statutes, and the whole profusion of blue laws foisted on the country by busybodies, as worse than useless and as an offense to the human spirit. "You cannot," he wrote, "legislate men into morality." The legislators, all too frequently sinners themselves, had no right to force men legislatively into virtue. Blue laws were made by hypocrites and thus produced more of the same. Each individual, Whitman held, should be responsible only to himself and to his God for his own behavior. Virtuous men are not created by law but by good moral principles and a decent environment.

"It is all folly," Walt wrote in one of his editorials, "to expect from law, the popular virtues, worth, and self-denial, which must come from entirely different sources—from the influence and example of home, from well-rooted principles, from a habit of morality. We have therefore little faith in laws that interfere with morals. We have no faith at all in the efforts of law to make men good."

The lawmakers, he said, "meddle with every thing, and derange every thing" for the purpose, among other things, of gulling the "great mass" of the people into accepting them as wise leaders. Behind the facade of such pretensions, the politicians practice favoritism, support special interests in matters such as the high tariff, exploit the poor, and maintain their privileged positions through all manner of chicanery.

What was the solution for this gulling of the public? Establish true democracy, Whitman answered. "Democracy would prevent all this harm," because its basic principles require that no man should benefit at the expense of another. Under this "beautiful and harmonious system," no individual would infringe upon the rights of another, and hence few laws (or politicians) would be necessary.

"While mere politicians, in their narrow minds, are sweating and fuming with their complicated statutes," he said, "this one single rule, rationally construed and applied, is enough to form the starting point of all that is necessary in government: *to make no more laws than those useful for preventing a man or body of men from* infringing on the rights of other men."

Whitman admitted that he had no consistent, logically constructed political philosophy: "I guess I don't, I should not desire to do so." He followed his democratic instincts. As the Democratic Party became more openly identified with slavery and the South, Whitman left it, became a Free-soiler and then a Republican and supporter of Lincoln. But in the end he lost interest in all political parties and organized groups, proclaiming instead his faith in the individual, in comradeship, in friendship and in manly love, in the genius of the "common people." He based his philosophy on universal human sympathy, on the ever-widening freedom of the masses of men. This universality, he said, was his "grand theme," and in it he rooted his democratic outlook.

The fullest expression of this philosophy was given in *Democratic Vistas,* a pamphlet he wrote in 1871, at the opening of the Grant era with its pervasive corruption. The Civil War had had a stunning impact on Whitman. "My experiences afterwards in the secession outbreak," he said, became one of the "three leading sources and formative stamps to my own character"—next only to the influences of his parental heritage and the Long Island environment. As a war nurse, he had witnessed slaughter and massive violence, the sufferings of the wounded, the courage of the simple soldier, the agonies of the dying. These Americans in their convulsions struck a mystical chord in Whitman. They were ordinary men and yet, "at the first tap of the drum," they sprang to arms, "not for gain, nor even glory, nor to repel invasion, but for an emblem, a mere abstraction"—the American flag and nation. *Democratic Vistas* was a response to his Civil War experiences. It may be considered, in its own way, an imperishable tribute to those "brave men" who gave their lives that this nation should have a new birth of freedom.

*Democratic Vistas* is a remarkable testament to the philosophy of freedom. Torrential, rhetorical, and imprecise, yet in its scope and inclusiveness, eloquence and faith in democracy, it is a stirring—and incredibly quotable—document of faith in humanity. The words and sentences throb with truths that are far above the mundane and ring with affirmations of life's triumphs. In its power to stretch the mind and enlarge the human horizon, *Democratic Vistas* is a major contribution to the world's literature of democracy.

At the risk of oversimplification of what is essentially a poetic and occasionally murky and repetitive rather than logical essay, one may say that in *Democratic Vistas* Whitman elaborates three chief points. First, he warns the nation against the prevailing cynicism, materialism, and corruption. Secondly, he underlines the greatness of America's destiny as a land of democracy, an empire of freedom to serve as a model for mankind, provided it consciously strives to fulfill its historic mission. Finally he develops the concept of democracy as a personal, not a governmental or political, ideal; as a philosophy that is in the deepest sense spiritual and religious (without being churchly) in that it elevates man's soul and liberates him from the bonds of vulgarity and selfishness.

In his criticism of post–Civil War America, Whitman was a prophet of rare anger. The nation, he wrote, had "just by a hair escaped destruction," and now it was wallowing in ugliness, "plentiful meanness and vulgarity," and universal corruption. State and federal legislatures were openly bought; politicians were the creatures of the moneyed men, especially the railroad magnates. In Whitman's own state, the political machine of the Tammany boss, William Marcy Tweed (1823–78), became a byword for corruption; the legislature at Albany, members of which received one hundred thousand dollars in bribes in 1872 alone, had given some forty million dollars of public money to the railroad speculators. In Washington, lobbyists spent some $436,000 in bribes to charter the Union Pacific Railroad, and nearly a million to get congressional subsidies for the Pacific Mail Steamship Company.

Whitman's contemporary, William Larrabee, a governor of Iowa, described the art of corruption as it was practiced in the United States in the latter part of the nineteenth century: "Outright bribery is probably the means least often employed by corporations to carry their measures. ... It is the policy of political corruption committees of corporations to ascertain the weakness and wants of every man whose services they are likely to need.... Men with political ambition are encouraged to aspire to preferment, and are assured of corporate support.... Briefless lawyers are promised corporate business.... Those in financial straits are accommodated with loans. Vain men are flattered and given newspaper notoriety.... Shippers are given advantage in rates over their competitors.... Influential constituents of doubtful members are sent for at the last moment to labor with the representatives.... Telegrams pour in upon the unsuspecting members.... Petitions are ... hastily circulated. ... Another powerful reinforcement of the railroad lobby is ... a subsidized press and its correspondents."

Outright or concealed bribery of politicians, office-holders, and members of the press was only one manifestation of the universal moral degeneration that Whitman found in American life at the time he was writing *Democratic Vistas*. He viewed the national scene "like a physician diagnosing some deep disease" after the "agony and bloody sweat" of the Civil War, and found it "appalling." America, he said, presented a spectacle ugly enough to dishearten any but the most optimistic believers in the noble ideal of democracy:

"The official services of America, national, state, and municipal, in all their branches and departments, except the judiciary, are saturated in corruption, bribery, falsehood, mal-administration; and the judiciary is tainted. The great cities reek with respectable as much as non-respectable robbery and scoundrelism. . . . Everywhere, in shop, street, church, theatre, bar-room, official chair, are pervading flippancy and vulgarity, low cunning, infidelity—everywhere the youth puny, impudent, foppish, prematurely ripe—everywhere an abnormal libidousness, unhealthy forms, male, female, painted, padded, dyed, chignon'd, muddy complexion, bad blood. . . ."

A picture straight out of Jeremiah, but one confirmed by other contemporary writers, such as Henry George, although not so eloquently. Whitman felt that the great challenge to America was to overcome this inner rot, the effects of "scrofulous wealth" and the "demonism of greed," to cleanse its soul and to strive actively for the fulfillment of the nation's destiny as the world's foremost example of democracy. Without such a reformation the United States, despite its vast prosperity and colossal power, "beyond Alexander's, beyond the proudest sway of Rome," would prove to be the "most tremendous failure" in history. But reform and moral uplift required conscious effort and will, a reaffirmation of democratic grandeur. "Thought your greatness to ripen for you like a pear? If you would have greatness, know that you must . . . pay for it with a proportionate price."

Whitman referred to his democratic philosophy as "personalism." This he defined in various ways, but in essence he meant by it the inner development of man to achieve his highest potential, rejecting personal greed and hoggish materialism, fulfilling himself in all his talents and aspirations as a moral member of society. To achieve this, it was necessary to reconsider the functions of government. It was not enough, Whitman wrote, for government merely to assert its physical authority or to exercise its police powers. The object of government, particularly democratic government, was far higher and nobler. It was to give opportunity for ordinary human beings to grow in all dimensions—"to develop, to open up to cultivation, to encourage the possibilities of all beneficent and manly outcroppage, and . . . the pride and self-respect latent in all characters." Such a democratic government was, in short, to be a "training-school for making first-class men."

"I say the mission of government, henceforth, in civilized lands," he wrote, "is not repression, and not authority alone, not even of law . . . —but higher than the highest arbitrary rule, to train communities through all their grades, beginning with individuals and ending there again, to rule themselves.

". . . For democracy . . . is the best, perhaps only, fit . . . formulater, general caller-forth, trainer, for the million, not for grand material personalities only, but for immortal souls. To be a voter with the rest is not so much. . . . But to become an enfranchised man, and . . . to stand and start without humiliation, and equal with the rest; to commence . . . the grand experiment of . . . the forming of a full-grown man or woman—that *is* something."

Thus Walt Whitman called America to greatness. He conceived of democracy, especially as he visualized it in the United States, as a unique form of civilization that, transcending ordinary politics and material strivings, should have for its sole aim the creation of a noble race of human beings unlike any others known in the past. Such were the dazzling vistas that the poet of democracy opened up for America, and beyond.

Come, I will make the continent indissoluble,
I will make the most splendid race the sun ever shone upon,
I will make divine magnetic lands,
With the love of comrades,
  With the life-long love of comrades.

I will paint companionship thick as trees along the
    rivers of America, and along the shores of the great
    lakes, and all over the prairies,
I will make inseparable cities with their arms about
    each other's necks,
By the love of comrades,
  By the manly love of comrades.

—*For You O Democracy*, 1860.

# 14

## *THE AMERICAN AS RADICAL:*

# Henry George *(1839–1897)*

*Perhaps the first approach to a critical diagnosis that made a rift in American complacency was Henry George's* Progress and Poverty.... *Through countless channels, George's ideas filtered out into varied types of American thought, helping to make the country at least dimly aware of the social question.*

—*Charles A. and Mary R. Beard,*
The Rise of American Civilization

In 1871, the year Whitman wrote *Democratic Vistas,* appeared a pamphlet, "Our Land and Land Policy," that was to be the precursor of a remarkable book, *Progress and Poverty*, published in 1879. Its author, Henry George, was, like Whitman, a printer and itinerant newspaperman. Both men despite their difference in temperament, shared with the liberal intellectuals of their day a sense of deep outrage at the corrupting power over American life wielded by the new plutocracy then emerging in the country.

Henry George was born in Philadelphia in 1839, one of eleven children of a lower-middle-class family. He was a child of the depression of the time and grew up in the period following the catastrophic panic of 1837, which caused wide and enduring havoc, especially among the poor. The panic destroyed real-estate values, produced a calamitous shortage of money, led to widespread business bankruptcies and bank failures, and closed 90 per cent of the nation's factories. In that atmosphere of gloom and hopelessness—akin to that of the Great Depression of 1929—George spent his early childhood. It colored his whole life. He never finished school. As a boy, he went to sea; after sailing the Pacific, he settled in California, where he supported himself in a humdrum way by printing and journalism. In 1880, the year after the publication of *Progress and Poverty* which made him famous, he moved to New York, where he lived the rest of his life.

*Progress and Poverty,* on which George's reputation rests and which is one of the few original works in its field ever written by an American, can best be appreciated in the light of contemporary economic and intellectual conditions. George made his basic observations of society and drew his generalizations in the 1860s and 1870s, the period that inaugurated America's Gilded Age. It was, and for the next half-century continued to be, an era of unrestrained capitalist enterprise and of ruthless exploitation of natural and human resources for private profit. It was an age of vast individual fortunes, piled up by a handful of entrepreneurs through the use of means and methods that shocked people accustomed to an earlier Protestant ethic. Politicians on all levels were openly bought or controlled by the aggressive new capitalists who operated either as predatory speculators, as did Jim Fisk and Daniel Drew, or through monopolistic trusts and corporations, such as John D. Rockefeller's Standard Oil Company.

Standard Oil, organized in 1872, was the first trust and served as a model for the others. Ida M. Tarbell's pioneering work, *A History of the Standard Oil Company,* which began as a series of articles in *McClure's* magazine in 1903, thus described John D. Rockefeller, who was a business genius: "Low-voiced, soft-footed, humble, knowing every point in every man's business, he never tired until he got his wares at the lowest possible figure. 'John always got the best of the bargain,' old men tell you in Cleveland today. 'Smooth,' a 'savvy fellow,' is their description of him."

A new breed of economic predators and industrial trusts—the Whiskey Trust, the Sugar Trust, the Steel Trust, the Copper Trust, to mention a few—with interlocking directorates that penetrated all business enterprise, controlled the political and economic life of the country. Systematically they used the machinery of government for their own private purposes.

"Senators," William Allen White, editor of the Emporia (Kansas) *Gazette,* wrote of this period in his autobiography, "elected in the days when machines and the ownership of machines were passing into the hands of a class-conscious, organized plutocracy had no obligations to the people of their state. . . . In Kansas, it was the railroads. In western Massachusetts, it was the textiles. In eastern Massachusetts, it was the banks. In New York, it was amalgamated industry. In Montana, it was copper. . . . The grade of senators, as far as intelligence went, was higher than the grade which the people selected, but on the whole . . . it was not representative government. Only a minority of the people of the United States had any control over the United States Senate. And that minority was interested in its own predatory designs."

In Henry George's day the plutocracy, which controlled government as well as educational institutions and the media of opinion formation, lacked the characteristics of older aristocracies—personal taste and a sense of public responsibility. The magnates of whiskey and sugar and cattle and railroads and timber and land despised politics and, except for personal charities, showed a monumental indifference to the social problems created by the industrial age they dominated. They equated "politician" with "crook" and, as a matter of course, acted accordingly. Gruff "Commodore" Cornelius Vanderbilt (1794–1877), one of the most conspicuous magnates of his day, bluntly described an honest politician as one who when bought stayed bought. An economist, Richard T. Ely, succinctly described in *The Independent* of August 28, 1890 the power of railroad interests: "You cannot turn in any direction in American politics without discovering the railway power. . . . Its power ramifies in every direction, its roots reaching counting rooms, editorial sanctums, schools and churches which it supports . . . , as well as courts and legislatures." In general, the new financial grandees looked upon government as a private trough, a brimming source of public-utility franchises, economic privileges, financial grants, and, of particular significance to Henry George's work, free land.

It should be remembered that America's first fortunes were made from the public lands. Cattle barons, grazing their herds on the federal domain, and railroad speculators and builders, heavily subsidized by government, built their mammoth wealth on the nation's basic resource. The railroads in particular were given lavish grants of land and hundreds of millions of dollars in subsidies. Beginning in 1850, when Congress gave the state of Illinois 2.7 million acres for the Illinois Central, a vast chunk of the public domain was given away to private railroad companies. Altogether 214 million acres—an area six times the size of the state of Illinois—were handed, a free gift, to the railroads in the West. In the 1860s, the Central Pacific and Union Pacific alone received sixty million dollars in cash plus forty-five million acres of public lands.

As Harry J. Carman and Samuel McKee put it in their *History of the United States:*

"Space forbids even a brief account of the fraudulent means often employed in securing public subsidies or of the corruption, wastefulness, and extravagance which characterized the expenditure of both private and public funds raised for railroad construction."

Nor were the railroad companies the only private interests that raided the public domain. Through dummy homesteading and other legal frauds, speculators acquired control of much of the nation's valuable land. By 1880 more than half of the country's best grazing, mineral, and timber lands had already been alienated. A large tenant class was being created. Of some four million farms, more than one million were being cultivated by nonowners.

Such was the land picture the young newspaperman-printer, Henry George, observed in the West. When he came east to New York, he was further dismayed by business panics, widespread poverty, and warlike strikes in the industrial areas. One of the great strikes of this period, that of the railroad workers in 1877, spread through several states (Pennsylvania, West Virginia, Maryland, Illinois, Missouri), led to pitched battles with many casualties (twenty-six were killed in Pittsburgh alone) and property damage estimated at about ten million dollars. This strike, as was the case with so many others at the time, was over wage cuts.

Economic conditions reminded George of his childhood and youth—nothing seemed to have changed except that the rich got fabulously richer and the poor were worse off. Stirred by what he called the "shocking contrast between monstrous wealth and debasing want," George was determined to discover the underlying causes of misery in a land of potential plenty. *Progress and Poverty,* which he completed in March 1879 and published, after paying for the plates himself, at the end of the year, contains his answers and proposed cures.

Fortunately for the originality of *Progress and Poverty,* George had no academic education. Had he been exposed to the political and economic theories then taught in American colleges and propagated by leading editors and preachers, he might have been intellectually intimidated and the springs of his creativity could have dried up. But, except for David A. Wells, chairman of the New York State Commission on Tax Reform, who advocated a single tax on monopolies in 1871, George was not influenced by any established "authorities" in the field of political economy. He did realize, however, that any serious challenge to the existing economic institutions and the ideas that shielded them was hazardous, as he wrote with some bitterness to Wells in 1871, when he was studying land policy and problems:

"Turn light into the caverns of ignorance, and the bats will whirr about your ears. Offer to lay hands upon vested wrongs, and you arouse the most bitter, the most unscrupulous assailants. I know the sickening part of it—how the very men you are doing your best to serve often turn upon you in their ignorance or worse. . . . Sometimes I feel disheartened when I see how little the people, and especially the laboring classes, appreciate their true interest, how easily they are deluded with words and led by demagogues, . . . and my habitual view of the future of the nation is far less rose-colored than it once was, but for all that the earnest honest man, who would do what he can in his day and generation, must go on."

The prevailing ideas that Henry George set out to challenge and defy were those of *laissez-faire* liberalism in economics and "social Darwinism" in political thought. In and out of academic halls, economics—or political economy, as it was known at the time—based on the theories of Adam Smith, David Ricardo, and John Stuart Mill, was considered a "finished product," an absolute science as fixed and immutable as the stars.

It is interesting to note that in 1876, *Publisher's Weekly* listed the following ten as the "most salable works on political economy" in the United States:—John Stuart Mill, *Principles of Political Economy* (two vols., 1848); Adam Smith, *The Wealth of Nations* (1776); Arthur L. Perry, *The Elements of Political Economy* (1865); John E. Cairnes, *Some Leading Principles of Political Economy Newly Explained* (1874); Henry Fawcett, *Manual of Political Economy* (1863); Amasa Walker, *Science of Wealth* (1866); Francis Wayland, *Elements of Political Economy* (1837); Horace Greeley, *Essays Designed to Elucidate the Science of Political Economy* (1870); Francis Bowen, *American Political Economy* (1870); and W. Stanley Jevons, *The Theory of Political Economy* (1871)—in that order.

Based upon the presumably cosmic laws of nature, the economic system was beyond human control. "It was held," Richard T. Ely tells in his autobiographical *Ground Under Our Feet* (1938), "that natural laws established certain fundamental principles for all times and places. It was only necessary that we should study these natural laws and follow them to attain the highest state of economic felicity possible to mankind."

To question the workings and expose the flaws of the economic system, or to propose reforms for social-economic improvement, was regarded as immoral and impious, an offense against God. Since the prevailing property system was held to be divinely ordained, any suggestion for government intervention or reform was nothing short of blasphemous —a meddling with the work of the Deity. Economic principles, said Professor Francis Bowen of Harvard, were the manifestation of the "wisdom and beneficence of the Deity, just as clearly as . . . the marvellous arrangement of the material universe."

In his popular textbook, *American Political Economy,* Bowen wrote: "Man cannot interfere with His work without marring it. The attempts of legislators to turn the industry of society in one direction or another, out of its natural and self-chosen channels, here to encourage by bounties and there to load it with penalties, to increase or diminish the supply of the market, to establish a *maximum* of price, to keep specie in the country, are almost invariably productive of harm. *Laissez faire;* 'these things regulate themselves,' in common phrase; which means, of course, that God regulates them by His general laws, which always, in the long run, work to good."

Not only must the divinely ordained economic system not be interfered with, but it was God's will that man should become materially rich. Poverty was a prime sin, a moral deficiency offensive to God and religion. Property, on the other hand, was sacred and wealth an object pleasing to Deity. Its acquisition "ennobled" man, in the words of Mark Hopkins (1802–87), president of Williams College and author of works on moral philosophy (among them *Lectures on Moral Science* and *The Law of Love and Love as a Law*).

On a popular level, these ideas on the sanctity of property found their widest echo in Russell H. Conwell (1843–1925), a Philadelphia Baptist minister, whose lecture, "Acres of Diamonds" (published in book form under the same title in 1890), was said to have been delivered by him to some 6000 audiences in the country. The Reverend Mr. Conwell, identifying poverty with impiety and wealth with happiness, told his listeners that there were riches (acres of diamonds) lying all around them, and that it was their moral duty to look for them: "Arise, ye millions . . . trust in God and man, and believe in the great opportunities that are right here . . . for business, for everything that is worth living for on earth." He said that every "man and woman ought to strive" for money and that those who were critical of the rich—among them men like Henry George—were nothing but "an envious, lazy crowd of unsuccessful persons." Conwell's crusading exhortation was: "I say, Get rich, get rich!" This spirit continued in the United States well into the twentieth century. President Calvin Coolidge, expressed a similar viewpoint succinctly when he said: "America's business is business."

Even more extreme were the social-economic ideas of another clergyman, the famous Congregational minister and lecturer Henry Ward Beecher (1813–77). In one of his sermons, given in 1877, two years before the publication of George's *Progress and Poverty,* Beecher orated: "Is the great working class oppressed? Yes, undoubtedly it is.... God has intended the great to be great and the little to be little.... I do not say that a dollar a day is enough to support a working man, but it is enough to support a man! ... Not enough to support a man and five children if a man would insist on smoking and drinking beer.... But the man who cannot live on bread and water is not fit to live." Beecher was one of the highest-paid lecturers in the United States.

The dominant scholarship of the period reinforced, on an intellectual and sophisticated level, the ideas preached by men like Conwell and Beecher. Foremost among the academic champions of the sanctity of property and social-economic inequality in Henry George's day was William Graham Sumner (1840–1910), professor of political science (and sociology) at Yale. Sumner was trained for the Episcopal priesthood, but he gave up the ministry for an academic career. He came under the influence of Herbert Spencer (1820–1903), an eccentric British Victorian writer, who, influenced by Darwin, composed numerous books on *Principles* of everything (biology, psychology, sociology, ethics). Spencer, of whom John Dewey observed drily that he had a "singular immunity from all intellectual contagion," was a dogmatist who generalized about humanity and society with a maximum of wordage and a minimum of data. He had an impact on a whole generation of Americans with ideas that came to be known as "social Darwinism."

"If we do not like the survival of the fittest," Sumner wrote with characteristic bluntness in one of his many articles on the subject, "we have only one possible alternative, and that is the survival of the unfittest. The former is the law of civilization; the latter is the law of anti-civilization."

As the author of *Folkways,* Sumner may in effect be considered one of the founders of American sociology. He collected a vast amount of data on the *mores* of mankind. His main work in this field, *Science of Society,* was published posthumously in four volumes by his student and collaborator, Professor A. G. Keller.

Against this background of barbaric social theory and, as it were, jungle morality, Henry George wrote *Progress and Poverty*. To him, as to such equally protesting contemporaries as Henry Demarest Lloyd (1847–1903), who wrote *Wealth Against Commonwealth* in 1894, and Edward Bellamy (1850–98), author of the utopian *Looking Backward* (1888), the theories of the "social Darwinists" were as shocking as the practices of the prevailing economic system, which the latter defended.

"The name of political economy," George wrote, "has been constantly invoked against every effort of the working classes to increase their wages or decrease their hours of labor. . . . Take the best and most extensively circulated text-books. While they insist upon freedom for capital, while they justify on the ground of utility the selfish greed that seeks to pile fortune on fortune, and the niggard spirit that steels the heart to the wail of distress, what sign of substantial promise do they hold out to the working man . . . ?"

George, who said that "we cannot safely leave political economy to college professors," accepted the American democratic premises as a fundamental approach to political and social problems. He believed in the Jeffersonian idea that men were equal (which Sumner ridiculed, as had Calhoun before him, as "an inherent absurdity"). He felt that human beings, and not impersonal historic forces were the center of the social universe ("the tide will not be changed by us," Sumner said); and that it was their inherent right so to organize or ameliorate their institutions as to achieve a decent and dignified existence for themselves. These were the basic assumptions on which George built his theory.

The title of his book pinpointed his subject with remarkable succinctness. Its subtitle, *An Inquiry into the Cause of Industrial Depressions and of Increase of Want with Increase of Wealth, the Remedy,* accurately described the content. *Progress and Poverty* consisted of three main themes integrated into a whole. One was an indictment of existing industrial society, with its widespread poverty and misery. The second was a philosophy of history, with its supposedly universal laws of progress and decline. The third and most original part was a proposed remedy for the existing evils of society.

George's initial statement of his study was both an attack on current conditions and an arresting challenge. Why, he asked, was there so much poverty in an age of science and technology? Why was there so much misery and stagnation in a period when inventions and machines were capable of creating wealth and well-being for everybody? The phenomenon of misery, he wrote, was not confined to the United States but was universal; complaints came "from all parts of the civilized world" where industrialism took root:

"In every civilized country pauperism, crime, insanity, and suicides are increasing. In every civilized country the diseases are increasing which come from overstrained nerves, from insufficient nourishment, from squalid lodgings, from unwholesome and monotonous occupations, from premature labor of children, from the tasks and crimes which poverty imposes upon women."

The United States was no exception to these conditions. George described American want amid potential riches as relentlessly as Karl Marx depicted European conditions.

"It is at last becoming evident," George wrote, "that the enormous increase in productive power which has marked the present century and is still going on with accelerating ratio, has no tendency to extirpate poverty or to lighten the burdens of those compelled to toil. . . . The march of invention has clothed mankind with powers of which a century ago the boldest imagination could not have dreamed. But in factories where labor-saving machinery has reached its most wonderful development, little children are at work; wherever the new forces are anything like fully utilized, large classes are maintained by charity . . . ; amid the greatest accumulations of wealth, men die of starvation, and puny infants suckle dry breasts; while everywhere the greed of gain, the worship of wealth, shows the force of the fear of want. The promised land lies before us like the mirage. The fruits of the tree of knowledge turn as we grasp them to apples of Sodom that crumble at the touch."

George did not exaggerate when he referred to "the greatest accumulation of wealth." The latter part of the nineteenth century witnessed the acquisition of individual American fortunes of staggering and unprecedented size. Such families as the Rockefellers, the Astors, the Goelets, the Harrimans, the Hills, the Rhinelanders, the Vanderbilts, and others amassed personal fortunes that ran into the scores and hundreds of millions of dollars each—in an era when taxation and social and labor legislation were at a minimum.

The cause of economic inequality, George concluded, lay in inadequate social organization. There was nothing in nature, he argued, that condemned men to poverty and suffering. The evils were entirely man-made, and hence correctible: "I assert that the injustice of society, not the niggardliness of nature, is the cause of . . . want and misery." He was sure that the root of the evil could be found in the prevailing system of land ownership. If that were properly reformed—through taxation—benefits would radiate out to the whole society.

In this connection, George developed a theory of history and psychology to explain his proposed land-reform program. First, he denied the concept that human progress was continuous or spontaneous. Actually, he argued, history records the rise and fall of numerous civilizations. "The earth is the tomb of the dead empires, no less than of dead men." Decline was due to poor social adjustments. If men do not, or cannot, organize their existence intelligently, for the benefit of the whole society rather than a handful, they stagnate and ultimately die. If they do adjust intelligently to social needs, they survive and flourish. This is what George meant by "progress."

Second, he rejected the notion that man was purely an animal, concerned only with satisfying his immediate physical needs and nothing else. Man, to be sure, had the physical necessities of an animal, but he was "an animal plus something else." Unlike other creatures, man was not satisfied with the needs of the moment. He was differentiated from other species by a constant yearning for things beyond immediate necessities or physical desires. He desired more than he had and imagined more than he saw. This "dissatisfaction" gave man a special dynamism:

"He is the only animal whose desires increase as they are fed; the only animal that is never satisfied. The wants of every other living thing are uniform and fixed. The ox of today aspires to no more than did the ox when man first yoked him. . . . All living things save man can only take, and care for, enough to supply wants which are definite and fixed."

Being an aspiring animal, man was capable of rising to heights beyond himself. "He is the mythic earth tree, whose roots are in the ground, but whose topmost branches may blossom in the heavens!" Hence it was a mistake to think of him as a selfish creature. Actually, he created civilization because of his capacity to experience feelings, emotions, and desires beyond the immediate material self:

"Shortsighted is the philosophy which counts on selfishness as the master motive of human action. . . . If you would move men to action, to what shall you appeal? Not to their pockets, but to their patriotism; not to selfishness, but to sympathy. Self-interest is, as it were, a mechanical force. . . . But there is in human nature what may be likened to a chemical force; which melts and fuses and overwhelms; to which nothing seems impossible . . . in loyalty to higher impulses men will give even life."

These "higher impulses" are the opposite of selfishness; they are unselfishness. In social terms, this meant cooperation among men for larger purposes. It was on this conception of cooperation, which George discerned in human nature, that he constructed both his theory of historic progress and his program of land reform:

"Here is the law of progress, which will explain all diversities, all advances, all halts, and retrogressions. Men tend to progress just as they come closer together, and by cooperation with each other increase the mental power that may be devoted to improvement."

The crux of George's philosophy lay in this human tendency to associate. For association involved living in proximity. This in turn led to population increases. As the population grew, so unavoidably did the value of the land on which people lived and worked. Land is the basis of all wealth and all production. It provides nourishment for men and raw materials for their industry. Control of land, George wrote, was the same as control of "all the fruits of labor." Those who own land, whether for speculation or rent, hold the key to wealth and the economic domination of society.

The people in general did not own or control the land on which they depended for their existence. In the cities especially, land values and rents kept rising, and the only beneficiaries were the landlords, even if they did nothing to improve their holdings. Land value was created entirely by people's use. A city plot, for example, was enhanced in value by such things as its strategic location, access to transportation, availability of markets, residential desirability. The landowner had nothing to do with these enhancements. Yet he reaped the profits from them. This, George said, was "unearned increment," and should be abolished for the benefit of the community as a whole.

He proposed a sweeping reform to eliminate both "unearned increment" and land monopoly. He suggested that all taxes should be eliminated and replaced by a single tax on land based on its increased and increasing value. In effect, this meant a tax on rent. Speaking of the landlords, he said: "We may safely leave them the shell, if we take the kernel. *It is not necessary to confiscate land; it is only necessary to confiscate rent.*"

Such a single tax, George was convinced, would have numerous advantages for society as a whole. It would once and for all eliminate land speculation by skimming off its profits. It would do away with large fortunes, decrease municipal congestion, provide the community with a steady (and fair) income, and free the users of the land from the parasitism of landlords. A single tax would also give men a chance to buy and own land for personal use and improvement, and by affording them an opportunity to build a secure and decent life, would banish misery from the earth:

"What I, therefore, propose, as the simple yet sovereign remedy, which will raise wages, increase the earnings of capital, extirpate pauperism, abolish poverty, give remunerative employment to whoever wishes it, afford free scope to human powers, lessen crime, elevate morals, and taste, and intelligence, purify government and carry civilization to yet nobler heights—is, *to appropriate rent by taxation*."

George seems to have been convinced that his single-tax proposal was not only a way of striking, as Charles A. Beard noted, "at the root of gross inequalities of wealth," but also a road to utopia. He was sure that his simple remedy, by merely eliminating one source of economic inequality, would naturally lead to the creation of a world full of creativity and happiness:

"To remove want and the fear of want, to give all classes leisure, and comfort, and independence, the decencies and refinement of life, the opportunities of mental and moral development, would be like turning water into a desert. The sterile waste would clothe itself with verdure, and the barren places where life seemed banned would ere long be dappled with the shade of trees and musical with the song of birds. Talents now hidden, virtues unsuspected, would come forth to make human life richer, fuller, happier, nobler."

Henry George and his book became famous. Within a quarter of a century of its publication, *Progress and Poverty* sold about two million copies—something of a record for a book of this character. It was widely praised. The *New York Herald* described it as "the most original, the most striking and important contribution which . . . has had no equal since . . . Adam Smith." In London, Karl Marx thought *Progress and Poverty* a significant work, although characteristically he believed it to be the "last attempt to save the capitalist regime." George's masterpiece was read by many capitalists, who, according to one historian, "weren't disturbed by his ideas," as well as by labor leaders and socialists, who adopted them at least temporarily.

In 1886, the now-famous George ran for mayor of New York City on a single-tax platform. He had the support of the Knights of Labor and the Socialists but was defeated by his Democratic opponent, Abram S. Hewitt, who received 90,000 votes against George's 68,000. The Republican candidate in that election, young Theodore Roosevelt, obtained only 60,000 votes. In 1897, George ran again for mayor and, while campaigning, died of apoplexy at fifty-eight.

George's influence is hard to gauge. His ideas took no permanent root in any political party, major or minor, but they did filter into American thought, affected public discussion, and penetrated the labor movement for a while. As the *Knights of Labor* publication wrote (January 15, 1887), "No man has exercised so great an influence upon the labor movement of today as Henry George, although never himself connected as a leader with any of the labor organizations of the country." But the influence did not last.

In general, Henry George widened the nation's awareness of the complexity and importance of economic-political problems. But his single-tax idea was not incorporated into any legislative act. Practical men could not take the single-tax panacea seriously. The major reason the program failed in practice was that it claimed both too much and too little. On the one hand, the single tax was supposed to cure all social ills as if by magic; on the other, it did not foresee the vast political implications of the tax program.

A tax on land, it became clear to critics, might regulate rents, but it was not apparent what else it could achieve. No tax could by itself solve such complex problems as child labor, conditions of work, wages, rates of investment, economic exploitation, political corruption, and a host of other issues created by industrial development and urban expansion. Experience has shown that such problems have to be regulated with infinite care and caution through an intricate network of separate legislative acts, governmental commissions, private organizations (notably trade unions), and civic bodies, all using a variety of techniques (including, among others, taxation of every kind). Even then, solutions are never perfect or final. Problems continue to arise and call for new methods and approaches. Despite the existence of a vast body of regulatory social legislation enacted since Henry George's day, utopia is still far away.

Perhaps a more serious criticism of the single-tax idea derived from its political implications. George himself said that his panacea would turn the state into "the universal landlord." What he did not realize was that such a single landlord—apart from being contrary to the whole American constitutional and federal system—would also become a single *political* master. Clearly, any one body that controlled the land also unavoidably dominated the livelihood and ultimately the liberties of the citizens. Thus the single-tax suggestion, although conceived by George in a spirit of democratic generosity and indignation at the fact of unnecessary misery, contained within itself the germs of political authoritarianism. The George idea was not accepted by the American nation.

His influence abroad seems to have been greater than in the United States. According to H. Schiffrin and Pow-Key Sohn, "The impact of Henry George's land value taxation theory was nothing less than global in scope, and his epochal *Progress and Poverty* . . . gained wider fame than any other political or socio-economic treatise emanating from an American pen."

Despite the ultimate failure of his proposal, Henry George made a valuable contribution to American thought by focusing attention on social evils, which eventually led to action and reform. His book, the work of an original mind, added a distinct chapter to the American political pattern.

# 15

## *THE AMERICAN AS PSYCHOLOGIST:* William James *(1842–1910)*

*By common consent James was far and away the greatest of American psychologists—it was a case of James first and no second.*

—*John Dewey, in* Journal of Philosophy (*September 1910*)

*I think as little of his philosophy as I do much of his psychology.*

—*Oliver Wendell Holmes to Harold Laski* (*March 29, 1917*)

*There is a sense in which James was not a philosopher at all. . . . Philosophy to him was rather . . . like a maze in which he happened to find himself wandering, and what he was looking for was the way out.*

—*George Santayana,* Character and Opinion in the United States (*1920*)

In William James American thought reached a breadth of view, a tolerance, and a felicity of expression unequaled since Jefferson. Professor of philosophy and psychology at Harvard for more than a quarter of a century (1880–1907), James was more than an erudite academic specialist. He went beyond specialization. His mind ranged over the spectrum of human experience with a curiosity that leapt the barriers of intellectual categories and established notions. It was an open mind —lively, probing, experimental, skeptical, endlessly exploring. The antithesis of a dogmatist, he accepted no fixed position so long as there was any doubt about it. "Philosophy for him," his Harvard colleague George Santayana said about him with affectionate irony, "had a Polish constitution; so long as a single vote was cast against the majority, nothing could pass."

James was a vital human being. "A mind, plus a man," a contemporary described him. He was generous in his attitudes toward people, deeply concerned with social problems, active in causes that stirred his sympathies. A thinker and a doer, he personified the finest characteristics of his country. In the words of John Dewey: "I love, indeed, to think that there is something profoundly American in his union of philosophy with life; in his honest acceptance of the facts of science joined to a hopeful outlook upon the future."

William James was born in New York City on January 11, 1842, into a brilliant if somewhat eccentric family. The Jameses were of Irish descent. Justice Oliver Wendell Holmes once said of his friend, "He seems to me typically Irish in his strength and his weakness." William's father, Henry James, Sr., was a radical intellectual, so learned and articulate that James Russell Lowell called him "the best talker in America." Santayana described the senior James, who was a disciple of Swedenborg, as an obscure sage, one of those "mystics of independent mind, hermits in the desert of business, and heretics in churches." A passionate believer in freedom, Henry James, Sr., encouraged his children to follow their personal intellectual bents without academic restraints. As a result, they developed a spirit of sturdy independence which made them "different." In later years someone said that William, the psychologist, wrote like a novelist, and his brother Henry, Jr., the novelist, wrote like a psychologist.

William's formal education was scientific. After studying at Lawrence Scientific School, he attended Harvard Medical School, where he earned his M.D. degree in 1870. Medicine was not his primary interest. Since it combined or impinged upon many disciplines—anatomy, physiology, chemistry, pharmacology, psychology—medicine was, for James, a broad avenue to both science and humanity. It opened numerous paths for discovery, evaluation, and speculation. Dr. James did not confine himself to any one discipline, but roamed among all of them, including the vast and practically uncharted fields of human emotions and beliefs, which he considered legitimate subjects for scientific inquiry and exploration.

James spent his creative years teaching at Harvard and lecturing in many parts of the world. He was a wonderfully stimulating lecturer, charming his hearers with a manner at once spontaneous, hesitant, conversational, and whimsical. His Harvard students were fascinated by this brisk and bearded professor, short and erect, who exuded an "intensely masculine" air in words and thought.

Among his students was the rambunctious Theodore Roosevelt, aged nineteen, who attended James' class on "Comparative Anatomy and Physiology of Vertebrates" in 1877–78. Young Teddy Roosevelt constantly challenged the professor with "largely irrelevant and far-fetched" arguments. James was amusedly patient with the young "limelighter." A classmate, Dr. Samuel Delano, recalled later: "I can see him [James] now . . . settling back in his chair, in a broad grin . . . and waiting for TR to finish." In later years, as Roosevelt became famous, James admired him for his robustness but disliked his lack of taste and discrimination. "His moral fibre is too irredeemably coarse," James said.

In classroom, Professor James was likely to wear tweeds, striped shirts, and flowing ties of exuberant hues. There was, a colleague said, "an occasional afterglow of Bohemia about him." But no one could mistake this surface bohemianism for shallowness or weakness. No matter what he wore or where he was, William James never lost his inner strength, the dignity of his bearing, or the authority of his utterances. Although in private conversation he was masterfully articulate and vigorously fluent, in his lectures he sometimes gave the impression of diffidence and hesitance. He would talk without prepared notes, struggling to catch a floating idea, peering into the distance, groping for the proper expression—which, on occasion, could be illustratively slangy. He created the impression that, philosophically speaking, he was likely to be more or less wrong, but that ideas and insights should always be given honest recognition. His lecturing was a special kind of artistry.

From a technical point of view, as John Dewey and others have pointed out, James' philosophy was "unsystematic." It did not have the rounded consistency of the traditional philosophers. It did not try to fit observable experience into preconceived frameworks or force stubborn facts into a universe of verbal perfection. Instead, James preferred to raise points exploratorily, look at them with a fresh eye, and treat them as phenomena that must have some meaning in the total fabric of life. Ideas and emotions were among those phenomena.

James' undogmatic approach reflected the American character. The lack of philosophic system was in itself a kind of system—the American democratic way of doing and of evaluating. It was "democratic" in the sense that everything was somehow important and useful somewhere to somebody, to some context. No wonder his ideas had a wide impact on American life and thought (educational institutions, pedagogical methods, psychological and philosophic studies).

James called his whole structure of thought "radical empiricism" and his method "pragmatism." In a lecture, "Philosophical Conceptions and Practical Results," given before the University of California Philosophical Union in 1898, James introduced the term "pragmatism." A year later, John Dewey took it up in his *Studies in Logical Theory*. The idea, however, was not original with James. It had, as he said, been postulated in 1878 by the philosopher Charles Saunders Peirce (1839–1914), author of *Illustrations of the Logic of Science,* who raised the question regarding the practical consequences of metaphysical arguments by asking: "If this were true, what actual difference would it make?" James' contribution to pragmatism was to extend Peirce's criterion of practicality to the world of ideas also. He asked: "What difference in action will a given difference in idea make?"

The emphasis of James' "radical empiricism" was on *facts,* which included *ideas*. As Professor Joseph Blau said, referring to James: "A tough-minded philosopher demands a system which leaves the universe in thought as open as it is in actuality." And James was tough-minded. He insisted that philosophic arguments be confined to observable phenomena and to matters derived from human experience. "Radical empiricism," he wrote in the preface to his *The Meaning of Truth,* "consists first of a postulate, next of a statement of fact, and finally of a generalized conclusion." Truth, in the view of pragmatism, was what worked. It was a way of looking at practicality and usefulness. James said of any idea: "It is useful because it is true," or conversely, "It is true because it is useful." He defined *true* as whatever idea starts the "verification process" and *useful* as the "completed function in experience."

In "A World of Pure Experience," James thus summarized the distinct features of his philosophy: "I give the name of 'radical empiricism' to my *Weltanschauung*. Empiricism is . . . the opposite of rationalism. Rationalism tends to emphasize universals. . . . Empiricism . . . lays the explanatory stress upon the part, the element, the individual, and treats the whole as a collection and the universal as an abstraction. . . . It is essentially a mosaic philosophy, a philosophy of plural facts, like that of Hume and his descendants, who refer these facts neither to Substances in which they inhere nor to an Absolute Mind that creates them as its objects. But it differs from the Humian type of empiricism in one particular which makes me add the epithet radical.

"To be radical, an empiricism must neither admit into its constructions any element that is not directly experienced, nor exclude from them any element that is directly experienced. For such a philosophy, the relations that connect experiences must themselves be experienced relations, and any kind of relation experienced must be accounted as 'real' as anything else in the system."

James did not deny the existence of supranatural or suprasensible phenomena. He merely insisted that, whether they existed or not, they should be kept out of any philosophic argument as unnecessary. Since they were extraneous and "trans-empirical," and hence not derived from direct experience, they added nothing to any meaningful (useful, workable) argument. "The only things that shall be debatable among philosophers," he wrote, "shall be things definable in terms drawn from experience." The latter, as he defined it, included the relations between things, which are "just as much matters of direct personal experience."

This empirical and pragmatic attitude also extended to religion and morality. James wrote in a period of religious ferment and controversy resulting from Darwin's theory of evolution. The Revised Version of the Bible, published in 1881 and 1885, as well as the science of textual Biblical criticism newly introduced from Germany, stirred up religious conflict over the nature of Biblical inspiration. The struggle between religious orthodoxy and theological liberalism resulted in a number of heresy trials, the most sensational of which was that of Charles A. Briggs (1892), who was suspended from the Presbyterian ministry. Books also entered the religious fray. Among them were John Fiske's *Outlines of Cosmic Philosophy* (1874), which attempted to reconcile Darwin with theology, and popular novels, such as Margaret Deland's best-selling *John Ward, Preacher* (1888) and Harold Frederic's *The Damnation of Theron Ware* (1896), which attacked sectarian intolerance. Colonel Robert G. Ingersoll (1833–99), a lawyer and Civil War veteran, became a national figure with his enthusiastic criticism of the established churches and his eloquent lectures on agnosticism. The author of books like *The Gods and Other Lectures* (1876) and *Some Mistakes of Moses* (1879), Ingersoll proclaimed his creed: "I do not deny. I do not know. But I do not believe."

In the wake of this national stir over religion, James published *The Varieties of Religious Experience* (1902), which consisted of his Gifford Lectures, delivered in England in 1901. It was, in itself, an original work, a searching contribution to a field long dominated by creedal fanaticism and theological obfuscation. James' stress was on "varieties" and "experience." He approached religion as an indispensable aspect of man's functioning and illustrated his arguments with a wealth of data from the religious experience and behavior of mankind. He did not advocate or attack any particular theology or religious form. He merely described the religious experience from the point of view of a psychologist, as an interesting manifestation of humanity:

"I am neither a theologian, nor a scholar learned in the history of religions, nor an anthropologist," he said in his introductory remarks. "Psychology is the only branch of learning in which I am particularly versed. To the psychologist the religious propensities of man must be at least as interesting as any other of the facts pertaining to his mental constitution."

In the American setting of the time, *The Varieties of Religious Experience* was a cool and memorable challenge to the extremists. To the fundamentalist bigots, James said in effect: You are absolutists, who make claims that are beyond any verification by reason or experience. To the agnostics and materialists, he said: Your materialism denies the moral law of the universe and your agnosticism, by suspending judgment, leads to passivity and pessimism, thereby undermining human life and vital experience.

For James accepted the idea of God as an essential element in what he conceived to be a "pluralistic universe." But his God was not that of the dogmatic fundamentalists. Their absolutist God, beyond human reach or experience, was to James inconceivable. "The absolute," he wrote, "neither acts nor suffers, nor loves, nor hates; it has no needs, desires, or aspirations, no failures or successes, friends or enemies, victories or defeats." As a finite human being—one who lives within a stream of sensed experience—James conceived God and religion as fitting into the pluralistic scheme of things. Any absolutism, even of such a lofty variety as that of Emerson, was open to serious criticism, as James wrote in *A Pluralistic Universe* (1909):

"What boots it to tell me that the absolute way is the true way, and to exhort me, as Emerson says, to lift mine eye up to its style, and manners of the sky, if the feat is impossible by definition? I am finite once for all, and all the categories of my sympathy are knit up with the finite world *as such,* and with things that have a history."

Underlying James' philosophy was the supreme importance of feelings and the efforts to give them shape. He regarded the emotions and the vast range of their expressions as the distinct characteristics of the human species. "Man's chief difference from the brutes," he wrote in *The Will to Believe* (1897), "lies in the exuberant excess of his subjective propensities. . . . Prune down his extravagance, sober him, and you undo him."

Characteristically, to James the world of feeling he proclaimed was not merely an abstraction but one that was applicable to individual human beings and their everyday existence. James had active sympathies for people. He was in love with life, cherishing experiences as they came. "Be not afraid of life," he wrote in *Is Life Worth Living?* "Believe that life is worth living, and your belief will help create the fact." After a week of lecturing to earnest and well-meaning people at Chautauqua, he could write irreverently to his family:

"I have learned a lot, but I'm glad to get into something less blameless but more admiration-worthy. The flash of a pistol, a dagger, or a devilish eye, anything to break the unlovely level of 10,000 good people —a crime, murder, rape, elopement, anything would do."

He enjoyed the unusual and even the ugly. Traveling widely on his lecture tours, he saw unattractive places, met boorish or dull people, and observed seemingly inane actions, but he was not shocked. On the contrary, he found in them manifestations of human life—expressions of the Old Adam—and, as such, meaningful. Every creature, he felt, had its own distinctness and experienced its own inwardness. In a pluralistic universe, each member of creation, in its own way, added to the enrichment of life, although it might not seem so outwardly. This was true even of his dog, of which James said whimsically: "His tail keeps wagging *all* the time, and he makes on me the impression of an angel hid in a cloud. He longs to do good." But as his biographer remarked, even dogs wagged for James.

In a famous lecture, "On a Certain Blindness in Human Beings," as well as in his book, *Talks to Teachers* (1899), he stressed the importance of the inner life of each individual. He criticized "the blindness with which we are all afflicted in regard to the feelings of creatures and people different from ourselves," and urged the widest kind of tolerance and understanding of each individual's intrinsic worth. This, he wrote: "commands us to tolerate, respect, and indulge those whom we see harmlessly interested and happy in their own ways, however unintelligible they may be to us. Hands off: neither the whole of truth nor the whole of good is revealed to any observer. . . . Even prisoners and sick-rooms have their special revelations."

James exulted in differences wherever he found them, in individuals as well as in groups, no matter how meaningless or preposterous they might appear to be. Differences meant a clash of ideas, which could result in new discoveries and fresh truths. "The obstinate insisting that tweedledum is *not* tweedledee is the bone and marrow of life," he wrote. "Look at the Jews and the Scots, with their miserable factions and sectarian disputes, their loyalties and patriotisms and exclusions—their annals now become a classic heritage, because men of genius took part and sang in them."

The best kind of society, he felt, was one that cherished differences and afforded opportunity for the expression of "peculiarities." This was especially true of those individuals, sometimes known as geniuses and whom he defined as men having the "faculty of perceiving in an unhabitual way," who differed from their fellow men by conspicuous talents. James shared with Emerson and Carlyle a belief in the superior role played by great men in history.

"The world," he wrote in *Memories and Studies* (1911), ". . . is only beginning to see that the wealth of a nation consists more than in anything else in the number of superior men that it harbors. . . . Geniuses are ferments; and when they come together as they have done in certain lands at certain times, the whole population seems to share in the higher energy which they awaken. . . . From the bare economic point of view the importance of geniuses is only beginning to be appreciated. How can we measure the cash-value to France of a Pasteur, to England of a Kelvin, to Germany of an Ostwald, to us here of a Burbank?"

True to his pluralistic philosophy, James did not subscribe to the essentially antidemocratic theory that all human development was due to great individuals alone. Genius was only one ingredient in the historic process; the other was the social milieu, the people who made up the community in general. A genius outside his time was sterile. "Not every 'man' fits every 'hour.' . . . A given genius may come either too early or too late. Peter the Hermit would now be sent to a lunatic asylum. John [Stuart] Mill in the tenth century would have lived and died unknown." Progress and creativity resulted only when the genius and the community, in the totality of its attitudes and values, were ripe for an interplay. As James explained in his article, "Great Men and Their Environment," *Atlantic Monthly,* 1880: "Social evolution is a resultant of the interaction of two wholly distinct factors—the individual, deriving his peculiar gifts from the play of physiological and infra-social forces, but bearing all the power of initiative and origination in his hands; and, second, the social environment, with its power of adopting or rejecting both him and his gifts. Both factors are essential to change. The community stagnates without the impulse of the individual. The impulse dies away without the sympathy of the community."

James did not believe that the importance of individuals in society was a contradiction of democratic theory. No society, he said, could function without intelligent leadership. Human progress depended upon the inventions and ideas of conspicuously talented individuals, who "show the way, and set the patterns, which common people then adopt and follow." In a democracy, the question was simply how to select the best leaders. In his lecture, "The Social Value of the College-Bred," delivered on November 7, 1907 and published in *McClure's* Magazine in February 1908, James stated that a democratic polity, more than any other, should be able to divine and select the "rightful leaders." Since the United States had no hereditary aristocracy, such leadership devolved upon the "alumni and alumnae of the colleges." Their function was to provide the society with the necessary wisdom, a "sense of ideal values," and, perhaps most of all, a critical "tone." Even if they were ridiculed by the "red-blood" stupid party, men of mind and education should stand up, he said, and assert their leadership: "'Les intellectuels!' What prouder club-name could there be than this one."

James' Harvard student and subsequent editor, Horace M. Kallen (1882– ), the distinguished philosopher of the New School for Social Research, further deepened these ideas with regard to American democracy. Applying James' concepts of a pluralistic universe and the importance of differentness to American life, Kallen developed the now well established theory of "cultural pluralism" to explain the extraordinary diversity and rich dynamism of American civilization. Kallen speaks of the "orchestration" of the diverse forces, persons, and ideas that make up modern America.

On virtually all levels, the implications of James' thought were democratic. His philosophy was rooted in a belief in human goodness and individual worthiness. As Ralph Barton Perry said of him, "While he saw men's weakness as well as their strength, he admired them for their strength instead of despising them for their weakness." James' attitude was that of universal love for all living things, regardless of their position or stage of development. All had a divine spark worthy of respect and cultivation. This intellectual position extended even to afterlife. Referring to a possibly overcrowded heaven, James wrote in *Human Immortality* (1898):

"The Deity that suffers us, we may be sure, can suffer many another queer and wondrous and only half-delightful thing. For my own part ... I am willing that every leaf that ever grew in this world's forests and rustled in the breeze should become immortal."

This philosophy of universal affection was at the base of James' political thought. He viewed democracy as a polity that depended upon good character and inner values, which he called "mystery," rather than mere external machinery. In this, he was at one with Emerson and Whitman. The "mystery" consisted of mutual respect and of an unswerving acceptance of public decisions without recourse to cruelty or violence. A democratic commonwealth was one founded on a regard for man and for humane values.

"Democracy is still upon its trials," James wrote.* "The civil genius of our people is its only bulwark, and neither laws nor monuments, neither battleships nor public libraries, nor great newspapers nor booming stocks; neither mechanical invention nor political adroitness, nor churches nor universities nor civil service examinations can save us from degeneration if the inner mystery be lost. That mystery . . . consists in nothing but two common habits . . . carried into public life—. . . . One of them is the habit of trained and disciplined good temper toward the opposite party when it fairly wins its innings. . . . The other is that of fierce and merciless resentment toward every man or set of men who break the public peace."

As a vital personality with strong convictions, James did not confine himself to the traditional ivory tower but participated in the struggles of his day. In fact, he had a deep distrust of inaction as inimical to the human character. "No matter how full a reservoir of *maxims* one may possess," he wrote in his classic *Psychology* (1892), "and no matter how good one's *sentiments* may be, if one have not taken advantage of every concrete opportunity to *act,* one's character may remain entirely unaffected for the better. With mere good intentions, hell is proverbially paved." James was an active liberal, espousing the causes of the weak and the oppressed, opposing cruelty and injustice wherever they came to his attention. "We are all ready to be savage in *some* cause," he said. "The difference between a good man and a bad one is the choice of the cause."

Primarily trained in scientific rather than political matters, he was influenced in his politics by the liberal weekly, *The Nation,* to whose crusading editor, Edwin Lawrence Godkin, he once wrote: "In the earlier years I may say that my whole political education was due to the 'Nation.' " This he later amended somewhat in a letter to his brother Henry: "I never said—Heaven bear me witness—that I had learned more from G. than from anyone. I said I had got more *political* education from him. You see the 'Nation' took me at the age of 22—you were already older and wickeder. . . ."

* "Robert Gould Shaw," *Memories and Studies,* p. 60–61.

As a fighting liberal—Santayana referred to him in this connection as "a sort of Irishman among the Brahmins"—James reflected the leftist positions of his time. He was, he said, in favor of the "under-dogs always." He was for labor and political reform, against lynching and against imperialism. His liberalism was no more disturbed by the prevailing and frequent labor unrest, often expressing itself in strikes of widespread violence, than was Jefferson's by Shay's Rebellion a century earlier. "Don't be alarmed about the labor troubles here," he wrote to his brother Henry in Europe. "I am quite sure they are a most healthy phase of evolution, a little costly, but normal, and sure to do lots of good to all hands in the end."

James pioneered in the cause of mental hygiene, working for the enlightened treatment of the mentally disturbed. Influenced by Clifford W. Beers' *A Mind that Found Itself,* for which he helped find a publisher, James became one of the founders of the National Committee for Mental Hygiene in 1909. In quest of funds for the committee, he wrote to John D. Rockefeller, Sr.: "During my life as a 'psychologist' I have had much to do with our asylums, and I have had so painfully borne in upon me the massiveness of human evil which the term 'insanity' covers, and the inadequacy of our arrangements for coping with it, that I long ago registered a vow that if I myself, by Heaven's grace, should ever be able to leave any money for public use it should be for 'insanity' exclusively . . . what should be regarded as a common functional disease is handled as a social stigma. . . . There must from now onward be a tremendous campaign waged for prevention and cure."

James was revolted by the prevailing political corruption and hypocrisy, as his older contemporaries Walt Whitman and Henry George had been. The political practices of the time, based on trickery and open chicanery, were offensive to reason and to ethical standards. Presidential campaigns, in particular, were orgies of bloated verbosity revolving primarily around the politicos' conception of "patriotism," which consisted of flagwaving, blowing on the embers of the Civil War, and fake righteousness. Referring to one such campaign, that of Republican presidential candidate James G. Blaine in 1884 (which, truth to tell, was not exceptional), James wrote in disgust:

"He is blind, and the whole section of Republicans whom he represents are blind, to the real life of the country . . . dead shibboleths are all they can think of. They live on hatred and prejudice against the Democratic name, as the Democrats live on hatred of the Republican name. If any decent Democrat be nominated, I shall be happy to vote him in, in order to get the present fossil Republican party permanently killed, and to be able four years later to drive out the Democrats in the same way in the name of a new national party with something of an intellectual character in purpose, which will devote itself to civil service and economical reform, and perhaps ultimately to certain constitutional changes of which we are in pressing need. Look at the Barnum advertisement called the Republican platform! Can you possibly wish to see a party like *that* cumber the earth any longer? I hope not."

James' particular indignation was aroused by the crop of jingoists, saber-rattlers, and imperialists that appeared on the American scene at the end of the nineteenth century. He hated them because they violated all his ethical and humane feelings. The new American nationalism, with its boastful drive for aggrandizement in all spheres, shocked him. "I am against all big organizations as such," he wrote to a friend, "national ones first and foremost; against all big successes * and big results; and in favor of the eternal forces of truth which always work in the individual and immediately unsuccessful way . . . , till history comes . . . , and puts them on the top." This opposition to mere bigness was to be developed further, and carried over into the economic sphere, by James' younger Boston contemporary, Louis D. Brandeis. James' most cutting remarks were directed against the American expansionists who, in the period of the Spanish-American War, advocated the muscular imperialist policy of the "white man's burden," even if it meant war against a weak people, as was actually the case in the Philippines.

In February 1899, when the Filipinos, under the leadership of Emilio Aguinaldo, learned that the United States would not grant the Philippines independence after the Spanish-American War, they broke into armed revolt. Although open resistance against an American army of seventy thousand men came to an end at the close of 1899, guerilla warfare continued for another three years. America's policy in the Philippines was widely condemned not only by William James but also by other influential citizens who supported the Anti-Imperialist League.

In letters to the press, James vehemently protested against American imperialism, which he considered "ignominious" and brutish.

"We see," he wrote to the *Boston Evening Transcript,* ". . . what an absolute savage . . . the passion of military conquest always is, and how the only safeguard against the crimes to which it will infallibly drag the

* The phrase "bitch-goddess success" has long been attributed to William James. But, as Burton E. Stevenson, editor of standard reference works, such as *The Home Book of Quotations,* wrote to me (March 20, 1958), "neither I nor the Library of Congress has been able to find [it] in his works." I have not either.

nation that gives way to it is to keep it chained for ever.... We are now openly engaged in crushing out the sacredest thing in this great human world—the attempt of a people [the Filipinos] long enslaved to attain to the possession of itself, to organize its laws and government, to be free to follow its internal destinies according to its own ideals.... Why, then, do we go on? First, the war fever; and then the pride which always refuses to back down when under fire.... We are to be missionaries of civilization, and to bear the white man's burden, painful as it often is.... The individual lives are nothing.... Could there be a more damning indictment of that whole bloated idol termed 'modern civilization' than this amounts to? Civilization is, then, the big, hollow, resounding, corrupting, sophisticating, confusing torrent of mere brutal momentum and irrationality that brings forth fruits like this!"

James' writings on war and peace were perhaps his most direct and important contributions to political thought. The problem of violence, as manifested in the individual and in society at large, naturally occupied the author of *Psychology*. He was concerned with the question of the use of force, its roots and possible cure, both as a psychologist and as a moralist. In his lectures, particularly on moral philosophy, and in his writings, he explored the intricate phases of the problem in an original and hard-headed fashion. His theories about war avoided the sentimentality of pacifists, whose well-intentioned phrases were little more than pious invocations (and hence permanently ineffectual), and the brutishness of militarists, whose exclusively martial ideals constantly endangered man's nobler potentialities.

The culmination of James' thinking on war is found in *The Moral Equivalent of War*. Published by the American Association for International Conciliation in 1910, the year of his death, the essay, in an edition of thirty thousand copies, stimulated discussion and was reprinted in popular magazines. But, coming out as it did on the eve of World War I, it had no immediate practical consequences.

The thought, however, has remained fresh to this day. Even Sigmund Freud, concerned as he was with human aggression, has not gone beyond James in this field. Two decades after James wrote his essay on war, Freud voiced similar views in an exchange of letters with Albert Einstein. On July 30, 1932, only a few months before Hitler seized power in Germany, Einstein wrote Freud a long letter saying that he was aware of man's "aggressive instinct" and "lust for hatred and destruction." He asked the famous Viennése psychoanalyst a question that has tormented humanity since the beginning of history: "Is there any way of delivering mankind from the menace of war?" Freud's lengthy reply (September 1932) agreed with Einstein (and James) in regard to man's "destructive instinct" which underlies war, but could offer no solution to the evil except in a recognition of the existence of hatred's "antagonist, Eros." Freud was pessimistic about peace: "In any case, . . . there is no question of getting rid entirely of human aggressive impulses . . ." In this regard, Freud differed from the more hopeful James.

In *The Moral Equivalent of War,* James began with the fundamental recognition that man was naturally an aggressive animal. It was folly and ignorance to assume otherwise. On this basic premise, James departed from the traditional liberals and pacifists. He felt that wisdom required a frank acknowledgment that human beings had a natural instinct, and consequently an insatiable need and desire, for violence. On a biologic level, man was not only an animal, but was capable of outanimaling in ferocity, so to speak, all other species.

"Man, biologically considered, and whatever else he may be into the bargain," James wrote, "is the most formidable of all beasts of prey, and, indeed, the only one that preys systematically on his own species. . . . A millennium of peace would not breed the fighting disposition out of our bone and marrow."

All human history, James pointed out, records this biologic fact of man's inherent aggressiveness. The annals of history are replete with war, glorified even by those who were by profession nonfighters: "Not only are men born to be soldiers, but non-combatants by trade and nature, historians in their studies, and clergymen in their pulpits, have been war's idealizers. They have talked of war as of God's court of justice . . . who can say what might have prevailed if man had ever been a reasoning and not a fighting animal? Like dead men, dead causes tell no tales, and the ideals that went under in the past, along with all the tribes that represented them, find today no recorder, no explainer, no defender."

James insisted that the aggressive instinct should not be considered as extraneous to humanity or rejected as pure evil. It is actually a vital part of mankind, of manhood, so to speak. The passions of organized violence, that is, war and systematized bloodshed, are vitally needful. War, even if vicariously experienced, stirs the imagination, brings "supremely thrilling excitement," breaks the deadening routine of daily existence (most men, Thoreau reminded us, lead lives of quiet desperation), and thereby wonderfully enlarges the horizons of humanity.

"The plain truth is that people *want* war . . ." James stated. "It is the final bouquet of life's fireworks. The born soldiers want it hot and actual.

The non-combatants want it in the background, and to feed imagination on and keep excitement going. . . . War is human nature at its uttermost."

Man's natural bloodthirstiness, he pointed out, required war as a kind of "sacrament," a form of "mystical blood-payment." In addition, war is also a preserver of the splendid qualities of courage and boldness and hardihood. Without it, "society would rot" away in softness. People would become flaccid in outlook and vapid in psychology. The earth would be transformed into a "world of clerks and teachers, of coeducation and zoophily, of 'consumers' leagues' and 'associated charities,' of industrialism unlimited, and feminism unabashed." Such a planet would be, James said, a "cattleyard."

This being the case, he thought it was psychologically unrealistic to talk about universal peace or worldwide disarmament. Such a radical cure would never do, even assuming that it was politically possible, because it ran counter to human nature. Actually, aggressiveness was needed in society—provided that it were properly used. As James said in his *Talks to Teachers:* "Pugnacity need not be thought of merely in the form of physical combativeness. It can be taken in the sense of a general unwillingness to be beaten by any kind of difficulty." Such a spirit, of "pugnacity and pride," was highly desirable and if properly stimulated would bring out the best in man or boy—would make him "rush at the difficult places with a sort of inner wrath at himself that is one of his best moral faculties."

It was at this point—the canalization of aggression—that James parted company with the militarists, who otherwise approved his views on human pugnacity. He proposed that the "savage virtues" be sublimated for social ends instead of social destructiveness. What James said, in effect, was that while human aggressiveness was both natural and desirable, war was neither, or at least need not be either. It was nonsense, he argued, to assume that war was an integral part of the operations of nature, as were the tides, for example, and hence unavoidable. War was man-made and man-manipulated, and as such, controllable. "For I know that war-making is due to definite motives and subject to prudential checks and reasonable criticisms, just like any other form of enterprise."

He therefore proposed a program of carefully planned substitutes, or "moral equivalents," for war. The martial spirit, so important for man and society, should be preserved through the channeling of community resources for the planned improvement of life in numerous ways. The youth of the population, for example, could be enlisted for a number of years to work on public projects—a proposal later carried out by the New Deal. The instincts for aggression could find an outlet in organized athletics. The virtues of hardihood could be kept fresh in physical adventures, such as exploration. The qualities of discipline could be preserved in military service, without the cruelty and degradation involved in actual warfare. In sum, James advised: Preserve the aggressive qualities, but "find some innocent way out."

By such "preventive medicine," as he called it, mankind might slowly learn to do without war. This program of sublimation, in effect an organized system of no war, required patience and planning. But in the long run, it was the only means of eliminating the endless scourge of war. As James said in his "Remarks at the Peace Banquet":

> We must cheat our foe, circumvent him in detail, not try to change his nature. In one respect war is like love. . . . Both leave us intervals of rest; and in the intervals life goes on perfectly well without them, though the imagination still dallies with their possibility. . . . How are old maids and old bachelors made? Not by deliberate vows of celibacy, but sliding on from year to year with no sufficient matrimonial provocation. So of the nations with their wars. Let the general possibility of war be left open, in Heaven's name, for the imagination to dally with. Let the soldiers dream of killing, as the old maids dream of marrying. But organize in every conceivable way the practical machinery for making each successive chance of war abortive. Put peace men in power; educate the editors and statesmen to responsibility. . . . Seize every pretext . . . for arbitration methods . . . ; foster rival excitements, and invent new outlets for heroic energy; and from one generation to another the chances are that irritation will grow less acute and states of strain less dangerous among nations. Armies and navies will continue, of course, and fire the minds of populations with their potentialities of greatness. But their officers will find that somehow or other . . . each successive 'incident' has managed to evaporate and to lead nowhere.

Thus William James—philosopher, psychologist, physician, scientist —added new dimensions to American thinking, always on the side of the generous, humane, and democratic aspirations of mankind in general. He was a universal American.

# 16

## *THE AMERICAN AS SKEPTIC:* Oliver Wendell Holmes *(1841–1935)*

> *I went to Justice Holmes to liven me up, and I had the most delightful talk. . . . He is ninety years old and gives no sign of it in his liveliness and vigor. He still swears like a trooper, enjoys a joke and makes plenty of them. . . . He told me that he had been trying to keep up his reading of philosophy. . . . He said, 'You know I can't take man quite so seriously as these other fellows do. It seems to me that he can't quite occupy the attention of God that they all think he does. I can't believe that if a comet, for instance, should hit the earth and knock it to smithereens that it would make such a very great difference to the universe.' . . . I came away completely cheered up with my horizon all changed.*
>
> —*Henry Stimson,* Diary (*November 1, 1930*)

When twentieth-century Americans speak of judges, they are likely to think first of Oliver Wendell Holmes. He had the superb qualities that symbolize greatness in a jurist—striving for truth, tolerance of ideas, skepticism in the face of dogma, urbanity of manner, grace of expression, philosophic balance and, in the words of Judge Learned Hand, "above all, humility before the vast unknown." There has never been another American judge quite like Holmes, the Boston Brahmin who graced the United States Supreme Court for nearly a third of this century. His impact on America, particularly in the crucial area of judicial thought and posture, has been pervasive and lingering.

Holmes was not merely *a* justice of the Supreme Court; he was a special kind of justice. His uncommonness derived not from any originality of particular juridical theories or precedent-shattering judicial decisions—he was often a dissenter from the majority on the Court—but from his personality. The Holmes character and style had a distinct flavor, as unique as a work of art. Peculiarly American in one sense—in his pragmatism plus humaneness—he was also exceptional in the American political-democratic tradition. A salty Yankee seasoned in intellectual brine, Holmes was a dedicated skeptic, cheerfully doubting the noblest tenets of his countrymen, and gleefully questioning the most devoutly held certainties of his philosophical friends.

Henry Stimson gives one example, that of Holmes' disagreement with the noted Harvard philosopher Royce (1855–1916): "He talked of his old arguments with Josiah Royce. He laughed and laughed over them. He said that the trouble with Royce was that whenever he, Holmes, got him cornered, he would take refuge in saying, 'Well, I am in the bosom of God'; while Holmes would reply, 'Nonsense, you are just in a rathole that I have cornered you in.' "

As free of cant as his predecessor John Marshall, whom he admired considerably, Holmes was blessed with that rare form of intellectual grace known as wit. In addition, his mind was fortified by a buoyancy positively Voltairean in its irreverence and cultivated by a philosophic curiosity that matched Jefferson's. According to Justice Felix Frankfurter, Holmes reminded judges that "in order to be weighty they need not be heavy." For all his erudition, Holmes was never heavy.

Oliver Wendell Holmes, Jr., was born in Boston on March 8, 1841, the son of a father whose reputation has been eclipsed by the subsequent renown of his son. Like the Adams family, the Holmeses belonged to the New England aristocracy. "All my three names," young Holmes wrote in the Harvard College album of the Class of 1861, "designate families from which I am descended. A longer pedigree of Olivers and Wendells may be found in the book called *Memorials of the Dead in Boston.*" From this line of ancestors, the future justice inherited much of his sturdy independence; from his father came his good humor and the sharpness of his wit. "Two and two," the father wrote in *The Poet at the Breakfast-Table,* "do not always make four, in the matter of hereditary descent of qualities. Sometimes they make three and sometimes five." It was five in the case of his son.

Oliver Wendell Holmes, Sr. (1809–94) was a celebrated figure whose rationalism and humor are reminiscent of another native Bostonian, Benjamin Franklin. The senior Holmes was a physician by profession and a writer by avocation. Professor in (and dean of) the Harvard Medical School, Dr. Holmes was the author of popular verse, psychological novels, and amusing books, the best known of which were the *Breakfast-Table* series (*The Autocrat at the Breakfast-Table,* 1858; *The Professor at the Breakfast-Table,* 1860). The witty professor did not spare even the profession of medicine, to which he contributed learned articles. "I firmly believe," he said in an address to the Massachusetts Medical Society, "that if the whole *materia medica* as now used could be sunk to the bottom of the sea, it would be all the better for mankind—and all the worse for the fishes."

The cheerful irreverence and raillery of the father seeped into the thought of the son. The wry humor and skepticism of Holmes the physician is echoed in the judge. "Of course everybody likes and respects self-made men," the senior Holmes wrote in *The Autocrat at the Breakfast-Table.* "It is a great deal better to be made in that way than not to be made at all." There is an echo of this in Justice Holmes' dissenting opinion in the Northern Securities Company case. In Holmes, Sr.'s *Pages from an Old Volume of Life* we have in a nutshell the son's basic approach to the philosophy of the law: "Of relative justice law may know something; of expediency it knows much; with absolute justice it does not concern itself."

Next to heredity and the immediate environment—"We are all tattooed in our cradles with the beliefs of our tribe; the record may seem superficial, but it is indelible," his father wrote—the most enduring influence on the younger Holmes' life was the Civil War. At its outbreak, when President Lincoln called for 75,000 volunteers, the twenty-year-old Harvard senior enlisted in the infantry. Characteristically, "he was walking down Beacon Hill with Hobbes' *Leviathan* in his hand," according to a contemporary, when he was informed that he had been commissioned a first lieutenant.

As an officer in the Twentieth Massachusetts Volunteers, young Holmes saw some of the bloodiest fighting of the war. He was wounded three times, twice severely and once almost mortally. At the Battle of Ball's Bluff (October 1861), Lieutenant Holmes was shot in the chest. He reports in his crisp diary: "I was hit at 4½ PM. . . . I felt as if a horse had kicked me and went over—1st Serg$^{t}$ Smith grabbed me and lugged me to the rear a little way & opened my shirt and . . . the two holes in my breast & the bullet. . . ." Years later he told a friend ironically, "When I was dying after Ball's Bluff, I remembered my father's saying that death-bed repentances generally meant only that the man was scared." After recovery, he returned to the front as a captain. During the Battle of Antietam (September 1862), he was shot in the neck. He wrote home the next day:

"My Dear Parents . . . Usual luck—ball entered at the rear passing straight through the Central seam of Coat & waistcoat collar coming out towa[rd] the front on the left hand side—yet it don't seem to have smashed my spine or I suppose I should be dead, or paralyzed or something— It's more than 24 h'rs & I have remained pretty cocky, only of course feverish at times. . . ." *

In "My Hunt After the Captain," published in the *Atlantic Monthly* in December 1862, Dr. Holmes told movingly how he had sought his "first-born" through many towns in Maryland and on the road to Philadelphia. He finally found him being fussed over by adoring ladies in the home of Mrs. Howard Kennedy in Hagerstown, twelve miles from Antietam. After a long convalescence, Holmes returned to duty, fought again in Maryland and at the Battle of Fredericksburg (May 1863), was once again wounded, this time by a piece of shrapnel that shattered his heel. He was finally mustered out of service on July 17, 1864, with the rank of lieutenant colonel.

Holmes never forgot the Civil War; it left an indelible imprint on his soul. Many decades later he wrote in a letter to Sir Frederick Pollock in 1920, "I loathe war—which I described when at home with a wound in our Civil War as an organized bore—to the scandal of the young women of the day, who thought that Captain Holmes was wanting in patriotism."

The Civil War battles, some of the most sanguinary in history up to that time, matured him as a man, steeled his character, and deepened his insight into the fragility of human existence: "As long as man dwells upon the globe, his destiny is battle, and he has to take the chances of war." He lost forever the easy optimism of his countrymen. To have proved himself in battle—in a war that tried the souls of men and tested the nation's existence—was to have undergone an experience which, Holmes said, was "incommunicable." Only battle-tested veterans, men who knew what it was to fear for life, what it meant to see their own

* His father diagnosed the wound: "*Through* the neck,—no bullet left in wound. Windpipe, food-pipe, carotid, jugular, half a dozen smaller, but still formidable vessels, a great braid of nerves, each as big as a lamp-wick, spinal cord—ought to kill at once, if at all. *Thought not* mortal, or *not thought* mortal—which was it?"

bodies bleeding and their comrades torn to pieces could understand the searing experience of war. Matchless, enduring, and elevating, the experience set him and his generation apart from their fellows. This is how Holmes put it, in a Memorial Day address to the veterans of the Grand Army of the Republic at Keene, New Hampshire, in 1884, in almost mystic tones:

"Through our great good fortune, in our youth our hearts were touched with fire. It was given to us to learn at the outset that life is a profound and passionate thing. While we are permitted to scorn nothing but indifference, and do not pretend to undervalue the worldly rewards of ambition, we have seen with our own eyes beyond and above the gold fields the snowy heights of honor, and it is for us to bear the report to those who come after us. . . . Our dead brothers still live for us, and bid us think of life, not death—of life to which in their youth they lent the passion and glory of the spring. As I listen, the great chorus of life and joy begins again, and . . . our trumpets sound once more a note of daring, hope, and will."

In the autumn of 1864, Lieutenant Colonel Holmes entered Harvard Law School, after considering and rejecting other possible careers, among them art and writing. There he formed a close friendship with William James, and they engaged in continuing philosophical arguments. But Holmes did not let philosophical speculation, in which he was to have a lifelong interest, interfere with his chosen profession. Even after graduation in January 1866 and admission to the bar the following year, he devoted himself to the technical study of the law with an absorption that baffled his friends. "For two or three months," Holmes wrote to "Dear Bill" James in December 1867, "I debauched o' nights in philosophy. But now it is law—law—law. My *magnum opus* was reading the *Critique of Pure Reason*." The next April he again wrote to James:

"Since I wrote in December I have worked at nothing but the law. Philosophy has hibernated in torpid slumber, and I have lain 'sluttishly soaking and gurgling in the devil's pickle,' as Carlyle says. It has been necessary—if a man chooses a profession he cannot forever content himself in picking out the plums with fastidious dilettantism and give the rest of the loaf to the poor, but must eat his way manfully through crust and crumb—soft, unpleasant, inner parts which, within one, swell, causing discomfort in the bowels."

Such concentration unavoidably assured Holmes' career. He had the qualities needed for success. Handsome, elegant, brilliant, hard-working, ambitious, he was bound to rise to eminence. The speculative William

James, observing his friend's single-minded pursuit of his legal career, remarked perceptively that "my Wendly boy" was "composed of at least two and a half different people. . . ." One was a philosopher, and the other a somewhat cynical and hard-minded lawyer bent on success. On the Supreme Court, Holmes was to show these distinct parts of his character on more than one occasion.

Success came with fair rapidity. At thirty he became lecturer on constitutional law at Harvard and editor of the *American Law Journal.* Three years later he edited and annotated the twelfth edition of Chancellor Kent's *Commentaries on American Law,* a four-volume work that was then the bible of American lawyers. In 1881, Holmes published *The Common Law,* consisting of the Lowell Lectures he had delivered the previous year and which became a landmark in the realistic study of American jurisprudence. It made his reputation as a jurist. His fame was now such that in 1882, at the age of forty-one, he was offered a professorship at Harvard and an appointment to the Judicial Supreme Court of Massachusetts. Holmes accepted the judgeship. "To think of it," his sprightly seventy-three-year-old father said with delight, "—my little boy a Judge and able to send me to jail if I don't behave myself."

In 1902, after Holmes had served on the Massachusetts bench for nearly twenty years (the last three as chief justice), Theodore Roosevelt appointed him to the United States Supreme Court. President Roosevelt knew Holmes' reputation as a legal scholar and admired him as a Civil War hero, but he first wanted to make sure that the Boston Brahmin judge was a liberal like himself, a man in "entire sympathy with our views." After the two Massachusetts senators, Henry Cabot Lodge and George F. Hoar, presumably reassured the President of the acceptability of Holmes' views, the appointment was confirmed by the Senate, in December 1902. Roosevelt, expecting in Holmes a pliable judge, was soon to be angrily disappointed.

For the white-haired Holmes, lean, erect, and sparkling at sixty-one, the appointment to the Supreme Court was the beginning of a great new career. He was to remain on the supreme bench, its ornament and its legend, through half a dozen presidential administrations until he resigned, still hale and racy, at ninety. By an historic coincidence, the humor of which would have delighted Holmes, the last case he heard on the Supreme Court was the first for a lawyer who was destined to become its chief justice within a quarter of a century. As Earl Warren relates the incident, he argued his first case before the Supreme Court on a Friday in June 1930; the next Monday Justice Holmes announced simply: "I won't be there tomorrow," and never returned to the Court. Chief Justice Warren, telling the incident, remarked that his friends have accused him of driving Holmes from the Supreme Court: "One look at you and he said 'I quit.'" Holmes died in 1935, ninety-four years old.

What Holmes had brought to the Supreme Court was not only a finely tempered and keenly cultivated mind but, more important, a special point of view, a philosophy of life and society that was not swayed by the winds of temporary doctrine or transient opinion. In a deeper sense, Holmes the Supreme Court justice, although called upon to deal with crucial questions of practical life, was above the battle in that he refused to become emotionally involved in the political currents or commitments of the moment, whether liberal, reformist, pacifist, or Socialist. Actually, he was not particularly interested in such currents. "As you know," he wrote to Harold Laski, "I am not much on politics." Not subject to what he called the "hydraulic pressure" of public opinion, Holmes occasionally surprised or shocked his liberal friends with judicial decisions that ran counter to prevailing emotions. Thus, taking a common-law position in defense of property, he dissented from the majority in the trustbusting Northern Securities Company case in 1904. And he again offended liberal opinion when he concurred, on the implied ground of national defense, with the majority in the sentencing of a Socialist leader in the free-speech case of Eugene V. Debs.

This case involved Eugene Victor Debs (1855–1926), founder of the American Socialist Party and its five-time presidential candidate. Under his leadership, the Socialist Party, which increased its presidential vote from about 97,000 in 1900 to nearly one million in 1920, dropped its Marxist phraseology but retained its Marxist ideology. Its 1912 platform, for example, blamed the capitalist system for nearly all the ills that afflict mankind, including armaments, crime, slums, child labor, insanity, and prostitution. Tried in Federal Court for advocating pacifism in World War I, Debs addressed the judge in September 1918, with brave eloquence before receiving sentence.

The case reached the Supreme Court on appeal, and Holmes, in *Debs v. U.S.* (1919), wrote the unanimous opinion of the Court upholding the sentence. He was not, of course, against free speech or against Debs as a socialist, although he despised both Debs and socialism. "I wonder," he wrote to Laski in April, "if Debs really has any ideas. What I have read of his discourse has seemed to me rather silly—and what he said about the judgment against him showed great ignorance." But, in a technical sense, Debs *did* violate the law, as Holmes wrote to Sir Frederick Pollock: "There was no doubt that the Jury was warranted in finding him [Debs] guilty or that the act [Espionage Act of 1917] was Constitutional. Now I hope the President will pardon him and some other poor devils with whom I have more sympathy." Holmes was unhappy about the whole thing. "I hated to have to write the *Debs* case," he admitted in a private letter to Herbert Croly in May, "and still more those of the other poor devils before us the same day and the week before. I could not see the wisdom of pressing the cases, especially when the fighting was over and I think it quite possible that if I had been on the jury I should have been for acquittal but I cannot doubt that there was evidence warranting a conviction on the disputed issues of fact." President Wilson refused to pardon Debs, but President Warren G. Harding did so in 1921.

To American liberals, those who most warmly admired Holmes, he was a baffling phenomenon. They expected him to pursue a consistently liberal line on the bench, but he eluded their pattern. His conception of the function of a judge was not theirs. John Dewey suggested that, if liberalism meant faith in human intelligence and respect for ideas as the supreme force in the solution of social problems, then Holmes was a liberal. If it meant an acceptance of prevailing doctrines of political reform just because they were regarded desirable or noble at any given moment in history, then he was hardly one. In truth, Holmes was a conservative much of the time and a pragmatist all the time. As Dewey said: "He has no social panacea to dole out, no fixed social program, no code of fixed ends to be realized." What Holmes was guided by was not tailored doctrine but skeptical philosophy and the experience of life.

There was a duality in Holmes as a judge. On the one hand he was a disciplined jurist bound by a profound respect for the law as it existed; on the other, he was a philosopher who viewed the human condition from the vantage point of universality. On one level, the law was a hard taskmaster, holding society together in an orderly framework of daily exigencies. On another level, the law, being pragmatic, local, and subject to amendment and alteration, had no cosmic significance. To a philosopher, no man-made statute really mattered much in the long view of history. This cosmic awareness tinctured Holmes' thinking and provided him with a pervasive skepticism—and humility—in areas that many men, including judges, considered certainties. Speaking before the Harvard Law School Association in New York in 1913, Holmes enunciated his judicial philosophy with almost Olympian detachment: "I have no belief in panaceas and almost none in sudden ruin. I believe with Montesquieu that if the chance of a battle—I might add, the passage of a law—has ruined a state, there was a general cause at work that made the state ready to perish by a . . . battle or a law. Hence I am not much interested one way or the other in the nostrums now so strenuously urged. I do not think the United States would come to an end if we lost our power to declare an Act of Congress void. . . . I do not pin my dreams for the future to my country or even to my race. I think it probable that civilization somehow will last as long as I care to look ahead—. . . perhaps also bred to greatness and splendor by science. I think it not improbable that man . . . may have cosmic destinies that he does not understand."

In Holmes' philosophy there was a kind of suspension of philosophy, at least of the traditional variety. Systematic philosophers, who seemed to know the answers to the most thorny problems of man and the universe, left him unconvinced. He was equally skeptical of moralists—"I naturally shrink from the moral tone," he wrote to Laski—and critical of dogmatists. He felt that none of the claimants to certainty really knew enough to substantiate their sweeping assertions about truth and the human condition. Large generalizations, including judicial decisions, were merely expressions of the "longing for certainty" to be found "in every human mind." But, he said, "certainty generally is illusion, and repose is not the destiny of man." Objecting to what he called "delusive exactness," Holmes insisted on intellectual humility and suspension of judgment in the presence of the unknown. "I think none of the philosophers sufficiently humble," he told William James in a letter in which he made some critical remarks on James' *Pragmatism*. And he wrote to Laski, "Why should we not be humble—why not willing to admit that the primordial wiggle of the first churning of chaos came before our time?"

The only thing that was meaningful, Holmes reiterated in his writings and speeches, was life itself—the plain, unvarnished reality of daily existence, with its joys and conflicts. The dynamism of human life was its own justification; it could not fit into preconceived theories. "From the point of view of the world," he said to the Boston Bar Association in March 1900, "the end of life is life. Life is action, the use of one's powers. . . . Life is an end in itself, and the only question as to whether it is worth living is whether you have enough of it." Holmes used a similar expression some eighteen years later in a letter to Sir Frederick

Pollock: "... Realize life as an end in itself. Functioning is all there is —only our keenest pleasure is in what we call the higher sort. I wonder if cosmically an idea is any more important than the bowels."

In a private letter to a friend, William James complained that Holmes' philosophy was "immature" and "unworthy" of a judge: "It is curiously childish to me." But to Holmes it was mature. Faith in life as a continuing struggle and experimentation was at the base of his approach to law. Nothing in human affairs, he held, was either sacrosanct or permanently fixed. Everything, including the federal Constitution, which Holmes had sworn to uphold, was flexible and subject to change. "The Constitution," he said in a famous statement, which echoed that of Jefferson a century earlier, "is an experiment, as all life is an experiment."

Holmes was one of the pioneers in the pragmatic study of jurisprudence. Even before Charles Sanders Peirce, William James and John Dewey developed the theories of pragmatism and revolutionized social thought in America, Holmes analyzed the law, not as an immutable system, but as an experimental process. In *The Common Law* he challenged the prevailing theories of natural law—which assumed absolute doctrines of eternal (unchanging) truths—with his assertion that the "life of the law has not been logic: it has been experience." Law, he went on to explain, was the product of time and experience, rather than handed-down dogma:

"The felt necessities of the time, the prevalent moral and political theories, intuitions of public policy, avowed or unconscious, even the prejudices which judges share with their fellow-men, have had a good deal more to do than the syllogism in determining the rules by which men should be governed."

Law, to Holmes, was not an *ought* but an *is*. Personal preferences or pet legal theories had little to do with the hard reality of law as it existed at any given time. Law was subject to alteration by orderly processes as a result of "felt necessities," but while on the statute books and backed by the sovereignty of government, it remained a brute fact of life. "When I talk of law," Holmes wrote to Laski in 1917, "I talk as a cynic. I don't care a damn if twenty professors tell me a decision is not law if I know that the courts will enforce it." The old veteran of the Civil War had no illusions about the sacredness of human life vis-à-vis the needs of government. Holmes frankly and cheerfully accepted the idea of the use of force as a social and political necessity—whenever the occasion arose.

Every society, he said, "rests on the death of men." Government does not hesitate to kill "when it sees fit and can."

"I think that the sacredness of human life," Holmes wrote to Pollock (in 1920), "is a purely municipal ideal of no validity outside the jurisdiction. I believe that force, mitigated so far as may be by good manners, is the *ultima ratio,* and between two groups that want to make inconsistent kinds of worlds I see no remedy except force."

Like Dewey, Holmes took a relativist position on moral values and judgments. Consistent with his rejection of natural law, he asserted the idea that truth in human relations was subject to changing conditions as seen and experienced by individuals. As such, its validity was personal instead of cosmic. To William James, of whose metaphysical theories he was dubious, he wrote in 1907: "I have been in the habit of saying that all I mean by truth is what I can't help thinking. The assumption of the validity of the thinking process seems to mean no more than that. . . . I have learned to surmise that my *can't helps* are not necessarily cosmic can't helps—that the universe may not be subject to my limitations; and philosophy generally seems to me to sin through arrogance. It is like the old knight-errants who proposed to knock your head off if you didn't admit that their girl was not only a nice girl but the most beautiful and best of all possible girls. I can't help preferring champagne to ditch water.—I doubt if the universe does."

Holmes developed his relativistic position concerning truth and values more fully in "Natural Law," an article published in the November 1918 *Harvard Law Review.* It is interesting, as Professor Arnold Brecht has pointed out in his comprehensive work, *Political Theory* (1959), that Holmes' relativism was close to that of pre–World War I German jurists and sociologists, whose writings the Justice "did not seem to know." (The essence of the relativist argument was that truth and value judgments, matters of personal preference, were not subject to scientific proof.)

Holmes felt that one man's choice of values was as good as another's —an opinion, Professor Brecht reminds us, almost identical with that expressed by Max Weber in his epochal 1904 article, " 'Objectivity' in Social Scientific and Social Political Knowledge." An individual may strongly assert his preferences and even fight for them, but he cannot prove them by reason or theorize them into universality. "I don't talk much of rights," Holmes said, "as I see no meaning in the rights of man except what the crowd will fight for."

Holmes' article in the *Harvard Law Review* is couched in terms more personal than is the wont of theoretical philosophers. It contains the quintessence of his relativistic and skeptical attitude toward both life and law:

"There is in all men a demand for the superlative, so much so that the poor devil who has no other way of reaching it attains it by getting drunk . . . this demand is at the bottom of the philosopher's effort to prove that truth is absolute and of the jurist's search for criteria of universal validity which he collects under the head of natural laws. . . . Certitude is not the test of certainty. . . . I love granite rocks and bayberry bushes, no doubt because with them were my earliest joys . . . others, poor souls, may be equally dogmatic about something else. . . . The jurists who believe in natural law seem to me to be in that naive state of mind that accepts what has been familiar . . . as something that must be accepted by all men everywhere . . . a right is only the hypostasis of a prophecy . . . behind these legal rights is the fighting will . . . to maintain them . . . ; but that does not seem to me the same thing as the supposed *a priori* discernment of a duty or the assertion of a preexisting right. A dog will fight for his bone."

Skepticism in the face of dogmas and relativism in regard to values underlay Holmes' legal thinking and help explain his role as the "Great Dissenter" on the Supreme Court. His dissents—in which Justice Louis D. Brandeis usually joined after his appointment to the Court in 1916—became celebrated for the independent position they embodied and for the matchless style in which they were couched.

Although Louis Dembitz Brandeis (1856–1941) is coupled with Holmes as a Great Dissenter, the two men were not intimate and did not altogether share the same philosophic outlook. Both were men of large liberal spirit, particularly in the field of free speech, but of widely different temperaments. Holmes' predilection was for legal and philosophical reasoning; Brandeis' propensity was for economic data. Holmes built his cases like a worldly philosopher; Brandeis constructed his like an academic social scientist. Holmes was an amused and amusing skeptic; Brandeis was a dead-serious believer in reform. "I'm afraid Brandeis has the crusading spirit," Holmes once said with ironic affection. "He talks like one of those upward-and-onward fellows."

It was that crusading spirit that had caused such a storm of opposition when President Wilson appointed Brandeis to the Supreme Court in January 1916. The most powerful conservatives of the day, among them seven former presidents of the American Bar Association (including William Howard Taft, Joseph H. Choate, and Elihu Root), opposed the nomination and attacked Brandeis' public as well as private life. "The propaganda in this matter," President Wilson wrote, "has been very extraordinary and very distressing to those who love fairness and value the dignity of the great professions." The opposition to Brandeis, partly motivated by anti-Semitism, was mainly due to his reputation as a liberal who had for years fought stubbornly for social justice and economic equality. Brandeis considered big business monopolies the greatest single danger to American democracy. He advocated government regulation of unrestrained economic bigness, protection of small business, freedom of labor to organize, and other social reforms, such as pensions, sick benefits, and unemployment insurance. He may justly be regarded as the father of the New Deal (of which he did not always approve, primarily because its governmental powers were becoming "too big").

To the advocacy of his social-economic reform program, in writings, speeches, and testimony before Congress, Brandeis brought a mastery of economic detail and a knowledge of the total national economy that was unprecedented, especially in a lawyer and judge. He had the rare gift of marshalling his ideas with a precision of language and (in the words of Charles A. Beard) "a display of stubborn and irreducible facts knit closely together" that was overwhelming in its impact. Before his appointment to the Court he had given freely of his time in the service of causes which he considered just and democratic.

"Some men," Brandeis said in 1911, "buy diamonds and rare works of art; others delight in automobiles and yachts. My luxury is to invest my surplus effort, beyond that required for the proper support of my family, to the pleasure of taking up a problem and solving, or helping to solve, it for the people without receiving any compensation. Your yachtsman or automobilist would lose much of his enjoyment if he were obliged to do for pay what he is doing for the love of the thing itself. So I should lose much of my satisfaction if I were paid in connection with public services of this kind. I have only one life, and it is short enough. Why waste it on things I don't want most? I don't want money or property most. I want to be free."

Brandeis' idealism and his known mastery of the complex data of modern life were the reason the equally reform-minded Woodrow Wilson selected him for the Supreme Court.

On the Court, Justice Brandeis' liberal position remained unchanged. In the fields of civil liberties and economic justice his judicial opinions were so unswerving that one prominent educator likened him to Lincoln.

"You two," Alvin Johnson wrote to Brandeis (November 1936), "seem to me the two most serenely implacable democrats in all history."

Brandeis upheld his social philosophy either in separate opinions or in concurrence with Holmes' dissents. The two justices continued to respect one another. "I don't see much of him," Holmes wrote to Laski in 1920, "except in Court but he is a great comfort to me." And again the next month: ". . . and that makes me think of Disraeli and the affection that he inspired, and that makes me ask whether loveableness is a characteristic of the better class of Jews. When I think how many of the younger men that have warmed my heart have been Jews I cannot but suspect it. . . . Brandeis, whom many dislike, seems to me to have this quality and always gives me a glow, even though I am not sure that he wouldn't burn me at a slow fire if it were in the interest of some very possibly disinterested aim. I don't for a moment doubt that for daily purposes he feels to me as a friend—as certainly I do to him."

Holmes did not, of course, always dissent, nor did he always agree with the liberal Brandeis. Much of the time, in fact, Holmes agreed with his "brethren" on the bench, the majority of whom were conservative in their economic outlook. He shared his fellow justices' antipathy for economic radicalism, but on grounds more sophisticated than theirs. He considered radical theorists and socialists fools or worse; they were "shriekers," whose proclaimed passion for economic equality, he said, was "merely idealizing envy." They simply had no grasp of the facts and meaning of life. The advocacy of "wholesale social regeneration" through "socialized property," Holmes wrote in the *Illinois Law Review* in 1915, was an "empty humbug." It ignored human beings as individuals with their immense range of talents, efforts and aspirations. "I never read a socialist yet from Karl Marx down," Holmes told Harold Laski, "and I have read a number, that I didn't think talked drool."

Holmes felt equal disdain for such American radicals as Henry George, Thorstein Veblen, and Eugene Debs. He disliked theories and legislative acts based upon them that involved the dangerous business of what he said was "tinkering with the institution of property." It is not too surprising, therefore, that he concurred with the conservative majority in about three fourths of the cases in which the Supreme Court held state legislation contrary to the Fourteenth Amendment.

The key words in the Fourteenth Amendment (1868), under which much state legislation in the economic sphere after the Civil War was challenged in the courts, were:

No State shall make or enforce any law which shall abridge the privileges or immunities of citizens of the United States; nor shall any State deprive any person of life, liberty, or property without due process of law."

The amendment was originally designed to provide protection for the civic rights of the newly enfranchised Negroes, but the *due process* clause was used increasingly by the federal courts to strike down social-economic legislation that was distasteful to conservative property interests—and that had nothing to do with the rights of Negroes.

In some cases, Holmes wrote the majority opinion for the Court. But his dissents, qualifying him for the exclusive title of the Great Dissenter, were Olympian in their disregard for precedent.

There were two general areas in which his dissents were conspicuous. One was his blunt rejection of dogmatic interpretations of the federal Constitution. The other was his approach to the problem of free speech.

Although he shared his colleagues' aversion for radicals and radical legislation, he did not accept the dogmatic economic and legal theories they used to justify their decisions. His rejection of dogmatism in Supreme Court rulings—in itself a major service in the cause of open-mindedness—is best seen in three important cases, those of *Lochner v. New York* (1905), *Truax v. Corrigan* (1921), and *Tyson Bros. v. Banton* (1927).

The Lochner case was of special significance because it was one of the first to deal with social legislation in the field of labor protection. It involved a New York state law limiting the hours of labor in bakeries to ten a day and a maximum of sixty a week. The act was passed under the general "police powers" of the state and was designed to protect the health of the bakers. Challenged as a violation of "liberty of contract" under the Fourteenth Amendment, the Supreme Court upheld the challenge by a vote of five to four, and declared the law invalid. The majority opinion, written by Justice Rufus W. Peckham, went beyond the immediate act and stated sweeping political-economic principles that all but destroyed the power of any states to legislate in the welfare field. "The act," Justice Peckham wrote, "is . . . an illegal interference with the rights of individuals, both employers and employees, to make contracts regarding labor upon such terms as they may think best."

In addition to that of Holmes, there was a dissenting opinion written by Justice John M. Harlan in which Justices Edward D. White and William Rufus Day concurred.

But Holmes' dissent became a landmark in sociological jurisprudence, in what Roscoe Pound has described as the pragmatic movement in the law that aimed at "putting the human factor in the central place." Holmes started out with a blunt rejection of Peckham's underlying assumptions. "This case," he wrote, "is decided upon an economic theory which a large part of the country does not entertain." Whether a judge personally liked a law or not, it was not his business to deny the "right of a majority to embody their opinions in law." The statute books were full of laws (many of them upheld in previous Supreme Court decisions) that were unwise or tyrannical—Sunday laws, lottery laws, school laws, tax laws—and yet within the right of the citizens to enact them. The New York state act regarding the bakers was in the same category. It was now being declared invalid, Holmes suggested, not because it violated the Fourteenth Amendment—it had nothing to do with that Amendment—but because it did not fit into the preconceived economic doctrines of the judges. "The Fourteenth Amendment," Holmes wrote in a passage that was to echo through the decades, "does not enact Mr. Herbert Spencer's Social Statics" (a teleological work, published in 1850, which contained the usual Spencerian generalizations unblemished by empirical data). The smuggling of dogmatic doctrines into the Constitution to justify the judges' economic bias was, in Holmes' view, bad law and bad policy.

"But a constitution," he continued, "is not intended to embody a particular economic theory, whether of paternalism and the organic relation of the citizen to the State or of *laissez faire*. It is made for people of fundamentally differing views, and the accident of our finding certain opinions natural and familiar or novel and even shocking ought not to conclude our judgment upon the question whether statutes embodying them conflict with the Constitution of the United States."

He took a similar position in *Truax v. Corrigan,* which involved labor, and in *Tyson Bros. v. Banton,* which concerned theater tickets. In both instances, Holmes rejected *a priori* theories and upheld the right of the states to legislate without hindrance by the Supreme Court. In *Truax v. Corrigan,* the Court invalidated an Arizona statute which provided that no injunctions could be issued against peaceful picketing. Chief Justice William Howard Taft, in a five-to-four decision, held that the Arizona act was unlawful in that picketing, being inherently an attack on property, violated the *due process* clause of the Fourteenth Amendment.

In his majority decision, Justice Taft wrote that picketing was "a direct invasion of the ordinary business and property rights" and that such experimentation as was involved in the Arizona law was unlawful:

"The Constitution was intended . . . to prevent experimentation with the fundamental rights of the individual." Professor Felix Frankfurter, a future justice of the Supreme Court, commented in *The New Republic* (1921) that the decision ignored American economic realities: "For all the regard that the Chief Justice of the United States pays to the facts of industrial life, he might as well have written this opinion as Chief Justice of the Fiji Islands."

Holmes dissented. He protested, with a touch of irony, against the dangers of "delusive exactness in the application of the Fourteenth Amendment" (by which the judges confused picketing, as a potential threat to business, with established property rights) and insisted that legislatures had a right to pass laws to remedy or redress evils. "Legislation may begin where an evil begins." He reiterated that it was not the Supreme Court's business to interfere with legislation on the ground that it did not coincide with the judges' economic theories:

"I must add one general consideration. There is nothing I more deprecate than the use of the Fourteenth Amendment beyond the absolute compulsion of its words to prevent the making of social experiments that an important part of the community desires, in the insulated chambers afforded by the several States, even though the experiments may seem futile or even noxious to me and to those whose judgment I most respect."

Similarly, in the Tyson case, in which the Supreme Court held that a New York state law setting a 50-cent limit on the mark-up of theater tickets was unconstitutional—taking away the rights of property without *due process*—Holmes dissented and repeated his belief that the powers of the legislature must not be curbed to fit the bias of the judges:

"I think the proper course is to recognize that a State legislature can do whatever it sees fit to do unless it is restrained by some express prohibition in the Constitution of the United States or of the State, and that Courts should be careful not to extend such prohibitions beyond their obvious meaning by reading into them conceptions of public policy that the particular Court may happen to entertain. . . . I am far from saying that I think that this particular law a wise and rational provision. That is not my affair. But if the people of the State of New York speaking by their authorized voice say that they want it, I see nothing in the Constitution of the United States to prevent their having their will."

In his dissents connected with the free-speech cases, Holmes was equally outspoken. Here he not only challenged the prevailing passions of intolerance—generated by World War I—but explored the difficult concepts and practices of free speech on a philosophical level reminiscent of Jefferson. Among the most important cases in which Holmes expressed his dissenting opinions were: *Abrams v. U.S.* (1919), *Gitlow v. N.Y.* (1925), *U.S. v. Schwimmer* (1928), and *Olmstead v. U.S.* (1928). These cases dealt with what he called the "free trade in ideas."

But here again his position was not an absolute one. Even in this crucial area of intellectual freedom, Holmes did not always dissent. As in other instances involving social legislation, so also in matters affecting freedom of speech he sometimes sided with the majority. This was particularly true in cases involving the national security, where the Civil War veteran took a high patriotic position. In such notable cases as *Schenck v. U.S.* (1919) and, as noted, *Debs v. U.S.*, both upholding limitations on freedom of speech in wartime, Holmes not only concurred with the majority but wrote the opinion for the Court.

The Schenck case concerned the general secretary of the Socialist Party, who was jailed under the Espionage Act of 1917 for sending through the mails, particularly to the armed forces, pacifist leaflets. The Supreme Court upheld the conviction. In handing down the opinion, Holmes formulated the famous "clear and present danger" doctrine as a test of free speech. He took the position that freedom of speech was not an absolute value, good at all times and at all places, but a relative one. His argument in *Schenck v. U.S.* was that speech was not being prohibited because the ideas involved were inherently undesirable, but because under certain circumstances—opposing recruitment and spreading demoralization among the troops in wartime, for example—words could endanger the war effort. What Holmes was saying in effect was that Schenck and other defendants similarly situated should remain in jail, not because they advocated pacifism and socialism but because they did so at the wrong time. "When a nation is at war many things that might be said in time of peace are such a hindrance to its effort that their utterance will not be endured so long as men fight." In other words, the test of freedom of speech was not its *substance* but its *circumstance.* He wrote in the Schenck case:

"We admit that in many places and in ordinary times the defendants in saying all that was said in the circular would have been within their constitutional rights [under the First Amendment]. But the character of every act depends upon the circumstances in which it is done. . . . The most stringent protection of free speech would not protect a man in falsely shouting fire in a theater and causing a panic. . . . The question in every case is whether the words used are used in such circumstances and are of such a nature as to create a clear and present danger that they will bring about the substantive evils that Congress has a right to prevent."

To a philosopher like Holmes, it must have been evident that the "clear and present danger" doctrine that justified limitation on freedom of speech was neither clear nor adequate. It could serve a momentary purpose, under pressures of war, but it was not sufficient to stand by itself as a doctrine governing man's rights and responsibilities in a free society. Moreover, the "clear and present danger" argument came perilously close to agreeing with the ultraconservatives and antidemocrats who have always held that freedom of speech was all right in its way, but not in a crisis. This was a manifest absurdity, and it would be surprising if Holmes was not troubled by it. For if freedom of speech had any meaning at all, it meant freedom to speak when it was unpopular to do so, precisely because it was unpopular. Obviously there is no problem when everybody agrees with everybody. Holmes himself said in the Schwimmer case (1928) that the principle of free thought meant "not free thought for those who agree with us but freedom for the thought that we hate."

It was this principle that Holmes developed in *Abrams v. U.S.* (1919), which followed hard on that of Schenck, and subsequent free-speech cases. His dissent in the Abrams case sounded as if he regretted his decision in Schenck; it was a complete reversal of his position. Just as he agreed with the majority that Schenck was guilty of distributing leaflets, so he disagreed with his colleagues that Abrams was guilty for doing almost precisely the same thing at approximately the same time. Jacob Abrams had thrown down from a loft in New York City leaflets urging that workers refuse to produce arms that were to be used for intervention in the Russian Revolution. Under the Espionage Act this was considered an "intent" to curtail or cripple the prosecution of the war, and Abrams was sentenced to twenty years in prison. The Supreme Court, with Justices Holmes and Brandeis dissenting, upheld the conviction. Technically, Holmes' dissent revolved around the meaning of the word *intent*. He did not regard Abrams' intent incitement enough to cause a direct limitation of war production. "Nobody can suppose," Holmes wrote, "that the surreptitious publishing of a silly leaflet by an unknown man . . . would present an immediate danger that its opinions would hinder the success of the government arms."

But Holmes went beyond the technicalities. He took the opportunity to explore the inner meaning of free speech, especially in a crisis, something he had failed to do in the Schenck case. Apart from intent, what was the real question in the Abrams case? It was, Holmes asserted, the right under the Constitution to express ideas and beliefs, no matter how silly, provided they were honestly held. He considered Abrams' socialist faith a "creed of ignorance and immaturity," but this was no excuse whatever for the government to punish him for his opinions. Like Voltaire and Jefferson before him, Holmes now elucidated the principles of free opinion in timeless terms. He rooted them in the Constitution as being integral to its whole spirit. The words, in the Abrams case, stand as a monument to intellectual freedom:

"Persecution for the expression of opinions seems to me perfectly logical. If you have no doubt of your premises or your power and want a certain result with all your heart you naturally express your wishes in law and sweep away all opposition.... But when men have realized that time has upset many fighting faiths, they may come to believe... that the ultimate good desired is better reached by free trade in ideas,—that the best test of truth is the power of the thought to get itself accepted in the competition of the market.... That, at any rate, is the theory of our Constitution. It is an experiment as all life is an experiment.... While that experiment is part of our system I think that we should be eternally vigilant against attempts to check the expression of opinions that we loathe and believe to be fraught with death."

Note the similarity to Jefferson. In his *Notes on the State of Virginia* (1785) Jefferson had written: "Reason and free inquiry are the only effectual agents against error.... They are the natural enemies of error, and of error only.... It is error alone which needs the support of government. Truth can stand by itself."

Holmes concluded this dissenting opinion by saying that he regretted he could not "put into more impressive words" this belief that in their conviction... the defendants [in the Abrams case] were deprived of their rights under the Constitution of the United States."

In the Gitlow and Schwimmer cases, Holmes continued and elaborated his reasoned defense of free expression. Benjamin Gitlow was convicted for publishing a revolutionary pamphlet. The Supreme Court upheld the sentence mainly on the ground that the Marxist pamphlet was a "direct incitement" to revolution. Holmes pointed out that his Schenck case criterion of "clear and present danger" did not apply to Gitlow, that the defendant's "redundant discourse" had little chance of starting a radical conflagration, and that there was no current danger of an attempt to overthrow the government by a small minority like that. In the absence of any such peril to the nation, Holmes could see no justification for punishing Gitlow for his opinions. Under the Constitution and in the free market place of ideas, Gitlow had a right to offer his opinions, even though they were inflammatory:

"It is said that this manifesto was more than a theory, that it was an incitement. Every idea is an incitement. It offers itself for belief and if believed it is acted on unless some other belief outweighs it . . . the only meaning of free speech is that they [beliefs] should be given their chance and have their way."

In the Schwimmer and Olmstead cases, both in 1928, Holmes extended his championship of freedom to include the advocacy of pacifism and the rejection of government-approved wiretapping. Rosika Schwimmer had had her application for citizenship rejected on the ground that she had been a pacifist. In his dissent, Holmes [Chief Justice Charles Evans Hughes, and Justices Brandeis and Stone also dissented] attacked the Court's decision on two main grounds: that her belief in pacifism was neither dangerous nor silly, and that even if it were both, she still had a right under the Constitution to voice it. "She is an optimist," Holmes wrote, "and states . . . her belief that war will disappear. . . . I do not share that optimism." But it was absurd to assume that hatred of war would not make her a good citizen. In the Olmstead case, which involved the tapping of a bootlegger's wire by federal agents to prove his violation of the prohibition laws, Holmes disagreed with the majority that such a procedure was lawful or constitutional. Wiretapping, he held, was a violation of the Fourth and Fifth amendments, and, as such, was a "dirty business." Evidence illegally obtained was a "criminal act." There was no justification for its use by the government, even for the apprehension of criminals. "We have to choose," Holmes wrote in his dissent, "and for my part I think it less evil that some criminals should escape than that the government should play an ignoble part."

Such was the over-all pattern of Holmes' thought. He was an unflinching realist, acutely aware of the relativity of values, moved by no dogmas, pursuing what he conceived to be the truth with an overpowering sense of philosophic humility. In human affairs, he took the long, detached view. But despite his Olympian aloofness, he could be stirred. When Alvin Johnson, in 1933, organized a committee to rescue European scholars driven out by Hitler, Felix Frankfurter asked Justice Holmes to be a sponsor. To Frankfurter's surprise, the Judge, then in his ninety-second year, eagerly accepted, saying: "I have never joined anything to promote a cause. This is different. Nothing less is involved than the history of civilization."

Holmes displayed a tolerant regard for the human mind, no matter what its direction. Without necessarily respecting the content of other people's ideas or convictions, he nevertheless championed their right to voice them. "With effervescing opinions as with the not yet forgotten champagnes," he wrote to the Harvard Liberal Club in 1920, "the quickest way to let them get flat is to let them get exposed to the air." He was in favor of what he called the "aeration" of ideas.

Holmes' greatness as a judge and jurist lies in this: Even in dissents, he spoke from the awe-inspiring platform of the Supreme Court in defense of the most crucial of all public values—freedom of the mind. The ideas embodied in his opinions and dissents became the intellectual property of his countrymen and ultimately even their laws. The skeptical Great Dissenter, in precisely that role, was the conscience of America, perhaps despite himself.

# 17

## *THE AMERICAN AS PRAGMATIST:* John Dewey *(1859–1952)*

*Dewey needs a great deal of building up and of following his principles into all sorts of questions of detail. But it's a noble work. Pity that their [Dewey and his Chicago school] style should be so dry and abstract.*
*—William James, November 15, 1903*

Influence is hard to measure, but that of William James on John Dewey seems to have been decisive. "William James' *Principles of Psychology,*" Dewey's daughter Jane wrote in a short biographic account of her father, "was much the greatest single influence in changing the direction of Dewey's philosophical thinking." Dewey himself admitted as much. In a *Personal Statement,* published in 1930, when he was seventy-one, he mentioned books as having had a limited impact on his intellectual development—with one exception: "It concerns the influence of William James. As far as I can discover, one specifiable philosophic factor which entered into my thinking so as to give it a new direction and quality, is this one. . . . It proceeded from his *Psychology* rather than from the . . . *Will to Believe,* his *Pluralistic Universe,* or *Pragmatism.*" Whatever the precise amount of influence, it is clear that the philosophic and psychological torch lighted by James was picked up by Dewey, seventeen years his junior.

In later years, Dewey claimed that his philosophy was fundamentally different from that of James. But James himself, admiring Dewey's work at the University of Chicago and hailing the younger philosopher as a "hero" despite the density of his language, thought that the difference between them was one of emphasis more than of substance. The objective critic sees the difference between the two men—both profoundly democratic and humanist—as one of temper and method. James was intuitive, Dewey logical. James was preoccupied with the whole spectrum of ideas, including metaphysical ones, as excitive and important in themselves (as a work of art is interesting and important). Dewey was concerned with ideas as instrumentalities of social impact.

John Dewey was almost a symbol of old-fashioned Americanism—a small-town descendant of New England farmers, practical, experimental, sturdy, thoughtful, and unassuming. He was born in Burlington, Vermont, on October 20, 1859. His father, Archibald Sprague Dewey, who served in the Civil War, was born in 1811, when James Madison was President. Since John Dewey lived to be ninety-three, dying in the last year of President Truman's administration, the two Deweys, father and son, between them spanned almost the whole period of American national history. John Dewey himself, in his thought and work, reflected not only basic American characteristics but also the revolutionary transformation that the United States underwent in his lifetime: from a rural society moving on horse-drawn wheels to an industrialized urban civilization plunging into an era of electronics and automation.

Dewey was brought up in an intellectual household. His father, who ran a grocery store in Burlington, had classical tastes. He knew Shakespeare, quoted Milton, and read Burns to his children. John Dewey was thus exposed to literary ideas early in life. After graduating from high school at fifteen, he attended the University of Vermont, which then had a faculty of eight and a curriculum of required courses that included Greek, Latin, ancient history, analytical geometry, and calculus. He also studied zoology, geology, and physiology, the last from a textbook by Thomas Henry Huxley. "From this book," Jane Dewey reports, "John Dewey derived an impressive picture of the unity of the living creature. This aroused in him that intellectual curiosity for a wide outlook on things which interests a youth in philosophic study."

In his senior year, Dewey took up philosophy. The course, based on Yale President Noah Porter's *Intellectual Philosophy* and Plato's *Republic,* was given by Professor H. A. P. Torrey, a follower of the Scottish school of intuitionists who contrasted with the English empiricists. In the course of his readings in philosophy, he encountered Auguste Comte and Friedrich Hegel. They opened a new world to the youth from Burlington.

After he graduated from the University of Vermont in 1879 and taught high school for a few years, Dewey went to Johns Hopkins, where he earned a Ph.D. in philosophy, as a student of the American Hegelian, Professor George S. Morris. Hegel, Dewey said, "left a permanent deposit in my thought"—as he had also on Karl Marx in Germany nearly half a century earlier.

Critics of Dewey's writing style must sadly agree that Hegel's influence was apparent. For Dewey was a plodding writer, whose ponderous style aroused widespread adverse comment. In the correspondence between Justice Oliver Wendell Holmes and Harold Laski there are some amusing remarks on the subject. After Laski wrote that he found Dewey "unreadable," Justice Holmes commented that he had not read him, but "I respect your stomach for long-winded books." A year later the Justice told how he was making up his mind about Dewey: "I am reading a book by John Dewey, *Experience and Nature*.... It is badly written in the sense that the style makes it more difficult than the thought—but even in the writing it gives me the feeling that Walt Whitman gives of the symphonic. Few indeed, I should think, are the books that hold so much of life with an even hand...."

Even after he struck out on a path of his own and ceased to be a Hegelian, Dewey continued to admire the acuteness and depth of the German thinker, of whom he said in later years: "There is greater richness and greater variety of insight in Hegel than in any other single systematic philosopher."

It took Dewey some fifteen years to drift away from Hegelianism. It was a painfully slow process, during which he turned Hegel upside down, so to speak. Gradually Dewey came to the conclusion that Hegel's basic metaphysical idea of the "absolute mind" dominating and shaping human institutions, had "no empirical support." The truth, Dewey thought, actually lay in the reverse. Empirically, it could be demonstrated that it was the cultural environment, and not the Hegelian "ready-made mind over against a physical world," that molded ideas and shaped men's beliefs and attitudes. Like William James, Dewey rejected absolutism and became, he said, "completely emancipated from [the] Hegelian garb." Whatever residue of Hegelianism may have been left in Dewey's philosophy, it had no apparent influence on his political thinking. Unlike other European Hegelians, Dewey did not develop into a Marxist.

He graduated from Johns Hopkins in 1884, then taught at the Universities of Minnesota, Michigan, and Chicago. At the new University of Chicago (established by John D. Rockefeller in 1892), Dewey taught for a decade (1894–1904) and did some of his most original work. Here, as director of the School of Education, he achieved renown with his experimental "new pedagogy." In 1904, he went to Columbia University, where he remained for most of his academic career and whence his influence radiated throughout the world. Active for well over sixty years, he became probably the most influential single academic figure and philosopher in America's intellectual history. He poured out his thought in hundreds of articles and books on an immense variety of subjects, including the main branches of philosophy and psychology, education, art, esthetics, logic, ethics, religion, metaphysics, epistemology, jurisprudence, politics, science, methodology, and the social sciences in general. He published close to forty books, ranging from his *Psychology* (1887) and *Critical Theory of Ethics* (1894) to *Culture and Freedom* (1939) and *Education Today* in 1946.

To appreciate Dewey's impact on American political and social thought, it is necessary to understand his philosophy of *instrumentalism*. This was a point of view and a method of social analysis that was to permeate American thinking about the world and its problems for nearly two generations. Dewey used the term, he said, for lack of a better word. Instrumentalism was designed to serve as a bridge between "something called 'science' . . . and something called 'morals.' " Its mechanism was a logic, which he defined as a "method of effective inquiry," that would at once supply a "theoretical solvent and a practical want."

Instrumentalism, as developed by Dewey in theory and applied by him to a whole range of practices, involved the fundamental notion that all ideas were regulative, or *instrumental,* in the sense that they contained within themselves plans of action. The validity of any idea was confirmed, or confuted, by its performance in specific tests or experiments. If an idea proved instrumental in any given context, if its usefulness was verified by experience, it could be considered "true." If it failed in any specific test—if it did not "check out"—it was invalidated and was hence not "true." Thus Dewey insisted that *truth* was not an absolute, not something rigidly fixed and universal in perpetuity, but a product of use and an instrument of practicality. As such, it varied not only in place, time, and circumstance, but also in the scale of values.

As an illustration of Dewey's instrumentalist position, Irwin Edman tells of an incident that took place in a seminar at Columbia. Dewey had been reiterating his basic idea that truth was tested by its use and hence was a flexible concept. A British woman student finally burst out in protest:

"But, professor, I have been taught to believe that true means true; that false means false, that good means good and bad means bad; I don't understand all this talk about more or less true, more or less good. Could you explain more exactly?"

Dewey replied mildly, "Let me tell you a parable. Once upon a time in Philadelphia there was a paranoiac. He thought he was dead. Nobody could convince him he was alive. Finally, one of the doctors thought of an ingenious idea. He pricked the patient's finger. 'Now,' he said, 'are you dead?' 'Sure,' said the paranoiac, 'that proves that dead men bleed. . . .' Now I'll say true or false if you want me to, but I'll mean better or worse."

One of the reasons for Dewey's influence in the area of political ideas and analysis was that he combined deed with thought. Unlike the traditional philosophers, he was averse to mere contemplativeness. He considered ideas instruments—the most powerful instruments—for shaping the environment. Given the interrelationship between ideas and action, it followed that nothing was absolutely stable. Human intelligence was in constant operation to change things—institutions, habits, attitudes, beliefs, and values. Dewey saw that change throughout society was not uniform. He identified two general types of change. One was comparatively slow, creating the impression of permanence and stability. This he called "structure." The other was relatively rapid. This he labeled "process." But neither "structure" nor "process" remains long unaltered. Regardless of the rhythm of change, according to Dewey, human intelligence always combines with action to alter the environment. "Every thinker," he wrote in his preface to *Characters and Events,* "puts some portion of an apparently stable world in peril."

What he suggested was that ideas should be used consciously and intelligently for the betterment of human life. This was at the root of his exaltation of action as a principle of human existence—a tenet he shared with William James. Who was better equipped to guide society into desirable channels than the philosopher with his special knowledge and insights? Dewey believed—and practiced his belief—that philosophy should be deliberately activist and participate in the practical problems of daily existence. That in itself was an integral part of his philosophy. He wrote on the flyleaf of *Characters and Events:*

"Better it is for philosophy to err in active participation in the living struggles and issues of its own age and times than to maintain an immune monastic impeccability. To try to escape from the snares and pitfalls of time by recourse to traditional problems and interests—rather than that, let the dead bury their own dead."

Dewey's activities illustrated his conviction that there was nothing more powerful than an idea. This was notably true in the field of education, with which his name and fame are indissolubly linked. Beginning with his experimental school at The University of Chicago in 1896 and continuing at Columbia from 1904 on, he directly influenced two generations of teachers and academic administrators. His guiding ideas and his practical experimentation, especially in the crucial area of elementary schools, wrought a revolution in American education. Insofar as education is a basic component of civilized life, it may be said that Dewey transformed the thoughts and habits of America as no other educator before him. The Progressive Education Association, founded in 1919 and discontinued in 1957, gave dynamic institutional form to his program and thereby helped propagate it all over America and beyond.

So far as a nation's educational system and its objectives are crucial, those who influence both wield power of incalculable if invisible measure. They deeply affect both behavior and institutions, including political ones. In the case of Dewey, his pedagogical ideas—an organic part of his general philosophy—triumphed to an extent that requires special analysis. They not only transformed America's school system but, in the process, added many levels of meaning to democratic thought and practice. First, was his basic assumption that schools must not be separated from daily life and that education should be integrated with practical experience. Second, his conception of human nature, which he regarded as flexible, changeable, and capable of continuous development. Third, his belief in the experimental process as the test of life and truth. Finally, his conviction that democracy had special values which both reflected and demanded the kind of "progressive education" he advocated. Dewey's educational thought was thus an integrated system that combined psychology, philosophy, politics, and social science, all of them in interaction.

The revolution Dewey brought about in American education can best be appreciated in terms of the conditions of the time. The American school system in the late nineteenth and early twentieth century was rigid, traditional, compartmentalized, isolated from the daily experiences of the pupils. The schools were poorly staffed by untrained teachers (receiving the "wages of unskilled labor," according to an 1872 report) and controlled by local politicians. There was neither a general program of national educational goals—various types of schools coexisted without connection in an atmosphere of pedagogical anarchy—nor a philosophy to make a meaningful tie between education and an expanding industrial society rooted in political democracy. Between the schools and the vigorous society around them, there were isolating walls. The two lived in separate worlds.

Dewey approached the educational situation and attacked the existing school system within a large framework of democratic thought. Democracy, as he defined it (in *Democracy and Education,* 1916) was "more than a form of government"; it was primarily "a mode of associated living, of conjoint communicated experience." As such, it had special needs, different from those of past societies. The difference lay essentially in economic dynamism and social mobility produced by modern science and industrialism. The new industrial age, Dewey saw as clearly as did Karl Marx in Europe, created revolutionary social change. It released human energies that affected ways of living and thinking. This continuing transformation necessitated, among other things, a thorough reexamination and reevaluation of the whole educational system and the philosophy behind it.

In *Democracy and Education,* Dewey wrote, "The widening of the area of shared concerns [political democracy], and the liberation of a greater diversity of personal capacities which characterize a democracy, are not of course the product of deliberation and conscious effort. On the contrary, they were caused by the development of modes of manufacture and commerce, travel, migration and intercommunication which flowed from the command of science over natural energy."

In the past, he pointed out, education had been based on a division of society into two major classes—"those who had to labor for a living and those who were relieved from this necessity." This division had roots in an economic system that consisted of a few owners and a multitude of slaves, and a theoretical, Aristotelian psychology that assumed the existence of unequal mental gifts among human beings. For more than two thousand years, he said, society operated on the theory that only a handful of men was capable of reason ("observation, meditation, cogitation, and speculation"), while the masses were moved by nothing but the lower appetites of human nature. Hence the organization of society into those capable of ruling (because they could learn and think) and those who were good only for labor.

Dewey rejected traditional psychology as unscientific and challenged the educational system as undemocratic. A libertarian society such as America could not continue to be educated in a framework based on ancient conceptions of hereditary superiors and natural inferiors. Modern education in a democracy must utilize the findings of psychology, which saw no proof of natural superiority based on status, and bring itself into line with the dynamism of an industrial society. This meant cutting across class barriers and opening educational opportunities to all the people.

"A society marked off into classes," Dewey wrote in *Democracy and Education,* "need be specially attentive only to the education of its ruling elements. A society which is mobile, which is full of channels for the distribution of a change occurring anywhere, must see to it that its members are educated to personal initiative and adaptability. Otherwise, they will be overwhelmed by the changes in which they are caught and whose significance they do not perceive."

It was not enough, Dewey argued, for the new education merely to dismiss ancient Greek philosophy or to change the theoretical symbols of old traditions. What was required was to reorganize the educational system by giving it a positive content and an integrated goal. The content was to consist of what is called "life situations," experiences that are understandable and ideas that are applicable to daily life. Students were to learn through practice, through questioning, through experimentation. Their interests were to be stimulated, and their values and attitudes shaped, not through inherited ideas or examples dictated to them by the teachers, but in a process of doing things freely in the classroom.

The goal of Dewey's educational philosophy was to serve "a truly democratic society" for the enjoyment of what he called "worthy leisure." Its purpose was to strengthen democracy by supplying the common people with wide opportunities for learning arts and skills. It sought to do so by the construction of a bridge over the long-accepted chasm between the cultural and the practical and thus unify society on levels of daily experience and action. The schools, in short, were to be harnessed directly to the service—and the level of understanding and interest—of the general population, rather than of a cultured elite.

Dewey lived to see his ideas on education and psychology transform the American school system and ultimately affect virtually every aspect of the nation's life. "Progressive education," in one form or another, penetrated the schools and homes. Dewey's name became a byword for what was both admirable and questionable in modern education. So great has been his educational influence that he has been blamed, often by poorly informed critics, for almost all the flaws in American schools, and even homes. In recent years, particularly as a result of increased juvenile delinquency throughout the nation and the reputed success of the Soviet Union's non-Deweyite educational system, he has been attacked not only for his pedagogical philosophy in general, but also for the excesses of fanciful educationalists experimenting in the name of "progressive education."

While much of the criticism is exaggerated and unjust to Dewey, it is not without some basis. Critics have four main arguments against American education as it has been developed by the disciples of Dewey:

1. *Education without content.* In its drive to please students by making them "happy," education has lost its inner meaning. The emphasis, particularly in training in the nation's teachers colleges, has been on method rather than on subject. Teachers' jobs depend upon the number of courses they take in "education"—*how* to teach. The *what,* or content, of education is of secondary importance.

2. *Sameness of values.* Since the stress is on method, it makes little difference what subject is being taught, so long as it holds the pupil's interest. The consequence has been that American schools, especially the high schools, have been overloaded with marginal and often frivolous subjects which have no cultural or serious educational value. Such subjects as woodworking, cooking, and trombone playing have the same educational rating (in that they lead to graduation) as mathematics, chemistry, or languages.

3. *Relativity of moral values.* The sameness of all subjects and the emphasis on "life situations" (play, immediate day-to-day experience, self-orientation), all but destroy discrimination in quality and moral principle. Since all things have more or less the same meaning, value judgments cease and the pupil is left to make his own unguided decisions as to what is "right" or "wrong."

4. *Lack of discipline.* Of all the criticisms leveled against the Dewey influence in education, this is probably the most serious. Lack of discipline in the schools has been a logical consequence of Dewey's pedagogic philosophy. His whole conception of the child—as a plastic being, with a personality to be respected, best developed only through doing, learning most effectively only when his interest is stimulated, capable of making choices, and a subject to be consulted ("coddled") in decisions regarding his own behavior—was bound to lead to a situation where neither teacher nor parent could possibly exert any meaningful authority. Yet both were expected to shape the child, to form his character, to provide him with leadership in the most impressionable years of life.

Dewey's critics argue that his whole conception of "education in a democracy and democracy in education," although plausible on the surface, contains within itself a grave contradiction. It has led to a dangerous oversimplification of the meaning of democracy and to a nearly fatal underestimation of the role of leadership in education.

Dewey, of course, knew better. In another context, that of politics, he wrote: "The fathers of our country belonged to an intellectual aristocracy; they shared in the intellectual enlightment of the eighteenth century. Franklin, Jefferson, John Adams, in their beliefs and ideas were men of the world. . . . Their free-thinking ideas did not prevent their being leaders. A generation later and it is doubtful if one of them could have been elected town selectman, much less have become a powerful political figure." ("The American Intellectual Frontier," *New Republic,* May 10, 1922)

Critics contend that Dewey's pedagogic influence, directly or indirectly reinforced (or elaborated upon) by Freudian psychology as applied to social institutions and behavior, must be held responsible for some of the moral chaos and intellectual sloppiness prevalent in the United States today. For example, Professor Richard La Piere in *The Freudian Ethic: An Analysis of the Subversion of American Character* (1959) argues that the Freudian ethic ("a doctrine of social irresponsibility and personal despair") has destroyed the crucial values of the older Protestant ethic and has undermined America's institutions of stability—homes, courts, schools. Of progressive education, he writes ironically: "The prime requisite for a truly progressive school is, therefore, complete freedom for the individual child to follow his personal inclinations"—to make him "wondrously adjusted to doing nothing at all."

Dewey's many defenders cite such charges as coming from sources that are biased against the philosophy of humanist liberalism. His enemies are considered "authoritarian" in politics as well as in religion.

In the field of political thought, Dewey did not develop an integrated theory. True to his general philosophy of pragmatism, he refused to be tied to a fixed conceptual framework of politics, preferring instead to be guided by events. He expressed his political ideas, occasionally with a theoretical slant, as they occurred and as they grew out of prevailing conditions at a given time. His politics, like his general philosophy, may thus be described as *instrumentalist.* Characteristically, his political ideas were molded as reactions to personal experience. This was in line with his theory that ideas did not exist as independent absolutes but were given substance through the "medium of individual temperament" and actions. "I reached fairly early . . . ," he wrote, "a belief in the intimate and indissoluble connections of means used and ends reached." Since thought and action are inseparable, it followed that the greater the individual's experience, the deeper and wider the forms of thought it shaped.

"I have usually . . . held an idea first in its abstract form . . . ," he explained. "Some personal experience, through contact with individuals, groups, or . . . peoples, was necessary to give the idea concrete significance. . . . I doubt if the force of the idea in the theory of social action would have come home to me without my experience in social and political movements."

It is understandable, therefore, that his political ideas and theories should have undergone changes, resulting from altered context of specific problems in different times. His political thought was thus a product of what the philosophers call "spatio-temporal conditions." He candidly admitted this in a letter, written on the eve of World War II, to his student, Chinese philosopher and Ambassador to the U.S. Hu Shih:

"You are quite right in suggesting that my political philosophy has changed in emphasis at least at various times, according to what was uppermost at the time. The economic collapse [of 1929], the reaction from the capitalistic orgies of the twenties, made me more socialistic than I had been—as in *Individualism Old and New* as well as in *Liberalism and Social Action*. . . . In my last change of emphasis, to which you refer, I have again been actuated by the principle of relativity."

At first, his political thought was unconnected with his technical philosophy and psychology. As a young teacher at the University of Michigan, he gave a course in political philosophy, discussing the usual topics (Hobbes, Locke, Rousseau, natural rights, jurisprudence) from the customary historical point of view. His personal position was that of an idealistic progressive; he supported William Jennings Bryan in 1892 (as he also did Theodore Roosevelt in the Bull Moose campaign of 1912), and believed in economic as well as political democracy. But these were general attitudes not integrated with his technical pursuits in philosophy.

He did not coordinate his political with his philosophic ideas until he moved to New York City. Here was a world different from the tree-lined campuses of Ann Arbor and Chicago. In America's greatest metropolis, the contrast between the promises of democracy and the practices of capitalism were so glaring that they roused the liberal intellectuals of the day to social reform. Dewey, with his pragmatic temperament and uncompromising honesty, was no exception. Challenged in mind and conscience, he responded with active participation in movements for the amelioration of conditions. The causes which engaged his active interest embraced the landscape of American liberalism—labor reform, progressive politics, improved schools, international peace, women's suffrage, individual justice, civil liberties. He became, in the words of Horace M. Kallen, "one of those rare philosophers whose life is his philosophy."

Kallen was for some thirty-five years professor of philosophy at the New School for Social Research, of which Dewey (with Charles A. Beard, Alvin Johnson and James Harvey Robinson) was one of the founders in 1919. Dewey was also first president of the People's Lobby; chairman of the League for Independent Political Action; head of a committee that exposed the fraudulent nature of Stalin's campaign against Trotsky; leading member of the international anticommunist Committee for Cultural Freedom. Referring to his full life of action, Professor Kallen said on Dewey's eightieth birthday: ". . . the philosopher has entered every one of the departments of the common life, the champion of freedom, of justice, of . . . tolerance. No person has been too unimportant, no cause too trivial, where a genuine issue of freedom was involved. Who can forget how he stood by Maxim Gorki when the hyenas of the yellow press were hounding him . . . ? Or how he marched in the parade that called for votes for women? As long as men will remember Sacco and Vanzetti they will remember Dewey's exposure of how these men were betrayed by class prejudice. Nor can one think of Leon Trotsky without thinking how Dewey championed his right to fair trial and true asylum. Where has there been a bondage which he has not sought to dissolve . . . , an oppressed minority for whose freedom he has not raised his voice?"

It was this continuous interaction between public activity and philosophic interest that led Dewey to formulate theories to fit events. He said of himself, "My ideas tend, because of my temperament, to take a schematic form in which logical consistency is a dominant consideration."

Dewey's theories of politics, never fully developed as a system, were as instrumentalist as his general philosophy and psychology. They were shaped by experience and intertwined with action. Under the impact of personal activities and travel abroad (China, Japan, Mexico, Turkey), his ideas underwent change. He insisted that the shifts were more in emphasis than in substance, but it is doubtful if the philosophic line between the two can be sharply drawn. The changes in his political position were more significant, certainly in their implications, than he was willing to admit. In his lectures in Japan in 1919, for example, he said that he was inclined to view the national state, once it had firmly established itself in power, as merely one of a number of instrumentalities in society. He compared the state to an orchestra conductor promoting and harmonizing the activities of other, "more voluntary forms of association." Its function was "limited to settling conflicts" among various competing groups. This was a theory fairly close to that of James Madison and the other founding fathers.

But in his Larwill Foundation Lectures at Kenyon College in 1926 Dewey dropped the "orchestra" theory of the state and replaced it with one that considered government ("there is no state without a government") the central instrument for the promotion of public welfare. The lectures were published in 1927 as *The Public and Its Problems,* which Dewey, in a letter to Hu Shih, said was "the best balanced of my writings . . . and also the most instrumental." Here, the change of position —from the idea of government as a kind of *primus inter pares* to that of its being an exclusive master—is a monumental one. The implications of Dewey's new conception would have shocked his liberal predecessors, notably Jefferson and Madison.

Defining the state as "the organization of the public effected through officials for the protection of the interests shared by its members," Dewey conceived of no restraints on the reach of its authority. As the sole welfare agent of society, Dewey wrote, government was a flexible instrument without "inherent limits" in the pursuit of its public objectives. Its functions must be left to fluid and variable needs and circumstances, and its activities must be judged only by its consequences, rather than by any preconceived moral–political criteria. Unlike the founding fathers with their dread of unrestrained political power, Dewey at this point visualized no need for any fences around governmental authority. On this crucial subject, which has always troubled political thinkers, Dewey's mind was open. "Our hypothesis," he wrote, "is neutral as to any general sweeping implications as to how far state activity may extend." He further developed the point in *The Public and Its Problems:*

"There is no more an inherent sanctity in a church, trade-union, business corporation, or family institution than there is in the state. Their value is also to be measured by their consequences. The consequences vary with concrete conditions; hence at one time and place a large measure of state activity may be indicated and at another time a policy of quiescence and *laissez faire*. Just as publics and states vary with conditions of time and place, so do the concrete functions which should be carried on by states. There is no antecedent universal proposition which can be laid down because of which functions of a state should be limited or should be expanded. The scope is something to be critically and experimentally determined."

What Dewey failed to realize was the terrible implications of this relativist political doctrine. Since government is an unrestrained machine for the solution of social problems, anything can obviously be justified in the name of public welfare and experimentation. Government thus conceived was pregnant with instability and dictatorship. A political mechanism, unchained by humane or moral considerations but activated only by the criterion of momentary usefulness, was a monster which ultimately could not avoid reliance on force. Dewey did not shy away from the use of force—if the ends justified it. He objected to coercion only if it was "wastefully" employed, that is, if it did not accomplish its objectives. He elaborated this position in *Characters and Events:*

"No ends are accomplished without the use of force. It is consequently no presumption against a measure, political, international, jural, economic, that it involves a use of force. Squeamishness about force is the mark not of idealistic but of moonstruck morals. But antecedent and abstract principles cannot be assigned to justify the use of force. The criterion of value lies in the relative efficiency and economy of the expenditure of force as a means to an end."

In his later years, Dewey again shifted his political position. This was a result of events in Europe. In the 1920s and 1930s, communists and fascists organized governments that were not far from Dewey's conception of the state as an amoral instrument uncontrolled by anything but utilitarian considerations. Lenin and Stalin, and Mussolini and Hitler, operating outside an established moral framework in the name of overriding utilitarianism, showed the ugly consequences of such an unchained monster state. Dewey, the passionate and embattled democrat, was dismayed by the practices of the totalitarians and once more changed his opinion. Writing on the eve of World War II, he candidly avowed his change of mind, declaring his faith in what was essentially Jeffersonian liberalism with emphasis on the human being as the core of organized society:

"I should now wish to emphasize more than I formerly did that individuals are the finally decisive factors of the nature and movement of associated life.... In rethinking this issue in the light of the rise of totalitarian states, I am led to emphasize the idea that only the voluntary initiative and voluntary cooperation of individuals can produce social institutions that will protect the liberties necessary for achieving development of genuine individuality."

The shortcomings in Dewey's thought, as it impinged on political institutions and actions, may be ascribed to his basic virtues. There was in his general political thinking a vein of naïveté astonishing in so seminal a mind; a trust in man's essential goodness not justified by history; a belief in human perfectability through education not proved by experience; a conviction that man has the capacity to organize his life intelligently to eliminate evil and injustice, based on a touching American idealism. Dewey's political thought was the large dream of a dedicated democrat who, in his unquenchable optimism, did not sufficiently consider the snares and dangers inherent in political power.

Dewey remained an optimist to the end of his life. On his eightieth birthday, speaking on "Creative Democracy: The Task Before Us," he reiterated his abiding trust in the potentialities of mankind. His final definition of democracy may be considered his testament: "Democracy is a way of life controlled by a working faith in the possibilities of human nature... as [it] is exhibited in every human being irrespective of race, color, sex, birth, and family, of material or cultural wealth.... Democracy is a way of personal life controlled... by faith in the capacity of human beings for intelligent judgment and action... democracy is belief in the ability of human experience to generate the aims and methods by which further experience will grow in ordered richness...."

# 18

## *THE AMERICAN AS NATIONALIST:*
# Theodore Roosevelt *(1858–1919)*

*Why, who can help but admire him? I differ with him on a great many questions, but they are the differences between men who both are seeking to do their best for the public good. Only he is doing it in the Republican way while I am trying to do it in a Democratic way.*
—*Franklin D. Roosevelt in an interview in* The New York Times (*January 22, 1911*)

*Thinking out loud, or at least seeming to do so, is one of [Theodore] Roosevelt's permanent contributions to the American political tradition. . . . He endued the cause of reform with the glamour of virility and vitality.*
—*John Dewey in* The Dial (*February 8, 1918*)

Theodore Roosevelt was the only Republican President in the twentieth century who combined dynamic action with a lively sense of social reform. In this respect he was closer to his younger kinsman, the Democrat Franklin D. Roosevelt, than to any Republican successor in the White House or, for that matter, any predecessor since Lincoln.

The reputation of Theodore Roosevelt—TR or "Teddy" to his contemporaries—has undergone changes since his presidency, which terminated in March 1909. In his own day, he was something of a fabulous figure on the American scene. Restlessly aggressive and immensely articulate, a coiner of stinging epithets and an activist for the sake of action, Roosevelt impressed himself upon his time as a colorful personality without peer in early-twentieth-century America. The period of TR's active political life—roughly from the time he became New York City's chief of police in 1895 to his candidacy for President on the Progressive Party ticket in 1912—may justly be described as the Roosevelt era.

TR came to personify American dynamism and activism to an extraordinary degree. Few public figures before him had so impressed their contemporaries (on both sides of the Atlantic) as did Theodore Roosevelt. The gleaming spectacles and the wide, white-toothed grin under the cavalryman's moustache became a symbol of masculine America. One Englishman referred to him as "a great wonder of nature." A "hearty, two-fisted fellow," Franklin Lane called him. A "lusty and bubbling enthusiast," said Amos Pinchot. John Dewey described him as "delirious with activity." The English writer and critic John Morley said that TR had "Napoleon's qualities." Rudyard Kipling, after seeing him for a "hectic half hour," thought him "scarce and valuable." A friendly colleague compared Roosevelt to a loudly chuffing engine, his steam always up. TR would sometimes rush to shake hands with a man whose hand he had just shaken, crying: "Bully! Splendid! Come in and see me!" and hurtle off.

There was more than mere animal magnetism to TR. He bubbled with ideas. He had an opinion on virtually every subject from art to zoology, and expressed himself with a torrential vigor which led his cool and scholarly rival, Woodrow Wilson, to remark drily, "I am told that he no sooner thinks than talks, which is a miracle not wholly in accord with the educational theory of forming an opinion."

Roosevelt's reputation faded after his death. Although his memory lived in the minds of many old-time progressives (such as Harold L. Ickes who, even as late as the New Deal, continued to regard TR as his greatest hero), a later generation of Americans failed to share their fathers' enthusiasm for the twenty-sixth President of the United States. For one thing, the aggressive nationalism tinged with militarism TR preached and believed in was distasteful to the Lost Generation of the post–World War I period. For another, Roosevelt's exhortatory political platitudes sounded hollow to those who lived through the period of the Great Depression and the New Deal. A shift in attitude toward TR did not begin until after World War II, when still another generation of Americans, living in a period of national uncertainty and international chaos, began to appreciate certain positive qualities that Roosevelt, the product of a more secure age, had possessed and proclaimed. Behind the torrent of words and often meaningless "he-man" activism, one may discover in TR a number of solid virtues—civic spirit, personal courage, self-reliance, and respect for the mind, for example—values important to preserve.

Theodore Roosevelt was born in New York City on October 27, 1858. His father, merchant-banker Theodore Roosevelt, was a seventh-generation New Yorker of Dutch descent. His mother, Martha Bulloch Roosevelt, a native of Georgia, was, unlike her Lincoln-Republican husband, a secessionist. Her adoring son described her as a "sweet, gracious, beautiful Southern woman" who remained "unreconstructed" to the end of her days.

Much of his character, his continuous aggressiveness and excessive activism, may be ascribed to what modern psychologists call over-compensation. Born physically weak, he suffered so much from asthma that one of his earliest memories was "sitting up in bed, gasping, with my father and mother trying to help me." He had weak muscles and was near-sighted.

"Having been a sickly boy, with no natural bodily prowess," he says in his *Autobiography* (1913), ". . . I was at first quite unable to hold my own . . . with other boys of rougher antecedents. I was nervous and timid. Yet from reading of the people I admired . . . I felt a great admiration for men who were fearless and who could hold their own in the world, and I had a great desire to be like them."

His father said to him: "You have the mind but not the body. . . . You must make your body. It is hard drudgery, but I know you will do it." Young Theodore took the challenge. "Bitterly conscious" of his physical inferiority, he decided to build his strength through rigorous training. He set up a gymnasium with bars and punching bag and learned to box. After a slow beginning, he became an expert boxer, good enough to knock out a desperado in a western barroom years later. He was always proud of his painfully acquired skill as a pugilist.

For the rest of his life he was to make a fetish of physical exertion, exposing himself to rigorous discipline and indulging in such adventures as big-game hunting. Once, thrown from a horse that landed on top of him, he remounted and leaped twenty fences despite a broken arm dangling at his side. On another occasion, in the far West, young Roosevelt pursued and finally caught a group of desperados through eleven days of blizzard. Thus, because he was born physically frail, he so over-compensated his deficiency that he made a lifelong philosophy of combativeness and of what he liked to call the "life of strenuous endeavor."

Biographer Carleton Putnam has described Roosevelt's unquenchable thirst for physical exertion as "unnecessarily heroic."

But activism and athleticism were only one aspect of TR's character. Another important facet was intellectualism. Side by side with a flamboyant pleasure in muscularity went a love of books and ideas. It was as if two personalities dwelt in TR: one was what his enemies called a showoff and blow-hard, a muscleflexer constantly relishing his physical prowess; and the other, a man of the mind, devouring books and hungrily reading poetry. Indeed, it has been suggested that TR was essentially a frustrated poet and scientist who happened to go into politics.

Roosevelt entered Harvard in 1876, at eighteen. His primary interest was then natural history. "My ambition," he says in his *Autobiography*, "was to be a scientific man" like Audubon and other naturalists. One of the classes he attended was that of zoology taught by Professor William James, whom, as we have seen, young Roosevelt—a "limelighter" in the words of a fellow student—used to challenge, to the wry amusement of the famous scholar. Roosevelt wanted to make science his life work, but his near-sightedness and the lack of opportunities for training in natural history at Harvard deflected this ambition. "I thoroughly enjoyed Harvard," he said later, "and I'm sure it did me good, but only in the general effect, for there was very little in my actual studies which helped me in afterlife."

Harvard, from which Roosevelt graduated in 1880, did not prepare him for a career in politics. Textbooks, particularly in the field of economics and politics, were remote from American realities and, above all, dogmatic in their point of view. As at Yale under the Spencerian influence of William Graham Sumner, so also at Harvard the economic doctrines of *laissez faire* were regarded as "canonical." The stress on devil-take-the-hindmost individualism in the economic sphere was vaguely offensive to the restless young New Yorker. Roosevelt comments in his *Autobiography:*

"All this individual morality I was taught by the books I read at home and the books I studied at Harvard. But there was almost no teaching of the need for collective action, and of the fact that in addition to . . . individual responsibility, there is a collective responsibility. Books such as Herbert Croly's *Promise of American Life* and Walter E. Weyl's *New Democracy* would generally at that time have been treated either as unintelligible or else as pure heresy."

Roosevelt's education did not cease with his graduation from Harvard. Reading and writing remained a passion for the rest of his life.

In a relatively short and thoroughly busy life, he published some thirty books, including works on history, biography, and natural history. He was a voluminous letter writer, pouring himself out in millions of words on practically everything.

As a reader of books, he was unequaled among the political figures of his time. He read widely and discriminately and had an astonishingly retentive memory. Van Wyck Brooks mentions in his *Notebook* that when he was at college, TR made a visit there and met the English author, W. H. Mallock. Roosevelt grasped the English writer's hand and "he poured forth a flood of comment on Mallock's views and books, every one of which he seemed to have read and remembered. It was like Niagara falling on a fern, for the little old man was stunned with confusion and pleasure."

As with everything else, Roosevelt had emphatic ideas about reading and literature. "The equation of personal taste is powerful in reading as in eating"; he said, "and within certain broad limits, the matter is merely one of individual preference, having nothing to do with the quality either of the book or the reader's mind. I like apples, pears, oranges, pineapples and peaches. I dislike bananas, alligator-pears and prunes. The first fact is certainly not to my credit, although it is to my advantage; and the second at least does not show moral turpitude. . . . A man with a real fondness for books of various kinds will find that his varying moods determine which of these books he at the moment needs. On the afternoon when Stevenson represents the luxury of enjoyment it may be safely assumed that Gibbon will not. The mood that is met by Napier's *Peninsular War,* or Marbot's *Memoirs,* will certainly not be met by Hawthorne and Jane Austen."

Roosevelt read much of the world's great literature in its original language—the *Chanson de Roland* in French and Ferrero's *Greatness and Decline of Rome* in Italian, for example. He had a special love for poetry. "I suppose," he wrote in 1915, "that everyone passes through periods during which he reads poetry; and some people, of whom I am one, also pass through periods during which they voraciously devour poets of widely different kinds." Among the poets whom he devoured were Horace and Pope, Schiller and Longfellow, Bret Harte and Kipling ("Kipling is an underbred little fellow . . . , but he is a genius"), Shelley and Tennyson, Poe and Coleridge, Emerson and Browning, as well as Dante and Whitman. He once compared the author of the *Divine Comedy* with the author of *Leaves of Grass,* saying that each expressed the "ordinary humanity of his day." His interest in American poetry was such that he found Edwin Arlington Robinson ("What a queer, mystical creature he is! . . . But he certainly has the real spirit of poetry in him.") a government job and tried to do the same for Bliss Carman.

Even as President, TR was an insatiable reader, possibly the greatest consumer of books since Jefferson. Unlike Woodrow Wilson and Herbert Hoover, who were, according to a White House aide, "incessant detective story readers," and unlike William Howard Taft and Calvin Coolidge, whose reading was confined to newspapers, Roosevelt consumed serious books at a fast and furious pace—and infected his whole family with his passion for reading. "The President," said Irwin Hood (Ike) Hoover, in his *Forty-Two Years in the White House* (1934), ". . . would just devour a book, and it was no uncommon thing for him to go entirely through three or four volumes in the course of an evening." Such reading was an emotional necessity to him.

"I find reading a great comfort," TR wrote to the English historian, George Otto Trevelyan, in 1904. "People often say to me that they do not see how I find time for it, to which I answer . . . that to me it is a dissipation . . . instead of an irksome duty . . . there are a great many books which ordinarily pass for 'dry' which to me do possess much interest—notably history and anthropology; and these give me ease and relaxation that I can get in no other way, not even on horseback."

As occupant of the White House, Roosevelt violated the century-old tradition that a politician should shun men of the mind. Unashamedly, he invited novelists, poets, philosophers and historians there. Characteristically, he also played host to pugilists and wrestlers, but the latter did not shock the politicians as much as the intellectuals did. Gerald W. Johnson remarks in *The Lunatic Fringe* (1957), "Roosevelt did more than any President since the Virginia dynasty to make it respectable to admit having read a book."

Roosevelt entered politics soon after he graduated from Harvard, at a time of all-pervasive corruption when gentlemen avoided political life as low and dirty. But as TR told his Alpha Delta Phi fraternity brothers, "I'm going to try to help the cause of better government." Against the advice of his wealthy and educated friends, he joined the Twenty-First District Republican Club in Manhattan and, in 1881, at twenty-three, was elected to the New York Assembly, where he served three successive terms.

The lower house of the New York state legislature was Roosevelt's first postgraduate school in politics. He found that while the majority of assemblymen were probably honest, an uncomfortably large number were crooked. "I never had anything in the nature of legal proof of corruption. . . ." he tells. "But three years' experience convinced me . . . that there were a great many thoroughly corrupt men in the legislature, perhaps a third of the whole number." The legislature was manipulated by a small group of men powerful in the economic life of the country. Soon after his election, a prominent lawyer friend asked TR to lunch and suggested that he play his hand cautiously. The lawyer explained that there existed an "inner circle of power" which included "certain big businessmen and the politicians, lawyers and judges." The young assemblyman was told that anyone who wanted to get ahead "in law, business or politics must have the backing of these forces." This conversation, Roosevelt relates in his *Autobiography,* "made such an impression that I always remembered it." He thus had his eyes opened to a fact that such critics of the American scene as Henry George had long proclaimed—that the masters of the American economy also controlled the political machinery of the nation. "It was," he said, "the first glimpse I had of that combination between business and politics which I was in after years so often to oppose."

After his experience in the legislature, where he began "rather timidly to strive for social and industrial justice," young Roosevelt left New York for the far West to recover from asthma. In the North Dakota Territory he ran a cattle ranch for three years, riding the range in buckskins, and taking tremendous enjoyment in what he called the masterful and virile West. Invigorated by the western outdoors, he returned to New York City, ran unsuccessfully for mayor against Henry George and Abram Hewitt (who won), and in 1889 (at thirty-one) was appointed member of the United States Civil Service Commission, on which he served under Presidents Benjamin Harrison and Grover Cleveland for six years. His subsequent political career moved rapidly.

In 1895, TR became president of the New York City Police Board, the equivalent of Police Commissioner today. By ejecting corrupt policemen and attacking the slums of New York, he garnered invaluable headlines in the newspapers. Two years later he became Assistant Secretary of the Navy under President McKinley. Following a brief but flamboyant experience as colonel of the "Rough Riders" in Cuba during the Spanish-American conflict which Roosevelt's friend, (subsequently his secretary of state) John Hay, described as "a splendid little war," TR achieved the stature of a national hero—which he never lost. The next year the Colonel, enhaloed by the reputation of his picturesque cavalry charge on Cuba's San Juan hill, was nominated and elected governor of New York. His name was now a household word. Having made an excellent record as governor, he was nominated for the vice-presidency on the Republican ticket in 1900.

The nomination, engineered by New York state Republican boss, Tom Platt, was not a reward for services performed but a way of getting the ebullient hero out of the state. TR was, in effect, "kicked upstairs," particularly since the vice-presidency was, both under the Constitution and in practice, an innocuous office. The machine politicians hoped to get rid of Roosevelt, knowing that as Vice-President he could do nothing. But shrewd Republican President-maker, Mark Hanna of Ohio, had his doubts. "Don't any of you realize," he said, "that there's only one life between this madman and the White House?" Hanna's worst fears were soon to be realized. In September 1901, half a year after TR was sworn in as Vice-President, President McKinley was assassinated. "That damned cowboy *is* in the White House," Mark Hanna said. Roosevelt was then just under forty-three years old—the youngest man ever to become President of the United States.

It was the beginning of a new era in the White House. The change in atmosphere was both personal and political. McKinley, the man whom TR succeeded, had been a gentle nonentity, a pleasant politician with no apparent enthusiasm either for thought or for action. He had been what the masters of the economy had long expected a President to be—a dignified figurehead. TR, with his penchant for brilliant phrase-making, once said of McKinley that he had "no more backbone than a chocolate eclair."

TR had definite views on the functions of the presidency. With few exceptions, Presidents had taken the position that their powers and duties were limited under the Constitution and that they could not, and should not, act for the national welfare unless there existed some specific legal authorization. But the history-minded Roosevelt knew that there had been some strong Presidents in the past. In his *Autobiography,* written after he left the White House, he made a distinction between what he called the Lincoln–Jackson and the Buchanan–Taft types of President. The latter he considered unwise, representing, he said, "simple weakness of character and desire to avoid trouble and responsibility." The Lincoln–Jackson type, on which TR modeled himself, appealed to him because of his admiration for both men, who in his view represented vigorous leadership.

"My view was," he explained in the *Autobiography,* "that every executive officer . . . was a steward of the people bound actively and affirmatively to do all he could for the people, and not to content himself with the negative merit of keeping his talents undamaged in a napkin. I declined to adopt the view that what was imperatively necessary for the nation could not be done by the President unless he could find some specific authorization to do it. My belief was that it was not only his right but his duty to do anything that the needs of the nation demanded unless such action was forbidden by the Constitution or by the laws. Under this interpretation of Executive power I did and caused to be done many things not previously done by the President and the heads of the departments. I did not usurp power, but I did greatly broaden the use of Executive power."

To understand Roosevelt's policies, it must be kept in mind that despite the vigor of his language and the animosity he aroused in conservative circles, he was no radical. TR actually hated radicals of every kind, referring to a man like Tom Paine as "a dirty little atheist" and making intemperate personal attacks on such active liberals as John Peter Altgeld. Roosevelt had no sympathy whatever for the progressive movements of his day and detested socialism as un-American. But as a shrewd politician, he knew that the Republican Party, in order to survive in what the New York *World* called a period of "social revolution," must adopt some reforms. This realization Woodrow Wilson also arrived at in connection with the Democratic Party.

Roosevelt, nevertheless, had a streak of liberalism. This was especially noticeable in his views on the multiple origin of the nation and on the role of minorities. To him America was a fusion of many races, and true Americanism was therefore not a matter of birthplace or nationality but of principle and character. If there were any line of division, he said in Spokane in 1903, it should not be drawn by creed or class but by conduct—"the line that divides the honest from the dishonest . . . good citizenship from bad." The essence of Americanism was to respect the individual, regardless of his origin or status, and to harmonize interests, no matter how diverse.

In this spirit, TR invited a Negro to dinner at the White House and appointed a Jew to a cabinet position. In November 1901, he outraged southern feeling by asking Booker T. Washington, the Negro scientist whose work at Tuskegee Institute he greatly admired, to dine with him. "The clamor aroused by the act," he said, "makes me feel as if the act was necessary." In 1906, he appointed Oscar S. Straus Secretary of

Commerce and Labor—the first cabinet position held by a person of Jewish faith (if one excludes the Confederacy's Secretary of State, Judah Benjamin) up to that time. All this was undoubtedly good politics, but it also expressed Roosevelt's strong bias in favor of racial and religious tolerance.

"I notice," he wrote to Straus in 1904, "that various Democratic papers . . . have endeavored to show that I have appealed to the Jew vote, the Catholic vote, etc. Now the fact is that I have not appealed to any man as Jew, as Protestant, or as Catholic, but that I have as strongly as in me lies endeavored to make it evident that each is to have a square deal, no more and no less, without regard to his creed. I hope that this country will continue in substantially its present form of government for many centuries. If this is so, it is reasonable to suppose that during that time there will be Presidents of Jewish faith, Presidents of Catholic faith. Now, my aim as President is to behave toward the Jew and the Catholic just as I should wish a Jewish or Catholic President to behave toward Protestants . . . as a good American should behave . . . without regard to the several creeds they profess or the several lands from which their ancestors have sprung."

In the field of economic and social policy, TR developed a special technique which, it must be admitted, was compatible with his character—talking reform while leaving fundamental problems unsolved. This was not hypocrisy; TR, a genuinely kindly man, really wanted to see all Americans enjoy a "square deal," but without in any way changing the basic economic and class structure of the country.

He asserted presidential power and influence in three general areas. One was in the field of labor relations, the second in the area of corporate monopoly, the third in foreign policy. In each of these spheres, he took a certain amount of action which, although rarely decisive or lasting, nevertheless was of significance in that it created precedents and crystallized public opinion.

In labor matters, Roosevelt was a liberal in speech. The labor movement of his time was weak, unrespected, and exposed to constant violence and harassment. Union leaders were widely regarded as alien agitators on the margin of criminality. Strikes were considered and treated as criminal acts against society, to be crushed by force. Only about a decade before TR entered the White House, his Democratic predecessor, Grover Cleveland, had sent federal troops to Chicago to cripple the Pullman employees' strike for better hours and wages. It was customary for working men, women, and children to labor from sunrise to sunset. Anyone who advocated a twelve-hour working day was considered—even by TR—an un-American socialist.

The American Federation of Labor, led by Samuel Gompers, struggled for union recognition against middle-class and governmental hostility. Its policy was to strengthen its position by opposing the employment of those who were not union members. One such case, that of a postal employee named Miller, gave President Roosevelt a chance to express his position in regard to labor. He had said, in a speech to the Brotherhood of Locomotive Firemen at Chattanooga in 1902: "I believe emphatically in organized labor," adding that he admired anybody who worked hard. But TR had no real understanding of the function of organized labor vis-à-vis the powerful corporations. In the case of the discharged Miller, Roosevelt reinstated him despite the vigorous protests of the American Federation of Labor that he was not a union member. The President replied characteristically in words that were highly patriotic and democratic but, by implication, inimical to organized labor:

"I am President of all the people of the United States, without regard to creed, color, birthplace, occupation, or social condition. My aim is to do equal and exact justice as among them all. In the employment and dismissal of men in the Government service, I can no more recognize the fact that a man does or does not belong to a union, as being for or against him, than I can recognize the fact that he is a Protestant or a Catholic, a Jew or a Gentile, as being for or against him."

Labor accordingly deserved no more (and no less) consideration or protection than capital. TR equated the feeble labor movement with the all-powerful business combinations. "We can no more afford to tolerate tyranny from a labor union than we can afford to tolerate it from a trust," the President wrote to his attorney general, Philander C. Knox. One is reminded of Anatole France's ironic remark about the French judicial system—that the law in its majestic impartiality prohibits rich and poor alike from sleeping under bridges.

Roosevelt's experience in the 1902 coal strike should have taught him a sharp lesson in labor-management relations. The United Mine Workers, pitifully underpaid, had gone out on a strike which the coal owners ("operators") refused to settle for many months. As coal was becoming scarce and people faced a winter without heat, President Roosevelt tried to mediate between the miners and the operators. His well-meaning move was attacked in the press as dangerous, the New York *Journal of*

*Commerce* criticizing TR's "uncontrollable penchant for impulsive self-intrusion." George F. Baer, representing the Wall Street-owned mines, refused to deal with what he called the "labor agitators," saying that the interests of the miners were best protected not by their union but "by the Christian men to whom God, in his Infinite Wisdom, has given control of the property interests of the country." Faced with such intransigence, Roosevelt, without legal authority to compel a settlement, called in the representatives of both the miners and the owners and forced an end to the strike by threatening to appeal to public opinion. The operators made a partial wage concession, and the President went on believing, or pretending to believe, that there was no difference in the power exercised by the labor unions and the industrial corporations.

It was with his policy regarding business monopolies that TR stirred keenest public interest. Gigantic corporations dominated the nation's economic life. Three trusts, oil, paper and steel, controlled three fourths of the total production in those fields. Concentration of industrial power, through interlocking directorates and financial manipulation, had gone so far that thousands of smaller businessmen, unable to meet the competition of the giant trusts (which fixed prices arbitrarily), were ruined. Throttling all competitors, the trusts rode roughshod over all opposition, controlling, as TR well knew, the political machinery, often including the judiciary, by means of social coercion, honorific rewards, or outright bribery. "The banks," said Grover Cleveland, during whose administration the J. P. Morgan syndicate made millions of dollars of profit in United States bonds, "have got the country by the throat."

Roosevelt was less passive about this stranglehold than his Democratic predecessor. He worried about the consequences of this concentrated economic power upon the country's democratic future. Both as a partisan Republican and a patriotic democrat, he felt that the economic domination of a plutocracy was fraught with ultimate danger to his own party and to the nation's political freedom. He was fully alive to the vigorous and widespread protest movements—on the part of farmers, workers, intellectuals, and the lower middle class—against Big Business and sensed that the time was ripe for some sort of action against the unprecedented monopolies.

In his *Autobiography,* he wrote: "There had been in our country a riot of individualistic materialism under which complete freedom for the individual . . . turned out in practice to mean perfect freedom for the strong to wrong the weak. The total absence of government control had led to a portentous growth in . . . corporations. In no other country in the world had such enormous fortunes been gained. . . . The power of the mighty industrial overlords of the country had increased with giant strides, while the methods of controlling them, or checking abuses by them, on the part of the people through the Government, remained archaic and therefore practically impotent."

The Sherman Antitrust Law of 1890, designed to control economic monopolies, was practically a dead letter. During the administration of Benjamin Harrison there had been only three indictments under the Sherman Act, only two in Cleveland's, and none in McKinley's. The Sherman Act was ineffectual for two main reasons. In the first place, government—generally in the hands of lawyers allied with or dependent upon business—was unwilling to prosecute. Second, the courts, made up of conservative judges, were unsympathetic to any legislation that involved meddling with the *laissez-faire* economic system.

"The Courts . . . had for a quarter of a century been on the whole the agents of reaction," TR continued in his *Autobiography,* "and, by conflicting decisions which, however, in their sum were hostile to the interests of the people, had left both the nation and the several States well-nigh impotent to deal with the great business combinations. . . . They had rendered these decisions sometimes as upholders of property rights against human rights . . . ; and sometimes in the name of liberty . . . , which secured to the powerful the freedom to prey on the poor and the helpless."

Roosevelt decided to do something about the situation. His objective was to try to break up the giant monopolies and thereby restore business competition. He was not opposed to business or the economic system. Again and again he repeated, or found it necessary to repeat, that he was not against property but only against monopoly. "When I ask that the question of trusts be taken up," he said in a speech at Boston in 1902, "I am acting in the most conservative sense in property's interest. When a great corporation is sued for violating the Anti-Trust Law, it is not a move against property, it is a move in favor of property." Similarly, in his message to Congress on December 2, 1902, he stated: "Our aim is not to do away with the corporations; on the contrary, these big aggregations are an inevitable development of modern industrialism. . . . We draw the line against misconduct, not against wealth."

The most famous case of TR's policy of enforcing the Sherman Act was that of the Northern Securities Company in 1902. It involved a merger of two great railroads, the Northern Pacific and the Chicago, Burlington and Quincy, an arrangement planned by the two financial giants J. P. Morgan and James J. Hill. When rumor of the merger reached Washington, TR expressed his opinion that it violated the Sherman Act. Whereupon Morgan went to the White House and, in the imperious tone of one feudal chieftain speaking to another, said to the President of the United States: "If we have done anything wrong, send your man [U.S. Attorney General Knox] to my man [one of Morgan's lawyers] and they can fix it up." "That," said the President, "can't be done. We don't want to fix it up." When Morgan left, TR remarked to his attorney general: "That is the most illuminating illustration of the Wall Street point of view. Mr. Morgan could not help regarding me as a big rival operator, who either intended to ruin all his interests or else could be induced to come to an agreement to ruin none."

Ignoring Morgan's displeasure, TR ordered suit brought against the Northern Securities Company for violating the Sherman Act and won the case. The United States Supreme Court, in 1904, upheld the decision and ordered the Northern Securities Company to dissolve. It was the first major triumph of Roosevelt's antitrust campaign; but it was somewhat marred by the position taken by Oliver Wendell Holmes, whom TR had recently appointed to the Court in the confident belief that the new justice shared his economic views. In the Northern Securities case, however, Holmes sided with the minority of the Court, reputedly causing TR to exclaim angrily: "I could carve out of a banana a Justice with more backbone than that."

Inevitably, TR's trustbusting made enemies in Wall Street. Morgan, for one, never forgave him. Amos Pinchot relates that some years after the Northern Securities case, Morgan visited his house and said to him furiously: "I don't like your friend Roosevelt; he's no good." He was so shaken by his sudden rage that he missed his footing, tripped on the steps and fell down the stoop. Such hostility did not trouble TR unduly. "These jacks in Wall Street," he said to the attorney general, ". . . never will understand that I am not against wealth because I make wealth obey the law. But they have to take their medicine."

In other domestic affairs President Roosevelt had no organized or prepared program. "I cannot say," he admitted, "that I entered the Presidency with any deliberately planned and far-reaching scheme of social betterment." Nevertheless his administration adopted a limited number of progressive measures, designed, he said, to help the American people "better themselves . . . politically, socially, and industrially."

During TR's second term (to which he was elected in 1904 by 7,628,834 votes against 5,084,491 for the Democratic candidate, Alton

B. Parker), a number of reform bills were passed. Among them were the Hepburn Act, regulating railroad rates; the Pure Food and Drug Act, providing penalties for use of injurious substances and false labeling; the Meat Inspection Act, requiring federal supervision of slaughtering sanitation. These, together with an important governors' conference on the conservation of natural resources, were Roosevelt's main achievements in the realm of social reform. They widened to a certain extent the area of governmental controls, but did not substantially alter the trend or complexion of the national economy. Indeed, despite TR's other antitrust suits, even against such giants as Rockefeller's Standard Oil Company, the monopolies grew richer and more powerful than ever. Real reforms—affecting the fundamental interests of the whole nation and extending the government's power to protect the economically weak and underprivileged—did not take place on any substantial scale for another third of a century, when another Roosevelt entered the White House.

In foreign affairs, TR's role had significance in two important respects. He was the first President in modern times to alert the American people to the fact that international politics was assuming importance in their lives; by precept and example, he served as teacher to the nation. He also helped crystallize public opinion concerning the role of power, and the meaning of the balance of power, in international relations.

Roosevelt's contribution to foreign policy can best be appreciated in terms of historic background and development. After the Civil War, the United States had grown and developed its vast resources in an atmosphere of security. Its flanks protected by two great oceans, the country felt no need to concern itself with foreign affairs or to pay much heed to the meaning of power in international relations. But TR, with his insatiable intellectual curiosity and sense of reality about the world, realized that the nineteenth-century era of isolation was coming to an end. America, with a population of some hundred million, was becoming too powerful and loomed too large in the eyes of the world to continue the luxury of nonparticipation in affairs abroad. Roosevelt also knew that the world's great powers, bristling with military and naval armament, were maneuvering dangerously to enhance their strategic and colonial positions on a global scale. At both extremes of the globe, mighty forces were at play, threatening existing international relationships. In Europe a newly united and powerfully militarized Germany was pushing its aggressive designs at such a tempo that it shook the precarious balance of power established at the Congress of Vienna in 1815. In the

Far East, the Japanese had emerged with astonishing rapidity from their medieval isolation to become a major naval and industrial power.

President Roosevelt was determined that the country should be awakened to this new age of power. In his inaugural address (March 4, 1905), he warned:

"We are the heirs of the ages. . . . We have become a great nation . . . , and we must behave as beseems a people with such responsibility . . . Power invariably means both responsibility and danger."

During the Spanish-American War, TR had advocated a course of military imperialism which angered pacifists, among them William James. But Roosevelt, following his conviction that the United States must play an active role in foreign affairs, inaugurated a policy of intervention in international affairs. He was not emotionally committed to any one nation, nor was he, like Woodrow Wilson in World War I, moralistic in his approach to foreign policy. TR thought of international politics in terms of power and and not in terms of righteousness. "Very early," he once said, "I learned through my reading of history . . . to pay heed to the needs of the nation from the international standpoint. . . . The most woeful example . . . of ruin . . . comes to a nation which cannot defend itself against aggression." A big-navy man, Roosevelt sent the United States fleet, painted a startling white, around the world to impress the nations with American power. "I never take a step in foreign policy," he said, "unless I'm assured that I shall be able eventually to carry out my will by force."

His foreign policy might be described as dynamic neutralism, consisting of the use of America's power—his "big stick"—to keep the international balance from tilting unduly. When the Russo-Japanese War broke out in 1904, TR quietly warned Germany and France that if they intervened against Japan the United States would "proceed to whatever lengths necessary." But when Japan surprised the world by defeating the Russians, Roosevelt moved to mediate and to prevent too great a weakening of Russia's power in the Pacific. Under TR's aegis, that Pacific war, seemingly as remote from America's interest as it was from its shores, was actually terminated by treaty in the United States—at Portsmouth, New Hampshire, in 1905. In 1906, at the Algeciras conference on the question of Morocco, TR's position in favor of France influenced the German Kaiser to back down. Roosevelt's skillful diplomacy won him the Nobel Peace Prize in 1906.

Characteristic of Roosevelt's use of power without squeamishness in defense of the national security was the acquisition of the Panama Canal

Zone. Considering a canal imperative for the protection of both United States coasts, Roosevelt supported a Panamanian rebellion against Colombia—which owned the vital strip of land. The United States then recognized Panama's independence and bought from it perpetual control of the Canal Zone—where the Canal was built and completed in 1915, in time for use in World War I. Roosevelt told two stories about the whole affair. At a cabinet meeting in which he buoyantly reported the "taking of Panama," he asked for a constitutional opinion on the subject. "Oh, Mr. President," Attorney General Knox said ironically, "do not let so great an achievement suffer from any taint of legality." Some years later, TR remarked to a friend:

"It is said that I started a revolution in Panama. The fact is, there had been fifty revolutions in Panama from time to time, but while I was President, I kept my foot on these revolutions; so that, when the Panama Canal situation arose, it was entirely unnecessary for me to start a revolution. I simply lifted my foot."

The Panama Canal was Roosevelt's last important achievement. His later years were anticlimax. He left the White House in 1909, a national and world hero—a "Yankee Prince," in the words of George M. Cohan—and soon found that there was nothing really left for him to do. Still relatively young at fifty, the ex-President, a combination of "St. Vitus and St. Paul," to quote a contemporary, had no outlet for his bursting energies. He went abroad, where he wandered for sixteen months. By the time of his return in July 1910, he was bitterly disappointed in his personally selected successor, William Howard Taft. In TR's opinion, the exceedingly obese Taft, characterized by Senator J. P. Dolliver of Iowa, as "an amiable island, entirely surrounded by men who knew exactly what they want," had surrendered the Republican Party to the reactionaries. In 1912, Roosevelt launched his own candidacy for President on the independent Progressive Party ticket, with the slogan "We stand at Armageddon, and We Battle for the Lord." But the sound and the fury did not prevail against the entrenched political machines. TR's Bull Moose campaign only succeeded in splitting the Republican vote (4,126,020 for Roosevelt and 3,483,922 for Taft), and electing Democrat Woodrow Wilson.

Roosevelt henceforth was a man lost and bewildered, with nowhere to go politically. His judgment of men and events seems to have deserted him. Frustrated and restless, he went abroad again, this time to explore the jungles of Brazil. "It was my last chance to be a boy," he said with unconscious pathos, thus confirming William James' opinion that even as an adult, Roosevelt suffered from *"Sturm und Drang* adolescence." Stricken with jungle fever and reduced to a gaunt skeleton, TR came home to a world which seemed to have no useful function for him. It was a case of other times, other heroes. He vented his impotent fury on President Wilson, whose policy of neutrality in the first phase of World War I Roosevelt characterized as "yellow." The final humiliation for TR was Wilson's refusal to let him, an aging and ailing civilian, raise a division of volunteers to fight in Europe.

TR's last months were saddened by illness and inactivity. Blind in one eye and partly deaf, his political opinions warped by hatreds, he died on January 6, 1919, of an embolism in the coronary artery. He was sixty; his strenuous and hectic life had come to an end "beset by a sense of inadequacy." But in the judgment of history, Roosevelt emerges a man who played a vigorous role in the shaping of the American political character and tradition.

# 19

## *THE AMERICAN AS LIBERAL:*
## Woodrow Wilson *(1856–1924)*

*Of course, as I once said about [John] Marshall, you can't really separate a man from the place he filled. His environment is part of him and Wilson was the nominal head of a great nation in a great war. But I never read anything of his that seemed to me anywhere near first rate—and I can't help surmising that his supposed idealism was Number One.*

*—Oliver Wendell Holmes*
*to Harold Laski (February 17, 1924)*

Thomas Woodrow Wilson was born in Staunton, Virginia, at the foot of the Blue Ridge Mountains four years before the Civil War, on December 28, 1856. Woodrow Wilson was the name he decided upon before achieving prominence. Autographs in his library books show that he had variously signed himself "Thomas W. Wilson," "Thomas Woodrow Wilson," "T.W. Wilson," and "T. Woodrow Wilson." The earliest influences upon him were southern and Presbyterian. He spent the first twenty-nine years of his life in the South, the family having moved first to Augusta, Georgia, and then to Columbia, South Carolina. Wilson's father, the Reverend Doctor Joseph Ruggles Wilson, was an eminent clergyman in whose house the Southern Presbyterian church was organized when the Civil War broke out. Presbyterianism was ingrained on both sides of Woodrow Wilson's Scotch-Irish family. His mother was the daughter of a Presbyterian minister in England. His grandfather, Thomas Woodrow, after whom he was named, and his uncle, James Woodrow, were likewise

Presbyterian clergymen. The future President himself received his elementary and college education in Presbyterian institutions—Davidson College in North Carolina and the College of New Jersey (which became Princeton University in 1896), from which he graduated in 1879. He studied law at the University of Virginia, practiced for a little over a year in Atlanta, then entered Johns Hopkins University, and received his Ph.D. there in 1886.

Wilson's academic career can be summarized briefly. In 1885, after publication of his doctoral dissertation, *Congressional Government,* he became associate professor of history and political economy at Bryn Mawr College, where he remained for three years. He then moved to Wesleyan University, where he taught the same subjects. Two years later, in September 1890, Dr. Wilson was appointed professor of jurisprudence and political economy at his alma mater, of which he became president in June 1902. As president of Princeton, Wilson achieved the prominence that ultimately catapulted him onto the national scene.

Wilson's successful educational reform program there, together with his brilliant articulateness as a lecturer, brought him to the attention of influential Democratic politicians and editors, such as George Harvey of *Harper's Weekly.* He was elected governor of New Jersey in 1910; his administrative record was so outstanding that two years later he was nominated Democratic presidential candidate, after forty-six ballots. Because the Republicans split between Theodore Roosevelt and William Howard Taft, Wilson, although he polled only about 40 per cent of the vote (some six million out of fifteen million) was elected President. His electoral college vote was 435 out of 531.

Wilson's rise to political eminence was thus comparatively swift and, to the nation in general, surprising. He was not nearly so well known as William Jennings Bryan, then the dominant figure of the Democratic party. Nor did he loom as a political hero like his Republican rival, Theodore Roosevelt. He had few of the qualities of the successful politician. He was unbending, intellectual, and cool. As the nation was soon to discover, he also had a powerful streak of idealism fortified by the stubbornness of an inherited Calvinism. "My ancestors," he said, "were troublesome Scotsmen, and among them were some of that famous group known as Covenanters."

Intellectually, the influences on Wilson were historical and literary. During his academic career, which spanned about a quarter of a century, he published half a dozen volumes of political and historical studies—among them *The State* (1889), *Division and Reunion, 1829–1889*

(1893), *George Washington* (1897), *A History of the American People* (five volumes, 1902), and *Constitutional Government in the United States* (1908), as well as five volumes of social and literary essays and studies. In addition, his 1912 campaign speeches were published as *The New Freedom: a Call for the Emancipation of the Generous Energies of a People* (1913). Only his two early books, *The State* and *Division and Reunion* were based on genuine research that earned him a deserved reputation as a scholar. The other works were more popularizations than original scholarship.

Wilson, indeed, did not possess a deep or wide education. He knew no foreign languages. He was not in touch with the scientific and technological developments of his age. He had no acquaintance with world literature. He cared practically nothing about music and art. His reading was confined mainly to the traditional English literary figures: Shelley, Keats, Tennyson, Browning, Arnold, Swinburne, and Wordsworth; Sir Walter Scott, Jane Austen, and Stanley Weyman; such essayists as Charles Lamb, Gilbert K. Chesterton, and Walter Bagehot, who was Wilson's particular favorite; such historians as Macaulay and Green.

Wilson felt that books of poetry, ballads, narratives, and novels served to stimulate the imagination, deepen the mind, and enrich the personal life. Literary books, he felt, were the true teachers of wisdom and sources of idealism, as well as of experience, including political experience. In 1895 he wrote:

"There is more of a nation's politics to be got out of its poetry than out of all its systematic writers upon public affairs and constitutions. Epics are better mirrors of manners than chronicles; dramas oftentimes let you into the secrets of statutes; orations . . . contain more history than parliamentary journals. It is not knowledge that moves the world, but ideals, convictions . . . opinions or fancies. . . ."

Wilson's reading practically stopped when he became an administrator, first at Princeton, then in the White House. As President, he read detective stories. In 1916, he frankly told a reporter: "I haven't read a serious book through for fourteen years."

In private life, Wilson had charm and courtesy; he also possessed a gift for jokes and mimicry. Like Abraham Lincoln he delighted in humorous anecdotes, and he enhanced them with hilarious imitations of Irish, Scottish, and Negro accents. His sense of humor, while professorial, at times had a Gallic flavor. Once a mother of one of his students suggested that he make Princeton coeducational. "Why?" he asked. She answered: "To remove the false glamor with which the two sexes see each other."

"My dear madam," replied the president of Princeton, "that is the very thing we want to preserve at all costs."

Wilson had a special love for limericks, of which he possessed a large store and which he enjoyed reciting. Louis Brownlow tells the story of President Wilson refusing to appoint Dixon Merritt to an Agriculture Department position on the ground that the latter was not in the Civil Service. Brownlow then won the President's heart, and incidentally the job for Merritt, by telling Wilson that the latter was a gifted limerick writer, and citing one of his samples:

Oh, a wonderful bird is the pelican
His mouth holds more than his belly can
He takes in his beak
Food enough for a week
I sometimes wonder how the hellican.

In public, however, Wilson showed little of his wit or quiet charm. He was shy, aloof, shrinking from the rough and tumble of political life. As President, he exerted no personal influence over members of Congress but managed his political and legislative affairs through the authority of the presidency and the adroit use of his executive power. Unlike Theodore Roosevelt, Wilson was not loved by his followers; indeed, it cannot be said of a man of his temperament that he really had followers. He was, rather, admired for the clarity of his ideas, his gift of phrase, and the integrity of his mind. He struck no sparks of enthusiasm. Wilson liked humanity, but not people. His political life was marred by his inability to maintain friendships. He permitted few intimates, and one after another, he alienated or broke with his most important political friends and supporters, among them men like George Harvey, Colonel Edward M. House (who called him "one of the most contradictory characters in history,") and Vice-President Thomas Marshall.

As President, Wilson had an aversion to taking advice and tolerated no independent counselors. His cabinet consisted of subordinates rather than strong personalities. "I have served him long and faithfully," his Secretary of the Interior, Franklin K. Lane, wrote privately with some bitterness in 1919, "under very adverse circumstances. It is hard for him to get on with anyone who has any will or independent judgment."

Arthur S. Link, Wilson's biographer and editor of his collected papers for the Princeton University Press, frankly professes bafflement at his subject's enigmatic personality. Professor Link feels that perhaps only a mindreader or psychiatrist could explain the contradictions in Wilson's character—"his craving for affection and his refusal to give friendship on equal terms, the warm idealism of his speeches and the sangfroid of many of his official relationships, the bigness of his political visions and the pettiness of his hatreds."

Despite his aloofness and the cloistered background of his academic career, Wilson had a special feeling for the needs and aspirations of the common people, with whom he had otherwise nothing in common. This was a great strength and a gift he shared with that other reserved intellectual democrat, Thomas Jefferson, like whom he also had a conspicuous ability to formulate political ideas. Wilson, unlike Jefferson, came to his liberal democratic ideas slowly and rather late in his career. Throughout most of his academic life, Wilson was more Hamiltonian than Jeffersonian, a conservative who reflected the classbound, parochial attitudes of his background.

In general, the early Wilson was a southerner with the traditional outlook and normal bias of the region from which he came. He had little knowledge of the rude world of American capitalism, of the ugly slums that pockmarked America's spreading industrial cities, of the cruel conditions of labor, including child labor, and the ruthless exploitation of women. It was during his later years at Princeton, particularly after he became president of the University and did a great deal of traveling and lecturing, that he came in contact with the raw reality and turbulence of American life. New Jersey itself was a growing industrial slum with all the accompanying diseases of unrestrained capitalism. The state was, in a sense, an adjunct to an immense financial and business area embracing New York, Pennsylvania, and Delaware. As the president of Princeton journeyed through the expanding urban region, his eyes were gradually opened to the harsh conditions of life in an industrial civilization. What he saw, heard, and sensed slowly but steadily transformed him from a professor of abstractions to a passionate advocate of social rights.

Wilson's liberal ideas were crystallized by the time he became governor of New Jersey. They were given their fullest expression in his 1912 campaign speeches, published under the title *The New Freedom.* In those speeches, Wilson reiterated three central themes. One was that the American economy was dominated by big business and special interests that were ruthless in their exploitation of the human and natural resources of the nation, and exerted an over-all power greater than that of the government of the United States. It was, he said, a tyranny that deprived the people of their natural rights and opportunities.

"By tyranny, as we now fight it, we mean control of the law, of legislation and adjudication, by organizations which do not represent the people, by means which are private and selfish. We mean, specifically, the conduct of our affairs and the shaping of our legislation in the interests of special bodies of capital. . . . We mean the alliance, for this purpose, of political machines with selfish business. We mean the exploitation of the people by legal and political means. We have seen many of our governments under these influences cease to be . . . governments representative of the people, and become governments representative of special interests, controlled by machines, which in their turn are not controlled by the people."

The second point Wilson made in *The New Freedom* was that government must no longer be subverted by big business and subservient to its special interests. Instead of "the combined capitalists and manufacturers" being, as they were at that time, "masters of the government of the United States," Wilson proposed that this "absolutely intolerable" relationship be reversed. He wanted the government restored to the American people and used for the benefit of the whole society, rather than for the business community.

"A great nation," he said, "cannot be tied with any particular set of interests. . . . No group of men less than the majority has a right to tell me how I have got to live in America. . . . The whole stability of a democratic polity rests upon the fact that every interest is every man's interest."

Wilson was aware that the American political tradition was hostile to strong central government and especially to legislation that might interfere with the economic processes. Both major parties, his own as well as the Republican, were committed to the practice of more or less impotent government. Wilson knew better than anyone that the advocates of limited national government, even more numerous in his own southern-influenced party than in the Republican, had history and powerful precedent behind them. Was it not Jefferson himself who had immortalized the notion of the less government, the better? For a Democrat to challenge the theory of weak government as a bulwark of democracy and states' rights, required a special kind of daring.

Wilson, in his advocacy of a positive role by the central government, could not ignore the arguments and beliefs held by the Jeffersonians. He paid tribute to Jefferson's democratic philosophy, but pointed out that the United States had undergone a profound economic and social transformation since the days when the sage of Monticello was in power. Wilson argued that certain specific attitudes applicable to the rural society which prevailed in the first days of the republic, had no reality in an age of industrialization. In Jefferson's time, there were no large numbers of landless urban laborers; there were no heavy industries, no great factories. But all that had changed radically. By the first part of the twentieth century, industrialization had brought with it human problems of a range and complexity undreamed of by the founders of the nation. These new problems required new solutions. In *The New Freedom,* Wilson justified governmental regulations in the field of labor, conditions of employment, and industrial relations:

"This dealing of great bodies of men with other bodies of men is a matter of public scrutiny, and should be a matter of public regulation. Similarly, it was no business of the law of the time of Jefferson to come into my house and see how I kept house. But when my house, when my so-called private property, became a great mine, and men went along dark corridors amidst every kind of danger in order to dig out of the bowels of the earth things necessary for the industries of a whole nation, and when it came about that . . . these mines . . . were owned by great stock companies, then all the old analogies absolutely collapsed and it became the right of the government to go down into these mines to see whether human beings were properly treated or not. . . . In these great beehives, where in every corridor swarm men of flesh and blood, it is the privilege of the government . . . to see that human life is protected, that human lungs have something to breathe."

Wilson's third point was that America needed to readjust to the new forces that had arisen. "The life of America is not the life that it was twenty years ago. . . . We have changed our economic conditions, absolutely, from top to bottom; and, with our economic society, the organization of our life. . . . We are facing the necessity of fitting a new social organization." What was required was, first, a larger participation of the people in their political affairs; and, second, the use of the machinery of government for harmonizing the infinitely varied and complex interests of the American society. Only thus could freedom, which underlay American democracy, be made secure and meaningful. Wilson conceived of freedom as social balance and harmony.

"What is liberty?" he wrote in *The New Freedom.* "You say of the locomotive that it runs free. What do you mean? You mean that its parts are so assembled and adjusted that friction is reduced to a minimum, and that it has perfect adjustment. . . . Human freedom consists in perfect adjustment of human interests and human activities and human energies."

These three themes—the obnoxious domination of America by special interests, the need for an assumption of social responsibility by government, and a revitalization of democracy—were not original with Wilson. They were in the air at the time, a part of the intellectual ferment and political protest that had been developing in the United States since the coming of industrialization. In one way or another, these ideas had been taken up, explored, and discussed by writers like Walt Whitman and Henry George, by political figures like Louis Brandeis and Theodore Roosevelt, by radical parties such as the Populists and Socialists.

Wilson was thus in line with the wide stream of American progressivism, but his espousal of these liberal ideas made a difference on two counts. He articulated progressive concepts with a special cogency and beauty of expression. What had hitherto sometimes sounded like wild radicalism became, in Wilson's deliberate prose, proposals of statesmanlike reasonableness. And, unlike other reform advocates, Wilson, by virtue of his political triumph in 1912, was in a position to carry into effect a liberal program. As President, he did institute a number of impressive reforms, among them railroad labor legislation, the Farm Loan Act, the Federal Trade Commission, and the Federal Reserve System. The Wilson reform program was cut short by the United States' involvement in World War I. But it served as a prelude to the later liberalization of the Democratic Party and as a precedent and example for the social legislation of the New Deal. As Governor Franklin D. Roosevelt wrote to Robert W. Bingham in 1931:

"President Wilson . . . said to me early in his first term something to this effect:—'It is only once in a generation that a people can be lifted above material things. That is why conservative government is in the saddle two-thirds of the time.' I am fully convinced that the cycle has swung again after twelve years and that it is our turn next."

As a public figure, Wilson is identified with the wide and repeated use of the word *democracy*. There was something almost obsessive in his repetition of the term and its applications. Certainly no man in American history before him had ever talked as much about democracy as did Wilson. He brought the word even into foreign affairs, applying an American domestic concept to international power conflicts. "The commands of democracy," he wrote, "are as imperative as its privileges."

"America is evidence of the fact," he said, unmindful of the Mexican War, "that no great democracy has ever entered upon an aggressive policy. Democracy has not been finally vindicated. The world must be made safe for democracy."

Rhetoric apart, Wilson visualized democracy as a political philosophy vital to American existence. Democracy to him was the link that bound together the states of the union. In addition to being a necessary American political ideal, is was also both a moral force and an energizer of the society. Democracy, Wilson insisted, was the main instrument for the release of the energies of the common people, providing them with unhampered opportunities for education and self-expression, something unavailable in any other polity. Like Jefferson and Lincoln, he believed that human gifts and abilities were widely scattered and could be found among the most humble as well as among the rich and exalted. The beauty of democracy was that it opened wide the gates of life to common humanity.

"Nature pays no tribute to aristocracy," he said, "subscribes to no creed or caste, renders fealty to no monarch or master of any name or kind. Genius is no snob. . . . It affects humble company as well as great. It . . . serenely chooses its own comrades, its own haunts, its own cradle even. . . . This is the sacred mystery of democracy, that its richest fruits spring up out of soils which no man has prepared and in circumstances amidst which they are the least expected. . . . The test of every American must always be, not where he is but what he is. That, also, is of the essence of democracy."

In this connection, Wilson proclaimed America a special creation of the Divinity to serve the purposes of freedom and equality. Like Walt Whitman, he equated democracy, justice and idealism with America. His speeches, particularly after 1912, were veritable paeans to the nation as a symbol of all that was great and pure in the human spirit. "Sometimes," he said, "people call me an idealist. Well, that is the way I know I am an American." The special, divinely ordained purposes of America, he asserted, were democracy and human liberty. "We are," he said in 1914, "custodians of the spirit of righteousness, of the spirit of equal-handed justice, of the spirit of hope." The nation was created, he reiterated in public speeches, to assert human rights for everybody.

This idealized view of the historic function of the country, with its missionary, Chosen-People flavor, was not actually chauvinistic or parochial. Wilson, a trained historian, was acutely conscious of the numerous ethnic elements that went into the making of the United States. Again and again, in public speeches and declarations, he hailed the immigrants and their indispensable contributions to the United States. One of the glories of America, he said, was that it was not one race but a people made up of all the races of Europe.

"Our American blood is not drawn from any one country, . . . not drawn from any one stock, . . . not drawn from any one language of the modern world . . ."

As Wilson saw it, the steady stream of immigration into America had had two unique consequences. One was the continuous replenishment of human energies and the revitalizing of hopes and ideals. "This," he said, "is the only country in the world which experiences this constant and repeated rebirth. Other countries depend upon the multiplication of their own native people instead of constantly drinking strength out of new sources." The immigrants came with dreams of a better life and passion for the improvement, not only of themselves, but also of the country that gave them the opportunity for a new life in freedom. He felt that so long as America kept her doors open to admit newcomers with dreams and aspirations, she would retain her greatness. In January 1915, he vetoed a bill requiring a literacy test for immigrants on the ground that it was morally wrong to exclude people who in the old world had had no opportunity for education. "Restrictions like these," he said in his veto message, "adopted earlier in our history as a nation, would very materially have altered the course and cooled the humane ardors of our politics."

The second consequence of immigration was to make the United States global-minded. Other nations, more ethnically integrated, were confined to their own strictly limited national outlook and concentrated on their own narrow national interests, but the United States, owing to its multiethnic composition, tended to take a world view, Wilson felt. "America," he said in 1915, "has been made up out of the nations of the world and is the friend of the nations of the world." A year later, May 1916, he extended and activated this global concept. "Because we are made up," he declared in a Memorial Day speech, "and consciously made up, out of all the great family of mankind, we are champions of the rights of mankind." It was while the United States was still neutral that Wilson gradually edged away from a position of aloofness toward active commitment in the world's struggle then raging abroad.

It is one of the ironies of modern history that Wilson, who was to have so profound an impact on the world politics of his time, knew very little about international affairs. His training, as we have seen, was entirely in the field of American history and English literature. He had no background in foreign affairs or in the institutions, politics, objectives, and history of other nations. During his academic career, he had shown scant interest in the international scene. In his first year in the White House, he reflected his own party's general isolationism and opposition to what was called "dollar diplomacy," the use of American power to protect economic interests abroad, especially in Latin America. But he was fated to become involved in foreign affairs, first in turbulent Mexico —where he sent troops to protect the American border—and later in the larger battle arena of Europe.

American involvement in World War I was one of the momentous events of modern times. For a variety of intricate reasons, Wilson took a by no means united nation into that global conflict. By and large, the country had been neutral and had hoped to remain so. But in his second Inaugural, Wilson hinted that neutrality was no longer a possible policy, saying: "We are provincials no longer. The tragic events of the thirty months of vital turmoil through which we have just passed have made us citizens of the world. There can be no turning back." Less than a month later, on April 2, 1917, he appeared before a crowded House of Representatives and, in the precise tones of a disciplined schoolmaster, his eyeglasses set firmly on his long nose, hair carefully brushed, chin protruding stubbornly, he took a manuscript from the pocket of his close-fitting frock coat and quietly proclaimed war against Germany. An eyewitness, Henry L. Stoddard, said that at that moment Wilson "was the coldest man I ever looked upon." Another man who witnessed the historic occasion was Edwin A. Alderman, president of the University of Virginia, who described the President's appearance: "The air . . . was tense with emotion. . . . Woodrow Wilson—the lithe figure, the bony structure of the forehead, the lean, long visage as of a Covenanter, somber with fixed purpose. . . . I was somehow reminded of the unbending lineaments and figure of Andrew Jackson, whom Woodrow Wilson resembled physically."

The words Wilson spoke echoed through America and the world. And in his war declaration are reflected his peculiar greatness and essential weakness.

"It is a fearful thing to lead this great and peaceful people into war," he stated, "civilization itself seeming to be in the balance. But the right is more precious than peace, and we shall fight for the things which we have always carried nearest our hearts—for democracy, for the right of those who submit to authority to have a voice in their own government, for the rights and liberties of small nations, for the universal dominion of right by such a concert of free peoples as will bring peace and safety to all nations, and make the world itself at last free. To such a task we can dedicate our lives and our fortunes, everything we are, everything we have, with the pride of those who know the day has come when America is privileged to spend her blood and might for the principles that gave her birth, and happiness and peace which she has treasured."

In historic perspective, it is clear that United States' involvement in World War I on the side of the Western allies was probably a necessity for the ultimate security of the American nation. This was especially true after the collapse of Czarism in Russia early in 1917, when it appeared that Germany, freed from the pressures of the eastern front, might be able to concentrate its forces in the west and defeat Great Britain and France. In that event, Germany would emerge the mightiest power on earth, dominating not only Europe but also Asia and, through its control of the seas, the other continents as well. This was an eventuality that a great nation like the United States, needing the freedom of the seas for its own growth, security, and development, could not possibly tolerate. In the last analysis, there were sound and realistic reasons for the United States to enter the war in Europe; to prevent any one country, in this instance imperial Germany, from destroying the other great nations and to preserve the balance of power in the world.

But Wilson did not talk that way. Instead of explaining to the American people the reasons that made it necessary to take the country into a war three thousand miles away from home, he indulged in a campaign of moralizing and rhetoric. The purposes of American participation in World War I obviously were realistic; the President's words were not. To proclaim, as did Wilson, that this was a war for democracy, was both unreal and untrue. Any student of the tragic conflict that was destroying Europe knew that it was a war neither for democracy, nor for justice, nor for freedom. It was, rather, a war of all the great imperialist powers, battling to the death for the preservation of their empires and their privileged positions in the world, and involving huge inequalities, especially where their colonies were concerned. Europe's imperialist belligerents, in all fairness, did not claim or pretend that they were fighting for anything so lofty as what Wilson proclaimed. The hard and cynical leaders of the belligerent countries—Clemenceau, Lloyd George, Orlando, among others—may well have been astonished to hear that they were fighting for democracy, for liberty, for justice, and for humanity.

One of Wilson's major weaknesses, which contributed to his final tragedy, was that he tended to confuse rhetoric with reality. He had a predilection for certain phrases and word combinations which, while sounding eloquent and high-toned, upon analysis proved to be either meaningless or ritualistic. He was particularly addicted to a rhetoric that had moralistic overtones. As William Bayard Hale pointed out in his tract, *The Story of a Style* (1920), Wilson loved the sound of certain locutions that he repeated again and again. "Mr. Wilson does not concur, he entirely concurs"; wrote Hale, not without irony, "he is seldom gratified, he usually is profoundly gratified; he does not feel pleasure, he experiences unaffected pleasure; he seldom says anything, but he is always privileged to say." Wilson's rolling rhetoric was perhaps defensible in an orator or political leader. But it was fraught with peril when applied to the infinitely complex realities of international politics and substituted for disciplined analysis.

Wilson went to Paris in 1919, filled with the missionary zeal and lofty idealism he had proclaimed throughout the war. In a Europe devastated by five years of unprecedented bloodshed, famine, and revolution, he was received with wild enthusiasm. A humanity utterly sick of war and hunger looked upon the American President as a veritable savior and accepted his idealistic proclamations and promises as gospel truth. Europeans knew that Wilson was speaking the truth when he said that America had neither ambitions as a world power nor desire for anyone's territory. He had come to the old world to secure freedom, justice, the self-determination of the formerly oppressed small nations, and a durable peace. At Paris, in 1919, he was the triumphant personification of American idealism. "We came into the world," he said there, "consecrated to liberty, and whenever we see the cause of liberty imperilled, we are ready to cast in our lot in common with the lot of those whose liberty is threatened. This is the spirit of the people of the United States."

But it did not work out that way. Wilson—stubborn, inexperienced, uninformed in the realm of international politics—was soon confronted by a welter of intrigues, national interests, ruthless ambitions, chauvinistic demands, cynical manipulations with which he was unfitted to cope. Step by step, he compromised his ideals, yielded to the pressures and persuasions of experienced European statesmen and leaders, and at the end managed to salvage only his great plan for peace, the League of Nations.

The hero of Europe, President Wilson returned to an unfriendly United States. The hostile atmosphere contributed to Wilson's "ordeal," the term used by one of his successors in the White House. He had failed to take the powerful leaders of Congress, especially the Republicans in the Senate, into his confidence. He had alienated a large section of the American people by some of his wartime measures. The nation seems to have been weary of his lofty rhetoric, of unaccustomed wartime exertions, and of internationalism. The Senate refused to ratify the treaty of Versailles which Wilson had brought with him from Europe and thereby destroyed the President's passionate hopes for an enduring peace through the League of Nations.

Stubborn and brave as ever, Wilson decided to take the peace treaty to the people, determined to inspire them with his ideals and convictions that the League of Nations was a desperate necessity for mankind. To his young Assistant Secretary of the Navy, Franklin D. Roosevelt, he said: "Unless this League goes through in some form or other, it will break the heart of the world." The President made speeches all the way from Washington to the West Coast, pleading support of the League, appealing to the pride and idealism of America. In Indianapolis, he said: "Opposition is not going to save the world. Negations are not going to construct the policies of mankind. . . . The only triumphant ideas in this world are the ideas that are organized for battle." In St. Louis, he said: "It is our business to prevent war, and if we do not take care of the weak nations of the world, there will be war." In Omaha, he said: "I would consider myself recreant to every mother and father, every wife and sweetheart in this country, if I consented to the ending of this war without a guaranty that there would be no other." In Sioux Falls, South Dakota, he said: "The peace of the world cannot be established without America. America is necessary to the peace of the world." In Coeur d'Alene, Idaho, he repeated: "There will be no reform in this world for a generation if the conditions of the world are not now brought to settled order, and they cannot be brought to settled order without the cooperation of America." In St. Paul, Minnesota, he said: "America is the only nation which can sympathetically lead the world in organizing peace." He told the people: "We Americans are the predestined mediators of mankind." All these splendid phrases were to be in vain.

In Pueblo, Colorado, on September 25, 1919, he gave his last speech —which contained the words: "There is one thing that the American people always rise to and extend their hand to, and that is the truth of justice, liberty and peace. We have accepted that truth, and it is going to lead us, and through us the world, out into pastures of quietness and peace such as the world never dreamed of before."

Then he was stricken with paralysis, from which he never recovered. Wilson may thus be said to have given his health and then his life for the cause of world peace, which he held to be greater than the cause of any one nation. He spoke for mankind.

As he lay stricken with paralysis, he saw many of his hopes shattered. In Europe, the harsh peace imposed upon defeated Germany and the dissolution of the Austro-Hungarian Empire, led to consequences which were ultimately to destroy everything Wilson had hoped for. An appalling inflation in Germany all but wiped out the life savings and security of the middle class and finally brought forth Hitler. In France, financial and political instability created insecurities which ultimately undermined the integrity of the Republic. In Italy, the parliamentary democracy was crushed by Mussolini's fascism. In Russia, the Bolsheviks instituted a machinery of terror which soon claimed millions of victims. In central Europe, all but one of the small states whose self-determination Wilson had championed and whose national existence he helped bring into being, became fascistic dictatorships. Virtually nowhere was the world "safe for democracy." In fact, Wilson's ideal of democracy was systematically being crushed everywhere.

At home, much of Wilson's record for liberalism was destroyed in the last years by the excesses of his own administration, which was darkened by reaction and hysteria. During the war, there had been an outbreak of intolerance, particularly against Germans, pacifists, and conscientious objectors. In many high schools and colleges, the German language was eliminated from the curriculum. While much of the hysteria and intolerance was spontaneous and self-generating, a good deal of it must be charged to Wilson himself. A President, especially in wartime, is in a supreme position of leadership and he can drastically affect, in one way or another, the moral tone of a nation and the prevailing climate of opinion. Wilson not only put no halt to the ugly passions stirred up by the war; his own administration compounded the evil through direct action of a nature that must forever be considered a disgrace. In December 1919, his attorney general, A. Mitchell Palmer, began a series of raids on radicals, using methods which had never before been seen in the United States, not even in the days of the Alien and Sedition Acts. In dozens of cities, arrests were made without warrant, Socialist offices were searched without any show of legality, documents were seized and impounded. In Detroit, more than a hundred men were herded into a cell measuring 24 by 30 feet and kept there for a week. In Hartford, Connecticut, federal authorities arrested even those who came to visit Palmer's victims in jail. Throughout the United States, more than six thousand men were arrested and kept in prison for days and weeks without warrant. The federal reign of terror set an example of illegality to the states. In the New York state legislature, five legally elected socialist representatives were denied their seats. The terror—there is no other word for it—extended to colleges, schools, publishing houses, and even to the United States House of Representatives, which, by a vote of 309 to 1, unseated Victor Berger, the Socialist Congressman from Milwaukee. Much of this wave of repression took place while Wilson was gravely ill and unable to exercise the powers and duties of the presidency. But he cannot be absolved of the moral responsibility for having done nothing to check the outbursts of hatred, violence, and political intolerance. He personally refused to pardon the widely beloved Eugene V. Debs for his pacifism, even though the war Debs had opposed was already over.

When the 1920 elections came, Wilson found his party and his policies and, by indirection, himself, overwhelmingly repudiated at the polls. The Democratic ticket in that year, headed by James Cox and Franklin D. Roosevelt, received a mere nine million votes against some sixteen million for the Republicans, led by Warren G. Harding and Calvin Coolidge. The extent of the revulsion of the American people against the war and the Wilson administration may be indicated by the fact that Debs, the Socialist candidate for the presidency, although in the federal penitentiary, received nearly one million votes—a Socialist Party record unexcelled before or since.

Wilson emerges a man of the most clashing contradictions. A genuine believer in democracy, he could tolerate the subversion of democracy at home; a passionate advocate of liberalism, he condoned and even encouraged the persecution of Socialists who claimed an advanced sort of liberalism. But when all this is said, he stands out as one of the major figures of our time by virtue of his impassioned advocacy of the ideal of peace—a vision which transcended his personal limitations. Here, his work was not in vain. His defeat in connection with the League of Nations was, in its way, a wry sort of triumph. "Wilson's failure was also his measure. It was probably the most colossal and heroic failure of modern times."

Wilson proved himself a tragic prophet. In September 1919 he said, "I can predict with absolute certainty that within another generation there will be another world war if the nations of the world do not concert a method by which to prevent it."

Twenty years later, almost to the day, the world was again engulfed in war.

The lesson taught by Wilson, in both its negative and creative aspects, was to be applied by his protégé and Democratic successor in the White House. Franklin D. Roosevelt was to remember the example of Woodrow Wilson.

# 20

## *THE AMERICAN AS REFORMER:* Franklin D. Roosevelt *(1882–1945)*

*A man in high public office is neither husband nor father nor friend in the commonly accepted sense of the words; but I have come to believe that Franklin stands in the memory of people as a man who lived with a great sense of history and with a sense of his obligation to fulfill his part as he saw it.*

*Eleanor Roosevelt,* This I Remember *(1949)*

It is fitting that this book should end with a study of Franklin Delano Roosevelt. FDR, as he came to be widely known, had a greater impact on twentieth-century America, and indeed on the world, than probably any other American in modern history. His work and achievements were of such dimensions that he left the United States transformed in its social and economic institutions—and, in fact, in its basic attitudes. He was one of the great revolutionists of our time—and he achieved his New Deal revolution through democratic means, without recourse to either fraud or violence.

Roosevelt's success as a democratic statesman derived from two fundamental sources: his love of life and his love of people. FDR had a zest for battle reminiscent of his uncle-in-law, Theodore Roosevelt, taking keen joy in struggle, especially political struggle. This combativeness was nourished by something that is uncommon among statesmen, a genuine affection for people and an intuitive sense of their feelings and ideas. His longtime secretary, Grace Tully, said:

"He liked everything about human beings. He always got something from a person. Why, old Moses Smith over at Hyde Park. The President would see him and stop and talk to him for half an hour. You know, he's no great mind. After he'd come away, the President would say, 'You know, ol' Moses has some good ideas.' He was very tolerant of stupidity. He disliked dishonesty and disloyalty."

A man of mercurial temperament and multifaceted personality, Roosevelt created contradictory impressions. The complexity of his character baffled observers. "As a human being," Adolf Berle said of FDR, "he is incomparably greater than any myth." Roosevelt's speech writer, friend, and biographer, Robert E. Sherwood, described him in his book *Roosevelt and Hopkins* (1948) as "... a man of infinite subtlety and obscurity—an artful dodger who could not readily be pinned down on specific points. ... He could be and was ruthless and implacable with those whom he considered guilty of disloyalty; but with those in his Administration who were inefficient or even recalcitrant or hopelessly inept, but loyal, he was 'a complete softy.' "

Roosevelt was a puzzle to his contemporaries, admirers and detractors alike, because he did not fit any category. An effective politician, he did not talk like one. A member of the upstate New York gentry, he embraced the cause of liberalism. A Harvard aristocrat, he believed in a Jeffersonian philosophy of human rights. He played politics like a master, but believed that the political game was not an end in itself but had a larger purpose. Tough and resourceful as a leader of men, he had an underlying human tenderness that sometimes made it impossible for him to appear unpleasant to those who sought his favor. Thus he sometimes created the impression of deviousness. Eleanor Roosevelt, in *This I Remember,* makes an effort to explain this puzzling aspect of her husband's character:

"Often people have told me that they were misled by Franklin. ... I have ... felt that he left them after an interview with the idea that he was in entire agreement with them. I would know quite well, however, that he was not, and that they would be very much surprised ... later. This misunderstanding not only arose from his dislike of being disagreeable, but from the interest that he always had in somebody else's point of view and his willingness to listen to it. If he thought it was well expressed and clear, he nodded his head and frequently said 'I see' or something of the sort. This did not mean that he was convinced of the truth of the arguments, or even that he entirely understood them, but only that he appreciated the way in which they were presented."

FDR's color, gaiety, and charm—General Hugh Johnson used to say of him that he could entice a canary into a cage—would have made him a memorable figure at any time. But he stands out, first, as the only American President to be elected four times; second, for his New Deal program; third, for his leadership in World War II. Each of these achievements would have given him a secure place in history; but combined, they establish him as a commanding figure.

Roosevelt's emergence on the historic stage was undramatic. He followed family tradition by going to Harvard and then entering politics. After serving in the New York State senate, young Roosevelt was appointed Assistant Secretary of the Navy by the newly elected Democratic President in 1912. Woodrow Wilson had no personal acquaintance with the obscure state senator from New York. But, in the words of Herbert Bayard Swope, "Wilson wanted a good upstate Democrat—and it was hard to find one. So, although he had always hated the Roosevelt name, Wilson named him to the minor cabinet."

The Navy post, in which Roosevelt served until 1920, marked the beginning of his maturation. In this period, he was exposed to the influences of four dissimilar men, each representing a distinct phase of the American character.

One was his immediate chief, Secretary of the Navy Josephus Daniels, a North Carolina prohibitionist and follower of William Jennings Bryan, with all the Methodist virtues and quirks of a pious southerner. The sophisticated young Roosevelt started out by mimicking the slow-speaking and provincial Southern Methodist and ended with a staunch admiration for his solid, old-fashioned qualities. In 1920, when the young Assistant Secretary accepted the Democratic vice-presidential nomination, he wrote in longhand a letter of genuine appreciation to his Tarheel "Chief," as he continued to call him: "You have taught me so wisely and kept my feet on the ground when I was about to skyrocket—and in it all there has never been a real dispute or antagonism or distrust. . . . please let me keep on coming to you to get your fine inspiration of real idealism and right living and good Americanism."

The other three influences on Roosevelt were Woodrow Wilson; Justice Louis Brandeis, for whose writings and ideas he had a deep respect; and Justice Oliver Wendell Holmes, whom he used to visit on Sunday afternoons.

In *This I Remember,* Eleanor Roosevelt writes, "President Wilson . . . had a profound effect on Franklin's thinking and political philosophy. Franklin admired him greatly, I know, and believed deeply in his ideas and ideals."

Wilson, an intellectual, a professional writer, an easy articulator of ideas, who was at the same time an outstanding political success, was an inspiration to young Roosevelt. Like Theodore Roosevelt, he served FDR as a model of what a gentleman in politics ought to be. President Wilson, moreover, was an outspoken liberal whose ideas struck a responsive chord in the mind of Roosevelt. The New Deal is full of echoes of *The New Freedom*. Justices Holmes and Brandeis widened Roosevelt's horizon in fields such as civil liberty and economic reform.

An even deeper influence on Roosevelt's life was the personal tragedy of his paralysis. After his defeat as vice-presidential candidate in 1920, he was stricken with polio which crippled his legs. The terrible illness that immobilized him was ultimately to enhance the power of his mind and spirit. The years of physical torment became years of preparation for his great historic role. A lesser man would have been crushed by the seeming disaster, but Roosevelt dredged from the depth of his being resources which he himself may not have known he possessed. In his crisis, he was helped by a profound feeling of hope which buoyed him up and gave him a strength and an assurance which nothing thereafter could shake. Henceforth, he was to fear neither defeat nor death. The years of his illness raised him above ordinary anxieties and provided an unshakable basis for his life's work.

During his invalidism, Roosevelt enlarged his mind through extensive reading and contact with people. Like Theodore Roosevelt, he was a lover of books. His main interests were biography and American history, especially naval history. Fascinated by attractively bound volumes, he was fond of commenting on their binding, design, print, and paper. He liked, on occasion, to think of himself as an author. Once, while he was governor of New York, he wrote to Arthur Krock of *The New York Times*, with jocular seriousness: "A lady palmist or fortune teller, sent me a horoscope the other day which showed that my real forte in life is writing and that I could become a highly successful AUTHOR. This is the first event in my life which has given me a real swelled head! Seriously, at this time of year I long to return to the ancestral fire, plant trees and write." Later, he published his major speeches in book form—*Whither Bound, Happy Warrior, On Our Way, Looking Forward*. He was a careful stylist, conscious of the impact of words. As President, he used to labor over and rewrite drafts of speeches prepared for him by gifted aides, including such eminent writers as Robert E. Sherwood, until he was satisfied that they had his own flavor and rhythm.

Another main source of influence upon Roosevelt during his convalescence was contact with a large number of people, among them businessmen, social-service workers, trade unionists, politicians, political scientists, and lawyers. Many of these contacts he made through the indefatigable Mrs. Roosevelt, who introduced him to trade unionists and opened his mind to the whole problem of labor exploitation and other consequences of industrial development.

"In the years of his illness," Frances Perkins writes in *The Roosevelt I Knew* (1946), "Mrs. Roosevelt developed a remarkable reportorial quality. She had always been an observant woman. She learned to be more observant and to be able to repeat in detail what she saw and heard. This was of priceless help to him, handicapped as he was, longing to be in touch with the people, and having to learn to take vicarious instead of direct personal experience . . . she brought him people with whom he could share the things going on in his mind. She realized she could introduce new and stimulating ideas through people who were thoughtful, had had a variety of experience, and wanted to know what he thought."

In later years, when the New Deal burst upon the country, the general impression was that it was something sudden and fortuitous. Actually the basic ideas which underlay the New Deal program had germinated in Roosevelt's mind by the time he was elected governor of New York in 1928. Even as a young man, his general stance had been that of a liberal, although his liberalism was still vague and undefined. As early as March 1912, addressing the People's Forum at Troy, New York, he spoke of the need to struggle "for the liberty of the community rather than the liberty of the individual." He then expressed himself in favor of such liberal policies as conservation of natural resources, help to farmers, and control of trusts. "I hope to God," he wrote to his wife when he was Assistant Secretary of the Navy, "I don't grow reactionary with advancing years." In his speech accepting the vice-presidential nomination (August 9, 1920), he came out in favor of liberalism and progress. The words were stereotyped, but the intention was clear.

"Some people have been saying of late: 'We are tired of progress, we want to go back . . .' " he commented. "They are wrong. This is not the wish of America! We can never go back. The 'good old days' are gone past forever; we have no regrets. For our eyes are trained ahead—forward to better new days. . . ."

Roosevelt regarded himself a Jeffersonian democrat. He was a student of Jefferson and, characteristically, preferred his ideas to those of Hamilton, who was then in fashion. In this connection, it is revealing to read a review of Claude Bowers' *Jefferson and Hamilton,* which Roosevelt wrote in the New York *Evening World,* December 3, 1925:

"For some years I have been, frankly, fed up with the romantic pulp which has . . . surrounded the name of Alexander Hamilton; and I have longed to write this very book, which now so much more ably comes from the delightful pen and untiring research of Mr. Bowers."

He then went on to point out that Hamilton, an opponent of democratic government, had organized the "compact forces, of wealth, of birth, of the press," while Jefferson could count only on the unorganized working people. In the great struggle between Hamilton and Jefferson, the reviewer continued admiringly, the latter remained the calm philosopher, unshaken in his faith in democracy and in the common people. Roosevelt concluded with what in retrospect seems a prophetic self-projection:

"I have a breathless feeling as I lay down this book—a picture of escape which this Nation passed through those first ten years; a picture of what might have been if the Republic had been finally organized as Alexander Hamilton sought. But I have a breathless feeling, too, as I wonder if, a century and a quarter later, the same contending forces are not again mobilizing. Hamiltons we have today. Is there a Jefferson on the horizon?"

Roosevelt's interest in Jefferson was unflagging. On August 1, 1931, in a letter to Josephus Daniels, referring to the restoration of the still privately owned Monticello, he wrote:

"Perhaps if we come into control in 1933, we can take some definite steps to make Monticello much more truly a national shrine than it is today. . . . Now that Virginia is getting excellent highways, there is no reason why a million people a year should not go there instead of fifty thousand." It was during Roosevelt's administration that the great monument to Jefferson was built in Washington, D.C., the national capital which the Virginian had done so much to create. At the dedication of the Jefferson Memorial on April 13, 1943, President Roosevelt, heavily burdened by World War II, made his painful way up the improvised platform and gave a moving address:

Today, in the midst of a great war for freedom, we dedicate this shrine to freedom. To Thomas Jefferson, apostle of freedom, we are paying a debt long overdue. . . . He faced the fact that men who will not fight for liberty can lose it. We, too, face that fact. He lived in a world in which freedom of conscience and freedom of mind were battles still to be fought through—not principles already accepted by all men. We, too, have lived in such a world. He loved peace and loved liberty—yet on more than one occasion, he was forced to choose between them. We, too, have been compelled to make that choice. . . . The words which we have chosen for this Memorial speak Jefferson's noblest and most urgent meaning, and we are proud indeed to understand and share:

> I have sworn upon the altar of God
> eternal hostility against every
> form of tyranny over the mind of man.

Much of the New Deal was foreshadowed by Roosevelt's governorship of New York state. As his close collaborator, Samuel Rosenman, pointed out in *Working with Roosevelt* (1952), the Governor dealt with measures and problems that were later to be duplicated on a national scale. Governor Roosevelt urged state action in such fields as farm relief, reforestation, conservation, old-age insurance, regulation of banks, public housing, public power, minimum-wage laws, regulation of public utilities, and a host of similar proposals made familiar by him as President. In all this, to be sure, he followed the progressive path of his predecessor, Governor Alfred E. Smith; but what is significant about Roosevelt's liberal program in New York is that it served as a trial run for future efforts for the nation at large. He was in the habit of expounding the idea, which he seems to have derived from Justice Louis Brandeis, that a great advantage of having forty-eight states was the opportunity of carrying out political and social experiments locally before applying them to the nation as a whole.

The governorship of New York served Roosevelt as a springboard to the presidency. Since it was a position which kept its occupant busy only about three months in the year, the period the legislature was in session, it left much leisure time for other pursuits. Governor Roosevelt used his spare time for the purpose of acquainting himself with every part of the state and making numerous political contacts. He traveled by car, and by boat on canals, to visit every county and most towns of the state. Going to villages that had never seen a governor before, he stopped and talked to all kinds of people—workers, farmers, businessmen. The result could have been foreseen. In 1930, he was reelected by the largest plurality ever received by a governor of New York state. Shortly after his reelection, he said to Edward Flynn, the shrewd and able Democratic boss of the Bronx: "Eddy, . . . I believe I can be nominated for the Presidency in 1932."

Roosevelt was now ready for the great task of the presidency. He had been storing away a vast amount of information, not only about

New York but about the whole country. His memory for facts has been described as prodigious. Once he learned something, and he did learn more from people and direct observation than from books, he never forgot it and sooner or later somehow put it to good use. His curiosity about the United States was inexhaustible. He used to astonish people by his fabulous knowledge of details relating to the remotest corners of the country. Flynn tells: "I have heard him talk cattle business in Texas, sheep business in Wyoming, citrus business in Florida and apple business in New York, with what was apparently an abundant knowledge of the subject, that seemed to have been obtained by dint of great study and research."

In his preparation for his presidential candidacy, Roosevelt set up an intricate network of communications at the grass roots. Through Louis Howe and other intimate advisers, he established and maintained contact with political figures, including obscure ones, throughout the country. But above all, he was probably the first major political figure in America to use the mass media and the mails as systematic instrumentalities for political purposes. The techniques he developed as governor he later applied as President.

Roosevelt employed the mails not only to maintain touch with the people but also as a barometer of public opinion. No letter, however humble, went unanswered. According to Howe, Roosevelt spent "precious moments poring over letters scribbled on butcher paper or ruled pages torn from a cheap pad." Simple people, living in isolated parts of the land, were touched by this attention and carried the name *Roosevelt* fresh in their memories. As governor and as President, he used the radio to appeal to his supporters to bring pressure on the legislators. His presidential "fireside chats" became a potent force in harnessing support for the New Deal and for communicating his ideas. In this manner, his sense of intimacy with the American people remained fresh and unbroken, supplying him not only with a sense of public opinion trends but also with a deep reservoir of political strength. He wrote to an unknown correspondent in March 1932, half a year before he was elected President:

"I was particularly interested in your comment on the importance of the radio. Time after time, in meeting legislative opposition in my own State, I have taken an issue directly to the voters by radio, and invariably I have met a most heartening response. Amid many developments of civilization which lead away from direct government by the people, the radio is one which tends on the other hand to restore direct contact between the masses and their chosen leaders."

As the presidential election period of 1932 approached, there was a feeling among many observers that the governor of New York was a man without convictions, inclined to carry the proverbial water pail on both shoulders. Despite his active record as governor, he had not impressed himself upon the country as a forceful personality. So experienced a political commentator as Harold Laski thought Roosevelt's campaign "evasive and timid." Justice Oliver Wendell Holmes, in a private reply written in November 1932, said that "Roosevelt, when I knew him struck me as a good fellow with rather a soft edge." But perhaps the most famous misreading of the character and destiny of FDR was done by Walter Lippmann who, in his column for January 8, 1932, said that Roosevelt, an amiable man given to two-faced platitudes, was nothing more than "a pleasant man, who, without any important qualifications for the office, would very much like to be President."

Roosevelt's reaction to such criticism was in keeping with his acute sense of political realities. He regarded himself as a practical politician who, in order to achieve anything, had first to be elected. His general position was: Get the votes first, and act afterwards. Both Samuel Rosenman and Rexford G. Tugwell, his close collaborators, quote him as making a remark that goes far to explain his character and his remarkable political success.

"You know the first thing a President has to do in order to put through good legislation?" he said. "He has to get elected! If I were now back on the porch at Hyde Park as a private citizen, there is very little I could do about any of the things that I have worked on. So don't throw votes away by rushing the gun—unless there is some good sound reason. You have to get the votes first—then you can do the good work."

He was sensitive to the fact that among the traditional weaknesses of liberals were doctrinal disagreement, carping criticism, and talk for its own sake. Once, after editorial criticism by Oswald Garrison Villard in the leading liberal weekly, *The Nation* (June 8, 1932), Roosevelt wrote him sharply: "I had hoped that in your more mature years you could find some way to be more truly useful to your country" than to spend energies in mere attacks, concluding with the tart advice that Villard should go vote for "my good friend Norman Thomas." FDR liked to repeat a remark made to him by Woodrow Wilson: "Roosevelt, we progressives never beat the conservatives because they, wanting to disturb nothing, and maintaining a purely defensive position, have the cohesiveness and resistance of a closed fist; but we, being determined to make progress and each knowing best how it should be done and being therefore utterly unable . . . to support any others of us, have about as much striking power as you'd expect from the fingers of an open hand, each pointing in a slightly different direction."

Roosevelt's election to the presidency, in November 1932, took place in a gloomy period in the life of the nation. The country was in economic distress as it had not been for a century. The Great Depression, which began with the stock-market crash on October 29, 1929, showed no signs of abating. Unemployment rose steadily and relentlessly. Every section of the country felt the terrors of economic insecurity. Within about a year of the stock-market collapse, practically every fourth worker in the country had lost his job. Of a total labor force of about 52 million, around thirteen million were out of work. Older salaried employees, despite their years of service, were fired ruthlessly. The fortunate ones who were still employed had their wages cut.

The distress was as widespread and catastrophic as a medieval epidemic. Agricultural income, after 1929, declined from seventeen billion dollars to hardly more than five billion. Farms were being foreclosed. In rural areas, such as Iowa, unrest and bitterness were so extensive that the situation exploded in direct action, carried out by farmers with shotguns. In the cities, the middle class was losing its savings and businessmen faced bankruptcy. Runs on banks were a common occurrence. By the time Roosevelt was inaugurated, 5504 banks had closed throughout the country. Desperate and hungry men roamed the city streets. Their plight inspired Tin Pan Alley's lyric: "Brother, can you spare a dime?" A particularly pathetic sight was that of formerly self-respecting men selling apples on streetcorners. "Hoovervilles," wretched tin shacks providing temporary shelter for the homeless, infested formerly prosperous communities. Soup kitchens and bread lines with long queues of the hungry were common in the cities. The economic system seemed to have collapsed, leaving unrelieved hopelessness and millions of wrecked homes.

In the White House, President Hoover was stubborn in his unwillingness to use governmental powers on the scale required for the relief of the national catastrophe. Men act, or do not act, out of their convictions, and those of Hoover were deeply held and sincerely felt. He was neither a callous nor a cruel man. As War Relief Administrator in Europe in World War I, he had shown both ability and philanthropic impulses. His record in the relief field was so outstanding that it made him a national figure and ultimately led to the White House in 1929. He was a hard-working, grimly earnest man guided by two inflexible assumptions. One was that the economic system, particularly the American capitalist structure, was the best in the world; it was, to all intents and purposes, a sacrosanct natural creation and hence not to be interfered with by any drastic legislation or otherwise. Given time and patience, the system, no matter how much out of kilter it might be at any moment, would automatically right itself. Hoover's second assumption, integrally connected with the first, was that government must not use its potential or actual power to meddle with social and economic affairs. He had what seems a lifelong hostility for and distrust of what he called "bureaucracy," meaning any person employed by government.

These convictions created in Hoover an ineradicable hostility to the use of governmental power, even for the relief of what was clearly a national disaster. According to him, the issue was not whether people should go hungry and cold in the United States; it was, rather, entirely a question as to the best method by which the problem could be solved. He was convinced that it could not and should not be solved through extensive governmental interference. "Economic depression," he said in his message to Congress in December 1930, "cannot be cured by legislative action or executive pronouncement." Governmental regulation of economic affairs, he said when he vetoed the Norris bill for the Muscle Shoals (later TVA) plant, was "not liberalism but degeneration." On August 11, 1932, in his acceptance speech for the presidential renomination, Hoover, despite the fact that the national economy was in desperate need of governmental assistance, said: "It does not follow, because our difficulties are stupendous . . . that we must turn to a State-controlled or State-directed social or economic system in order to cure our troubles. That is not liberalism . . . it is tyranny." As he conceived his function, his primary duty as chief executive, at a moment when the country was stricken with catastrophe, was to see to it that the budget was balanced.

It was against this background that Franklin D. Roosevelt and his New Deal must be understood.

In his acceptance speech in Chicago, July 2, 1932, Roosevelt took direct issue not only with the policies of Hoover but with the Republican President's fundamental political philosophy. He boldly proclaimed that it *was* the duty of the government to act for the welfare of the nation. The American people, he said, wanted only two things. One was work, "with all the moral and spiritual values that go with it"; the other was a reasonable measure of security. It was the government's obligation to provide them with those elementary necessities. "Our Republican leaders," he said in challenge to Hoover, "tell us economic laws—sacred, inviolable, unchangeable—cause panic which no one could prevent. But while they prate of economic laws, men and women are starving. We must lay hold of the fact that economic laws are not made by Nature. They are made by human beings." He then concluded with his famous promise: "I pledge you, I pledge myself to a New Deal for the American people."

Credit for the phrase "New Deal," acknowledged by FDR, belongs to Mark Twain, whose Connecticut Yankee had remarked that when half a dozen men cracked the whip over the backs of a thousand of their fellows, "what the nine hundred and ninety-four other dupes needed was a new deal." In regard to another phrase made famous by Roosevelt—"the forgotten man" (first used by him in a radio speech in April 1932)—credit belongs to William Graham Sumner. Ironically, Sumner used "The Forgotten Man" as the title of a lecture in 1883, referring not to the underprivileged, as did FDR, but to the average middle-class citizen who worked and saved and paid the cost of political inefficiency.

As Roosevelt took his oath of office in March 1933, he laid his hand on the passage in the Bible that begins, "For now we see through a glass, darkly. . . ." It was a dark time, but the President electrified the nation with the phrase: "First of all, let me assert my firm belief that the only thing we have to fear is fear itself." Fearless himself, he pledged immediate action.

Then began the famous Hundred Days. Roosevelt convened the Seventy-third Congress into special session and for the next hundred days he and his Brain Trusters, a group of economists, lawyers, and college professors, working night after night, produced fifteen major legislative acts unexcelled in range, scope, and variety. Their total effect was to inaugurate an historic change in America by extending federal power into crucial areas of the nation's life.

The legislation was of two types—short- and long-range. The first was designed to give swift and immediate relief to the hungry, the homeless, and those threatened with bankruptcy and foreclosure. The second type of program was aimed at restoring the economy on all levels, including the agricultural and industrial sectors. Twenty-six new government agencies were finally set up, ranging alphabetically from AAA (Agricultural Adjustment Administration) through WPA (Works Progress Administration).

Among the alphabetical agencies, which critics were later to deride but which were remarkable acts of political improvisation, one of the most dramatic was the NIRA (National Industrial Recovery Administration). It was designed to establish voluntary cooperation between government and industry, to raise wages, regulate working hours, create employment, increase purchasing power, revive business, and establish a code of fair competition. NIRA, later shortened to NRA and thrown out by the Supreme Court as unconstitutional, was an example of Roosevelt's acute sense of experimental action. In making his radio appeal for NRA, he said:

"If all employers will act together to shorten hours and raise wages, we can put people back to work.... When Andrew Jackson...died, someone asked, 'Will he go to Heaven'? And the answer was, 'He will if he wants to.' If I am asked whether the American people will pull themselves out of this depression, I answer, 'They will if they want to.' I cannot guarantee the success of this nation-wide plan, but the people of this country can guarantee its success. I have no faith in 'cure-alls' but I believe we can greatly influence economic forces. I have no sympathy with the professional economists who insist that things must run their course and that human agencies can have no influence on economic ills. One reason is that...professional economists have changed their definition of economic law every five or ten years for a very long time."

The following timetable will show the range and swiftness of the revolutionary New Deal legislation:

On March 9, 1933, the day on which Congress convened, the Emergency Banking Act was passed.

On March 10, an economy bill reduced government expenditures.

On March 16, FDR proposed the AAA to end farm surpluses and increase farm prices.

On March 21, the President sent to Congress an elaborate relief program, including the FERA (Federal Emergency Relief Administration), to give five hundred million dollars to the states as direct relief; the CCC (Civilian Conservation Corps) to provide employment for a quarter of a million young men; PWA (Public Works Administration) to spend billions on construction, to supply jobs throughout the nation.

On March 29, FDR recommended to Congress the establishment of SEC (Securities and Exchange Commission), to protect investors against fraudulent stock issues and manipulations.

On April 10, he proposed the establishment of the TVA (Tennessee Valley Authority).

On April 13, he recommended HOLC (Home Owners Loan Corporation), to slow down mortgage foreclosures.

On April 20, he took the nation off the gold standard.

On May 17, he asked Congress to create the NIRA.

In June, he signed the FDIC (Federal Deposit Insurance Corporation), to insure bank deposits up to $5000.

All this was done in a little more than three months. "The effort," said a presidential adviser, "is not to destroy our institutions but to save them from the poison of unlimited greed."

Subsequently, other New Deal programs and agencies were added, among them the National Housing Authority, the Social Security Act (1935), the Agricultural Adjustment Act (1938), The Fair Labor Standards Act (1938), and the National Labor Relations Act—which became a veritable Magna Carta for American labor.

Even the arts and the theater were not neglected. The unprecedented Federal Arts Project became an important part of the New Deal. Its purpose was to "conserve the talents and skills of artists who, through no fault of their own, found themselves on the relief rolls . . . ; to encourage young artists of definite ability . . . ; to integrate the arts in general with the everyday life of the community." More than 350 separate art projects were put into operation throughout the United States. It was the first time that the American national government had given serious attention to the creative aspects of American life. Frances Perkins, Roosevelt's Secretary of Labor, said: "It's time to treat ourselves to some civilization."

Another interesting example of Roosevelt's creative political imagination and range of interests was his proposal to set up a shelter belt to check soil erosion on the Great Plains. One day, as he was going through reports on the devastation caused by erosion in the West, he casually inquired why it would not be a good idea to plant trees as windbreaks and soil protection. "Man," he said, "cannot change all the forces of weather, but he can modify his own surroundings." So he allocated a million dollars for a shelter-belt program, which at the time caused considerable ridicule as being another example of the boondoggling and wasteful New Deal. But the thousands of Chinese elms, pines, cedars, and other hardy trees have become a widely admired achievement in saving the Great Plains from further devastation. Similarly, the monumental TVA, with its 650-mile navigable channel, flood protection, irrigation, and hydroelectric power installations, revolutionized the life and the economy of seven southern states. The New Deal also built or completed other great dams, among them the gigantic Grand Coulee across the Columbia River in Washington; Boulder (Hoover) Dam, with the largest man-made lake in America and an annual power output of about six billion kilowatt hours; Shasta Dam in California's Sacramento Valley; Bryant Dam in California's Central Valley; and numerous other projects and structures that have increased the nation's wealth, power, and resources beyond calculation. The livcliness and scope of Roosevelt's imagination is illustrated in a story told by his wife. One night during World War II, he said to her: "It would be interesting to see if we can't do something about the deserts in the Middle East." "Heavens!" she exclaimed, "do you mean we're going to have to face some new problems?" FDR replied: "They are a result of man's mismanagement. What man has destroyed, should be replaced."

In his second presidential campaign in 1936, FDR promised to continue his New Deal and to widen the program to achieve the prosperity and security for the whole nation that he had promised four years earlier. At Madison Square Garden, he delivered in 1936 one of the great and characteristic speeches of his career, its underlying motif being, "We have just begun to fight." Much of the essential Roosevelt, his joy in battle, his political aggressiveness, his sense of triumph, is crystallized in that speech:

"For twelve years this Nation was afflicted with hear-nothing, see-nothing, do-nothing Government. The Nation looked to Government but the Government looked away. Nine mocking years with the golden calf, three long years of the scourge! Nine crazy years at the ticker and three long years in the bread lines! Nine mad years of mirage, and three long years of despair! ... For nearly four years, you have had an Administration which instead of twirling its thumbs, has rolled up its sleeves. We will keep our sleeves rolled up.... I should like to have it said of my first Administration that in it, the forces of selfishness and lust for power met their match. I should like to have it said of my second Administration that in it these forces met their master."

Roosevelt was triumphantly reelected in 1936, carrying every state of the union but Maine and Vermont, thus giving rise to the gibe that "as Maine goes, so goes Vermont." But his second administration was not so creative or productive as the first. For one thing, the New Deal program had run into trouble with the Supreme Court. For another, international crises began more and more to absorb the energies and attention of the President.

The conservative Supreme Court had struck down many of Roosevelt's major acts of legislature as unconstitutional. Between January 1935 and May 1936 the Court, often by simple majorities of five to four, invalidated no less than twelve New Deal statutes. It was an unprecedentedly large number of invalidations for so short a period of time, and it infuriated the President.

In his anger at the so-called Nine Old Men who, Roosevelt charged, willfully blocked "the need to meet the . . . challenge of one-third of a Nation, ill-nourished, ill-clad, ill-housed," FDR proposed his so-called "Court packing" plan in 1937. Designed to bring younger blood to the Court, the plan proposed the appointment of an additional justice for every incumbent above the age of seventy. It created a furor throughout the country. Roosevelt was accused of a plot to destroy the most sacred foundation of the American Constitution, which the nation's conservative interests regarded as their last bulwark against radicalism. The storm of protest was so intense that FDR was forced to drop the plan; nevertheless he achieved his objective. A century and a quarter earlier, Jefferson had said grimly of an equally conservative Supreme Court, "Few die, none resign." Now, age and death did remove the most diehard conservatives from the Supreme Bench; they were replaced by sympathizers with FDR's program—Hugo Black, Felix Frankfurter, William O. Douglas, Robert H. Jackson, and Frank Murphy. By the end of Roosevelt's third administration, he had created a new Court made up of justices whose ideas were close to his own.

The struggle over the Court, together with declining unemployment and a stabilization of the economy, tended to slow down the reform impetus of the New Deal. But more important than the domestic development was the deepening crisis abroad. The second Roosevelt administration coincided with the rise of intensified military preparations of the fascist Axis in Europe and the aggressive Japanese in the Pacific. Roosevelt understood, earlier than did the American people in general, the actual and potential menace to freedom represented by the forces of Nazism, fascism, and militarism. He watched the spreading terror of totalitarianism with dismay. The Spanish Civil War, which broke out in 1936 and which was a test of the military power of Hitler and Mussolini, seemed to him an "unfortunate and terrible catastrophe." On October 5, 1937, in his "quarantine speech" in Chicago, he warned the nation that the "epidemic of world lawlessness is spreading"; and although the United States was determined to keep out of foreign entanglements, he hinted that it might be impossible to do so: "We cannot insure ourselves against the disastrous effects of war and the dangers of involvement."

Involvement in global war came with the Japanese attack on Pearl Harbor on December 7, 1941. Henceforth, FDR's energy was devoted to the mobilization of the vast American resources and the conduct of a war of worldwide dimensions. In World War II, Roosevelt, in alliance with the British and Russian leaders, headed a gigantic, earthgirdling coalition of forces on a scale unmatched in the history of mankind.

In his war aims, Roosevelt, solidly backed by a virtually unanimous nation, had only one overriding objective. It was not the maintenance of empire or territorial expansion or capitalism, but peace and freedom for all mankind. Roosevelt was fighting for the same broad objectives that had been proclaimed by his Democratic predecessor in the White House a score of years earlier. Woodrow Wilson had formulated his international program in his Fourteen Points; Roosevelt proclaimed the Four Freedoms. Wilson had proposed a League of Nations as a permanent institution for the settlement of international disputes; Roosevelt offered the world the United Nations for the achievement of the same goal. Peace and freedom everywhere in the world, as he put it in the Four Freedoms message, were the aims which embodied the historic idealism of the American nation, of which Roosevelt was the living symbol to all of mankind during World War II.

One month before Pearl Harbor FDR had said: "The American people have made an unlimited commitment that there shall be a free world." The draft of his last speech to be delivered at the Jefferson Day dinner, written on the eve of his death on April 12, 1945, was a proclamation of his hope for peace: "The work, my friends, is peace, more than an end of this war—an end to the beginnings of all wars, yes, an end, forever, to this impractical, unrealistic settlement of the differences between governments by the mass killing of peoples." He concluded with words which, symbolically, were an echo of the opening of his first Inaugural, when he rejected the fear of fear, by now saying: "The only limit to our realization of tomorrow will be our doubts of today. Let us move forward with strong and active faith."

FDR died of sheer physical and mental exhaustion, in the fullness of his political power and world influence, dedicated to a cause he considered greater than the interests of any one people or nation—freedom from the scourge of war and from the terrors of dictatorship. Final victory came within a few weeks after his death. He died as he had lived—a fighter.

FDR's personality is not easy to evaluate. Definitive judgment will have to wait the verdict of history. He is a character of perennial fascination. Hundreds of books have been written about him. Undoubtedly many more will follow. He has legions of ardent admirers and unforgiving enemies. He has been enshrined by his followers as the patron saint of the Democratic Party and, indeed, of the democratic ideal in general, as the annual Roosevelt Birthday dinners indicate. He has been diabolized by his enemies as evil incarnate.

Politically, FDR was neither altogether a lion nor entirely a fox. Like any successful political figure, he possessed in good measure the qualities of both. But he was not any more Machiavellian or more crafty than such equally shrewd and successful politicians as Jefferson or Lincoln. FDR, a superb operator of the American political mechanism, was constantly aware that democracy, to be successful, required a succession of intricate compromises to achieve both consensus and a measure of social harmony. Such compromises often looked like evasions or dishonesty, but in the democratic process they were essential to the attainment of necessary objectives. As Senator Hubert H. Humphrey of Minnesota, a follower of FDR, put it: "You are really doing your cause little or no good to be untimely, to take unnecessary risks. You merely bleed yourself white and lose your effectiveness. In fact, you may be destroyed. I'll never forget what Franklin D. Roosevelt once said. He said . . . that a man frequently had to make little compromises in order to be around to make great decisions." Roosevelt was a masterful manipulator of the democratic machinery and the political forces at play in that immense aggregation of interests, geographic sections, economic combinations, ethnic and religious groupings that make up the United States of America.

This is one aspect of Roosevelt's historic significance. The other, an equally important one, is his willingness and ability to use the powers given to and inherent in the federal government for the general welfare. Unlike his immediate predecessor in the White House, FDR not only did not fear government, he gloried in it, he understood it, he believed in it, and he was ready at all times to use it for any purposes he considered desirable for the well-being of the nation and its citizens. This unhesitating use of governmental authority and influence in virtually every phase of the nation's life, including the arts, was unprecedented. It altered the fundamental pattern of American politics. Herein lies the enduring significance of the Roosevelt revolution, as it has been aptly called.

One of the measures of Roosevelt's stature is the hostility he aroused. Political hatreds are a normal accompaniment of vigorous political action, but the depth of animosity for FDR has been of a quality, duration and intensity unmatched in the annals of American history. The hatred applied not only to Roosevelt himself but also to his remarkable wife, to his family, to members of his cabinet, and even, as he pointed out ironically in one of his speeches, to his little Scottish terrier, Fala. No lie, innuendo, gossip, or distortion was too mean to serve FDR's detractors.

Three main reasons probably account for the protracted rage of his foes. The first, and perhaps the most important, is the fact that Roosevelt and his program destroyed the monopoly of power held by the American plutocracy and its middle-class allies for three quarters of a century. From the Civil War to the New Deal, American political power had been directly or indirectly in the hands of big business. Even FDR's strongest predecessors, including Theodore Roosevelt and Woodrow Wilson, had been unable to control or mitigate to any extent the stranglehold the masters of the national economy held on the country's political institutions. FDR succeeded where no other President or political leader before him had been able to, without in any way weakening the capitalist system—in which he believed—or reducing the immense wealth of the industrial corporations.

Roosevelt managed to break the monopoly of the oligarchy by bringing into being strong countervailing powers. One of these was the force of the organized farmers, to whom the New Deal brought the unwonted security of guaranteed agricultural prices. The other was the force of organized labor, which was supplied with institutional, political, and moral assistance by the New Deal. "Franklin," Eleanor Roosevelt says in *This I Remember*, "has been accused of giving labor too much power, but his effort was simply to equalize the power of labor and capital. As a close student of history, he knew how great and unhampered capital's power had been during some previous Administrations."

It would have been too much to expect of human nature for those who had so long wielded a monopoly of power not to resent Roosevelt, even though the far-ranging New Deal had saved capitalism from chaos or possibly even dictatorship. They could not forgive FDR, particularly since they knew that he disliked them and made no secret of his contempt for them. "They are unanimous in their hate for me," he said, during the 1936 campaign, "—and I welcome their hatred." Nor did he endear himself to them when, in reaction to their continued baiting, he indulged in ridicule at their expense. Referring to his big-business opponents in a speech in Chicago in October 1936, he said:

"Some of these people really forget how sick they were. But . . . I have their fever charts. I know how the knees of all of our rugged individualists were trembling four years ago and how their hearts fluttered. They came to Washington in great numbers. Washington did not look like a dangerous bureaucracy to them then. Oh, no! It looked like an emergency hospital. All of the distinguished patients wanted two things—a quick hypodermic to end the pain and a course of treatment to cure the disease. They wanted them in a hurry; we gave them both. And now most of the patients seem to be doing very nicely. Some of them are even well enough to throw their crutches at the doctor."

The second reason for the hostility to FDR is more subtle. The business community and its allies, long accustomed to wielding power through bankers, corporation lawyers, and others who belonged to their intimate circles, were genuinely shocked when Roosevelt brought in a host of advisers and officials not of their class or milieu. FDR surrounded himself with and appointed to high office men whose origins, professions, religions, college affiliations, and ideas had barred them from the inner circles of power and influence in the past. Around Roosevelt were professorial theorists like Rexford Guy Tugwell and Raymond Moley, Mugwumps like Harold L. Ickes, liberals like Felix Frankfurter, mavericks like Henry Wallace, social-service workers like Harry Hopkins and Frances Perkins. Among FDR's intimate advisers were members of minority religions, such as Benjamin Cohen and Thomas Corcoran. But above all, it was the intellectuals close to Roosevelt, the so-called longhairs, the "men who never met a payroll," who outraged dominant middle-class opinion. The New Deal intellectuals, full of enthusiasm for a better America and devoid of respect for those who, in their view, had brought misery and mismanagement upon the country, were an especial affront to the conservatives. Unable to beat the New Deal at the polls, the latter vented their rage on Roosevelt and all he stood for. Their enmity, continuing well beyond the New Deal era, knew no bounds.*

* An example is Clare Boothe Luce, former congresswoman from Connecticut and wife of the prominent Republican publisher, Henry Luce. Mrs. Luce said of FDR's Party: "The Democratic Party has a vested interest in Depression at home and in war abroad. Its leaders are always troubadours of trouble; crooners of catastrophe. Public confusion on vital issues is Democratic weather. A Democratic President is doomed to proceed to his goals like a squid, squirting darkness all about him." In 1944, at the height of the mortal struggle against fascism abroad, Mrs. Luce said that Roosevelt was "the only American President that ever lied us into war." In 1949, a New Jersey Republican, John W. Hopper, even went so far as to transmit his hatred of FDR to his heirs, stating in a codicil to his will: "I also hereby bequeath to my children and their descendants down through the ages to come a

A third reason for the animosity to Roosevelt was the belief, sincerely held by many, that the New Deal was communistic. There was a tendency on the part of the New Deal's opponents to label any political reform a product of Red machinations. In conservative circles, "That Man in the White House" was regarded as a traitor to his class. Roosevelt and his aides soon found that in this matter feeling was so deep and irrational that there was no sensible way of coping with it. They simply had to trust to history to convince public opinion that native American reform was a totally different species of action and philosophy from imported communism.*

There were also, of course, many sincere New Deal critics who knew the difference between progressivism and communism. These were troubled by an aspect of the New Deal which had nothing to do with economic radicalism. Liberals like Amos Pinchot and Louis D. Brandeis were worried about the extent of governmental operations and the widespread penetration of federal activities into the life of the nation. As old-fashioned progressives, they were imbued with the conviction that big government tended to lose its democratic character and to become a vast bureaucratized mechanism, endangering the traditional liberties of the people. Their criticism was not leveled at the objectives of the New Deal, which in principle they approved, but at its political consequences.

The consequences of the New Deal have been incalculable and still continue. Weak government, strictly limited to its prescribed constitutional functions as envisioned by the founding fathers, came to an end

---

priceless heritage—the knowledge that I, their father and grandfather, had no share, not even once, in the installation or perpetuation of the Roosevelt dynasty. ... With this knowledge they may always hold up their heads in pride." As late as May 8, 1959, the *New York Daily News* editorialized: "It's a toss-up whether Hitler, Roosevelt or Stalin was the most to blame for the present upset and hate-filled state of the world." In January 1960, President Eisenhower's Secretary of Commerce, Frederick H. Mueller, could still refer to the New Dealers and their successors, the Truman Fair Dealers, as "sour-bellied left-wingers," "pink-tinted pundits and egg-heads," a "motley crew" of "aristocratic parasites and Skid Row bums."

* Much of the hysteria that afflicted the country, in the form of so-called McCarthyism, in the early 1950s had its roots in the period of the New Deal, when it was assaulted as having sheltered and spawned communist agents in government offices. Early in 1952, when this writer published an article on Harold L. Ickes, he received a letter which, among other scurrilities, said: "Ickes was a mastiff in a sick and corrupt kennel of Communist feists or Roosevelt poodles." This letter was typical of millions of others received by FDR and all of those connected with the New Deal.

under FDR. Today it is a universally accepted idea that government has functions and obligations far beyond the traditional ones of national defense, international relations, and coinage. Today the government of the United States, as a result of institutions created and precedents set by the New Deal, plays an ever-widening role in the daily lives of all the people. As the United States moves into the space age, it will probably find government assuming greater and greater obligations, including responsibility for matters which the American political system had not traditionally considered its domain: among them culture, science, the arts, health, higher education, leisure, and whatever else may be involved in the national commitment to the "pursuit of happiness."

As for Franklin D. Roosevelt, one thing is certain: he was one of the major democratic figures and molders of our time. His dramatic personality, combined with political genius and creative statesmanship, guarantee him a conspicuous position in that small gallery of Americans whose accomplishments continue to shine with glory.

# Selected Bibliography


Aaron, Daniel, *Men of Good Hope*. New York, Oxford, 1951

Adams, Charles Francis, *ed., The Works of John Adams,* with a Life of the author, etc. 10 vols. Boston, Little, Brown, 1850–1856

Adams, John, *Works* (as above). Vol. III. A Dissertation on the Common and the Feudal law. Vol. IV. Novanglus; etc. *and* Thoughts on Government. Vol. V–VI. Defense of the Constitutions, etc. Vol. VI. Discourses on Davila

Adams, John Quincy, *Diary, 1794–1845;* American diplomacy and political, social, and intellectual life from Washington to Polk. Ed. Allan Nevins. New York, Scribner, 1951

Adams, Randolph Greenfield, *Political Ideas of the American Revolution*. Durham, N.C., Trinity College, 1922; New York, Barnes & Noble, 1958

Arrowrood, Charles Flinn, *ed., Thomas Jefferson and Education in a Republic*. New York, McGraw-Hill, 1930

Baehr, Harry W., Jr., *The New York Tribune Since the Civil War*. New York, Dodd, Mead, 1936

Baker, Ray Stannard, *Woodrow Wilson, Life and Letters*. 8 vols. Garden City, Doubleday, Page, 1927–1939

———, *Woodrow Wilson and World Settlement*. Garden City, Doubleday, Page, 1922

——— and Wm. E. Dodd, *eds. The Public Papers of Woodrow Wilson*. 2 vols. New York, Harper, 1925

Barker, Charles A., *Henry George*. New York, Oxford, 1955

Basso, Hamilton, *Mainstream*. New York, Reynal & Hitchcock, 1943

Beale, Howard K., *Theodore Roosevelt and the Rise of America to World Power*. Baltimore, The Johns Hopkins, 1956

Beard, Charles A., *Economic Origins of Jeffersonian Democracy*. New York, Macmillan, 1915

———, *The Rise of American Civilization,* with Mary R. Beard. 2 vols. in one. New York, Macmillan, 1927, 1956

Becker, Carl, *The Declaration of Independence;* reprinted with an Introduction. New York, Knopf, 1941

Beer, Clifford W., *A Mind That Found Itself*. New York, Longmans, Green, 1908; Garden City, Doubleday, Doran, 1935

Bent, Silas, *Justice Oliver Wendell Holmes: A Biography*. New York, Vanguard, 1932

Benton, Thomas Hart, *Thirty Years' View (1820–1850)*. 2 vols. New York, D. Appleton, 1854, 1856

Beveridge, Albert J., *Life of John Marshall*. 4 vols. in 2. Boston & New York, Houghton, Mifflin, 1929

Bishop, Joseph B., *Theodore Roosevelt and His Time*. 2 vols. New York, Scribner, 1920

Blau, Joseph L., *Men and Movements in American Philosophy*. New York, Prentice-Hall, 1952

Blum, John M., *The Republican Roosevelt*. Cambridge, Harvard, 1954

Bolling, J. Randolph *et al.*, *Chronology of Woodrow Wilson,* together with his most notable addresses, a description of the League of Nations and League of Nations Covenant. New York, Stokes, 1927

Bowen, Francis, *American Political Economy*. New York, Scribner, Armstrong, 1877

Bowers, Claude G., *Jefferson and Hamilton*. Boston & New York, Houghton, Mifflin, 1925

———, *Jefferson in Power*. Boston, Houghton, Mifflin, 1936

———, *The Young Jefferson, 1743–1785*. Boston, Houghton, Mifflin, 1945

Boyd, Julian Parkes, *ed.*, *The Declaration of Independence;* evolution of the text in facsimiles. Washington, Library of Congress, 1943

Brant, Irving, *James Madison*. 4 vols. Indianapolis & New York, Bobbs, Merrill, 1941–1953

Brecht, Arnold, *Political Theory: The Foundations of Twentieth-Century Political Thought*. Princeton, 1959

Brownlow, Louis, *A Passion for Politics*. 2 vols. Chicago, University of Chicago, 1955, 1958

———, *The President and the Presidency,* Chicago. Public Administration Service, 1949

Bryce, James, *The American Commonwealth*. 2 vols. London, Macmillan, 1888

Buchler, Justus, *ed.*, *The Philosophy of Peirce*. London, K. Paul, Trench, Trubner, 1940

Burke, Edmund, *ed.*, *Annual Register*. A compleat history of the late war, etc. Dublin, J. Exshaw, 1763

Butterfield, Lyman H., *Letters of Benjamin Rush*. 2 vols. Princeton, 1951

Calhoun, John C., *Works*. Ed. R. K. Crullé. 6 vols. New York, Appleton, 1854–1855. Vol. I. A Discourse on the Constitution *and* A Disquisition on Government. Vol. VI. South Carolina Exposition

Carlson, Oliver, *The Man Who Made News: James Gordon Bennett*. New York, Duell, Sloan & Pearce, 1942

Carman, Harry J., and Samuel McKee, Jr., *A History of the United States*. Boston & New York, Heath, 1931

Carnegie, Andrew, *The Gospel of Wealth*. New York, Century Co., 1900

Child, Lydia Maria, *Letters from New-York*. Boston, J. Munroe, 1843

Chinard, Gilbert, *Jefferson et les idéologues d'après sa correspondence inédite avec Destutt de Tracy, etc.* Baltimore, The Johns Hopkins, 1925

Commager, Henry S., *The American Mind*. New Haven, Yale, 1950

Conwell, Russell H., *Acres of Diamonds*. New York, Harper, 1915

Corwin, Edward S., *John Marshall and the Constitution*. New Haven, Yale, 1921

Crane, Milton, *The Roosevelt Era*. New York, Boni & Gaer, 1947

Croly, Herbert, *Promise of American Life*. New York, Macmillan, 1909

Current, Richard N., with J. G. Randall, *Lincoln the President: The Last Full Measure*. New York, Dodd, Mead, 1955

Curti, Merle E., *Growth of American Thought*. New York & London, Harper, 1943

Curtis, George Ticknor, *Constitutional History of the United States,* from the Declaration of Independence to the close of the Civil War. 2 vols. New York, Harper, 1895–1896

Dauer, Manning, *The Adams Federalists*. Baltimore, The Johns Hopkins, 1953

Destler, Chester McA., *American Radicalism, 1865–1901*. New London, Connecticut College, 1946

Dewey, John, *Characters and Events*. 2 vols. New York, Holt, 1929

———, *The Child and the Curriculum* (1902). 23rd impression. University of Chicago, 1934

———, *Democracy and Education*. New York, Macmillan, 1916

———, *Freedom and Culture*. New York, Putnam, 1939

———, *Human Nature and Conduct*. New York, Holt, 1922

———, *Individualism, Old and New*. New York, Minton, Balch, 1930

———, *Interest and Effort in Education*. Boston, Houghton, Mifflin, 1913

———, *Liberalism and Social Action*. New York, Putnam, 1935

———, *Philosophy and Civilization*. New York, Minton, Balch, 1931

———, *The Public and Its Problems*. New York, Holt, 1927

———, *Reconstruction in Philosophy*. New York, Holt, 1920

*Dictionary of American Biography*. Allen Johnson and Dumas Malone, eds. 22 vols. New York, Scribner, 1928—

Dodd, William E., *Statesmen of the Old South*. New York, Macmillan, 1911. *See also* Baker, Ray Stannard

Donald, David, *Lincoln Reconsidered*. New York, Knopf, 1956

Dorfman, Joseph, *The Economic Mind of American Civilization*. 5 vols. New York, Viking; Toronto, Macmillan; 1946–1959

Douglass, Frederick, *Lectures on American Slavery*. Buffalo, Geo. Reese, 1851

DuPont de Nemours, P. S., *Correspondence with T. Jefferson*. Tr. L. Lehman. Baltimore, The Johns Hopkins, 1931

Ely, Richard T., *Ground under Our Feet*. New York, Macmillan, 1938

Emerson, Ralph Waldo, *Complete Works,* ed. E. Waldo Emerson. 12 vols. Boston & New York, Houghton, Mifflin, 1903. Vol. IV. Representative Men. Vol. VI. The Conduct of Life.

*F.D.R.: His Personal Letters,* ed. Elliott Roosevelt. New York, Duell, Sloan & Pearce, 1947–1950

Foner, Philip S., ed., *Basic Writings of Thomas Jefferson*. New York, Wiley, 1944

Frank, John P., *Cases and Materials on Constitutional Law* (1952 and Supplement). Chicago, Callaghan & Co., 1952, 1955

*The Federalist*. Commentary on the Constitution by Alexander Hamilton, James Madison, and John Jay, ed. Paul Leicester Ford. New York, Holt, 1898

Frankfurter, Felix, *Mr. Justice Holmes and the Supreme Court*. Cambridge, Harvard, 1938

Freeman, Douglas Stouthall, *George Washington: A Biography*. 6 vols. New York, Scribner, 1948–1954

Freidel, Frank, *Franklin D. Roosevelt*. 3 vols. Boston, Little, Brown, 1952–1956
Gabriel, Ralph H., *The Course of Democratic Thought*. New York, Ronald, 1941
Garrison, William Lloyd, *The Story of His Life as Told by His Children*. 4 vols. I–III. Boston & New York, Houghton, Mifflin, 1889; IV. New York, Century, 1894
George, Henry, *Complete Works*. 10 vols. New York, National Single Tax League, 1871–1897
———, *The American Republic*. Fourth of July oration, San Francisco. Thomas' printer, 1877
———, *Progress and Poverty*. New York, Henry George copyright, 1879; Appleton, 1881
George, Henry, Jr., *The Life of Henry George*. Garden City, Doubleday, 1900
*George Washington's Rules of Civility*, ed. Moncure D. Conway. New York, United States Book Co., 1890
Goldman, Eric, *Rendezvous with Destiny*. New York, Knopf, 1952
Grattan, C. Hartley, *The Three Jameses: A Family of Minds*. New York, Longmans, Green, 1932
Gregory, Daniel Seely, *Christian Ethics*. Philadelphia, Eldredge & Bro. 1881
Gunther, John, *Roosevelt in Retrospect*. New York, Harper, 1950
Hacker, Louis M., *Alexander Hamilton in the American Tradition*. New York, McGraw-Hill, 1957
———, *The Shaping of the American Tradition*. New York, Columbia, 1947
Hale, William B., *The Story of a Style*. New York, Huebsch, 1920
Hamilton, Alexander. *Works*. Constitutional Edition, ed. Henry Cabot Lodge. 12 vols. New York, Putnam, 1904
———, *A Full Vindication of the Measures of Congress,* etc. New York, Jas. Rivington, 1774
———, *Industrial and Commercial Correspondence;* anticipating (and including) his report on manufactures, ed. A. H. Cole. Chicago, A. W. Shaw, 1928
———, *The Farmer Refuted,* etc. New York, Jas. Rivington, 1775
Hand, Learned, *The Spirit of Liberty,* ed. Irving Dilliard. New York, Knopf, 1953
Handlin, Oscar, *Race and Nationality in American Life*. Boston, Little, Brown; Garden City, Anchor Books, 1957
———, *The Uprooted*. Boston, Little, Brown, 1951
Haraszti, Zoltan, *John Adams and the Prophets of Progress*. Cambridge, Harvard, 1952
Hartz, Louis, *The Liberal Tradition in America*. New York, Harcourt, Brace, 1955
Heckscher, August, *ed., The Politics of Woodrow Wilson*. New York, Harper, 1956
Helper, Hinton R., *The Impending Crisis of the South*. New York, A. B. Burdick, 1860
Herndon, William H., with Jessie W. Weik, *Abraham Lincoln: The True Story of a Great Life*. 2 vols. New York, Appleton, 1896
Higgs, Henry, *The Physiocrats*. London, Macmillan, 1897
Hofstadter, Richard, *The Age of Reform: From Bryan to F.D.R.* New York, Knopf, 1955

———, *The American Political Tradition and the Men Who Made It.* New York, Knopf, 1951
———, *Social Darwinism in American Thought.* Philadelphia, University of Pennsylvania, 1944
Holmes, Oliver Wendell, *The Autocrat of the Breakfast Table.* Boston, Houghton, Mifflin, 1892. *The Poet . . .*, 1889. *The Professor . . .*, 1883.
———, *Pages from an Old Volume of Life,* Boston, Houghton, Mifflin, 1883
Holmes, Oliver Wendell, Jr., "Dead, Yet Living." Address delivered Memorial Day 1884. Boston, Ginn, Heath, 1884
———, *Touched with Fire.* Civil War Letters and Diary of O. W. Holmes, Jr., 1861–1864. Cambridge, Harvard, 1946
Hook, Sidney, *ed., John Dewey: Philosopher of Science and Freedom.* New York, Dial, 1950
Hoover, Herbert C. *American Individualism.* Garden City, Doubleday, 1922
———, *The New Day;* Campaign Speeches of 1928. Stanford (Cal.) University, 1929
———, *The Ordeal of Woodrow Wilson.* New York, McGraw-Hill, 1958
———, with Calvin Coolidge, *Campaign Speeches of 1932.* Garden City, Doubleday, 1933
Hoover, Irwin Hood, *Forty-two Years in the White House.* Boston & New York, Houghton, Mifflin Co., 1934
House, Edward M., *The Intimate Papers of Colonel House,* ed. Charles Seymour. Boston, Houghton, Mifflin, 1926–1928
Howe, Mark de Wolfe, *ed., Holmes-Laski Letters;* the Correspondence of Mr. Justice Holmes and Harold J. Laski, 1916–1935. 2 vols. Cambridge, Harvard, 1953
———, *Holmes-Pollock Letters;* the Correspondence of Mr. Justice Holmes and Sir Frederick Pollock, 1874–1932. 2 vols. Cambridge, Harvard, 1941
Hughes, Rupert, *George Washington.* 3 vols. New York, Morrow, 1926–1930
Jackson, Andrew, *Correspondence with Calhoun.* Washington, D. Green, 1831
James, William, *Essays in Radical Empiricism* (incl. "A World of Pure Experience"). Ed. Ralph Barton Perry. New York, Longmans, Green, 1912
———, *Human Immortality.* Boston, Houghton, Mifflin, 1898
———, *The Meaning of Truth.* New York, Longmans, Green, 1927
———, *Memories and Studies.* New York, Longmans, Green, 1911
———, *The Moral Equivalent of War.* International Conciliation No. 27, February 1910
———, *Pragmatism,* New York, Longmans, Green, 1909
———, *Psychology,* New York, Holt, 1915
———, *Talks to Teachers* (incl. "On Some of Life's Ideals"). New York, Holt, 1904
———, *Varieties of Religious Experience.* New York, Longmans, Green, 1902
———, *The Will to Believe,* and other essays. New York, Longmans, Green, 1917
Jefferson, Isaac, *Memories of a Monticello Slave.* Charlottesville, University of Virginia, 1951
Jefferson, Thomas, *Autobiography,* introduction by Dumas Malone. New York, Capricorn Books, 1959
———, *The Complete Anas.* Ed. F. B. Sawvel. New York, Round Tables Press, 1903

———, *Notes on the State of Virginia*. Ed. Wm. Peden. Chapel Hill, University of North Carolina, 1955

———, *The Papers of,* to 1789. Julian P. Boyd, editor-in-chief. 15 vols. Princeton, 1950—

———, *The Writings of,...* Published by the Order of the Joint Committee of Congress on the Library. Ed. H. A. Washington. 9 vols. Washington, Taylor & Maury, 1853–1854

*John Taylor of Caroline, Prophet of Secession,* preface by W. E. Dodd. John P. Branch Historical Papers of Randolph-Macon College, Vol. II, No. 364, June 1908

Johnson, Gerald W., *The Lunatic Fringe*. Philadelphia, Lippincott, 1957

Kallen, Horace M., *ed., The Philosophy of William James, Drawn from His Own Works*. New York, The Modern Library, 1925

Kilpatrick, Carroll, *ed., Roosevelt and Daniels: A Friendship in Politics*. Chapel Hill, University of North Carolina, 1952

Koch, Adrienne, *Jefferson and Madison: The Great Collaboration*. New York, Knopf, 1950

———, *The Philosophy of Thomas Jefferson*. New York, Columbia, 1943

———, with William Peden, *The Selected Writings of John and John Quincy Adams*. New York, Knopf, 1946

Kohn, Hans, *American Nationalism*. New York, Macmillan, 1957

Konefsky, Samuel J., *The Legacy of Holmes and Brandeis*. New York, Macmillan, 1956

———, *ed., The Constitutional World of Mr. Justice Frankfurter*. Selected opinions. New York, Macmillan, 1949

Lane, Franklin K., *Americanism*. Addresses [1915 Conventions] by Woodrow Wilson and Theodore Roosevelt. Veterans of Foreign Wars, 1926

Lansing, Robert, *The Peace Negotiations:* A Personal Narrative. Boston, Houghton, Mifflin, 1921

La Piere, Richard, *The Freudian Ethic*. New York, Duell, Sloan & Pearce, 1959

Laski, Harold J., *The American Democracy*. London, Allen & Unwin, 1949

Lee, Richard Henry, *The Letters of,...* collected and ed. by Jas. C. Ballogh. 2 vols. New York, Macmillan, 1911–1914

Lerner, Max, *America as a Civilization*. New York, Simon & Schuster, 1957

———, *ed., The Mind and Faith of Justice Holmes*. New York, Modern Library, 1954

*The Letters of William James*. 2 vols. Boston, Atlantic Monthly Press, 1920

Lief, Alfred, *ed., The Dissenting Opinions of Mr. Justice Holmes,* New York, Vanguard, 1929

———, *The Social and Economic Views of Mr. Justice Brandeis*. New York, Vanguard, 1930

———, *Representative Opinions of Mr. Justice Holmes,* New York, Vanguard, 1931

Lincoln, Abraham, *The Collected Works of,...* Published by the Abraham Lincoln Association, Springfield, Ill. Ed. Roy P. Basler. 9 vols. New Brunswick, Rutgers, 1953–1955

———, *Complete Works*. Ed. J. G. Nicolay and John Hay. 2 vols. New York, Century Co., 1894

———, Gettysburg Address; the first and second drafts now in the Library of Congress. Washington, Library of Congress, 1950

Link, Arthur S., *Wilson*. 2 vols. Princeton, 1956

———, *Woodrow Wilson and the Progressive Era*. New York, Harper, 1954

*Literary History of the United States*. Ed. Robert E. Spiller and others. 3 vols. New York, Macmillan, 1948

Lloyd, Henry Demarest, *Wealth against Commonwealth*. New York, Harper, 1896

Loth, David, *Chief Justice John Marshall and the Growth of the Republic*. New York, Norton, 1949

Lowell, James Russell, *The Works of,...* 8 vols. Boston, Houghton, Mifflin, 1892. Vol. V. Political Essays. Vol. VIII. The Bigelow Papers

Madison, James, *Letters and Other Writings*. Published by Order of Congress. 4 vols. Ed. Wm. Cabell Rives. Philadelphia, Lippincott, 1839

Malone, Dumas, *Jefferson and His Time*. Boston, Little, Brown, 1948

Marke, Julius, B., *ed., The Holmes Reader*. New York, Oceana, 1955

Marshall, John, *The Writings of,... upon the Federal Constitution*. Boston, J. Munroe, 1839

Martineau, Harriet, *Retrospect of Western Travel*. 2 vols. in one. New York, C. Lohman; 3 vols. London, Saunders & Otley, 1838

Mason, Alpheus T., *Brandeis: A Free Man's Life*. New York, Viking, 1946

———, *Free Government in the Making*. New York, Oxford, 1949

———, *The Supreme Court from Taft to Warren*. Baton Rouge, Louisiana State, 1958

Matthiessen, F. O., *The James Family*. New York, Knopf, 1947

McKee, Samuel, Jr., *History of the United States*, with Harry J. Carman. Boston & New York, Heath, 1931

Moley, Raymond, *After Seven Years*. New York, Harper, 1938

Montaigne, Michel de, *Essays*. Tr. Chas. Cotton. 3 vols. London, Reeves & Turner, 1877

Montesquieu, Charles de Secondat, baron de, *The Spirit of Laws*. Tr. Thos. Nugent. London, G. Bell, 1878

Mudge, Eugene T. *The Social Philosophy of John Taylor of Caroline*. New York, Columbia, 1939

Nettels, Curtis P., *George Washington and American Independence*. Boston, Little, Brown, 1951

Nevins, Allan, *The Evening Post*. New York, Boni & Liveright, 1922

———, *Ordeal of the Union*. 4 vols. New York, Scribner, 1947–1950

Niebuhr, Reinhold, *The Irony of American History*. New York, Scribner, 1952

———, *Pious and Secular America*. New York, Scribner, 1958

Nock, Albert Jay, *Henry George, An Essay*. New York, Morrow, 1939

O'Neill, James M., *Religion and Education under the Constitution*. New York, Harper, 1949

Padover, Saul K., *Jefferson*. New York, Harcourt, Brace, 1942

———, *Thomas Jefferson and the National Capital*. Washington, Government Printing Office, 1943

———, *Thomas Jefferson on Democracy*. New York, Appleton-Century, 1939; Mentor Book, 1946

———, *ed., The Complete Jefferson;* his major writings, published and unpublished, except the Letters. New York, Duell, Sloan & Pearce, 1943

———, *The Complete Madison;* his basic writings. New York, Harper, 1953

———, *A Jefferson Profile;* as revealed in the Letters. New York, John Day, 1956

———, *The Mind of Alexander Hamilton.* New York, Harper, 1958

———, *The Washington Papers;* basic selections from the public and private writings. New York, Harper, 1955

———, *Wilson's Ideals.* Washington, American Council on Public Affairs, 1942

Parrington, Vernon L., *Main Currents in American Thought.* 3 vols. in one. New York, Harcourt, Brace, 1930

Perkins, Frances, *The Roosevelt I Knew.* New York, Viking, 1946

Perry, Ralph Barton, *In the Spirit of William James.* New Haven, Yale; London, H. Milford, 1938

Pollack, Ervin H., *ed., The Brandeis Reader.* New York, Oceana, 1956

Presidents. *The Addresses and Messages.* 1789–1846. New York, E. Walker, 1846

———. *Messages and Papers.* 1789–1897. Washington, Govt. Printing Office, 1899

Putnam, Carleton, *Theodore Roosevelt.* 2 vols. New York, Scribner, 1958

Randall, John G., *Lincoln the President: The Last Full Measure,* with Richard N. Current. New York, Dodd, Mead, 1955

Randolph, Sarah N., *The Domestic Life of Thomas Jefferson,...* by his great-granddaughter. Cambridge, Harvard, 1939

Ratner, Joseph, *ed., The Philosophy of John Dewey.* New York, Holt, 1928

Rauch, Basil, *ed., The Roosevelt Reader.* New York, Rinehart, 1957

Roosevelt, Eleanor, *This I Remember.* New York, Harper, 1949

Roosevelt, Franklin D., *The Happy Warrior, Alfred E. Smith.* Boston & New York, Houghton, Mifflin, 1928

———, *Nothing to Fear;* selected Addresses, 1932–1945. Foreword by Harry Hopkins. Boston, Houghton, Mifflin, 1946

———, *The Public Papers and Addresses of,...* with introduction by F.D.R. Ed. Samuel I. Rosenman. 9 vols. New York, Random House, 1938–1950

Roosevelt, Theodore, *An Autobiography.* New York, Macmillan, 1913

———, *The Works of,...* Executive Edition. 8 vols. New York, Collier, 1910

Rosenman, Samuel I., *Working with Roosevelt.* New York, Harper, 1952

Rossiter, Clinton, *Seedtime of the Republic: The Origin of the American Tradition of Political Liberty.* New York, Harcourt, Brace, 1953

Sandburg, Carl, *Abraham Lincoln: The Prairie Years.* 2 vols. New York, Harcourt, Brace, 1926

Santayana, George, *Character and Opinion in the United States.* New York, Scribner, 1920

———, *Persons and Places.* New York, Scribner, 1944

Savelle, Max, *Seeds of Liberty: The Genesis of the American Mind.* New York, Knopf, 1948

Saveth, Edward N., *Understanding the American Past.* Boston, Little, Brown, 1954

Schachner, Nathan, *Alexander Hamilton.* New York & London, Appleton-Century, 1946

Schilpp, Paul A., *The Philosophy of John Dewey.* Evanston & Chicago, Northwestern University, 1939

Schlesinger, Arthur M., Jr., *The Age of Jackson.* Boston, Houghton, Mifflin, 1945

———, *The Age of Roosevelt.* 3 vols. Boston, Houghton, Mifflin, 1957–1960

Schneider, Herbert Wallace, *A History of American Philosophy,* New York, Columbia, 1946

Schurz, Carl, *Reminiscences.* 2 vols. New York, Doubleday, 1907–1909

Sherwood, Robert E., *Roosevelt and Hopkins.* New York, Harper, 1948

Spain, August O., *The Political Theory of John C. Calhoun.* New York, Bookman Associates, 1951

Sparks, Edwin Earle, *ed., The Lincoln-Douglas Debates of 1858.* Springfield, Trustees of Illinois State Historical Library, 1908

Stern, Philip Van Doren, *The Life and Writings of Abraham Lincoln.* New York, Random House, 1940

Stoddard, Henry L., *As I Knew Them:* Presidents and Politics from Grant to Coolidge. New York & London, Harper, 1927

———, *Horace Greeley.* New York, Putnam, 1946

Stoddard, William O., *John Adams and Thomas Jefferson.* New York, White, Stokes & Allen, 1887

Story, Joseph, *Commentaries on the Constitution.* 3 vols. Boston, Hilliard, Gray, 1833

Sumner, William G., *The Challenge of Facts,* and other essays. New Haven, Yale, 1914

———, *Essays.* 2 vols. New Haven, Yale, 1934

———, *The Science of Society.* 4 vols. New Haven, Yale, 1927

Tarbell, Ida M., *The History of the Standard Oil Company.* 2 vols. New York, McClure, Phillips, 1904

———, *The Nationalizing of Business 1878–1898.* New York, Macmillan, 1936

Taylor, John, *Arator.* Being a series of Agricultural Essays, etc. Petersburg, Va., Witworth & Yancey, 1818

———, *An Enquiry into the Principles & Tendency of Certain Public Measures.* Philadelphia, Thos. Dobson, 1794

———, *An Inquiry into the Principles & Policy of the Government, etc.* Fredericksburg, Va., Greene & Cary, 1814; New Haven, Yale, 1950

———, *Construction Construed & Constitution Vindicated.* Richmond, Va., Shepherd & Pollard, 1820

———, *New Views of the Constitution of the United States,* Washington, the Author, 1823

———, *Tyranny Unmasked.* Washington, Davis & Force, 1822

Thomas, Benjamin Platt, *Abraham Lincoln: A Biography.* New York, Knopf, 1952

Thoreau, Henry David, *The Journal.* Ed. B. Torrey and F. H. Allen. 14 vols. Boston, Houghton, Mifflin, 1949

———, *The Writings of,...* biographical sketch by R. W. Emerson. 11 vols. Boston & New York, Houghton, Mifflin, 1893–1894

———, *On the Duty of Civil Disobedience.* London, The Peace Pledge Union, 1943

———, *Walden.* New York, Modern Library, 1950

———, *A Week on the Concord and Merrimack Rivers.* Boston & Cambridge, J. Munroe; New York, Putnam; Philadelphia, Lindsay & Blackiston, 1849

———, *Anti-slavery and Reform Papers* (with *A Yankee in Canada*). Boston, Ticknor & Fields, 1866

Tocqueville, Alexis de, *Democracy in America*. Tr. H. Reeve; revised and annotated by F. Bowen. 2 vols. New York, Century, 1898

Trent, William P., *Southern Statesmen of the Old Regime*. New York, Crowell, 1897

Tugwell, Rexford G., *The Democratic Roosevelt: A Biography*. Garden City, Doubleday, 1957

Van Buren, Martin, *Autobiography*. Washington, American Historical Society, 1918

Van Doren, Carl C., *The Great Rehearsal:* The Story of the Making and Ratifying of the Constitution. New York, Viking, 1948

Walker, Amasa, *The Science of Wealth*. Boston, Little, Brown, 1866

Webster, Daniel, *Works,* with a biographical memoir by E. Everett. 6 vols. Boston, Little, Brown, 1853

Weems, Mason Locke, *A History of the Life and Death, Virtues and Exploits of Gen. George Washington, with curious anecdotes, etc.* Philadelphia, Lippincott, 1918

Weyl, Walter E., *The New Democracy*. New York, Macmillan, 1914

White, Leonard D., *The Jeffersonians*. New York, Macmillan, 1951

White, Morton G., *The Origin of Dewey's Instrumentalism*. New York, Columbia, 1943

White, William A., *Autobiography*. New York, Macmillan, 1946

Whitman, Walt, *The Complete Writings of,...* Paumanok edition. 10 vols. New York, Putnam, 1902

———, *Democratic Vistas*. Washington, J. S. Redfield, 1871

———, *Leaves of Grass* (1855). Philadelphia, D. McKay, 1883

———, *Specimen Days in America* (1882–1883). London, Routledge, 1906

Williams, Roger, *The Bloody Tenent yet More Bloody* (1644). Providence, Narragansett Club Publications, Series 1, 1870

Wilson, Woodrow, *Congressional Government*. Boston, Houghton, Mifflin, 1885

———, *Constitutional Government in the United States*. New York, Columbia, 1921

———, *Division and Reunion 1829–1889*. New York, Longmans, Green, 1893

———, *The New Freedom: A Call for the Emancipation of the Generous Energies of a People*. New York, Doubleday, 1918

———, *The State and Federal Governments of the United States*. Boston, Heath, 1889

———, *State Papers and Addresses,* ed. with analytical index by Allan Nevins. New York, G. H. Doran, 1918

Wiltse, Charles M., *John C. Calhoun: Sectionalist, 1840–1850*. New York, Bobbs, Merrill, 1951

Wolfe, Don M., *The Image of Man in America*. Dallas, Southern Methodist University, 1957

Wright, Benjamin F., *A Source Book of American Political Theory*. New York, Macmillan, 1929

# Index

## *About the Author*

Mr. Padover, a professor on the graduate faculty of the New School for Social Research, has lectured widely in the United States, Asia, and Africa under the auspices of the State Department. He is the author of seventeen books, including five on Jefferson—one of them the celebrated biography. Among his other well-known works are *The Living United States Constitution, The Complete Madison, The Mind of Alexander Hamilton,* and *Wilson's Ideals.* The recipient of innumerable awards, honors, and fellowships, Mr. Padover is now teaching at the Universities of Tokyo and Malaya. *The Genius of America* represents a lifetime of research and thought.